CD-ROM
in
Book

sAMs
Teach Yourself

ASP.NET

in **24**
Hours

Scott Mitchell

IMPLETE STARTER KIT

800 East 96th St., Indianapolis, Indiana, 46240 USA

Sams Teach Yourself ASP.NET in 24 Hours Complete Starter Kit

Copyright © 2003 by Sams Publishing

International Standard Book Number: 0-672-32543-8

Library of Congress Catalog Number: 2002114148

Printed in the United States of America

First Printing: June 2003

06   05   04   4

Trademarks

All terms mentioned in this book that are known to be trademarks or service marks have been appropriately capitalized. Sams Publishing cannot attest to the accuracy of this information. Use of a term in this book should not be regarded as affecting the validity of any trademark or service mark.

Warning and Disclaimer

Every effort has been made to make this book as complete and as accurate as possible, but no warranty or fitness is implied. The information provided is on an "as is" basis. The author and the publisher shall have neither liability nor responsibility to any person or entity with respect to any loss or damages arising from the information contained in this book or from the use of the CD or programs accompanying it.

Bulk Sales

Sams Publishing offers excellent discounts on this book when ordered in quantity for bulk purchases or special sales. For more information, please contact:

U.S. Corporate and Government Sales
1-800-382-3419
corpsales@pearsontechgroup.com

For sales outside of the U.S., please contact:

International Sales
+1-317-428-3341
international@pearsontechgroup.com

ASSOCIATE PUBLISHER
Michael Stephens

ACQUISITIONS EDITOR
Neil Rowe

DEVELOPMENT EDITOR
Mark Renfrow

MANAGING EDITOR
Charlotte Clapp

PROJECT EDITOR
Matthew Purcell

COPY EDITOR
Publication Services, Inc.

INDEXER
Publication Services, Inc.

PROOFREADER
Publication Services, Inc.

TECHNICAL EDITOR
Mike Diehl

TEAM COORDINATOR
Cindy Teeters

INTERIOR DESIGNER
Gary Adair

COVER DESIGNER
Alan Clements

PAGE LAYOUT
Publication Services, Inc.

GRAPHICS
Tammy Graham
Laura Robbins

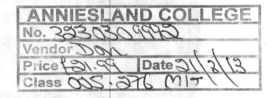

Contents at a Glance

Contents

Hour 5   Visual Basic .NET Variables and Operators   111

Hour 6   Visual Basic .NET Control Structures   137

About the Author

As editor and main contributor to 4GuysFromRolla.com, a popular ASP/ASP.NET resource Web site, **Scott Mitchell** has authored hundreds of articles on Microsoft Web Technologies since 1998. In addition to his vast collection of online articles, Scott has written four previous books on ASP/ASP.NET: *Sams Teach Yourself Active Server Pages 3.0 in 21 Days* (Sams); *Designing Active Server Pages* (O'Reilly); *ASP.NET: Tips, Tutorials, and Code* (Sams); and *ASP.NET Data Web Controls Kick Start* (Sams). Scott has also written a number of magazine articles, including articles for Microsoft's *MSDN Magazine* and *asp.netPRO*.

Scott's non-writing accomplishments include speaking at numerous ASP/ASP.NET user groups across the country and at ASP.NET conferences. Scott has also taught numerous ASP.NET classes at University of California, San Diego, Extension. In addition to teaching and writing, Scott also is a software developer. He works as an independent consultant and has authored and sold a number of commercial software applications. Scott recently completed his master's degree in computer science at the University of California, San Diego.

Dedication

This book is dedicated to my dog Sam. You're such a good girl!

Acknowledgments

The past six months have been quite busy for me writing-wise. Over this duration I wrote a total of approximately 800 pages, churning out two books (the one you have in your hands now and *ASP.NET Data Web Controls Kick Start*, also by Sams Publishing). This feat would not have been possible if it weren't for the untiring patience and undying support of my fiancée, Jisun. You make life unbearably fun, dear.

Furthermore, neither this book nor any of my others would have been possible without my wonderful family. Their unwavering love and support has made me the man I am today.

Thanks also to Neil Rowe, Mark Renfrow, Jan Fisher, and the entire editorial team at Sams Publishing.

We Want to Hear from You!

As the reader of this book, *you* are our most important critic and commentator. We value your opinion and want to know what we're doing right, what we could do better, what areas you'd like to see us publish in, and any other words of wisdom you're willing to pass our way.

As an associate publisher for Sams, I welcome your comments. You can email or write me directly to let me know what you did or didn't like about this book—as well as what we can do to make our books better.

Please note that I cannot help you with technical problems related to the *topic* of this book. We do have a User Services group, however, where I will forward specific technical questions related to the book.

When you write, please be sure to include this book's title and author as well as your name, email address, and phone number. I will carefully review your comments and share them with the author and editors who worked on the book.

E-mail: feedback@samspublishing.com

Mail: Michael Stephens
           Sams Publishing
           800 East 96th Street
           Indianapolis, IN 46240 USA

For more information about this book or another Sams title, visit our Web site at www.samspublishing.com. Type the ISBN (excluding hyphens) or the title of a book in the Search field to find the page you're looking for.

Introduction

As the World Wide Web continues its meteoric growth, Web sites have matured from simple collections of static HTML pages to data-driven dynamic Web applications. For example, Web sites like eBay and Amazon.com are much more than simple HTML pages—they're actual applications that are accessed through the Internet. While there are many competing technologies for building data-driven Web sites, this book shows how to use Microsoft's popular ASP.NET technology for creating Web applications.

ASP.NET Web applications are composed of individual ASP.NET Web pages. As we will see in numerous examples throughout this book, these ASP.NET Web pages can display HTML, collect user input, and interact with databases. ASP.NET Web pages contain a mix of both HTML markup and source code. It is the source code of an ASP.NET Web page that allows for the most advanced features, such as accessing data from a database or sending an e-mail from an ASP.NET Web page. The source code of an ASP.NET Web page can be written in any one of a number of different programming languages. This book will be using Microsoft's Visual Basic .NET programming language. Don't worry if you've never programmed in Visual Basic or have never even programmed at all. Starting with Hour 5, "Visual Basic .NET Variables and Operators," we will spend three hours examining programming language concepts and the Visual Basic .NET syntax.

To ease ASP.NET Web page development, Microsoft provides a free development editor, the ASP.NET Web Matrix Project. We will be using the Web Matrix Project throughout this book to create our ASP.NET Web pages. The Web Matrix Project simplifies creating both the HTML markup and source code portions of ASP.NET Web pages. The HTML markup for an ASP.NET Web page can be quickly created by using the Web Matrix Project's What You See Is What You Get (WYSIWYG) graphical editor. With this WYSIWYG editor, you can simply drag and drop various HTML elements onto an ASP.NET Web page, moving them around with a few clicks of the mouse.

With its Code Builders, the Web Matrix Project also simplifies creating the source code portion of an ASP.NET Web page. When using a Code Builder, you simply need to supply values for a few options. Following this, the Code Builder automatically generates the source code to accomplish a given task based on the values you supplied earlier. For example, in Hour 14, "Understanding SQL, the Language of Databases," we will discuss how to use one of the Web Matrix Project's Code Builders to quickly generate the source code needed to retrieve data from a database.

This book is geared for developers new to ASP.NET, whether or not you've had past experience with HTML or programming languages. By the end of this book, you'll be able to create your own dynamic, data-driven Web applications using ASP.NET.

I hope you enjoy reading the book as much as I enjoyed writing it.

Happy Programming!

Scott Mitchell
mitchell@4guysfromrolla.com

PART I

Getting Started with ASP.NET

Hour

HOUR 1

Getting Started with ASP.NET

ASP.NET is an exciting Web programming technology pioneered by Microsoft that allows developers to create *dynamic Web pages,* whose content is dynamically generated whenever the Web pages are requested. For example, once you log on, the front page of Amazon.com will show books it recommends for you, based on your previous purchases. This is a dynamic Web page because it is a single Web page whose content is customized based on what customer is visiting the page.

In this book we'll examine how to create dynamic ASP.NET Web sites quickly and easily. Before we can start creating our first ASP.NET Web page, though, there are three components we must set up and install. The first of these is the .NET Framework, which is the technology that ASP.NET needs in order to function.

In addition to the .NET Framework, we need to install an ASP.NET editor. An editor is a software application that allows us to create and edit ASP.NET Web pages. Since ASP.NET Web pages are simple text files, any text editor will work (such as Microsoft Notepad). If you've created Web sites before, though, you know that using tools like Microsoft FrontPage makes the development process much easier than using a generic text editor like Notepad. This is the case for ASP.NET, as well. In this book we will be using a free ASP.NET editor called the ASP.NET Web Matrix Project. The .NET Framework and the ASP.NET Web Matrix Project are both included in the CD-ROM accompanying this book.

The third and final piece we will need to install is a Web server. Fortunately, the ASP.NET Web Matrix Project comes with a Web server. Note that if you are using Windows 2000 or Windows XP Professional, your computer may already have a Web server installed; however, you can still use the Web server included with the ASP.NET Web Matrix Project.

This chapter will be focusing on getting everything set up properly in order to start creating ASP.NET Web applications. While it would be nice to be able to jump straight into creating ASP.NET Web pages, it is important that we first take the time to ensure that the pieces required for ASP.NET are correctly installed and configured.

In this chapter we will cover these points and tasks:

- What is ASP.NET?
- System requirements for using ASP.NET
- Software that must be installed prior to using ASP.NET
- Installing the .NET Framework
- Setting up the ASP.NET Web Matrix Project
- Examining the Web Matrix Project Web Server
- Creating a simple ASP.NET Web page and viewing it through a Web browser

What Is ASP.NET?

Have you ever wondered how dynamic Web sites like Amazon.com work behind the scenes? As a shopper at Amazon.com, you are shown a particular Web page, but the content on the Web page is dynamic, based upon your preferences and actions. For example, if you have an account with Amazon.com, when you visit Amazon.com's home page, your name is shown at the top, and a list of personal recommendations is presented farther down the page. When you type a book's title into the search text box, a list of matching books appears. When you click a particular book's title, you are shown the book's details along with comments from other users and an overall rating. When you add the book to your shopping cart and check out, you are prompted for a credit card number, which is then billed.

Web pages in Web sites whose content is determined dynamically based upon user input or other information are called *dynamic Web pages*. For example, any Web site's search engine page is an example of a dynamic Web page, because the content of the search page is based upon the search criteria entered by the user and the documents on the Web server. Another example is Amazon.com's personal recommendations. The books and products that Amazon.com suggests when you view the page are different from the books and products suggested when someone else views these pages. Specifically, the recommendations at Amazon.com are generated by products you have viewed as well as previous purchases you have made.

The opposite of dynamic Web pages are *static Web pages*, which contain content that does not change. HTML pages, for example, are static Web pages. An HTML Web page on a Web site with the following HTML markup is considered static:

```
<html>
<body>
  <b>Hello, World!</b>
</body>
</html>
```

The reason such a page is considered a static Web page is that regardless of who views the page or what external factors there might be, the output will always be the same: the text, "Hello, World!" in a bold font. The only time the content of a static Web page changes is when someone edits the page and saves it over the old version.

Virtually all Web sites today contain a mix of static and dynamic Web pages. Rarely will you find a Web site that has just static Web pages, because they are so limited in their functionality.

By learning ASP.NET, you will be learning how to create Web sites that contain dynamic Web pages. It is important to understand the differences between how a Web site serves static Web pages versus dynamic Web pages.

Competing Web Programming Technologies

ASP.NET is only one of many technologies that can be employed to generate dynamic Web pages. ASP.NET is the successor to Active Server Pages (ASP), which was Microsoft's earlier dynamic Web page creation technology. Similar technologies include PHP, JSP, and ColdFusion.

Personally, I find ASP.NET to be the easiest and most powerful technology of the bunch, which is why I'm writing a book about ASP.NET instead of one of these other technologies. Furthermore, ASP.NET is head and shoulders above ASP. If you've created ASP scripts in the past, you'll no doubt find that you can do the same things you did in ASP by using ASP.NET but in a fraction of the time.

If you have experience developing Web applications with other Web programming technologies, such as ASP, PHP, or JSP, you may already be well versed in the material covered in the next two sections. If this is the case, feel free to skip to the "ASP.NET System Requirements" section.

Serving Static Web Pages

If you've developed Web sites before, you likely know that a Web site requires a *Web server*. A Web server is a software application that continually waits for incoming *Web requests*, which are requests for a particular URL (see Figure 1.1). The Web server examines the requested URL, locates the appropriate file, and then sends this file back to the client who made the Web request.

FIGURE 1.1
The Web server handles incoming Web requests.

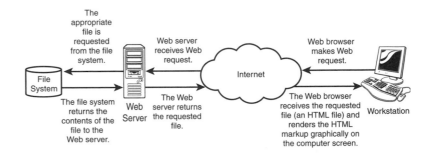

For example, when you visit Amazon.com, your Web browser makes a Web request to Amazon.com's Web server for a particular URL. If you are viewing the details for a particular book, the URL may end something like /index.html. Amazon.com's Web server translates this requested URL into an actual file residing on the same computer where the Web server resides. The server returns the contents of the file, which is then rendered by your browser. Here the file /index.html might contain HTML markup that displays Amazon.com's home page.

This Web server model is adequate for serving static pages, whose content does not change. However, such a simple model is insufficient for serving dynamic pages, because the Web server merely returns the contents of the requested URL to the browser that initiated the request. That is, the contents of the requested URL are not modified in any way based on external inputs.

Serving Dynamic Web Pages

With a static Web page, the contents are just HTML tags that describe how the page should be rendered on a user's Web browser. Therefore, when a static Web page is requested, the Web server can simply send the Web page's content, without modification, to the requesting Web browser.

This simple model won't work for dynamic Web pages, where the content of the Web page can be dependent upon various factors on a per-visitor basis. To accommodate this dynamic content, dynamic Web pages contain source code that is *executed* when the page is requested (see Figure 1.2). When the code is executed, it produces HTML markup as its result, which is then sent back to the visitor's Web browser.

FIGURE 1.2

The content of a dynamic Web page is created by executing the dynamic Web page's source code.

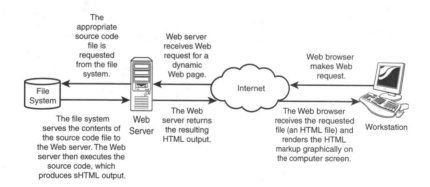

This model allows for dynamic content because the content for a dynamic Web page isn't actually created until the Web page is requested. For example, imagine that we wanted to create a Web page that displays the current date and time. If we wished to do this using a static Web page, someone would need to edit the Web page every second, continually updating the previous time on the page to the current time. Clearly, this isn't feasible.

With a dynamic Web page, source code can retrieve the current date and time. Say that one particular user visits this page on April 4, 2003, at 4:15:03 p.m. When the Web request arrives at this time, the dynamic Web page's code is executed, which obtains the current date and time and returns it to the requesting Web browser. The visitor will see displayed in the browser the date and time: April 4, 2003, 4:15:03 p.m. If another visitor requests this page 7 seconds later, the dynamic Web page's code will be executed, which will obtain the current date and time (April 4, 2003, 4:15:10 p.m.) and will return it to the requesting Web browser, where it will be displayed.

Figure 1.2 is, in actuality, a slightly oversimplified model. Commonly, the Web server and the execution of the dynamic Web page source code are *decoupled*. That is, when a Web request arrives, the Web server determines whether the requested page is a static Web page or a dynamic Web page. If the Web page is static, the Web page's contents are sent directly back to the browser that initiated the request (as shown in Figure 1.1). If, however, the requested Web page is dynamic—say an ASP.NET Web page—the Web server hands off responsibility for executing the page to the *ASP.NET engine* (see Figure 1.3). When the Web server receives a Web request, it examines the requested file's extension. If the extension is .aspx, then the Web server knows the requested page is an ASP.NET Web page and therefore hands off the request to the ASP.NET engine.

FIGURE 1.3

Execution of an ASP.NET Web page is handled by the ASP.NET engine.

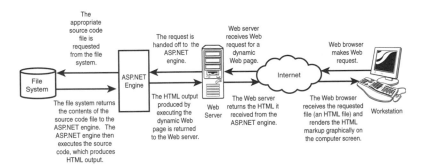

The ASP.NET engine is a piece of software that knows how to execute ASP.NET Web pages. Other Web programming technologies, such as ASP, PHP, and JSP, have their own engines, which know how to execute ASP, PHP, and JSP pages, respectively.

Recall that when a dynamic Web page is executed, its result is HTML output. When the ASP.NET engine executes an ASP.NET Web page, the engine generates the Web page's resulting HTML output. This HTML output is then returned to the Web server, which then returns the HTML to the browser that initiated the Web request.

ASP.NET System Requirements

Recall that your browser doesn't know or care that your Web site uses ASP.NET Web pages. (From here on throughout this book, dynamic Web pages that are executed by the ASP.NET engine are referred to as *ASP.NET Web pages*.) However, for a Web server to be able to execute ASP.NET Web pages, it needs to have the ASP.NET engine (which is what executes the ASP.NET Web page) installed. In order to install the ASP.NET engine, the computer must be running Microsoft Windows 2000, Microsoft Windows XP, or Microsoft Windows Server 2003.

Microsoft's Windows Server 2003 is Microsoft's latest Windows variant. This version of Windows is designed for use on a server, which is a computer that typically does nothing but handle particular types of requests from remote computers. For example, a machine may function as a Web server, meaning its sole purpose is to handle incoming Web requests, or a machine may be designed to be a mail server, in which case it handles incoming and outgoing email traffic.

Because Microsoft Windows Server 2003 is an operating system geared toward these special-purpose machines, it is very unlikely that your personal computer is using Microsoft Windows Server 2003.

If your personal computer is running on one of these three operating systems, you can work through the examples in this book using your own computer. You can install a Web server on your personal computer that will serve the ASP.NET Web pages you will be creating throughout this book. (We'll examine how to install a Web server in the section "Serving ASP.NET Web Pages from Your Personal Computer," coming later in this chapter.)

What if Your Computer Doesn't Have the Necessary Operating System Installed?

If your personal computer does not have Microsoft Windows 2000, Microsoft Windows XP, or Microsoft Windows Server 2003 as its operating system, then you cannot serve ASP.NET Web pages from your local computer. If this is the case, you have two options. The first is to purchase one of these operating systems. The second is to use a *Web hosting company*, which has a number of Internet-accessible computers for individuals or other companies to place their Web sites. These computers contain Web servers that are accessible from any other computer on the Internet. You might want to contact one of these Web hosting companies and set up an account with it.

There are literally thousands of Web hosting companies to choose from, ranging dramatically in price, performance, features, support, and other qualities. A great place to start shopping for a Web hosting company is at Web sites like `http://www.tophosts.com` or `http://www.hostindex.com`. These Web sites catalog the thousands of Web hosting companies and allow you to search through their databases looking for companies that match your price range, feature needs, and so forth.

Once you do choose a Web hosting company that you'd like to do business with, be sure to contact the company and make certain it supports ASP.NET development.

When setting up an account, you can ask the company to register a *domain name* for you. A domain name is the text that a person would enter into the Web browser to visit your Web site. (For example, the domain name of Microsoft's site is `microsoft.com`. For my personal Web site, I might choose `scottmitchellinfo.com`.)

Of course, you can only choose a domain name that has not already been registered by somebody else. To determine whether your desired domain name is still available, visit `http://www.netsol.com`, where you can enter a domain name to check on its availability.

Once your Web hosting account is set up, you can move Web pages to the computer where your account is hosted. Then you, or anyone else on the Internet, can visit these pages. If you upload a Web page named `index.htm` and your domain name was `bobshomepage.org`, anyone could view the `index.htm` page by typing `http://www.bobshomepage.org/index.htm` into the browser's Address bar.

If you are not running Windows 2000, Windows XP, or Windows Server 2003, you should still install the .NET Framework on your computer, as well as the ASP.NET Web Matrix Project. The ASP.NET Web Matrix Project is a free tool we will be using to help us create our ASP.NET Web pages. To run the ASP.NET Web Matrix Project, we need to have the .NET Framework installed, as well. Instructions for these tasks are given in upcoming sections in this chapter.

Getting Started with a Web Hosting Company

Before you can create an account with a Web hosting company, you need to find a suitable company, and in order to execute ASP.NET Web pages, you need to find a Web hosting company that supports ASP.NET. The easiest way to find such a company, in my opinion, is to check sites like TopHosts.com and HostIndex.com, which list hundreds of Web hosting companies. You can search these sites' databases for Web hosting companies that meet certain criteria, such as cost per month, geographical location, Web server platforms used, and other criteria.

> Because you will need a Web hosting company that provides ASP.NET support, consider searching for Web hosting companies that use Windows 2000 as their Web server platform.

Costs for Web hosting companies can range from a few dollars per month to hundreds or thousands of dollars per month, based on the features provided. Additionally, most Web hosting companies have a setup fee in the $50 to $100 range. On top of the Web hosting costs, you will probably want to register a domain name, which costs $35 per year.

When choosing a Web hosting company, pick one that has *FTP* support. FTP (or File Transfer Protocol) is a protocol that allows transferring of files from one computer to another. The reason is that throughout this book we will be using a free Web development editor from Microsoft called the Web Matrix Project. In order to use the Web Matrix Project to edit and create Web pages on a Web host's computer, the Web host must provide FTP support.

> If you do not have Windows 2000, Windows XP, or Windows Server 2003 installed on your home computer, you may become a bit agitated that you have to shell out money every month to create and test the ASP.NET Web pages you will be creating throughout this book.
>
> Fortunately, there is a Web hosting company that has free Web hosting: Brinkster.com. Unfortunately, there is no FTP support with the free account, meaning that you cannot use the ASP.NET Web Matrix Project editor; rather, you have to type the content of your files into a textbox on the Brinkster Web site.

Once you have picked out a Web hosting company and have double-checked that it supports ASP.NET development, contact the company's sales staff to create an account.

What About Using a Web Hosting Company Even Though You Have the Necessary Operating System Installed?

You may be wondering whether even with Windows 2000, Windows XP, or Windows Server 2003 installed on your personal computer, you should choose to use a Web hosting company instead. This depends on what you want to accomplish. If you simply want to learn ASP.NET and not create a public Web site that others can visit, you are better off running the examples locally, on your own machine. If, however, you want to create a public Web site that anyone else can visit via Web browser, you should consider creating an account with a Web hosting company.

Can I Host a Web Site from My Personal Computer?

Readers who have always-on broadband connections, such as through a cable modem or DSL, and have a static IP address may be able to host a Web site from their personal computers. For more information on this option, contact your broadband provider.

If you want a public Web site, I'd personally recommend that you go with a Web hosting company. Setting up your computer to host a public Web site can be a difficult process and, if not done correctly, can leave your computer open to a number of security threats. For example, in July 2001 an Internet worm named Code Red spread quickly across the Internet, infecting Microsoft Web servers. (A *worm* is a program that replicates and distributes itself over a computer network.) Specifically, the worm defaced Web pages by adding the following text: "HELLO! Welcome to http://www.worm.com! Hacked By Chinese!" (For more information on the Code Red worm, see: http://www.cert.org/advisories/CA-2001-19.html.) By setting up a public Web server on your personal computer, you open yourself up to this sort of attack.

To summarize, if you want to create a public ASP.NET Web site, consider using a Web hosting company. Otherwise, develop your ASP.NET Web site locally, as it will save you money and does not require that you be online to create, edit, and test your ASP.NET Web pages.

Serving ASP.NET Web Pages from Your Personal Computer

In order to serve ASP.NET Web pages from your personal computer, you will need to install Microsoft's .NET Framework and a Web server. The steps for installing these two components can be found in the upcoming sections "Installing the .NET Framework" and "Installing a Web Server." Additionally, you will want to install an ASP.NET editor that you can use to create and edit ASP.NET Web pages. I recommend Microsoft's ASP.NET Web Matrix Project, which is a free editor provided by Microsoft (and included on the book's CD). The steps for installing the Web Matrix Project can be found in the section "Installing the ASP.NET Web Matrix Project."

If you plan on having a Web hosting company serve your ASP.NET Web pages, you won't need to install the Web server or .NET Framework on your personal computer. You will, however, need an editor, so you should still install the Web Matrix Project.

Installing the .NET Framework

The first step in serving ASP.NET pages from your personal computer is installing the .NET Framework, which is included on the accompanying CD. Start by installing the *.NET Framework Redistributable*, which contains only the essential pieces needed to run an ASP.NET Web site. This lightweight version is available on the accompanying CD in a 21MB file named `dotnetredist.exe`.

After you have installed the .NET Redistributable, you can optionally install the *.NET Framework SDK* (for software development kit). This optional installation contains full documentation, samples, tutorials, a free database product called Microsoft Database Engine (MSDE), and other goodies. The .NET Framework SDK is packaged into a single file called `setup.exe`, which is a 131MB file. Unfortunately the .NET Framework SDK can only be installed if your computer's operating system is Windows NT, Windows 2000, or Windows XP.

> If you are running Microsoft Windows Server 2003, you should already have the .NET Framework installed. Similarly, if you are running Windows 2000 or Windows XP and have installed Microsoft's Visual Studio .NET, the .NET Framework should already be installed.

The .NET Framework is also available to download from Microsoft's Web site at either `http://www.asp.net` or `http://msdn.microsoft.com/net`.

Starting the Installation Process

To begin installing the .NET Framework, locate and double-click the `dotnetredist.exe` file on the accompanying CD. This will begin the .NET Framework Redistributable setup, displaying the splash screen shown in Figure 1.5. The redistributable is simple enough to setup: merely click the Next button after the splash screen and the installation process will complete automatically.

After installing the .NET Framework Redistributable you can optionally install the .NET Framework SDK, assuming your computer is using Windows 2003 Server, Windows XP Professional, or Windows 2000 as its operating system. If you decide to install the .NET Framework SDK and your operating system does not currently have Microsoft's Internet Information Services (IIS) Web server installed, you may be prompted with the dialog box shown in Figure 1.4, which warns you that IIS should probably be installed prior to setting up the .NET Framework SDK. However, it does not need to be installed at this point, and we will discuss installing IIS and other Web servers in the "Installing a Web Server" section later in this chapter. For now, just click the Continue button.

FIGURE 1.4

If you do not have IIS installed, you will be shown this dialog box.

 IIS is Microsoft's commercial-grade Web server that ships with Windows 2000, Windows XP Professional, and Windows Server 2003. Even if you are running one of these operating systems, though, IIS might not be installed, depending on the setup options you specified when installing your operating system.

 In order to install the .NET Framework, you need to have the latest version of Microsoft Windows Installer. If you are installing the .NET Framework on Windows XP or Windows Server 2003, you should already have the latest version of the Windows Installer. If you are installing on an earlier version of Windows, however, you may not have the latest version of Installer. Don't worry, though. When installing, if you do not have the most recent version, the setup program will inform you and then, with your permission, automatically download the latest version of the Windows Installer.

You should now see the .NET Framework Installation Setup splash page, which is shown in Figure 1.5.

FIGURE 1.5

The first screen of the .NET Framework installation.

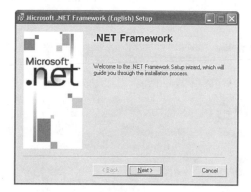

At this point you will need to step through two screens, selecting various options. To proceed to the first of these screens, push the Next button. This screen, shown in Figure 1.6, allows you to choose what pieces of the .NET Framework SDK you want installed. I would encourage you to keep the default options. However, if you are not interested in having sample applications and code installed, feel free to unselect the SDK Samples check box. Once you have made your selection, click the Next button.

FIGURE 1.6

Choose what pieces of the .NET Framework SDK to install.

The new screen allows you to specify the destination folder the .NET Framework will be installed in (see Figure 1.7). Again, I would encourage you to use the default choice. Also, the screen allows you to choose whether you want the environment variables registered. Leave this check box checked.

FIGURE 1.7

This screen allows you to specify where to install the .NET Framework.

Once you click the Next button from this screen, the .NET Framework will be installed onto your computer, which can take several minutes. Once the .NET Framework has been successfully installed on your computer, the next step is to install the editor we will be using to create and edit our ASP.NET Web pages: the ASP.NET Web Matrix Project!

Installing the ASP.NET Web Matrix Project

As we discussed earlier, ASP.NET Web pages, being dynamic Web pages, contain a mixture of HTML markup and source code. These pages, like static HTML Web pages, are simple text files and can therefore be created and edited with any text editor. Given this, installing the ASP.NET Web Matrix Project is optional, because you could decide to create your ASP.NET Web pages through a text editor like Microsoft's Notepad.

However, the Web Matrix Project was designed specifically for editing ASP.NET Web pages and contains many useful features and tools not found in generic text editors. Furthermore, the ASP.NET Web Matrix Project comes with a built-in Web server. Therefore, by installing the Web Matrix Project, you do not need to install a separate Web server, such as IIS.

The ASP.NET Web Matrix Project Web Server can only serve ASP.NET Web pages for Windows 2000, Windows XP, and Windows Server 2003. Even if you do not have one of these operating systems installed, you should still install the ASP.NET Web Matrix Project, as you can use it to edit ASP.NET Web pages on a remote computer, as well.

In fact, all of the examples used in this book were created with the Web Matrix Project and were tested using the Web server included with the Web Matrix Project. Additionally, many of the powerful tools provided by the ASP.NET Web Matrix Project are used in the book, so it is assumed that you have this editor installed. For these reasons, I strongly encourage you to take the few moments needed to install ASP.NET Web Matrix.

There are other editors available that are designed specifically for editing ASP.NET Web pages. These include Microsoft's Visual Studio .NET and Macromedia's DreamWeaver MX. However, these editors can be prohibitively costly. DreamWeaver MX can run you $400 to $800, depending on the version, while Visual Studio .NET's price range runs from $100 to $2,500. The ASP.NET Web Matrix, on the other hand, is free.

Starting the Web Matrix Installation Process

The Web Matrix Project is included on the accompanying CD. To install it, double-click the file webmatrix.msi. This will begin the installation process, and you should see the splash screen shown in Figure 1.8.

FIGURE 1.8

The Web Matrix installation starts with the splash screen.

Once you click the splash screen's Next button, you will be taken to a screen that displays the Web Matrix Project license agreement. Following this you will be prompted to enter customer information, such as your name and organization. After this screen you are allowed to specify any custom setup options. Simply keep the default options. Finally, you will be shown a screen that lists your installation options. After clicking Next here, the Web Matrix Project will begin to be installed on your system.

A Quick Tour of the Web Matrix Project

The ASP.NET Web Matrix Project is a sophisticated editor for creating and editing ASP.NET Web pages either locally or remotely. Throughout the course of this book, we will be using the Web Matrix Project to create and edit our ASP.NET Web pages. Many of the editor's features will be examined and discussed when they are first used.

Before we move on, though, let's take a moment to examine some of the basic features of the Web Matrix Project. To launch the Web Matrix Project, go to Start, Programs, Microsoft ASP.NET Web Matrix Project, ASP.NET Web Matrix.

> If you installed the ASP.NET Web Matrix Project but have yet to install the .NET Framework, you will get an application exception dialog box when attempting to run the Web Matrix Project.

Once the application loads, you should be prompted with a dialog box to create a new file (see Figure 1.9). If you want to create a new file, you can select the type of file in the upper right corner of the dialog box; the types of files, as you can see in Figure 1.9, are ASP.NET Page, ASP.NET User Control, HTML Page, and so on. Additionally, you can specify the directory the file should be placed in, its filename, and other attributes.

FIGURE 1.9

Create a new ASP.NET Web page named `MyFirstPage.aspx`.

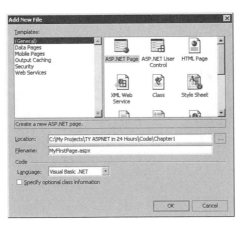

Creating Our First ASP.NET Web Page

Let's create a new ASP.NET Web page. If your computer has Windows 2000, Windows XP, or Windows Server 2003 installed, you can develop and test your ASP.NET Web pages locally, on your own computer's file system. To do this, create a new file named `MyFirstPage.aspx`. Leave the language as Visual Basic .NET and leave the Specify optional class information check box unchecked.

> Web servers use requested URL file extensions to determine how to handle Web requests. It is important that your ASP.NET Web pages end with the extension `.aspx`, so that the Web server knows to have the ASP.NET Web page executed by the ASP.NET engine.

If You Are Using a Web Hosting Company

If your computer is not using Windows 2000, Windows XP, or Windows Server 2003 and you have already created an account with a Web hosting company, you might be able to use the ASP.NET Web Matrix Project to remotely edit files on your Web hosting company's computer. Your Web hosting company needs to support FTP, however.

To create an FTP connection to your Web hosting company's computer, close the New File dialog box shown in Figure 1.9 by clicking Cancel. Then go to the Workspace menu and choose Add FTP Connection. This will display the dialog box shown in Figure 1.10. Here you are prompted to enter the FTP Site, Port, User Name, and Password for the FTP connection, as well as the Web URL, which is the URL where your Web site resides.

FIGURE 1.10

The Web Matrix Project allows you to work on files remotely via FTP.

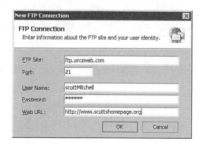

> To determine what values to put in the FTP Site, Port, User Name, and Password boxes, contact your Web hosting company.

Once you make a connection to your Web hosting company's computer, an FTP folder
will be added to the Workspace window in the upper right corner. To create a new file,
right-click the FTP folder name and select Add New Item (see Figure 1.11). This will
then display the Add New File dialog box shown in Figure 1.9. Create a new file named
`MyFirstPage.aspx`. Leave the language as Visual Basic .NET and leave the Specify
optional class information check box unchecked.

FIGURE 1.11
*To create a new file
on your Web hosting
company's computer,
right-click the FTP
folder and select Add
New Item.*

Providing the Content for `MyFirstPage.aspx`

Upon your creating the new file, a new window should appear within the ASP.NET Web
Matrix Project with a cursor flashing inside of it. Go ahead and type a message, such as "Hello,
World!" and then save the file. Figure 1.12 shows a screen shot of what you should be seeing.

FIGURE 1.12
*The ASP.NET Web
page contains the text
"Hello, World!"*

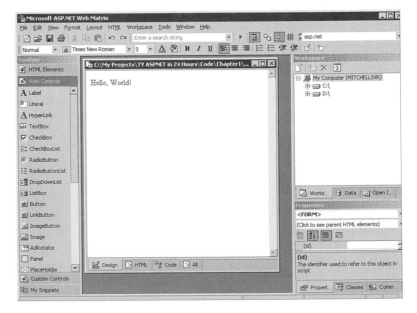

Not only can we type in the text we wish to appear in the ASP.NET Web page, but we can also format it. For example, select the text Hello World and click the Format menu. From here you can format the text as bold, italic, or strikethrough; indent it; change its foreground and background color; and so on.

Viewing the ASP.NET Web Page

At this point we have created and saved a very simple ASP.NET Web page called MyFirstPage.aspx, which simply displays "Hello, World!" Let's view this ASP.NET Web page through a browser.

If you created the ASP.NET Web page locally (because your computer is running Windows 2000, Windows XP, or Windows Server 2003), you must first start the ASP.NET Web Matrix Project Web browser. Begin by hitting F5 or going to the View menu and selecting Start. This will pop up the dialog box shown in Figure 1.13. This dialog box allows you to specify the *application directory* and the *application port*. Simply leave the default selections as are and click Start. (For information on the Application Directory and Application Port settings, refer to the sidebar "Understanding the Application Directory and Application Port.")

FIGURE 1.13

When starting the Web Matrix Web Server, you can specify both the application directory and application port.

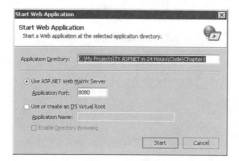

Understanding the Application Directory and the Application Port

When a Web request arrives, the Web request is in the form of a URL, such as http://www.someserver.com/someFile.htm. Recall that the Web server must determine what file the URL request is referring to. Essentially, the Web server has specified an *application directory,* which is a directory on the computer's file system. To locate the file for a Web request, the Web server starts the search at this application directory. Imagine that the application directory is C:\SomeDirectory. When a Web request for http://www.someserver.com/someFile.htm arrives, the Web server will look for the file C:\SomeDirectory\someFile.htm; if a Web request for http://www.someserver.com/dir1/file2.htm arrives, the Web server will look for the file C:\SomeDirectory\dir1\file2.htm.

When you start the Web Matrix Project Web server (by hitting F5 or going to View/Start), the default application directory is the directory where the ASP.NET Web page currently being edited resides.

Recall that a Web server listens for incoming Web requests, and when a Web request arrives, the server retrieves the needed file and sends it back to the requesting source. Such an incoming Web request is a communication from one computer to another. When computers communicate with one another, they must specify what *port* the communication is intended for.

Ports, identified by numbers ranging from 0 to 65,535, are used to simplify communication. Since a computer may be receiving a number of communications from other computers, an application that is expecting incoming messages can opt to listen to a specific port. This way, when the application listening to a specific port receives a message, it can be certain that the message was intended for it and not some other application. For example, Web servers typically listen to port 80.

After you click Start, the Web Matrix Web Server will start up, Internet Explorer will launch, and the ASP.NET Web page will load. Figure 1.14 shows a screenshot of the Web page being viewed through Internet Explorer.

FIGURE 1.14

A Web page displaying "Hello, World!" is shown.

Note that the address in Internet Explorer is `http://localhost:8080/MyFirstPage.aspx`. When requesting a Web page from a Web server installed locally on your machine, you will always use the name `localhost`. The `:8080` portion indicates that the Web request is being made to port 8080 (instead of the default, port 80).

When the Web Matrix Web Server is started, an icon will be added to your computer's taskbar (see Figure 1.15). You can stop the Web Matrix Web Server by right-clicking this icon and choosing the Stop option, as shown in Figure 1.16.

FIGURE 1.15

A taskbar icon is added when you start the Web Matrix Web Server.

FIGURE 1.16

Choose Stop to halt the Web Matrix Web Server.

When the Web Matrix Web Server is started, you must specify an Application Directory. Once this directory has been specified, you can use the Web server to view ASP.NET Web pages in that directory, or in any of its subdirectories. However, if you want to view an ASP.NET Web page that resides in a different directory, you must either stop the first Web server before starting the second, or you must start the second Web server instance using an Application Port setting that differs from the first Web server's.

Also, when you exit the Web Matrix Project the Web server does not automatically stop. Be sure to manually stop the Web Matrix Web Server after exiting from the editor.

If you are using a Web hosting company, you can view your ASP.NET Web page by launching your Web browser and entering the appropriate URL. For example, if your Web hosting company has set up the domain name http://www.AcmeWebSite.com to point to your Web site on its servers, you can view the ASP.NET Web page MyFirstPage.aspx by visiting http://www.AcmeWebSite.com/MyFirstPage.aspx.

Installing a Web Server

If you have installed the Web Matrix Project, then you already have installed a Web server on your computer. (If you have yet to install the Web Matrix Project, please take a moment to do so; see the "Installing the ASP.NET Web Matrix Project" section for more information.) In fact, the Web Matrix Web Server was the Web server used to test all of the examples in this book.

If you are running Windows 2000, Windows XP Professional, or Windows Server 2003 (hereafter referred to simply as local Web servers), however, you can install Microsoft's Internet Information Services (IIS) Web server, as well, and use that when testing your ASP.NET Web pages.

Windows XP Home edition does not come with IIS. To view ASP.NET Web pages through Windows XP Home, you will need to use the Web Matrix Project Web Server.

Table 1.1 contains a list of Windows operating systems and what Web server options they support, if any. Note that Windows 98 and Windows ME cannot use the Web Matrix Web Server or IIS. Therefore, if you are using one of these two operating systems, you must host your ASP.NET Web pages with a Web hosting company. Table 1.1 also shows that the IIS Web server cannot be used with Windows XP Home.

TABLE 1.1 Web Server Options for a Variety of Operating Systems

Windows Version	Web Matrix Web Server	IIS	Requires Web Hosting
Windows 98			X
Windows ME			X
Windows NT	X	X	X
Windows XP Pro	X	X	
Windows XP Home	X		
Windows Server 2003	X	X	

IIS and the Web Matrix Project Web Server are two very different Web servers. IIS is a professional-grade Web server used by many large Web sites, while the Web Matrix Project Web Server was not designed for use as a production Web server. In fact, the Web Matrix Project Web Server is limited in that it can only accept Web requests that originated from the same computer on which it is installed. Even with the Web Matrix Project Web Server running on a machine with an always-on connection to the Internet, no one outside will be able to have a request fulfilled by this Web server.

This may seem too restrictive, but it was put in place to protect users from Internet worms like Code Red. Also, the Web Matrix Project Web Server was designed for developers to test out their own ASP.NET Web pages, not for running Web sites. For these reasons, the designers of the Web Matrix Project Web Server decided to have the Web server accept only local incoming Web requests.

I encourage you to use the Web Matrix Project Web Server, but if you have a local Web server installed and you want to use IIS as your Web server, feel free. IIS may already be installed, depending on the options you chose when installing your operating system.

If IIS is not installed, you can install it via the following steps:

1. Go to the Control Panel and select Add or Remove Programs.

2. When the Add or Remove Programs dialog box comes up, click the Add/Remove Windows Components button (the third button down on the left-hand column). This will pop up a dialog box that lists the Windows Components you can add or remove.

3. Scroll down until you see the Internet Information Services (IIS) line item and simply check the box, as shown in Figure 1.17. Then click Next, and IIS will be installed.

FIGURE 1.17

Select the IIS check box from the list of Windows components.

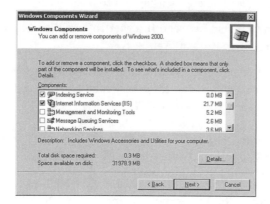

Summary

By installing the .NET Framework and the ASP.NET Web Matrix Project, which includes a Web server, you have set up your computer so that you can create and test ASP.NET Web pages. While you can install the .NET Framework on any version of Windows from Windows 98 on, keep in mind that in order to work with ASP.NET, you must be using Windows 2000, Windows XP, or Windows Server 2003 as your operating system.

Without one of these three operating systems, you will need to have your ASP.NET Web pages hosted on a computer that does meet this requirement. Fortunately, there are thousands of companies out there that provide such a service. If you decide to host the ASP.NET Web pages on a remote computer, you should still install the .NET Framework and the ASP.NET Web Matrix Project.

Now that we have installed and configured all of the pieces needed to develop ASP.NET Web pages, we're ready to dig into ASP.NET! The first step, which we'll tackle in the next chapter, is understanding the various pieces of an ASP.NET Web page and how they work together.

Q&A

Q **What is the main difference between a static and a dynamic Web page?**

A A static Web page has static content, whereas a dynamic Web page's content is generated each time the page is requested.

Q **What options for developing ASP.NET applications are available to a reader whose computer is not running Windows 2000, Windows XP, or Windows Server 2003?**

A The reader can decide to purchase one of these operating systems or can develop ASP.NET Web pages remotely by using a Web hosting company.

Q **What are the differences between Internet Information Services (IIS) and the ASP.NET Web Matrix Project Web Server?**

A IIS is Microsoft's commercial-grade Web server and is designed to handle Web requests from remote computers. IIS is very robust and is used on some of the most visited Web sites, such as www.microsoft.com. The ASP.NET Web Matrix Project, on the other hand, is designed as a lightweight Web server for developers to use in testing their ASP.NET Web pages. Due to its purpose, the ASP.NET Web Matrix Project Web Server does not handle remote Web requests.

Q **Can the Web Matrix Project still be used as ASP.NET editor even if the computer is running Windows 98, Windows ME, or Windows NT?**

A Yes. However, to use the Web Matrix Project, you must first install the .NET Framework. Recall that if your computer is running Windows 98 or Windows ME, you can install the .NET Framework only via the .NET Framework Redistributable. Once you've installed the .NET Framework and the ASP.NET Web Matrix Project, you can access the files on a remote Web host by using the Web Matrix Project's built-in FTP capabilities.

Workshop

Quiz

1. What is the difference between a static Web page and a dynamic Web page?
2. What is the purpose of the ASP.NET engine?
3. True or false—ASP.NET Web pages can be served from computers using the Windows ME operating system.
4. What software packages must be installed to serve ASP.NET Web pages from a computer?

5. When should you consider using a Web hosting company to host your ASP.NET Web pages?

6. What software packages must be installed to edit ASP.NET Web pages that reside on a Web host computer?

Answers

1. The HTML markup for a static Web page remains constant until a developer directly modifies the HTML markup. The HTML markup for a dynamic Web page, on the other hand, is automatically produced every time the Web page is requested by a Web visitor.

2. When the Web server receives a request for an ASP.NET Web page, it hands off the request to the ASP.NET engine, which then executes the requested ASP.NET Web page and returns its HTML markup to the Web server. The ASP.NET engine allows for the HTML markup of an ASP.NET Web page to be dynamically generated for each request.

3. False. ASP.NET Web pages can be served only from computers running Windows 2000, Windows XP, or Windows Server 2003.

4. For a computer to serve ASP.NET Web pages, the .NET Framework must be installed. Additionally, a Web server must be installed.

5. You should consider using a Web hosting company if your computer is not running one of the operating systems that can serve ASP.NET Web pages. Additionally, if you want your ASP.NET Web pages to be accessible via the Internet, you should consider using a Web hosting company.

6. To edit an ASP.NET Web page that resides on a Web hosting computer, you can use the Web Matrix Project.

Exercises

This chapter does not have any exercises. We'll start with exercises in future chapters, once we become more fluent in creating ASP.NET Web pages.

HOUR 2

Understanding the ASP.NET Programming Model

Before we can start creating ASP.NET Web pages, it is important that we have a solid understanding of the ASP.NET programming model. As we'll see in this hour, ASP.NET Web pages are comprised of two portions: a source code portion and an HTML portion. In this hour's first section, "Examining the HTML Markup Portion of an ASP.NET Web Page," we'll examine what belongs in the HTML portion of an ASP.NET Web page.

In this hour we'll also see the the Web Matrix Project editor in action a number of times. Because we'll be using this editor throughout the book, please do take the time in this hour to familiarize yourself with the Web Matrix Project.

In this hour we will cover the following:

- What content belongs in the HTML portion of an ASP.NET Web page
- A quick primer on HTML semantics and syntax

- The syntactical differences between valid XHTML and HTML
- Using the Web Matrix Project to create a new ASP.NET Web page
- Viewing an ASP.NET Web page through a Web browser
- Adding HTML controls to the HTML portion of an ASP.NET Web page
- Adding Web controls to the HTML portion of an ASP.NET Web page
- The similarities and differences between HTML controls and Web controls

Examining the HTML Markup Portion of an ASP.NET Web Page

As we discussed in the previous hour, there are some fundamental differences between static Web pages and dynamic Web pages, the most profound one being that dynamic Web pages contain a mix of HTML markup and source code. Whenever a dynamic Web page is requested, its source code is executed, generating HTML markup. This dynamically generated HTML markup is then sent back to the requesting client.

In this section we are going to be looking at the HTML markup portion of a dynamic Web page. In the upcoming section "Examining the Source Code Portion of an ASP.NET Web Page," we'll look at one of the more interesting parts of dynamic Web pages—the source code.

A Brief HTML Primer

HTML markup, as you probably already know, specifies how data should be displayed in a Web browser. For example, to have a Web browser display a message in bold, you could use the following HTML markup:

```
<b>This will be in bold.</b>
```

HTML is composed of *tags* that specify how the data between them should be rendered in a Web browser. A tag is denoted by

```
<tagName>... some content ...</tagName>
```

Here `<tagName>` is referred to as the start tag and `</tagName>` is referred to as the end tag. The semantics of an HTML tag applies formatting to the content between the start and end tags; the formatting applied depends upon the tag name. As we saw earlier, text is made bold by placing it between `<b>` and `</b>` tags. (The `<b>` tag specifies that the content it contains be made bold.)

There is a plethora of HTML markup tags that you can use to specify formatting in a Web page. Such a discussion, however, is beyond the scope of this book. For more information on HTML, be sure to check out *Sams Teach Yourself HTML and XHTML in 24 Hours*, or go online to http://www.w3schools.com/html/.

Not all HTML tags have a start and closing tag. For example, the <br> tag, which specifies a line break, does not have a matching close tag, nor does the <hr> tag, which displays a horizontal line. Similarly, one can use the paragraph tag (<p>) without a closing tag like so:

```
This is one paragraph.
<p>
And this is another.
<p>
And yet another.
```

However, you can use starting and closing paragraph tags like so:

```
<p>This is one paragraph.</p>
<p>And this is another.</p>
<p>And yet another.</p>
```

Nested Tags

HTML tags can be *nested*, meaning that one set of HTML tags can appear within another. For example, if you wanted to have a Web page display a message in both italics and bold, you would use both the <i> tag and <b> tag like so:

```
<i><b>This is both italic and bold</b>, whereas this is just italic</i>
```

In this example the <b> tag is said to be *inside* the <i> tag. (Throughout this book I will also refer to nested tags as one tag being *contained within* the other, or *enclosed within*.)

The semantics of nested tags is fairly straightforward. In our example the <i> tag indicates that everything within it should be formatted using italics. Next the <b> tag indicates that everything within it should be bold. Therefore, the text "This is both italic and bold" will be formatted using both bold and italics. Next the </b> tag appears, which is the bold closing tag. This ends the bold formatting. However, the italic formatting is still in effect, so the text ", whereas this is just italic" will appear in italics. Finally, the closing italics tag is reached (</i>), and the italic formatting ends.

There's no reason why the <b> tag must be inside the <i> tag and not the other way around. That is, you could also do

```
<b><i>This is both italic and bold</i>, whereas this is just bold</b>
```

Here the <i> tag is contained within the <b> tag. Again, the text "This is both italic and bold" will be both bold and italic, but the text ", whereas this is just bold" will be bold but not italic.

These past two examples are instances of *properly nested tags*. Note that in our last example the <i> tag that is contained within the <b> tag has both its starting and closing tags (<i> and </i>) before the closing <b> tag (</b>). An *improperly nested tag* is one whose start tag is contained within a tag but whose closing tag is not. The following HTML markup is an example of an improperly nested tag:

```
<i><b>This is both italic and bold</i>, but this is just bold</b>
```

Notice that the <b> tag's starting tag is contained within the <i> tag, but the <b> tag's closing tag is not. Therefore, the <b> tag is improperly nested.

HTML, however, allows for improperly nested tags. When viewed through a Web browser, this improperly nested HTML markup will display the text "This is both italic and bold" in both italic and bold, and ", but this is just bold" in bold.

> Avoid using improperly nested tags, as they make the HTML harder for people to read. Also, as we will see later in this hour, various pieces of the HTML markup portion of ASP.NET Web pages require that tags *not* be improperly nested.

Case Sensitivity

HTML tag names are *not case sensitive;* that is, the casing of the tag names is irrelevant. For example, a bold tag can be specified using <b> or <B>. The <table> tag can be specified using <tAbLE> or <TABLE>. Additionally, the case of the start or close tag need not match the others. That is,

```
<b>This is bold.</B>
```

will have the same effect as

```
<B>This is bold.</B>
```

or

```
<B>This is bold.</b>
```

A Brief Look at XHTML

XHTML is a variant of HTML that has stricter formatting rules. Specifically, XHTML requires that its tags be properly nested tags and that all tags appear in lowercase. That is, to create an HTML table using XHTML, you must use <table>, not <TABLE> or any other casing variation.

Additionally, XHTML documents require that every tag has a matching close tag. That means to use the paragraph tag, you can't simply use <p> but instead must use <p>...</p>. For a tag that doesn't have a closing tag, such as <br> or <hr>, XHTML requires that you use the following variation:

and

<hr />

The /> is a shorthand notation to specify that there is no content between the starting and closing tags. Using <tagName /> is synonymous to using <tagName></tagName>.

> The X in XHTML stands for *XML*. XML, which stands for *extensible markup language*, is a language that uses tags for describing data. XML has strict formatting criteria that XHTML adopts, such as case sensitivity, properly nested tags, and requiring every tag to have a closing tag. For more information on XML and XHTML, be sure to pick up a copy of *Sams Teach Yourself XML in 24 Hours* and *Sams Teach Yourself HTML and XHTML in 24 Hours*.

As we'll see in the "Look at ASP.NET Web Controls" section later in this hour, the HTML portion of an ASP.NET Web page can contain a number of items referred to as Web controls. These Web controls appear like ordinary HTML tags but require the stricter XHTML formatting rules.

Creating the HTML Portion of an ASP.NET Web Page by Using the Web Matrix Project

Creating the HTML portion of an ASP.NET Web page is fast and easy with the Web Matrix Project's *WYSIWYG editor*.

WYSIWYG stands for What You See Is What You Get. The Web Matrix Project hastens Web design by allowing designers simply to drag and drop HTML elements onto the Web page. Similar WYSIWYG editors can be found in other editors, like Visual Studio .NET, Microsoft FrontPage, and Macromedia's DreamWeaver.

To follow along, start the ASP.NET Web Matrix Project by going to Start, Programs, Microsoft ASP.NET Web Matrix Project, ASP.NET Web Matrix. Create a new ASP.NET Web page named HTMLExample.aspx. (If you want, you can place the newly created ASP.NET Web page in a directory other than the directory suggested by the Add New File dialog box.)

When creating ASP.NET Web pages for the examples in this book, please leave the Language option as the default (Visual Basic .NET) and leave the Specify Optional Class Information checkbox unchecked unless otherwise specified.

If you are using a Web hosting company, first create an FTP connection to your Web hosting company and then create a new ASP.NET Web page by right-clicking the FTP connection name in the Workspace pane and selecting Add New Item.

Figure 2.1 shows what you should be seeing at this point. The window in the middle of the screen represents the ASP.NET Web page just created. Note that this window has four tabs along its bottom left-hand corner. The first one, the one selected by default, is the Design tab. The other three tabs, in order, are HTML, Code, and All.

FIGURE 2.1

The Design tab is the default tab when creating or opening a file.

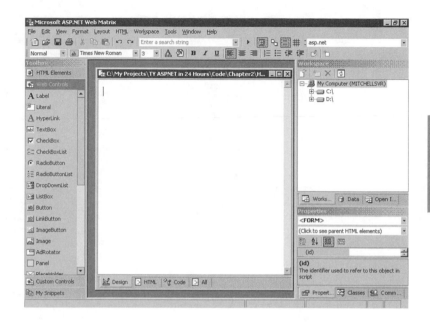

The Design tab displays the *designer*, which is the Web Matrix Project's WYSIWYG editor. Using the designer, you can simply type in the content you want to appear on your ASP.NET page. If you want to add HTML elements to the ASP.NET Web page, you can simply select them from the Toolbox on the left and drag them onto the designer. We'll see how to do this shortly.

The next tab is the HTML tab, which contains the actual HTML markup of your ASP.NET Web page. Take a moment to click the HTML tab. Notice that even though we have yet to add any HTML content to our ASP.NET Web page, some HTML content already exists. Specifically, there is an <html> tag, which has nested within it <head> and <body> tags. Inside the <body> tag is a <form> tag, and inside the <form> tag is an *HTML comment*. Figure 2.2 contains a screenshot of the HTML tab.

> An HTML comment is text in an HTML document that is not displayed by the Web browser. HTML comments are delimited by <!-- and -->.

FIGURE 2.2

The HTML tab contains the HTML markup for the ASP.NET Web page.

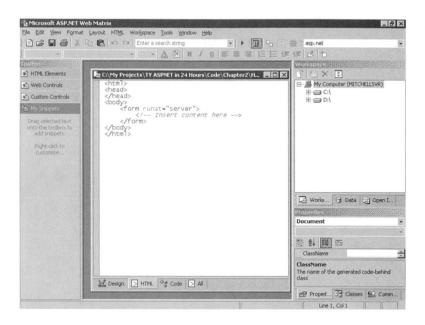

You may have noticed that the `<form>` tag in Figure 2.2 contains a `runat="server"` attribute. This is not a standard HTML attribute. In fact, the `<form>` tag in Figure 2.2 tag is not an HTML element at all!

In an ASP.NET Web page, HTML elements that contain the `runat="server"` attribute are known as *HTML controls*. We'll discuss what, exactly, HTML controls are and their place in an ASP.NET Web page later on in this hour in the "Look at ASP.NET HTML Controls" section.

The Code tab displays just the source code portion of the ASP.NET Web page. The All tab displays both the source code and the HTML portions of the ASP.NET Web page. We'll examine these two tabs in further detail in the section "Examining the Source Code Portion of an ASP.NET Web Page."

Editing the HTML Content by Using the Designer

To edit the ASP.NET Web page's HTML content, you can either use the designer, or you can type the HTML in by hand using the HTML tab. Let's first examine how to create some HTML markup using the designer. Specifically, let's add an HTML table that lists some popular Internet Web sites—Yahoo!, Google, MSN, and Lycos—along with their logos. Start by switching back to the Design tab. The first thing to add is an

HTML table. Go to the HTML menu and select Insert Table. Choosing this option will show the dialog box in Figure 2.3. Here you can enter the number of columns and rows you want to display in your table, as well as the table's overall width and height.

FIGURE 2.3

When inserting an HTML table, you must specify the number of rows and columns as well as the table's width and height.

Choose a table with two columns and four rows and an overall width and height of 300 by 500. In the first column we will display the name of the Web site, and in the second column we will display the Web site logo.

To add the Web site names, simply click inside the first column of each row and type in the Web site's name. Figure 2.4 shows a screenshot of the table after the names have been added.

FIGURE 2.4

The first column contains the name of four Web sites.

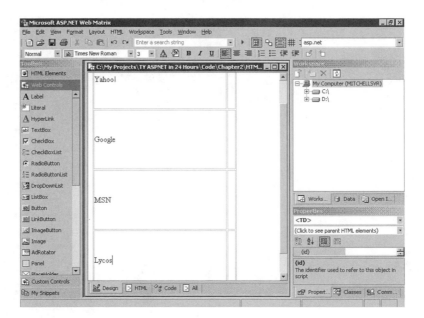

As you can see in Figure 2.4, after typing in the name of the Web site in the first column, the second column is squeezed over so that it is only a thin sliver. Don't worry; once we start to add content to the second column, this column's width will adjust to accommodate its content.

Notice that the name of each Web site is displayed left-justified in a fairly plain-looking font. Let's spruce things up a bit by centering the name of each Web site and displaying each name in a bold, Arial font.

To accomplish this, simply select the text of a particular Web site. Once it is selected, you can make the text centered by going to the Format menu and selecting Bold. Next, to center the text that is still highlighted, go to the Format menu and select Align Center. Finally, to make the font of the still-selected text Arial, simply click on the list of fonts that is positioned beneath the Cut, Copy, and Paste icons near the top left-hand corner. (The Cut, Copy, and Paste icons are the scissors, paper, and clipboard icons found directly beneath the View, Format, and Layout menu headers.)

Figure 2.5 shows a screenshot of the Web Matrix Project after this formatting has been applied to all four Web site names.

FIGURE 2.5

The Web site names have been centered, bolded, and changed to Arial font.

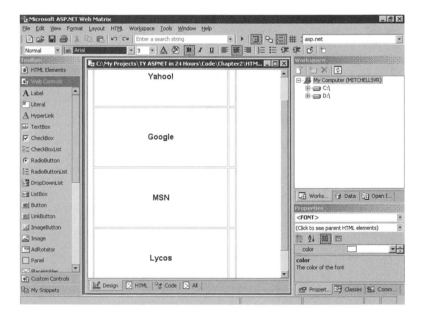

In addition to the Format, Bold and Format, and Align Center menu options, you can also make selected text bold by clicking the bold toolbar or by pressing Ctrl+B. To center the selected text, you can click the centered toolbar icon.

Now let's add the logos for each of the Web sites in the second column. To accomplish this, start by clicking the HTML Element tab of the *Toolbox*. The Toolbox, which is the leftmost pane in the Web Matrix Project, contains four tabs:

1. HTML Elements
2. Web Controls
3. Custom Controls
4. My Snippets

Each tab contains a number of elements underneath it. Only one tab's elements are displayed at a time, so to view another tab's elements, you must click that tab.

When the Web Matrix Project starts up, the Web Controls tab is selected by default. This means that when you first load up the Web Matrix Project, you will see the Web Controls elements in the Toolbox.

We'll be discussing what Web controls are later this hour in the "Look at ASP.NET Web Controls" section.

Once you click the HTML Element tab, you should see the HTML Element tab's elements, which include Label, TextBox, TextArea, Password, Button, and so on. A screenshot of the HTML Elements tab selected is shown in Figure 2.6.

To add one of the HTML Elements to your ASP.NET Web page, first click the element you wish to add. Holding down the mouse button, move the mouse pointer over the location you want the element to be placed, and then release the mouse button.

As you can see from Figure 2.6, one of the HTML elements in the HTML Element tab is an Image element. We'll use this HTML element to add the Web site logos in the second column of the table. Start by dragging and dropping four Image HTML elements into the designer, one in each of the second columns of each of the four rows. Figure 2.7 shows a screenshot of what you should see once the four Image elements have been added to the designer.

FIGURE 2.6

FIGURE 2.6

The HTML Elements tab contains elements that can be dragged and dropped into the designer.

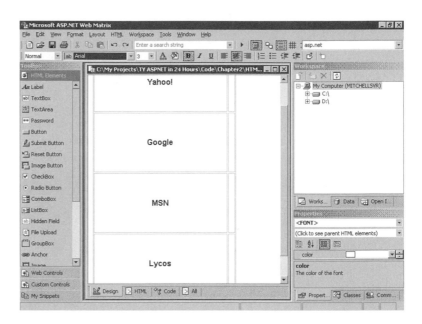

Note that each image element currently is displayed as a red X. This is because we have yet to specify the URL of the image. Each Image element has an `src` property that specifies the URL of the image. To edit the properties of an HTML element, locate the Properties pane in the lower right-hand corner. The Properties pane lists the property names and values of the selected HTML element.

FIGURE 2.7

An Image element has been added to each row in the table.

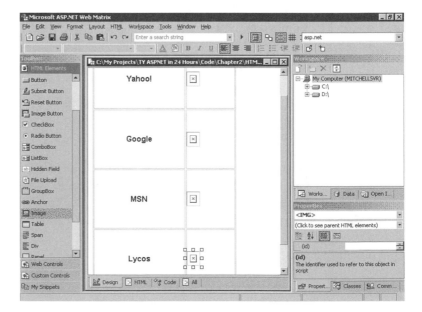

To specify the Image element's src property, select one of the Image elements. This should populate the Properties pane with the Image's properties. Scroll down the Properties pane until you find the src property. By default, this is a blank string, meaning that no value for the src property has been specified. For each company's logo, type in the company's name followed by .gif. For instance, for the Google logo enter the src property as Google.gif.

After entering the src values for the four Image elements, each Image element will still be displayed as a red X. This is because the designer is looking for the file named Google.gif, MSN.gif, and so on. In order to have the Image element display the actual image and not a red X, you need to download these logos from the Internet to your personal computer (or to the Web hosting company's computer if you are using a Web hosting company). It is important that these images be placed in the same directory as the ASP.NET Web page that uses them.

The images may be placed in a different directory than the ASP.NET Web page, but then the src property must be altered accordingly. For example, if the image is placed in a subdirectory named images, the src property for the Google logo should be set to images/Google.gif.

To download the Web site logos to your home computer, simply visit the Web sites (such as www.google.com) and search for the logo on the Web site's home page. Once you have located the logo, right click the logo and choose Save Picture As, being sure to save the logo in the same directory as the ASP.NET Web page that references them.

Once you have added the four images, you may notice that the images are taller or wider than you like. To adjust an image's height or width, you can alter its width and height properties. To specify that an image should have a width of, say, 100 pixels, simply set its width property to a value of 100.

At this point we've created the HTML content for an ASP.NET Web page using the designer. Note that we did not have to write a single line of HTML markup; rather, we simply chose various menu options, dragged and dropped HTML elements from the HTML Elements tab, and set properties via the Properties pane.

To test your ASP.NET Web page, first save it, and then view it as discussed in Hour 1, "Getting Started with ASP.NET." That is, if you are hosting the ASP.NET Web pages locally, hit F5 or go to View, Start. This will start the ASP.NET Web Matrix Project Web Server (if it's not started already) and automatically visit the page using Internet Explorer. If you are using a Web hosting company, save the ASP.NET Web page, fire up your Web browser of choice, and point it toward the appropriate URL.

Figure 2.8 contains a screenshot of the ASP.NET Web page when viewed through a Web browser. Note that what the user visiting the page sees is what we saw in the designer; this is why the designer is referred to as a What You See Is What You Get (WYSIWYG) editor.

FIGURE 2.8

The ASP.NET Web page when viewed through a browser.

Take a moment to click the HTML tab, which is the tab to the right of the Design tab at the bottom of the window containing the content of your ASP.NET Web page. Clicking the HTML tab will show you all of the HTML markup generated for you automatically by the Web Matrix Project's WYSIWYG editor.

> To enter the HTML markup for an ASP.NET Web page's HTML portion by hand, click the HTML tab in the ASP.NET Web page's window (the tab to the right of the Design tab).

Editing the HTML Content by Using the HTML Tab

Some Web designers feel more comfortable creating an HTML document by typing in the HTML markup by hand rather than using a WYSIWYG editor. Although entering the HTML markup by hand is not as efficient as dragging and dropping HTML elements onto the designer, entering the HTML markup manually allows for finer control over the HTML markup, as well as its positioning and indentation.

Let's recreate the table with the Web site names and logos that we created in the "Editing the HTML Content by Using the Designer" section, but this time entering the HTML markup by hand.

Start by creating a new ASP.NET Web page named HTMLMarkupByHand.aspx. Next click the HTML tab. At this point you should see the default HTML content that is inserted into every new ASP.NET Web page by the Web Matrix Project, specifically

```
<html>
    <head>
    </head>
    <body>
        <form runat="server">
            <!-- Insert content here -->
        </form>
    </body>
</html>
```

Now we need to enter the HTML markup to display the table with the four Web site names and logos. Listing 2.1 contains the HTML content that you should enter.

LISTING 2.1   A Two-Columned Table Is Displayed

```
 1: <html>
 2:     <head>
 3:     </head>
 4:     <body>
 5:         <form runat="server">
 6:             <table width="300" height="500">
 7:                 <tr>
 8:                     <td align="center">
 9:                         <font face="Arial"><b>Yahoo!</b></font>
10:                     </td>
11:                     <td align="center">
12:                         <img src="Yahoo.gif" width="100">
13:                     </td>
14:                 </tr>
15:                 <tr>
16:                     <td align="center">
17:                         <font face="Arial"><b>Google</b></font>
```

continues

LISTING 2.1   Continued

```
18:                    </td>
19:                    <td align="center">
20:                      <img src="Google.gif" width="100">
21:                    </td>
22:                  </tr>
23:                  <tr>
24:                    <td align="center">
25:                      <font face="Arial"><b>MSN</b></font>
26:                    </td>
27:                    <td align="center">
28:                      <img src="MSN.gif" width="100">
29:                    </td>
30:                  </tr>
31:                  <tr>
32:                    <td align="center">
33:                      <font face="Arial"><b>Lycos</b></font>
34:                    </td>
35:                    <td align="center">
36:                      <img src="Lycos.gif" width="100">
37:                    </td>
38:                  </tr>
39:                </table>
40:            </form>
41:        </body>
42: </html>
```

Note that the <html>, <head>, <body>, and <form> tags from lines 1–5 and lines 40–42 already are present. All you have to do is type in the HTML content from lines 6 to 39.

> The line numbers shown in Listing 2.1 should *not* be typed into the HTML document. These line numbers are present simply to make it easier to refer to specific lines of code in the listing.

Once you type in the HTML markup in Listing 2.1, save the ASP.NET Web page and view it through a browser. What you see in your Web browser should be similar to Figure 2.8.

> If you are serving ASP.NET Web pages locally from your computer, when I say to view an ASP.NET Web page through a browser, I mean start the Web Matrix Project, if necessary, and visit the page in your Web browser. This can be accomplished simply by pressing F5 or going to View, Start in the Web Matrix Project.
>
> If you are using a Web hosting company, when I say to view an ASP.NET Web page through a browser, I mean fire up your Web browser of choice and visit the appropriate URL.

2

If you enter HTML markup in the HTML tab and then switch to the Design tab, you can see what your HTML markup will look like when viewed through a browser. Beware, however, because when switching to Design mode, the HTML markup you entered in the HTML tab is automatically formatted to XHTML. This means by simply navigating from the HTML tab to the Design tab and then back to the HTML tab, the HTML markup you entered can be altered.

Web designers who prefer entering HTML markup by hand will find this "feature" an annoying one. Fortunately, the Web Matrix Project allows you to disable the Design tab, which protects your hand-written HTML markup from being altered.

To do this, go to the Tools menu and select the Preferences option. This will cause a dialog box to be displayed. This dialog box has three top-level options in its left pane: (General), Text Editor, and Web Editing. Select the Web Editing option, which will display the Web editing preferences, as shown in Figure 2.9.

FIGURE 2.9

The Preferences dialog box allows you to specify the preferences for the Web Matrix Project.

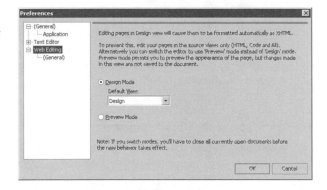

To disable the Design pane, select the Preview Mode option instead of the Design Mode option. Once this change has been made, you will need to close and reopen any open ASP.NET Web pages being edited in the Web Matrix Project to have the change take effect. When you reopen your ASP.NET Web page, notice that the four Design, HTML, Code, and All tabs have been replaced by two tabs: Source and Preview (see Figure 2.10).

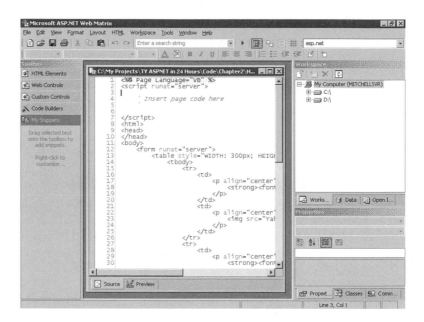

When working in Preview Mode, only two tabs are shown: Source and Preview.

The Source tab is synonymous to the All tab in Design Mode. That is, the Source tab shows both the HTML and source code portions of the ASP.NET Web page. The Preview tab shows the ASP.NET Web page's HTML output when viewed through a browser (like the Design tab in Design Mode). However, the Preview tab cannot have Toolbox elements dragged and dropped onto it, nor can you simply type in content via the Preview tab.

Notice that the Source tab displays line numbers along the left-hand column. These line numbers are not part of the ASP.NET Web page's source code or HTML. Rather, they exist so that developers can discuss portions of the ASP.NET Web page with one another.

When using the Preview Mode, you can no longer use a WYSIWYG editor. Rather, you have to enter all of the HTML markup by hand. The benefit of this is that if you are planning on entering the HTML markup by hand, using the Preview Mode guarantees you that the Web Matrix Project will not alter the HTML markup you wrote.

Figure 2.11 shows a screenshot of the `HTMLMarkupByHand.aspx` page when viewed through the Preview tab.

FIGURE 2.11

The Preview tab shows how the HTML content will look when viewed through a Web browser.

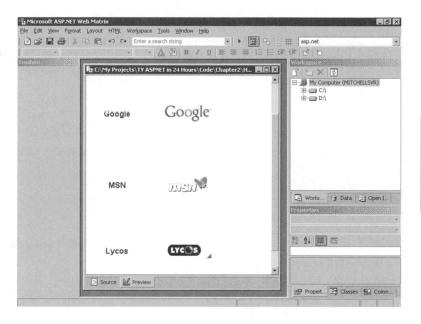

Examining the Source Code Portion of an ASP.NET Web Page

Now that we've examined the HTML portion of an ASP.NET Web page, let's turn our attention to the source code portion. As we saw in Figure 2.1, the Web Matrix Project contains four tabs when in Design Mode. In the last section we examined the Design and HTML tabs; here we will look at the two remaining tabs, Code and All.

If you have the Web Matrix Project set in Preview Mode, you will see only two tabs: Source and Preview. Please take a moment to change the Web Matrix Project back to Design Mode.

Create a new ASP.NET Web page named `SourceCodeExample.aspx`. Be certain that you create the new ASP.NET Web page only after leaving the default Language option as Visual Basic .NET.

Visual Basic .NET is commonly abbreviated as VB.NET.

ASP.NET Web pages can have their source code portion written in one of two programming languages: Visual Basic .NET or C#. In this book all of our code examples will use Visual Basic .NET. For more information on Visual Basic .NET consult Hours 5 through 7.

The Code tab lists the source code content in the ASP.NET Web page. Go ahead and click on the Code tab. You should see a screen similar to that shown in Figure 2.12.

Note that the only content present in the Code tab is the following two lines:

```
' Insert page code here
'
```

FIGURE 2.12

The Code tab contains the source code portion of the ASP.NET Web page.

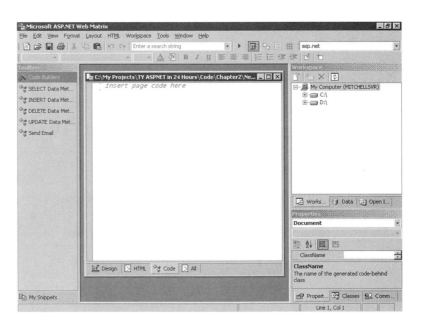

These lines are *comments*. Comments are lines in the source code that are ignored by the ASP.NET engine, much like HTML comments are HTML markup that is ignored by the Web browser. In Visual Basic .NET, any content on a line of code that follows an apostrophe is considered to be a comment. In the Web Matrix Project, such lines of code are italicized and colored green.

If you created the ASP.NET Web page with the Language option as C#, you will
see two lines slightly different from the ones above. Specifically, you will see

```
// Insert page code here
//
```

If this is the case, please close the file and create a new file, but this time
select Visual Basic .NET as the Language choice.

2

A Quick Object-Oriented Programming Primer

In ASP or PHP, two other dynamic Web page technologies, the source code portion of an
ASP or PHP Web page is executed serially, from top to bottom. That is, if the source
code section contains five lines of code, the first line of code is executed first, followed
by the second, then the third, the fourth, and finally the fifth. This programming paradigm,
where one line of code is executed after another, is known as *procedural programming*.

ASP.NET Web pages, however, use *object-oriented programming,* a programming paradigm
that contains *objects*. A key construct of any object-oriented programming language is the
class, which abstractly defines an object. Classes contain *properties*, which describe the state
of the object, and *methods*, which provide the actions that can be performed on the object.
Objects are concrete instances of classes abstractions.

Whew! This all likely sounds very confusing, but a real-world analogy should help.
Think, for a moment, about a car. What things describe a car? What actions can a car
perform?

A car can have various properties, like its make, model, year, and color. A car also has a
number of actions it can perform, such as drive, reverse, turn, and park.

In object-oriented terms, an object's actions are referred to as its methods.

This assimilation of properties and actions (from here on referred to as methods) abstractly
defines what a car can do. The reason this assimilation of properties and methods is an
abstraction is because it does not define a specific car; rather, it describes features common
to all cars. This collection of properties and methods describing an abstract car is a class in
object-oriented terms.

An object is a specific instance of a class. In our analogy an object would be a specific
instance of the car abstraction, such as a year 2000, forest green Honda Accord. The

methods of the car abstraction can then be applied to the object. For example, to drive this Honda to the store, I'd use the drive method, applying the turn method as needed. When I reached the store I'd use the park method. After making my purchases, I'd need to back out of the parking spot, so I'd use the reverse method, and then the drive and turn methods to get back home.

The programming language we will be examining throughout this book—and in detail in Hour 5, "Visual Basic .NET Variables and Operators"—is *Visual Basic .NET*, which is Microsoft's latest version of its Visual Basic programming language. It, like C#, is an object-oriented programming language.

Examining Event-Driven Programming

Another important construct of the programming languages used to create ASP.NET Web pages is the *event* and its corresponding *event handler*. An event, as its name implies, is an action that can occur; the event handler is a piece of code that is executed when the event occurs. Programming languages that include support for events are called *event-driven*.

When an event occurs, it is commonly said that the event has *fired*. Furthermore, an event handler, when run, is referred to as having been *executed*. Therefore, when an event fires, its event handler executes.

As we saw in the last section, classes contain properties and methods. The properties describe the state of the abstraction, whereas the methods describe the actions that can be invoked. We can meld the notion of event-driven programming with object-oriented programming by augmenting the class to include events.

In our earlier analogy we likened the abstract definition of a car to a class, with properties model, make, year, and color, and methods drive, reverse, turn, and park. Let's augment our car class by adding events. One event a car might have is starting. This is the event that occurs when the driver turns the key in the ignition. Another event might be stepping on the accelerator; yet another might be stepping on the brake.

For events to be useful, they need to be paired with an event handler. An event handler is a block of source code that is executed when the event it is specified to deal with fires. The event handler for the car's starting event, for example, might contain code that instructs the starter to start turning the crankshaft.

You can think of ASP.NET Web pages as event-driven programs. The source code portion of the ASP.NET Web page contains event handlers.

Out-of-Order Execution

With procedural programming the code is executed sequentially, from the first line of code to the last. If you have had experience with technologies like ASP or PHP in the past, you know that these technologies use procedural programming languages. With procedural programming you know that code on line 5 will execute before code on line 10.

With event-driven programming, however, there are no such guarantees. The only serial portions of code in an event-driven program are those lines of code within a particular event handler. There is no way to determine, however, the order that the event handlers will be called.

Looking back at our car analogy, imagine that our starting event has an event handler that had the following two lines of code:

```
Begin Starting Event Handler
  Send signal to starter to start turning the crankshaft
  Send signal to fuel injector to send fuel to the engine
End Starting Event Handler
```

When the starting event fires, the starting event handler is executed. The first line of code in this event handler will fire first, followed by the second. But imagine that our complete source code for the car consisted of two event handlers, one for starting and one for stopping.

```
Begin Starting Event Handler
  Send signal to starter to start turning the crankshaft
  Send signal to fuel injector to send fuel to the engine
End Starting Event Handler

Begin Stopping Event Handler
  Send signal to brake drums
  Decrease fuel injector's output
End Stopping Event Handler
```

Even though the starting event handler appears before the stopping event handler, this does not imply that the starting event handler will execute prior to the stopping event handler. Because an event handler is executed only when its corresponding event fires, the order of execution of these event handlers is directly dependent on the order of the events that are fired. The important thing to keep in mind is that the order of the event handlers in the source code has no bearing on the order of execution of the event handlers.

The code used to describe the Starting and Stopping events is not actual VB.NET code but is instead *pseudocode*. This is not code recognized by any particular programming language, but instead is a made-up, verbose, English-like language commonly used when describing programming concepts.

Executing Source Code when an ASP.NET Web Page Is Visited

There are some predefined events that are associated with an ASP.NET Web page. The event that you'll use over and over again in your ASP.NET Web pages is the page's *load event*. When the ASP.NET engine begins execution of an ASP.NET Web page, it fires the ASP.NET Web page's load event. Therefore, if we want to provide source code that is executed immediately after the Web page is requested, we must provide an event handler for this event.

To provide an event handler for the load event, you have to create an event handler through the following *declaration:*

```
Sub Page_Load(sender as Object, e as EventArgs)
  'The code to execute when the page's load event fires
  'goes here...
End Sub
```

If this code looks confusing, don't worry; we'll discuss Visual Basic .NET's syntax in greater detail in Hour 5, "Visual Basic .NET Variables and Operators." For now, just accept that if you want to create an event handler for the page's load event, you must use this preceding code.

It is important that you leave the event handler declaration as is. The only parts you can change are the italicized parts (*sender* and *e*). You can change these variable names to any valid VB.NET variable name. However, for consistency, you are encouraged to leave these variable names as *sender* and *e*.

It's been mentioned that the page's load event fires when the ASP.NET engine starts executing the ASP.NET Web page. Recall that the job of the ASP.NET engine in executing an ASP.NET Web page is to obtain the HTML content of the ASP.NET Web page and then to send that content back to the Web server, which sends it back to the browser that initiated the Web request. Furthermore, we have seen how the ASP.NET engine processes standard HTML content; it just sends it as is to the Web server.

But what if we want our ASP.NET source code to emit HTML, returning it to the Web server? Our ASP.NET source code can emit HTML content by using the `Response.Write()` method. The `Response.Write()` method takes a single argument: the string to be sent back from the ASP.NET engine to the requesting Web browser.

The `Response.Write()` method is one of many built-in methods that we can use in our ASP.NET Web page; we'll be examining this method and many others in the next two hours.

When referring to a method, it is common practice to place a pair of parentheses at the end of the method name, as in `RenderControl()`, to distinguish it from a property.

We know that the ASP.NET engine executes an ASP.NET Web page's source code, obtaining its HTML content. Additionally, the ASP.NET engine returns the ASP.NET Web page's HTML markup found in the HTML portion. But what is evaluated first? Does the ASP.NET Web page execute the source code first and then return the HTML present in the HTML portion? Or does it first return the HTML and then execute the source code?

To answer that question, let's examine the use of the `Response.Write()` method in the `Page_Load` event handler. By using `Response.Write()` in the `Page_Load` event handler, we can determine, by examining the HTML returned to the Web browser, what is evaluated first—the source code or the HTML portion of the ASP.NET Web page.

To run this experiment, start by creating an ASP.NET Web page named `SourceCodeExample.aspx` and then click on the Code tab. Replace the two comment lines with the following code:

```
Sub Page_Load(sender as Object, e as EventArgs)
  Response.Write("<i>This is from the Page_Load event handler.</i>")
End Sub
```

Next click the HTML tab and replace all of the HTML content in the HTML tab with the following single line of HTML markup:

```
<p>This is from the HTML portion.
```

Finally, save the ASP.NET Web page and then view it through a browser. You should see the output shown in Figure 2.13.

FIGURE 2.13

The message is displayed in italics.

Notice that the message *"This is from the Page_Load event handler."* appears before the message "This is from the HTML portion." This does not indicate that the source code portion of the ASP.NET Web page is evaluated before the HTML portion; rather, it indicates that the Page_Load event handler executes prior to the HTML portion's being evaluated.

Viewing the Source Code and HTML Portions of the ASP.NET Web Page

Recall that when the Web Matrix Project is in Design Mode, there are four tabs: Design, HTML, Code, and All. At this point we've seen the first three tabs, but we've yet to look at the fourth.

If you still have the SourceCodeExample.aspx file open, click its All tab. (If you have closed the SourceCodeExample.aspx file, reopen it.) Figure 2.14 contains a screenshot of the Web Matrix Project with the All tab selected for the SourceCodeExample.aspx file.

FIGURE 2.14

The All tab shows both the source code and HTML portions of the ASP.NET Web page.

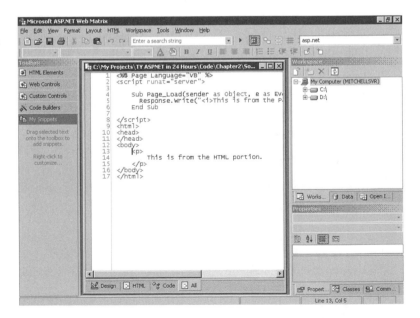

In Preview Mode the Source tab is equivalent to the Design Mode's All tab. That is, the Source tab shows both the ASP.NET Web page's source code and its HTML markup.

Listing 2.2 contains the complete source code and HTML content found in the All tab of Figure 2.14.

LISTING 2.2   The All Tab Contains the Source Code and HTML Markup of the ASP.NET Web Page

```
1: <%@ Page Language="VB" %>
2: <script runat="server">
3:
4:     Sub Page_Load(sender as Object, e as EventArgs)
5:       Response.Write("<i>This is from the Page_Load event handler.</i>")
6:     End Sub
7:
8: </script>
9: <p>This is from the HTML portion.
```

The code on lines 4 through 6 should look familiar, as it's the code we entered in the Code tab in the previous section. Additionally, the HTML content on line 9 should look familiar, as it's the HTML markup we entered in the HTML tab in the past section. The remaining content—lines 1, 2, and 8—was automatically entered by the Web Matrix Project.

Line 1 contains a *page directive* that specifies which programming language the ASP.NET source code section is using. A directive is a line of code that contains information about some facet of the ASP.NET Web page. The ASP.NET engine, when executing an ASP.NET Web page, uses the information provided by directives. For example, the page directive on line 1 of Listing 2.2 tells the ASP.NET engine that the source code section is written in Visual Basic .NET (VB is an abbreviation for Visual Basic).

Directives use the following syntax:

```
<%@ DirectiveName Property1="Value1" Property2="Value2" ... %>
```

When talking about directives, it is common to refer to a directive by its *DirectiveName*. One directive that we will have on every ASP.NET Web page is the page directive, which is the directive that has the form

```
<%@ Page Property1="Value1" Property2="Value2" ... %>
```

There are a number of page directive properties, such as Language, Debug, Trace, and many others. The Language property, as you can see in line 1 in Listing 2.2, is automatically entered by the Web Matrix Project when you create a new ASP.NET Web page. The

Language property specifies which *server-side programming language* the ASP.NET Web page is using. The programming language used in the ASP.NET Web page's source code section is referred to as a server-side programming language because the source code is executed on the Web server.

Recall that when you create a new ASP.NET Web page in the Web Matrix Project, you can specify the Language option to be either Visual Basic .NET or C#. If you choose the default, Visual Basic .NET, the Web Matrix Project will set the Language property to VB; if, however, you choose C# as the language, the Web Matrix Project will set the Language property to C#.

We will see other directives in upcoming hours, as well as additional page directive properties other than Language. For now, understand that the Web Matrix Project automatically enters a page directive specifying the server-side programming language.

The other content in Listing 2.2 that is automatically entered by the Web Matrix Project is the opening <script> tag on line 2 and the closing </script> tag on line 8. Notice that the <script> tag on line 2 has a runat="server" attribute. When the ASP.NET engine is executing the ASP.NET Web page, it locates all <script> blocks that have a runat="server" attribute. It then executes the code within these <script> blocks.

<script> blocks *without* the runat="server" attribute are considered to be HTML markup and therefore do not have their code processed by the ASP.NET engine.

Recall that an ASP.NET Web page is composed of a source code portion and an HTML portion. The source code portion is the portion within the <script runat="server"> tags. When you enter source code via the Code tab, the source code is placed in the <script runat="server"> tag that is automatically created by the Web Matrix Project.

A Look at ASP.NET HTML Controls

When creating a new ASP.NET Web page by using the Web Matrix Project, the ASP.NET Web page is created with some default HTML markup and source code already inserted. The inserted HTML markup is shown in Listing 2.3.

LISTING 2.3   The Default HTML Inserted into Each ASP.NET Web Page by the Web Matrix Project

```
1: <html>
2:     <head>
3:     </head>
4:     <body>
5:         <form runat="server">
6:             <!-- Insert content here -->
7:         </form>
8:     </body>
9: </html>
```

2

> To see the HTML automatically inserted into an ASP.NET Web page by the Web Matrix Project, create a new ASP.NET Web page and then click the HTML tab.

Note that the HTML markup on line 5 contains a <form> tag with a runat="server" attribute. With ASP.NET, HTML elements that contain the runat="server" attribute are referred to as *HTML controls* and are treated differently by the ASP.NET engine than HTML elements that do not contain the runat="server" attribute.

Recall that when a Web server receives a request for an ASP.NET Web page, it hands off the request to the ASP.NET engine, which executes the Web page and returns the resulting output HTML to the Web server, which then returns it to the browser that initiated the Web request. When the ASP.NET engine is executing a page and it comes across HTML elements, such as a <p> tag or the markup Hello, World!, it simply passes on the HTML content as is.

However, if the ASP.NET Web page encounters an HTML control—that is, an HTML element with the runat="server" attribute—it performs special handling.

To understand the handling performed, it is important to comprehend the role of the .NET Framework, which is the software library you installed in Hour 1. Understand that the .NET Framework contains a number of classes that can be used by *.NET-compatible programming languages*. A .NET-compatible programming language is one that uses the .NET Framework. To do so, it must be an object-oriented programming language and adhere to other technical specifications that are beyond the scope of this book.

How HTML Controls Are Represented in the .NET Framework

Recall that when an ASP.NET Web page is executed by the ASP.NET engine, those HTML elements with the `runat="server"` attribute are considered HTML controls and are handled differently by the ASP.NET engine than HTML elements without this attribute. Each HTML control is represented by a class in the .NET Framework. For example, to create a textbox in an HTML page, you can use the following HTML markup:

```
<input type="text" id="myTextBox">
```

You can make this textbox an HTML control by adding the `runat="server"` attribute like so:

```
<input type="text" id="myTextBox" runat="server">
```

When the ASP.NET engine executes the ASP.NET Web page that contains the textbox HTML control, it creates an instance of the `HtmlInputText` class. This class has properties and methods that abstractly define an HTML textbox. These properties include `ID`, `Size`, and `Value`, among others.

All HTML controls share a method called `RenderControl()`, which examines the properties of the HTML control and produces resulting HTML output based upon those properties.

For example, imagine that there is an instance of the `HtmlInputText` class with its `Size` property set to 10, its `ID` property set to `myTextBox`, and its `Value` property set to "I am an HTML control textbox." When this HTML control's `RenderControl()` method is called, the following HTML markup will be produced:

```
<input type="text" id="myTextBox" size="10" value="I am an HTML control
textbox." />
```

This is the HTML markup that is then sent to the browser that made the Web request.

Notice that the `<input>` tag rendered by an HTML control has a `/>` to close the tag. This is because the HTML produced by HTML controls is XHTML compliant. Recall that XHTML requires that all tags have a matching close tag. The `/>` is a shorthand way of writing

```
<input ...></input>
```

For now realize that the ASP.NET engine, when executing an ASP.NET Web page, starts by looking through the HTML portion of the ASP.NET Web page. If it finds HTML content that does *not* contain the `runat="server"` attribute, it simply returns the HTML content as is. If, however, it finds an HTML element with the `runat="server"` attribute—meaning that the HTML element is an HTML control—then an instance of the appropriate class is created, and its properties are set. This object's `RenderControl()` method is then called, and the HTML returned by this method is what is returned, along with the other HTML, by the ASP.NET engine.

This description of the ASP.NET engine leaves two questions:

- Recall that the ASP.NET engine creates an object from a particular class based upon the HTML control it encounters. How does the ASP.NET engine determine what the appropriate class is for the HTML control?

- Once an instance of this class has been created, how does the ASP.NET engine know how to set the properties of the class?

The answer to both questions can be found by examining how the ASP.NET engine executes the ASP.NET Web page. As we've discussed, when the ASP.NET engine comes across an HTML element with the `runat="server"` attribute, it notes that the element is an HTML control. Now the ASP.NET engine must create an object (an instance of a class) from the class in the .NET Framework that abstractly defines this particular HTML control.

This class is determined by examining the HTML element itself. For example, if the user is using an HTML control to create a textbox, the HTML control's markup will appear as

```
<input type="text" runat="server" ...>
```

The ASP.NET engine sees that it's an `<input>` tag and that its `type` attribute is set to `text`, so the ASP.NET engine creates an instance of the `HtmlInputText` class. If, on the other hand, the HTML control's markup appeared as

```
<input type="radio" runat="server" ...>
```

the ASP.NET engine would create an instance of the `HtmlInputRadioButton` class.

Once an instance of the appropriate class is created, the ASP.NET engine still needs to set the properties of the object. Again, the ASP.NET engine determines the value of these properties by examining the HTML control's markup. For example, if the markup appears as

```
<input type="text" runat="server" size="10" id="myTextBox">
```

the ASP.NET engine will create an instance of the `HtmlInputText` class and set the object's `Size` property to 10 and its `ID` property to `myTextBox`.

Correctly setting the properties of the HTML control's corresponding class instance is important because these properties affect the HTML output produced by the object's RenderControl() method.

What Benefits Do HTML Controls Have over HTML Markup?

From our discussion thus far, it may seem like HTML controls don't provide any functionality that cannot be obtained by using standard HTML markup. As we saw earlier, when the HTML control

```
<input type="text" id="myTextBox" runat="server" size="10">
```

is rendered into HTML, its resulting HTML output is

```
<input type="text" id="myTextBox" size="10" />
```

The only differences between the HTML control markup and the resulting HTML output seem to be the removal of the runat="server" attribute and the addition of a />.

The benefit of using HTML controls is that HTML controls can be programmatically referenced from the ASP.NET Web page's source code portion. They are referenced in code by the id attribute provided in the HTML control's markup. For example, to create an HTML control textbox with an id of myTextBox, we would use the following HTML markup:

```
<input type="text" id="myTextBox" runat="server" />
```

Recall that when the ASP.NET engine encounters this HTML control, it converts the control into an instance of the HtmlInputText class (an object). This object is given the same name as the id attribute of the HTML control. That is, the object is named myTextBox.

Also recall that the ASP.NET engine will call the RenderControl() method of the textbox HTML control myTextBox. This method returns the HTML markup that corresponds to the HTML control; this HTML markup depends upon the value of the various properties of the HTML control. In order to dynamically alter the HTML markup returned by the RenderControl() method, we can programmatically specify the value of myTextBox's properties.

For example, imagine that we want to create an ASP.NET Web page that has a textbox that has as its value the current date and time. To accomplish this, we can add an HTML control textbox and then, in the Page_Load event handler, set the HTML control textbox's Value property to the current date and time.

Let's create such an ASP.NET Web page. Start by creating a new ASP.NET Web page named `CurrentDate.aspx`, and then go directly to the All tab and edit the source code and HTML markup so that it is identical to Listing 2.4.

LISTING 2.4 An HTML Control Textbox Displays the Current Date and Time

```
 1: <%@ Page Language="VB" %>
 2: <script runat="server">
 3:
 4:   Sub Page_Load(sender as Object, e as EventArgs)
 5:     currentDT.Value = DateTime.Now
 6:   End Sub
 7:
 8: </script>
 9: <html>
10: <body>
11:     <form runat="server">
12:         <input type="text" runat="server" id="currentDT" />
13:     </form>
14: </body>
15: </html>
```

On line 12 we added an HTML control textbox whose `id` attribute is set to `currentDT`. On lines 4–6 we have the `Page_Load` event handler, which contains just one line of code that sets the `Value` property of the `currentDT` object to the current date and time.

> Make sure that when you create the HTML control textbox on line 12 that you don't forget the `runat="server"` attribute. If you omit this important attribute, the ASP.NET engine will treat the textbox as standard HTML markup and will not create an HTML control object.

Now view the ASP.NET Web page through a browser. You should see a textbox whose value is the current date and time, as in Figure 2.15.

FIGURE 2.15

The textbox contains the current date and time.

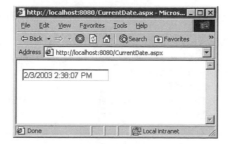

If you forget to add the `runat="server"` attribute to the HTML control on line 12, you will get a compile time error when trying to view the ASP.NET Web page. This is because the ASP.NET engine cannot find the `currentDT` object referenced on line 5.

Much of the code of Listing 2.4 may seem foreign to you. Don't worry; over the next few hours, we'll be examining ASP.NET Web pages in greater detail, as well as using Visual Basic .NET. The important lesson to take away from Listing 2.4 is that the power of HTML controls lies in the fact that they can be programmatically accessed from the ASP.NET Web page's source code portion.

A Look at ASP.NET Web Controls

ASP.NET Web controls are server-side controls that can be included in the HTML portion of an ASP.NET Web page. Web controls are declared with the following syntax:

```
<asp:WebControlName runat="server" Property1="Value1" Property2="Value2"
    ... PropertyN="ValueN"></asp:WebControlName>
```

The semantics of Web controls are identical to HTML controls'. Each Web control has a corresponding class in the .NET Framework. When the ASP.NET engine is executing an ASP.NET Web page and comes across a Web control, it creates an instance of the correct class and sets the created object's properties to the properties specified in the Web control's markup. Also, each Web control contains a `RenderControl()` method that, when called, produces HTML markup. Furthermore, Web controls can be referenced programmatically, just like HTML controls.

There are Web controls designed for just displaying text, such as the Label and Literal Web controls. There are Web controls designed for accepting user input, such as the TextBox, DropDownList, RadioButton, and CheckBox Web controls. And there are Web controls for displaying a collection of data, such as the DataGrid and DataList Web controls.

We will discuss the Label and Literal Web controls in detail in Hour 6, "Visual Basic .NET Control Structures." The TextBox Web control is examined in Hour 7, "Working with Objects in Visual Basic .NET"; the DropDownList, RadioButton, and CheckBox Web controls in Hour 8, "ASP.NET Web Controls for Displaying Text." The DataGrid is introduced in Hour 14, "Understanding SQL, the Language of Databases," and examined in greater detail in Hours 18 through 20. The DataList is studied in Hour 15, "Displaying Data with the DataGrid Web Control."

Dragging and Dropping Web Controls on an ASP.NET Web Page

Web controls can be quickly added to an ASP.NET Web page by dragging and dropping them from the Toolbox into the Web Matrix Project designer. Let's create an ASP.NET Web page that displays a TextBox Web control that itself displays the current date and time; we'll add the needed Web control by dragging and dropping it onto the designer.

Start by creating an ASP.NET Web page named `CurrentDateWebControl.aspx`. Next make sure that you are in the Design tab.

> If you have the Web Matrix Project in Preview Mode, the Design tab will not be present. In order to be able to drag and drop Web controls onto the designer, you must specify in the Preferences that you want to be in Design Mode. Refer back to the "Editing the HTML Content by Using the HTML Tab" section for more information on Design Mode and Preview Mode.

Click the Web Controls tab of the Toolbox (if it is not already selected). You should see a list of the Web controls available, which include Label, Literal, Hyperlink, TextBox, CheckBox, and so on. Figure 2.16 shows a screenshot of what you should see.

FIGURE 2.16
The Web Controls tab in the Toolbox lists the available Web controls.

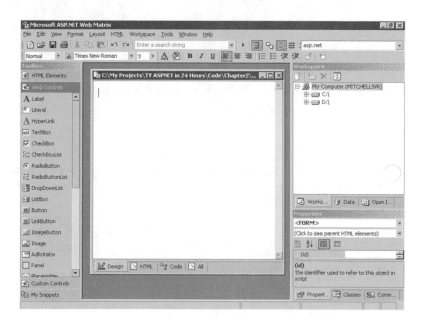

Drag and drop the TextBox Web control onto the designer. When you click the TextBox, it should become highlighted, and the Properties pane in the lower right-hand corner should list the various properties of the selected TextBox Web control. In the Properties pane, change the (ID) property from the default TextBox1 to currentDT. Figure 2.17 shows a screenshot of what you should see once you make this change.

FIGURE 2.17

The (ID) property in the Properties pane has been changed to currentDT.

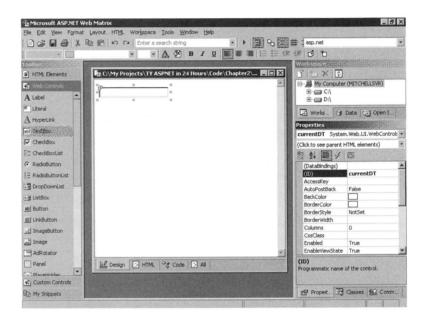

Now click the Code tab and enter the following source code:

```
Sub Page_Load(sender as Object, e as EventArgs)
    currentDT.Value = DateTime.Now
End Sub
```

Notice that the source code that we have just added to the Code tab of our CurrentDateWebControl.aspx file is the same source code used in Listing 2.4, specifically lines 4 through 6.

Finally, click the All tab. In the All tab you should see the content presented in Listing 2.5.

LISTING 2.5 The Content in the All Tab

```
 1: <%@ Page Language="VB" %>
 2: <script runat="server">
 3:
 4:     Sub Page_Load(sender as Object, e as EventArgs)
 5:         currentDT.Text = DateTime.Now
 6:     End Sub
 7:
 8: </script>
 9: <html>
10: <head>
11: </head>
12: <body>
13:     <form runat="server">
14:         <asp:TextBox id="currentDT" runat="server"></asp:TextBox>
15:         <!-- Insert content here -->
16:     </form>
17: </body>
18: </html>
```

Note that the content in Listing 2.5 is nearly identical to the content in Listing 2.4. The only difference is that instead of an HTML control, a Web control is used.

Line 14 of Listing 2.5 shows the markup produced by the Web Matrix Project when we dragged and dropped the TextBox Web control onto the designer.

Note that the ID property of the Web control—currentDT—is set to the (ID) property specified in the Properties pane.

Dragging and dropping Web controls from the Toolbox onto the designer has a number of advantages. First, it's quicker than typing in the Web control name. Second, you can set the properties via the Properties pane instead of having to type them in manually. And third, the runat="server" attribute is automatically added for you.

The Differences between HTML Controls and Web Controls

Having seen two examples—one that uses an HTML control and one that uses a Web control—that perform the same task, you may be wondering why there are both Web controls and HTML controls. Why not just have HTML controls or just Web controls? In fact, the majority of HTML controls have Web control equivalents (such as the HTML control textbox and the Web control TextBox).

The reason HTML controls exist is to ease porting a Web page that was created using a dynamic Web page technology other than ASP.NET to an ASP.NET Web page. Imagine that you already had a page that has a number of <input> tags for collecting user input. If you wanted to convert this page to an ASP.NET Web page and you had only Web controls at your disposal, you would have to change each <input> tag to its corresponding Web control, which would be time consuming. With HTML controls, however, you would simply need to add the runat="server" attribute to these <input> tags.

> If you are creating a new ASP.NET Web page and encounter a situation where you can choose between an HTML control and a Web control, such as when needing a textbox, choose to use a Web control. Web controls typically contain more properties than HTML controls, meaning that you, the developer, have more control over their appearance and functionality. Also, as we saw in the previous section, Web controls can be easily dragged and dropped from the Toolbox into the Design tab, whereas HTML controls must be entered by hand in the HTML or All tabs.

There are times, however, when you need to use an HTML control because there is no corresponding Web control that has the same functionality. For example, to upload a file from the user's computer to the Web server, you need to use an HTML control; there is no corresponding Web control.

> Uploading a file from the user's computer to the Web server is beyond the scope of this book. For information on this topic, check out Tribikram Rath's article "Uploading in ASP.NET," available online at http://www.4GuysFromRolla.com/webtech/091201-1.shtml.

Summary

We covered quite a bit of material in this hour, starting with an examination of the HTML portion of an ASP.NET Web page. Here we saw how to drag and drop HTML elements onto the Web Matrix Project's WYSIWYG designer. We also saw how to change the appearance of HTML content in the designer by using the options under the Format menu. In addition to using the WYSIWYG designer, the Web Matrix Project also allows you to enter HTML markup by hand via the HTML tab.

After studying the HTML portion of an ASP.NET Web page, we moved on to the source code portion. Here we went over a crash course in object-oriented programming, as well as event-driven programming. We then saw how to provide code that would be executed each time an ASP.NET Web page is first visited.

This hour wrapped up with an examination of HTML controls and Web controls. Web controls, which we will be using extensively throughout the ASP.NET examples in this book, can be added to an ASP.NET Web page simply by dragging and dropping the appropriate Web control from the Toolbox onto the designer. When an ASP.NET Web page is executed by the ASP.NET engine, the Web controls and HTML controls on the page are converted into objects and eventually have their `RenderControl()` method executed, which returns the HTML markup created by the HTML control or Web control based on its properties. The main benefit of HTML controls and Web controls is that they can be programmatically accessed from the ASP.NET Web page's source code.

The examples we've examined in this hour and the previous one have been pretty simple ones with limited real-world application. In the next hour we'll create a more practical ASP.NET Web page with more involved HTML and source code portions.

Q&A

Q Must an ASP.NET Web page contain both an HTML portion and a source code portion?

A No. Either may be left out, or both may be left out—except if both are left out, your ASP.NET Web page has no content, which makes it a pretty uninteresting Web page!

Q Why are we building all of our ASP.NET Web pages by using Visual Basic .NET as the server-side programming language?

A I chose to use Visual Basic .NET for this book because it is, in my opinion, an easier language to comprehend for developers who may be newer to programming than C#.

Visual Basic .NET syntax reads much more like everyday English, whereas C# uses more cryptic symbols. Furthermore, Visual Basic .NET is not case sensitive, whereas C# is case sensitive. Languages that are not case sensitive are typically easier to pick up for those new to programming.

Q How can I find out the various properties that are allowable for each Web control?

A One way to determine what properties you can set for a particular Web control is to drag and drop the Web control onto your ASP.NET Web page's designer. Next click on the Web control, and in the Properties pane in the lower right-hand corner, you will see a listing of the Web control's properties. Additionally, there is extensive documentation available through the Web Matrix Project that lists the properties, methods, and events of the various Web controls. We'll look at using this built-in documentation in future hours.

Workshop

Quiz

1. What does WYSIWYG stand for?

2. Is the following HTML properly nested?

```
<html><body>
<h1>My First Web Page</h1>
These are a few of my favorite <i>things:
<ol>
  <li>Jisun</li>
  <li>ASP.NET</li>
  <li>Basketball</li>
</ol></i>
</body></html>
```

3. In Design Mode, why might the HTML markup you entered manually in the HTML tab be altered when switching between the HTML tab and the Design tab?

4. What does the following line of code in your ASP.NET Web page do?

```
<%@ Page Language="VB" %>
```

5. What is the name of the event handler you would use to have code execute each time the ASP.NET Web page is loaded?

6. What attribute distinguishes HTML controls from other HTML elements?

7. How can one add a Web control to an ASP.NET Web page?

Answers

1. What You See Is What You Get.

2. Yes. There are no tags whose start tag appears after another tag's start tag (call that tag *t*) but whose end tag appears after *t*'s end tag.

3. The designer ensures that the HTML it is working with is XHTML compliant. Therefore, the HTML markup you write by hand in the HTML tab may be slightly altered to conform to XHTML standards.

4. It is a page directive that specifies that the server-side programming language being used is Visual Basic .NET.

5. The Page_Load event handler. This event handler is written in code as

```
Sub Page_Load(sender as Object, e as EventArgs)
  'The code to execute when the page's load event fires
  'goes here...
End Sub
```

6. The runat="server" attribute.

7. There are two ways. First, you can simply drag and drop the appropriate Web control from the Toolbox onto the designer. Second, you can enter the Web control by hand in the HTML tab, much like you must enter HTML controls by hand.

Exercises

The aim of these exercises is to help you familiarize yourself with the Web Matrix Project editor.

1. The HTMLExample.aspx ASP.NET Web page we created in the "Creating the HTML Portion of an ASP.NET Web Page by Using the Web Matrix Project" section contained an HTML <table> tag that was added by going to the HTML menu and selecting the Insert Table... option. Once an HTML table has been added to a Web page, it is easy to set the table's various display properties.

   For this exercise, open up the HTMLExample.aspx Web page in the Web Matrix Project. If you click the HTML table so that it is highlighted, you will find that its properties are displayed in the Properties pane. For this exercise set the border property to 3 and the cellPadding property to 5. Also, try setting the bgColor property. Notice that when you select this property from the Properties pane, you can choose from an array of colors. You are invited to try setting the various HTML table properties to view their effect on the table in the designer.

2. For this exercise we want to add a message to the top of the `HTMLExample.aspx` Web page that reads: "Here Are Some Popular Search Engines." This text should be centered, appear at the top of the Web page, and be displayed in a bold, Arial font.

To accomplish this, start by positioning the cursor in the designer immediately before the HTML table. Hit Enter a few times to create some space. Then type in the text "Here Are Some Popular Search Engines." Once you have entered this text, select it with the mouse. Then choose the Arial font from the font dropdown list near the upper left-hand corner. Next make the text bold by going to the Format menu and selecting Bold. Finally, center the text by going to the Format menu and choosing the Align Center option.

As with the previous exercise, you are encouraged to experiment with the Web Matrix Project's formatting capabilities. See how the text looks with different fonts and formats. Note that you can add bulleted lists, numbered lists, and so on.

HOUR 3

Creating Our First ASP.NET Web Page

In the last two hours, we've spent quite a bit of time talking in very high-level terms about ASP.NET Web pages and the ASP.NET programming model. We've looked at how to configure our computer to serve ASP.NET Web pages, and we've looked at the role of the Web server. We've examined the HTML and source code portions of an ASP.NET Web page and looked at HTML controls and Web controls. We've created some very simple ASP.NET Web pages and have seen how to use the Web Matrix Project to create these pages.

In this hour we turn from these high-level discussions to actually building a useful ASP.NET Web page that illustrates the concepts discussed in the last two hours. Specifically, we'll be creating an ASP.NET Web page that serves as a financial calculator. This hour will focus on building the ASP.NET Web page, with only a light discussion of the source code and Web controls used. In the next hour, however, we will look at the ASP.NET Web page created in this hour in much more depth.

Fire up the Web Matrix Project and get ready to start creating your first practical ASP.NET Web page!

In this hour we will cover

- Creating the design requirements for the financial calculator
- Creating the user interface
- Adding the needed Web controls to the ASP.NET Web page
- Writing the code for the ASP.NET Web page's source code portion
- Testing the ASP.NET Web page

Specifying the Design Requirements

Throughout this book we will be creating a number of ASP.NET Web pages, which involves creating both the ASP.NET Web page's HTML and its source code. When writing any piece of software, whether a Windows desktop application or a dynamic Web page, there are a number of development stages. First and foremost we need to decide what the purpose of the software is, along with what features and functionality the software should provide. After this we must sit down and actually write the software. Finally, we need to test the software and fix any bugs or errors that arise.

These three steps—design, development, and testing—should always be performed when creating an ASP.NET Web page, but too frequently, developers jump straight to the coding task without spending enough time in the planning stage. This initial planning stage, sometimes called the *design requirements* stage, is vital for the following reasons:

- It lays down a road map for the software project. Having a road map allows us to determine how much progress we've made at a given point, as well as how much we have left to accomplish.
- The design requirements spell out precisely what the software will provide.

To get into the habit, we will spend a bit of time discussing what features will be present and what user interface will be employed in the ASP.NET Web page we will be creating in this hour.

Without spending adequate time in the design requirements stage, you would be unable to accurately answer your boss when he asks, "How much longer will this take," or "How much progress have you made?" Additionally, agreeing on a list of feature requirements—a task typically performed during the design requirements stage—avoids any confusion at the conclusion of the project; otherwise, your boss and client might wonder why a feature they thought was going to be present was not.

Formulating the Features for Our Financial Calculator

An important step in the design requirements process is to list the features you plan on providing in your application. So far I have just mentioned that we will be creating a financial calculator, but let's take the time to specifically define the features we want to provide.

For our financial calculator let's build a loan calculator designed to determine the monthly payments for a fixed home *mortgage*. To determine the monthly payments required for a fixed mortgage, three inputs are needed:

1. The amount of money being borrowed (the principal)
2. The loan's annual interest rate
3. The duration of the loan—typically 15 or 30 years (the loan's term)

The output of our financial calculator, along with these three inputs, gives us the features of our financial calculator. In a sentence: Our financial calculator will compute the monthly payment of a fixed mortgage when provided the amount, duration, and interest rate of the mortgage.

Deciding on the User Interface

After describing the features that the application will have, the next stage in the design requirements phase is to create a user interface. The user interface, or UI for short, is the means by which the user interacts with the application. How will the user enter these inputs? How will the results be displayed?

With large applications the user interface portion of the design requirements phase can take quite a while and be very involved. For our financial calculator, however, the user interface is fairly straightforward and will exist on a single Web page.

Essentially, our users need to be able to do two things: enter the three inputs discussed earlier and see the result of the calculation. These inputs can be entered via TextBox Web controls. The output of the financial calculator should show the mortgage's monthly cost.

Figure 3.1 contains a screenshot of the ASP.NET Web page financial calculator when first visited by the user. Note the three textboxes for the three inputs. Additionally, there is a button labeled Compute Monthly Cost that the user is instructed to click once having entered the required inputs.

FIGURE 3.1

The user is asked to enter the three inputs.

Figure 3.2 contains a screenshot of the financial calculator after the user has entered the requested inputs and has clicked the Compute Monthly Cost button. Note that the output shows how much money the mortgage will cost per month.

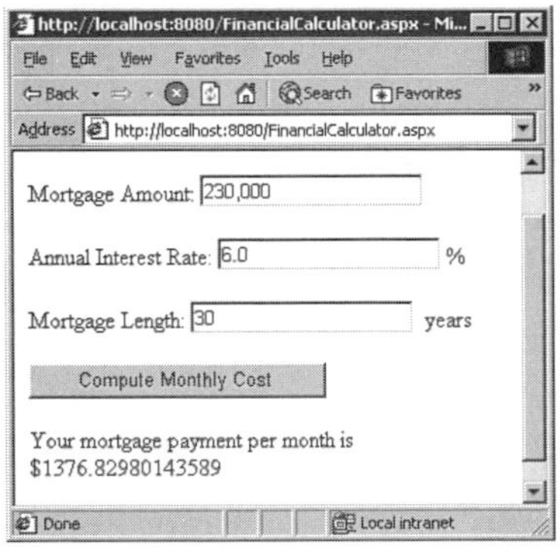

FIGURE 3.2

The monthly cost of the mortgage is shown.

In order to display the output of our calculation, we need to add a Label Web control to our ASP.NET page. This Label Web control will display the result of the calculation. Therefore, we should place this Label Web control in the ASP.NET Web page precisely where we want the final output to appear. As you can see from Figure 3.2, I have created the financial calculator so that the output appears below the input TextBoxes.

Creating the User Interface

Now that we've completed the design requirements phase and have decided what features our financial calculator will provide, as well as how the interface will appear to the user, it's time to actually start creating our ASP.NET Web page.

The first task is to create the user interface (or UI), which is considered the HTML portion of our ASP.NET Web page. To construct this UI, we'll add a TextBox Web control for each of the three inputs, as well as a Button Web control that, when clicked, will perform the necessary computations.

After creating the user interface, we will turn our attention to writing the needed source code to perform the financial computations.

To start creating our user interface, launch the Web Matrix Project and create a new ASP.NET Web page named FinancialCalculator.aspx, making certain to use the Visual Basic .NET Language option (the default). Before we add any content to the HTML portion of our ASP.NET Web page, first take a moment to turn on *glyphs*, which are markers in the designer that indicate the location of HTML controls and Web controls. To turn on glyphs, go to the View menu and choose the Glyphs option.

With glyphs activated, you should see, in your Design tab, two yellow tags that mark the beginning and end of your form HTML control. Figure 3.3 contains a screenshot of the Web Matrix Project with glyphs enabled.

FIGURE 3.3

Turning on glyphs uses markers to display invisible HTML controls and Web controls.

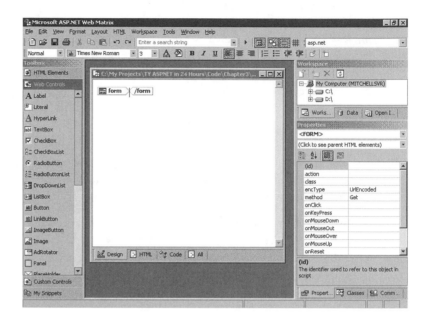

If you do not see a Design tab for your ASP.NET Web page and instead see only Source and Preview tabs, you have the Web Matrix Project in Preview Mode and need to change to Design Mode. Refer back to the "Editing the HTML Content by Using the HTML Tab" section from Hour 2, "Understanding the ASP.NET Programming Model," for information on switching back to Design Mode.

Recall from our discussion in the previous hour that the Web Matrix Project automatically inserts a form HTML control in the HTML portion of your ASP.NET Web pages. The <form> tag is inserted in an HTML control because it has the runat="server" attribute, as can be seen by clicking the HTML tab (see Figure 3.4).

FIGURE 3.4

The HTML portion of the ASP.NET Web page contains a form HTML control.

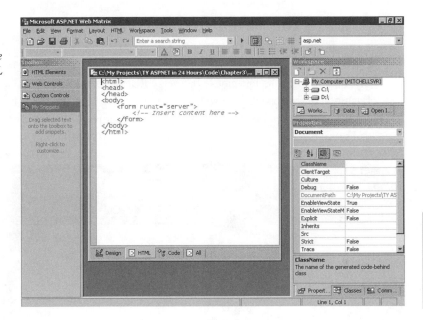

The form HTML control is commonly referred to as a *Web form* or *server-side form*. The remainder of this book will refer to form HTML controls as either Web forms or server-side forms.

When creating an ASP.NET Web page that accepts user input—such as our financial calculator, which accepts three inputs from the user—it is required that the Web controls for user input (the TextBoxes, DropDownLists, CheckBoxes, and so on) be placed within a Web form. We will discuss why this needs to be done in Hour 9, "Web Form Basics."

Because our user input Web controls need to be within the Web form, it is important that we turn on glyphs so that we can see the Web form's start and finish. Then we can be sure that the controls we drop onto the designer from the Toolbox actually end up between the Web form's start and end tags, as opposed to before or after the Web form.

Adding the Three TextBox Web Controls

Let's start by adding the TextBox Web controls for our user's three inputs. First make sure that you are in the Design tab. Next place your mouse cursor between the Web form glyphs and click the left mouse button so that the designer receives focus and there is a flashing cursor between the Web form glyphs. Create some space between the Web form's start and end tags by hitting enter a few times. You should see something similar to Figure 3.5.

FIGURE 3.5

Hit Enter to create some space between the Web form start and end tags.

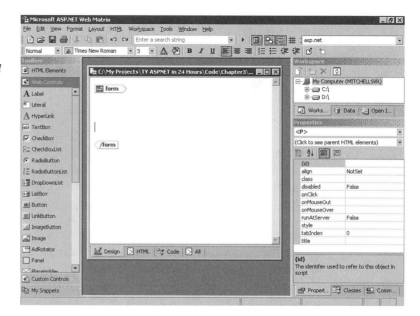

Before we drag a TextBox Web control to the designer, let's first create the title for the textbox we're going to add. Because the first input is the amount of the mortgage, start by typing in this title: **Mortgage Amount:.**

Next we want to add a TextBox Web control after this title. To accomplish this, make sure that the Web Controls tab from the Toolbox is selected, and then drag a TextBox control from the Toolbox and drop it into the designer after the "Mortgage Amount:" title. Take a moment to make sure your screen looks similar to the screenshot shown in Figure 3.6.

FIGURE 3.6

At this point you should have a title and a single textbox, both inside the Web form tags.

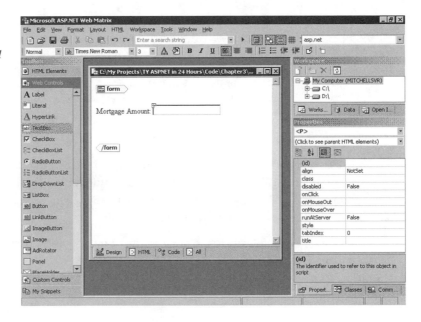

When dragging and dropping the TextBox Web control from the Toolbox, it is very important that the Web Control tab be selected so that you are indeed dragging and dropping TextBox Web controls. If the HTML Elements tab is selected on the Toolbox, you'll be placing standard HTML textboxes (textboxes without the runat="server" attribute present).

If you do not use TextBox Web controls, you will not be able to reference the values that the user entered in the TextBoxes in the source code portion of the ASP.NET Web page. Therefore, be certain that when dragging and dropping TextBoxes onto the designer for this exercise, you are dragging TextBox Web controls, not HTML textboxes.

Currently, the TextBox Web control we just added has its ID property set to TextBox1. Because we will later need to refer to this ID in order to determine the value of the beginning retirement balance entered by the user, let's choose an ID value that is representative of the data found within the TextBox. Specifically, change the ID property to loanAmount.

To change a Web control's ID property, click the Web control in the designer, which will load the Web control's properties in the Properties window in the lower right-hand corner. Scroll to the top of the Properties pane until you see the ID property. This is the property value that you should change. Note that in the list of properties in the Properties pane, the ID property is denoted as (ID).

Now let's add the second textbox, the mortgage's interest rate. Add it just as we did the previous TextBox Web control by first creating a title for the TextBox. Type in the title **Annual Interest Rate:**. Next drag and drop a TextBox Web control after this title and change the TextBox's ID property to rate.

Finally, add the third textbox, the duration of the mortgage. Start by adding the title **Mortgage Length:**, and then drag and drop a TextBox Web control after the title. Set this TextBox's ID to mortgageLength.

You might want to type in some text after each TextBox Web control to indicate the units that should be entered into the textbox. For example, after the "Annual Interest Rate" textbox, you might want to add a percent sign so that the user knows to enter this value as a percentage. Similarly, you might want to enter the word "years" after the "Mortgage Length" TextBox.

Figure 3.7 contains a screenshot of the Design tab after all three input TextBox Web controls have been added.

The screenshot in Figure 3.7 shows the TextBox Web control titles in the standard font. Feel free to change the font or the aesthetics of the HTML portion however you see fit. Just be sure to have three TextBox Web controls inside of the Web form.

FIGURE 3.7

A screenshot of the Design tab, shown after all three TextBox Web controls have been added.

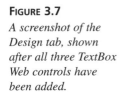

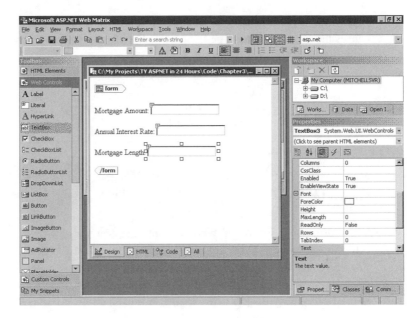

Adding the Compute Monthly Cost Button

After the user has entered inputs into the three TextBox Web controls, we want to be able to take that information and perform our financial calculation. Realize, though, that when the ASP.NET engine executed the ASP.NET Web page, it converted the TextBox Web controls into HTML <input> tags.

As we'll discuss in much greater detail in the next hour, "Dissecting Our First ASP.NET Web Page," when the users visit the FinancialCalculator.aspx ASP.NET Web page via their browsers, they are receiving HTML that contains a <form> tag and, within it, three <input> textbox tags. This HTML markup, when rendered by a browser, displays three textboxes, as shown in Figure 3.7. In order for the calculation to take place, the inputs entered by the user must be submitted back to our ASP.NET Web page (FinancialCalculator.aspx). Once our ASP.NET Web page receives these user-entered values, it can perform the financial computation and return the results.

In order for an HTML form to be submitted, the user needs a button that, when clicked, causes the form to be submitted. We can add such a button by adding a Button Web control to our ASP.NET Web page.

> We will discuss the specifics involved with collecting and computing user input in Hour 9, "Web Form Basics."

To add a Button Web control, first ensure that the Web Controls tab in the Toolbox is selected. Then drag the Button Web control from the Toolbox onto the designer, dropping it after the last input title and textbox.

When dropping a Button Web control onto the designer, the button's caption reads "Button." To change this, click the button and then in the Properties pane change the `Text` property from `Button` to `Compute Monthly Cost`. This will change the caption on your button to "Compute Monthly Cost." Also, while in the Properties pane, change the button's `ID` property—listed in the property pane as (ID)—from the default `Button1` to `performCalc`.

Take a moment to make sure that your screen looks similar to the screenshot in Figure 3.8.

FIGURE 3.8

A Button Web control has been added.

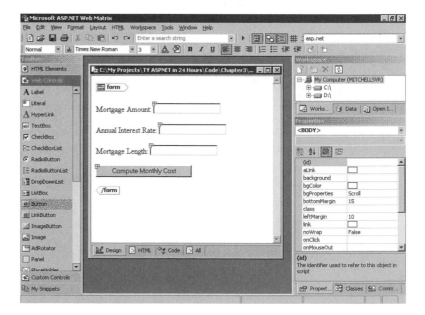

Creating a Label Web Control for the Output

The final piece we need to add to our user interface is a Label Web control that will to display the output of our financial calculation. Because the Label Web control will display the output (the amount of money the mortgage costs per month), the Web page's final result will appear wherever you place the Web control. Therefore, if you want the output to appear at the bottom of your ASP.NET Web page, simply drag and drop a Label Web control after the existing content in the designer. If you want the output to appear at the top of the Web page, place it before the existing content in the designer.

To add the Label Web control, drag and drop it from the Toolbox and onto the designer. Once you have added the Label Web control, you will see that it displays the message "Label." The Label Web control displays the value of its Text property, which is configurable via the Properties pane. Figure 3.9 is a screenshot of the designer with the Label Web control added.

FIGURE 3.9

A Label Web control has been added to the ASP.NET Web page.

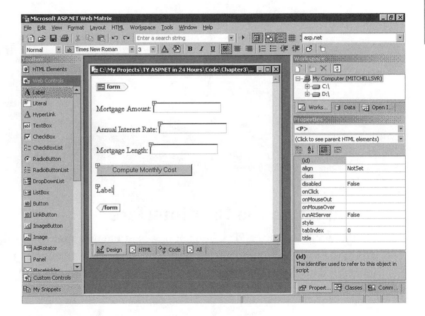

Because we don't want this label to display any content until the user has entered their three inputs and the calculation has been performed, clear out the Label's Text property. To clear out a property value for the Label Web control, first click the Label Web control so that its properties are loaded in the Properties pane. Then, in the Properties pane, locate the Text property and erase the Text property value by clicking the Text property's value and hitting backspace until all of the characters have been erased.

Once you clear out the Label's Text property, the designer will show the Label Web control as its ID property, enclosed by brackets. Currently, the Label Web control's ID property is Label1, meaning that in the designer you should see the Label Web control displayed as: [Label1]. Go ahead and change the ID property of the Label Web control from Label1 to results, which should change the label's display in the designer from [Label1] to [results]. Figure 3.10 shows a screenshot of the designer after the Label Web control's property has been changed to results.

FIGURE 3.10
The Label Web control's ID has been changed to results.

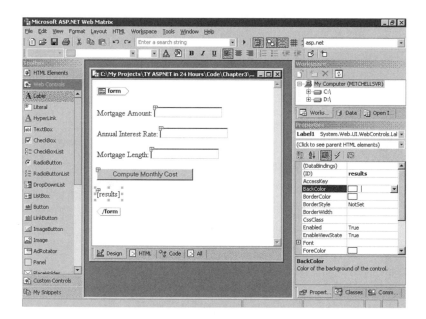

Completing the User Interface

At this point we have added the vital pieces of the user interface. This was accomplished using the Web Matrix Project's WYSIWYG editor in a fraction of the time it would have taken to enter the HTML markup and Web control syntax manually.

> To fully appreciate the amount of HTML markup the Web Matrix Project generated for us automatically, click the HTML tab.

If you want to add additional user interface elements at this time, perhaps a bold, centered title at the top of the Web page or a brief set of instructions for the user, feel free to do so.

Now that we have created the HTML portion of the ASP.NET Web page, we are ready to create the source code portion in the next section.

> HTML markup and Web controls not used for user input may appear either within the Web form tags or outside of these tags. The only things that *must* be placed within the Web form tags are the Web controls that collect user input (the TextBoxes and Button).

Writing the Source Code for the ASP.NET Web Page

3

Now that we have completed the HTML portion of our ASP.NET Web page, all that remains is the source code. The source code will read the user's inputs and perform the necessary calculations to arrive at the monthly cost for the mortgage.

In the previous hour we looked at the Page_Load event handler. This event handler, which you can include in your ASP.NET Web page's source code portion, is executed each time the Web page is loaded. We will not be placing the source code to perform the monthly mortgage cost calculation in this event handler, though, because we do not want to run the calculation until the user has entered the loan amount, interest rate, and duration, and has clicked the Compute Monthly Cost button.

Button Web controls have a Click event, which fires when the button is clicked. Therefore, what we want to do is write our own event handler and associate it with the Compute Monthly Cost button's Click event. This way, whenever the Compute Monthly Cost button is clicked, the event handler that we provide will be executed. All that remains, then, is to place the source code that performs the computation inside this event handler.

Adding event handlers to a Button Web control's Click event is quite easy to accomplish with the Web Matrix Project. From the designer, simply double-click the Button whose Click event you would like to provide an event handler for. Once you double-click the Button Web control, you will be whisked to the Code tab, where you should see the following source code already entered:

```
Sub performCalc_Click(sender As Object, e As EventArgs)

End Sub
```

These two lines of code are the shell for the button's Click event handler. Note that the event handler is named performCalc_Click. More generally, it is named *buttonID_Click*, where *buttonID* is the value of the button's ID property. (Recall that after adding the Button Web control, we changed its ID from Button1 to performCalc.)

Any code that you write between these two lines will be executed whenever the performCalc button is clicked. Because we want to compute the monthly cost of the mortgage when the performCalc button is clicked, the code to perform this calculation will appear within the performCalc_Click event handler.

Reading the Values in the TextBox Web Controls

In order to calculate the monthly cost of the mortgage, we must first be able to determine the values entered by the user into the three TextBox Web controls. Before we look at the code to accomplish this, let's take a step back and reexamine Web controls, a topic we touched upon lightly in the previous hour.

Recall from Hour 2's discussion that when the ASP.NET engine is executing an ASP.NET Web page, Web controls are handled quite differently from standard HTML elements. Standard HTML markup is passed directly from the ASP.NET engine to the Web server without any translation; with Web controls, however, an object is created that represents the Web control. The object is created from the class that corresponds to the specific Web control. That is, a TextBox Web control has an object *instantiated* from the TextBox class, whereas a Label Web control has an object *instantiated* from the Label class.

> Recall that a class is an abstract blueprint, whereas an object is a concrete instance. When an object is created, it is said to have been *instantiated*. The act of creating an object is often referred to as *instantiation*.

Each of these classes has various properties that describe the state of the Web control. For example, the TextBox class has a Size property that indicates how many columns the textbox has. Both the TextBox and the Label classes have Text properties that indicate that Web control's text content.

> The classes that represent various Web controls are classes in the .NET Framework. We will discuss how to find the properties, methods, and events for these classes in future hours.

The primary benefit of Web controls is that their properties can be accessed in the ASP.NET Web page's source code section. Because the `Text` property of the TextBox Web control contains the content of the textbox, we can reference this property in the Compute Monthly Cost button's `Click` event handler to determine the value entered by the user into each textbox.

For example, to determine the value entered into the Mortgage Amount textbox, we could use the following line of code:

```
loanAmount.Text
```

When the ASP.NET engine creates an object for the Web control, it names the object the value of the Web control's `ID` property. Because `loanAmount` is the ID of the Mortgage Amount TextBox Web control, the object created representing this Web control is named `loanAmount`. To retrieve the `Text` property of the `loanAmount` object, we use the syntax `loanAmount.Text`.

> Don't worry if the syntax for retrieving an object's property confuses you. We will be discussing the syntax and semantics of Visual Basic .NET in greater detail in Hour 5, "Visual Basic .NET Variables and Operators."

The Complete Source Code

Listing 3.1 contains the complete source code for our ASP.NET Web page. Take a moment to enter the source code shown below into the `performCalc` Button's `Click` event handler. (You should do this from the Code or All tab.)

> Keep in mind that the line numbers shown in Listing 3.1 should *not* be typed in as well. The line numbers are present in the code listing only to help reference specific lines of the listing when discussing the code.

LISTING 3.1 The Computation Is Performed in the performCalc Button's Click Event Handler

```
1: Sub performCalc_Click(sender As Object, e As EventArgs)
2:   'Specify constant values
3:   Const INTEREST_CALCS_PER_YEAR as Integer = 12
4:   Const PAYMENTS_PER_YEAR as Integer = 12
5:
6:   'Create variables to hold the values entered by the user
7:   Dim P as Double = loanAmount.Text
```

continues

LISTING 3.1 Continued

```
 8:    Dim r as Double = rate.Text / 100
 9:    Dim t as Double = mortgageLength.Text
10:
11:    Dim ratePerPeriod as Double
12:    ratePerPeriod = r/INTEREST_CALCS_PER_YEAR
13:
14:    Dim payPeriods as Integer
15:    payPeriods = t * PAYMENTS_PER_YEAR
16:
17:    Dim annualRate as Double
18:    annualRate = Math.Exp(INTEREST_CALCS_PER_YEAR * Math.Log(1+ratePerPeriod)) - 1
19:
20:    Dim intPerPayment as Double
21:    intPerPayment = (Math.Exp(Math.Log(annualRate+1)/payPeriods) - 1) *
       payPeriods
22:
23:    'Now, compute the total cost of the loan
24:    Dim intPerMonth as Double = intPerPayment / PAYMENTS_PER_YEAR
25:
26:    Dim costPerMonth as Double
27:    costPerMonth = P * intPerMonth/(1-Math.Pow(intPerMonth+1,-payPeriods))
28:
29:
30:    'Now, display the results in the results Label Web control
31:    results.Text = "Your mortgage payment per month is $" & costPerMonth
32: End Sub
```

An in-depth discussion of the code in Listing 3.1 will have to wait until the next hour. For now, simply enter the code as is, even if there are parts of it you don't understand. One thing to pay attention to, though, is in lines 7 through 9. In these three lines we are reading the values of the three TextBox Web controls and assigning the values to variables.

If the source code in Listing 3.1 has you hopelessly lost and confused, don't worry. The point of this hour is to get you creating a useful ASP.NET Web page quickly; we will take the time needed to dissect the HTML and source code portions of this ASP.NET Web page in the next two hours.

The mathematical equations used to calculate the monthly interest cost can be found at http://www.faqs.org/faqs/sci-math-faq/compoundInterest/. A more in-depth discussion of these formulas can be found at http://people.hofstra.edu/faculty/Stefan_Waner/RealWorld/Summary10.html.

Testing the Financial Calculator

Now that we have completed the HTML and source code portions of our ASP.NET Web page, it's time to test. First make sure that you have saved the ASP.NET Web page since entering the source code in Listing 3.1. Next view the ASP.NET Web page through your browser. When first visiting the page, you should see three empty textboxes and the Compute Monthly Cost button, as shown in Figure 3.11.

FIGURE 3.11

When the ASP.NET page is first visited, three textboxes await user input.

Now go ahead and enter some values into the textboxes and then click the Compute Monthly Cost button. When this button is clicked, the monthly cost is displayed beneath the textboxes and button, as shown in Figure 3.12.

FIGURE 3.12

The output of the financial calculator is displayed when the Button is clicked.

Testing Erroneous Input

Part of testing is not only testing expected inputs but also testing unexpected ones. For example, what will happen if the user enters into the Mortgage Length textbox a value of "Jisun"? Obviously, this is not a valid number of years. Entering such an erroneous value will cause a run-time error, as shown in Figure 3.13.

FIGURE 3.13

A run-time error will occur if the input is not in proper format.

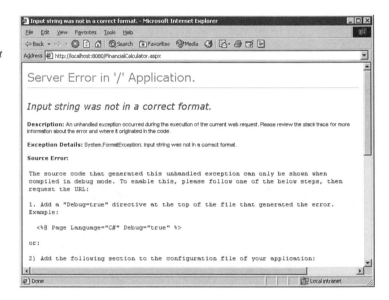

Errors such as those shown in Figure 3.13 are an eyesore. Rather than displaying such error messages when the user enters erroneous input, it would be better to display a simple error message next to the textbox(es) with erroneous input, explaining that the input is not in the right form.

The process of ensuring that user input is in the correct format is known as *input validation*. Fortunately, input validation is incredibly easy with ASP.NET. We'll examine ASP.NET's input validation features in Hour 12, "Validating User Input with Validation Controls."

Earlier in this hour we discussed the importance of planning the user interface and functionality of an ASP.NET Web page prior to creating the page. Not only is it important to plan how the ASP.NET Web pages should work, but it is also important to plan on how to ASP.NET Web page should behave when things don't necessarily go according to plan.

Summary

In this hour we saw how to create our first useful ASP.NET Web page. We started by outlining the features we wanted to include in our ASP.NET Web page, including the output and needed inputs. We then briefly discussed what the user interface should look like.

Next we implemented the user interface by completing the HTML portion of the ASP.NET Web page. Using the Web Matrix Project's WYSIWYG editor, it was simply a matter of typing in the textbox labels and dragging and dropping the needed TextBox, Button, and Label Web controls.

After the HTML portion, the source code portion was entered. The code to perform the calculation was inserted in an event handler for the Compute Monthly Cost button's Click event. This had the effect of having the entered code executed whenever the user clicked the Compute Monthly Cost button.

Finally, we tested the ASP.NET Web page by visiting it with a Web browser and entering some values for the three textboxes.

In this hour we did not spend much time discussing the source code or the specifics of the Button Web control's Click event and corresponding event handler. We will touch upon these issues in detail in the next two hours.

Q&A

Q Can I use HTML controls instead of Web controls for the textboxes in the HTML portion of the ASP.NET Web page?

A Yes, but I would advise against it, in large part because the Web Matrix Project's Toolbox does not contain support for dragging and dropping HTML controls. Rather, you would have to enter the markup for the HTML controls by hand in the HTML tab. That is, there are no HTML controls in the Web Matrix Project's Toolbox, just Web controls and HTML elements.

Additionally, we will be using Web controls extensively throughout this book, so I would encourage you to familiarize yourself with adding Web controls to an ASP.NET Web page and consider using HTML controls only when an example explicitly mentions their use.

Q How do I associate "event code" with a Web control that I've placed on a Web Form?

A In this hour we saw how to have the Button Web control's Click event associated with an event handler provided in the source code section. We accomplished this by simply double-clicking the Button Web control in the designer. Realize that, behind the scenes, the Web Matrix Project is performing a number of steps when you double-click the Button. Each Web control has a *default event*. When the Web control is double-clicked in the designer, an event handler is created for this default event. (Note that the Button Web control's default event is the `Click` event.)

Adding an event handler for an event other than a Web control's default event involves a more thorough discussion than we are ready for at this point. We'll examine adding event handlers for events other than the Web control's default event in the next hour.

Q What would happen if I placed the financial calculation code in the `Page_Load` event instead of the button `Click` event handler?

A Recall that the source code in the `Page_Load` event handler executes every time the ASP.NET Web page is requested. When the page is visited for the first time by the user, the user has yet to enter the loan principal, interest rate, and duration. Therefore, in attempting to compute the calculation, we will get an error.

Because we want to perform the calculation only *after* the user has provided the required inputs, the source code for the calculation is placed in the button's `Click` event handler.

Workshop

Quiz

1. Why is the design requirements phase of software development an important one?

2. How can one add a TextBox Web control to an ASP.NET Web page using the Web Matrix Project?

3. Why did we add a Label Web control to our ASP.NET Web page's HTML portion?

4. What will the ASP.NET Web page's output be if the user enters invalid characters into the textboxes—for example, if under the Mortgage Amount textbox, the user enters "Scott"?

5. How do you add an event handler for a Button Web control's `Click` event with the Web Matrix Project?

6. When using a TextBox Web control, what property is referenced to determine the value entered by the user?

Answers

1. The design requirements phase outlines the specific features for the software project and also outlines the user interface. It is an important stage because by enumerating the features, you—and your boss and client—can easily determine the current progress of the project. Furthermore, there is no ambiguity as to what features should and should not be included.

2. To add a TextBox Web control, simply click the TextBox Web control from the Toolbox and drag it onto the designer.

3. A Label Web control was added to the ASP.NET Web page's HTML portion to indicate where the output of the financial calculator would appear. Without using a label, we could output the results using only Response.Write() statements. Recall from the previous hour that this would have the effect of omitting the results before the HTML portion of the ASP.NET Web page. By using a Label Web control, then, we have more flexibility over where the output appears in the HTML portion.

4. If the user provides invalid input, a run-time error will occur.

5. To add an event handler for a Button Web control's Click event, simply double-click the button that you wish to add an event handler for.

6. The Text property contains the value entered by the user. To reference this property in an ASP.NET Web page's source code portion, we can use

    `TextBoxID.Text`

Exercises

1. In this hour we saw how to use the Web Matrix Project to create an ASP.NET Web page with TextBox Web controls, a Button Web control, and a Label Web control. Using this knowledge, let's create an ASP.NET Web page that will prompt the user for his name and age. Once the user provides this information and clicks the submit button, the ASP.NET Web page will display a message whose content depends on the user's age.

    This ASP.NET Web page will need to have two TextBox Web controls, a Button Web control, and a Label Web control. Set the TextBox Web controls' ID properties to name and age. The Button Web control should have its Text property set to Click Me. Set the Label Web control's ID property to results and clear out its Text property. You will then need to create an event handler for the Button Web control's Click event—recall that this is accomplished by simply double-clicking the Button in the designer.

Now, in the `Click` event handler, you need to determine what message to display, based on the user's age. The code for this will look like

```
If age.Text < 21 then
  results.Text = name.Text & ", you are a youngster!"
End If

If age.Text >= 21 AND age.Text < 40 then
  results.Text = name.Text & ", you are an adult."
End If

If age.Text >= 40 then
  results.Text = name.Text & ", you are over the hill!"
End If
```

Once you have entered the preceding source code into the Button Web control's `Click` event handler, save the ASP.NET Web page and test it by visiting it through a browser.

2. For more practice with the Web Matrix Project, take a moment to enhance the user interface of the `FinancialCalculator.aspx` Web page we created in this hour. A couple suggested enhancements, of many possible, include displaying the TextBox Web control titles in a more appealing font and adding some text at the top of the Web page explaining the purpose of the financial calculator.

HOUR 4

Dissecting Our First ASP.NET Web Page

In the previous hour we created our first practical ASP.NET Web page, a financial calculator that computed the monthly cost of a mortgage. In building this example, we examined the steps that needed to be taken to construct the ASP.NET Web page's HTML and source code portions. These steps included adding the appropriate Web controls, creating an event handler for the Button Web control's Click event, and writing source code to perform the particular calculation.

Although we covered the steps required to build the ASP.NET Web pages, we didn't delve into the details of each step. In this hour we will reexamine the FinancialCalculator.aspx page and the steps needed to create the page, but this time focusing on the details to a greater degree.

In this hour we will cover these topics:

- The differences between the ASP.NET Web page's content and the HTML returned to the Web browser
- When Web control events fire

- How to create event handlers for events other than a Web control's default event
- How to edit the declaration of an ASP.NET Web control easily

Understanding How the Web Controls Are Rendered

Recall from our discussions in Hour 1, "Getting Started with ASP.NET," and Hour 2, "Understanding the ASP.NET Programming Model," that when an ASP.NET Web page is requested by a Web visitor, the ASP.NET engine executes it, returning the HTML that is then sent to the user's Web browser. The HTML returned by the ASP.NET engine is the HTML produced by the source code portion along with the HTML markup in the HTML portion.

The HTML portion of an ASP.NET Web page can contain both static HTML and Web controls. In the `FinancialCalculator.aspx` example, we used a number of Web controls, including TextBox Web controls, a Button Web control, and a Label Web control. When the ASP.NET engine executes an ASP.NET Web page, the Web controls on the Web page are converted into HTML markup; the resulting HTML markup is dependent upon the properties of the Web controls.

For example, take a moment to examine the complete contents of the `FinancialCalculator.aspx` Web page. To do this, open up the `FinancialCalculator.aspx` file in the ASP.NET Web Matrix Project and click the All tab (or simply refer to Listing 4.1).

LISTING 4.1 The Complete Contents of the `FinancialCalculator.aspx` ASP.NET Web Page

```
 1: <%@ Page Language="VB" %>
 2: <script runat="server">
 3:
 4:     Sub performCalc_Click(sender As Object, e As EventArgs)
 5:       'Specify constant values
 6:       Const INTEREST_CALCS_PER_YEAR as Integer = 12
 7:       Const PAYMENTS_PER_YEAR as Integer = 12
 8:
 9:       'Create variables to hold the values entered by the user
10:       Dim P as Double = loanAmount.Text
11:       Dim r as Double = rate.Text / 100
12:       Dim t as Double = mortgageLength.Text
13:
14:       Dim ratePerPeriod as Double
15:       ratePerPeriod = r/INTEREST_CALCS_PER_YEAR
16:
17:       Dim payPeriods as Integer
18:       payPeriods = t * PAYMENTS_PER_YEAR
19:
```

LISTING 4.1 Continued

```
20:        Dim annualRate as Double
21:        annualRate = Math.Exp(INTEREST_CALCS_PER_YEAR *
                   Math.Log(1+ratePerPeriod)) - 1
22:
23:        Dim intPerPayment as Double
24:        intPerPayment = (Math.Exp(Math.Log(annualRate+1)/payPeriods)
                   - 1) * payPeriods
25:
26:        'Now, compute the total cost of the loan
27:        Dim intPerMonth as Double = intPerPayment / PAYMENTS_PER_YEAR
28:
29:        Dim costPerMonth as Double
30:        costPerMonth = P * intPerMonth/(1-Math.Pow(intPerMonth+1,
                   -payPeriods))
31:
32:
33:        'Now, display the results in the results Label Web control
34:        results.Text = "Your mortgage payment per month is $" &
                   costPerMonth
35:     End Sub
36:
37: </script>
38: <html>
39: <head>
40: </head>
41: <body>
42:    <form runat="server">
43:         
44:        <p>
45:        </p>
46:        <p>
47:        </p>
48:        <p>
49:        </p>
50:        <p>
51:            Mortgage Amount:
52:            <asp:TextBox id="loanAmount" runat="server"></asp:TextBox>
53:        </p>
54:        <p>
55:            Annual Interest Rate:
56:            <asp:TextBox id="rate" runat="server"></asp:TextBox>
57:            %
58:        </p>
59:        <p>
60:            Mortgage Length:
61:            <asp:TextBox id="mortgageLength" runat="server"></asp:TextBox>
62:             years<!-- Insert content here -->
63:        </p>
64:        <p>
```

4

continues

LISTING 4.1   Continued

```
65:                    <span style="FONT-SIZE: 12pt; FONT-FAMILY: Courier;
                           mso-bidi-font-size: 10.0pt; mso-fareast-font-family:
                           'Times New Roman';
                           mso-bidi-font-family: 'Times New Roman';
                           mso-ansi-language: EN-US;
                           mso-fareast-language: EN-US; mso-bidi-language: AR-SA">
66:                    <asp:Button id="performCalc" onclick="performCalc_Click"
                           runat="server" Text="Compute Monthly Cost "></asp:Button>
67:                </span>
68:        </p>
69:        <p>
70:        </p>
71:        <p>
72:            <asp:Label id="results" runat="server"></asp:Label>
73:        </p>
74:        <p>
75:        </p>
76:     </form>
77: </body>
78: </html>
```

The complete contents of the FinancialCalculator.aspx Web page are divided into two parts: the source code portion and the HTML portion. The source code portion is defined by the contents within the server-side script block, which starts on line 2 and ends on line 37. The HTML portion starts immediately after the source code portion, on line 38, and continues through the remainder of the contents.

The source code portion contains an arbitrary number of event handlers, such as the Page_Load event handler or, as shown in Listing 4.1, an event handler for a Button Web control's Click event (lines 4–35). The contents of the source code portion can be viewed exclusively in the Web Matrix Project by clicking the Code tab.

The HTML portion contains the HTML markup generated by adding Web controls and static HTML via the designer. For example, on line 51 you can see the HTML static text "Mortgage Amount:," which is what we typed into the designer. The HTML portion also includes the Web controls. Recall that Web controls have the following syntax in the HTML portion:

```
<asp:WebControlName runat="server" ...></asp:WebControlName>
```

Line 52 shows the syntax for the TextBox Web control that we added after the "Mortgage Amount:" text.

The only required property for a Web control is runat="server". Other properties might be present, depending on what properties for the Web control have been specified via the

Properties pane. For example, recall that when we added the TextBox Web control for the loan amount, we set the ID property to loanAmount. This is why, on line 52, the TextBox Web control has the ID property specified as loanAmount:

```
<asp:TextBox id="loanAmount" runat="server"></asp:TextBox>
```

As you can see by examining the HTML portion in Listing 4.1, using the designer to create the user interface of the ASP.NET Web page adds a lot of odd-looking and, at times, superfluous HTML markup. This is one downside of using the designer.

An alternative to using the designer is to enter the HTML markup by hand via the ASP.NET Web page's HTML tab. Some developers prefer this approach. For this book, however, we will use the designer for two reasons: First, its GUI, WYSIWYG nature allows for a much quicker development time; second, those readers who are not familiar with HTML would find using the HTML tab to enter the HTML markup by hand a daunting task.

Comparing the Contents of the ASP.NET Web Page to the HTML Received by the User

Listing 4.1 shows the contents of the FinancialCalculator.aspx ASP.NET Web page. However, when a user requests this Web page, the Web browser receives the HTML output generated by the ASP.NET engine. This resulting HTML shows precisely how the various Web controls are converted into HTML markup. Listing 4.2 shows the HTML returned by FinancialCalculator.aspx when a user first visits the page through a browser.

LISTING 4.2 The HTML Returned by FinancialCalculator.aspx when First Visited by a User

```
 1: <html>
 2: <head>
 3: </head>
 4: <body>
 5:     <form name="_ctl0" method="post" action="FinancialCalculator.aspx"
                id="_ctl0">
 6: <input type="hidden" name="__VIEWSTATE"
            value="dDwtMjA5NTYyODY5MTs7PieSu11aDAUD02BSUuOXUlZ8PS3r" />
 7:
 8:           
 9:          <p>
10:          </p>
11:          <p>
12:          </p>
13:          <p>
14:          </p>
15:          <p>
```

continues

LISTING 4.2 Continued

```
16:                   Mortgage Amount:
17:                   <input name="loanAmount" type="text" id="loanAmount" />
18:            </p>
19:            <p>
20:                   Annual Interest Rate:
21:                   <input name="rate" type="text" id="rate" />
22:                   %
23:            </p>
24:            <p>
25:                   Mortgage Length:
26:                   <input name="mortgageLength" type="text" id="mortgageLength" />
27:                    years<!-- Insert content here -->
28:            </p>
29:            <p>
30:                   <span style="FONT-SIZE: 12pt; FONT-FAMILY: Courier;
                              mso-bidi-font-size: 10.0pt; mso-fareast-font-family:
                              'Times New Roman'; mso-bidi-font-family: 'Times New Roman';
                              mso-ansi-language: EN-US; mso-fareast-language:
                              EN-US; mso-bidi-language: AR-SA">
31:                   <input type="submit" name="performCalc" value="Compute
                              Monthly Cost " id="performCalc" />
32:                   </span>
33:            </p>
34:            <p>
35:            </p>
36:            <p>
37:                   <span id="results"></span>
38:            </p>
39:            <p>
40:            </p>
41:      </form>
42: </body>
43: </html>
```

Note that the HTML in Listing 4.2 contains no server-side script blocks and no source code. Furthermore, Listing 4.2 contains no Web control syntax. Instead, the Web controls have been converted to their equivalent HTML markup. For example, the TextBox Web control defined on line 52 in Listing 4.1 appears to the user as an <input> textbox (see line 17 in Listing 4.2).

The important concept to grasp here is that the makeup of the actual ASP.NET Web page and the HTML received by the user's Web browser are not one and the same. Since all ASP.NET Web pages are converted into valid HTML, this means that any Web browser can request and display an ASP.NET Web page. In fact, the Web browser doesn't know or care whether the page it is requesting is an ASP.NET Web page or not, because the ASP.NET Web page returns HTML markup just like any static Web page does.

Examining the Web Form

Recall that the Web Matrix Project automatically adds a Web form to each and every ASP.NET Web page that you create. A Web form, as discussed in the last hour, "Creating Our First ASP.NET Web Page," is a form HTML control that has the syntax

```
<form runat="server">
  ...
</form>
```

Web forms are necessary when creating ASP.NET Web pages that collect a user's input and do some sort of action based on that input. The `FinancialCalculator.aspx` Web page is an example of such a page—the user needs first to supply the loan amount, the mortgage rate, and the loan duration in order to have the monthly mortgage cost computed.

As with Web controls, HTML controls are converted into HTML markup depending upon their property values. The Web form is of particular interest, and its rendered form can be seen on lines 5 and 6 in Listing 4.2. As you can see, the Web form is converted into two tags: a standard HTML `<form>` tag and a hidden `<input>` tag.

The hidden `<input>` tag is worth discussing, but let's hold off on this talk until later. We'll return to a more detailed look at Web forms in Hour 9, "Web Form Basics."

4

Examining when the Events of a Web Control Fire

As we saw in the previous hour, Web controls can have events. For example, we have seen that the Button Web control has a `Click` event. In Hour 2 we discussed the fact that events can be associated with event handlers. An event handler is a piece of source code that is executed whenever its associated event fires. With the `FinancialCalculator.aspx` example, we created an event handler for the Button Web control's `Click` event that computed the monthly cost of the mortgage based upon the user's input.

But when do events fire? From the name of it, one might expect the Button Web control's `Click` event to fire immediately after the user has clicked the button, but this isn't exactly the case. Recall from our discussions in Hour 1 that there is a sharp distinction between the client (the Web browser requesting the Web page) and the server (the Web server retrieving the requested Web page). The only way for the client and the server to communicate with one another is by having the client make a Web request to the Web server. For example, if the client wants to access a particular Web page, it must request the Web page from the Web server, which will then send the Web page's HTML content to the client.

When an ASP.NET Web page that contains a Button Web control is requested, the Button Web control is rendered into an HTML `<input type="button" ... />` tag (see line 31 in

Listing 4.2), which displays a button in the user's Web browser. When this button is clicked, the postback form in the ASP.NET Web page is submitted. This causes the Web browser to re-request the ASP.NET Web page, passing along various bits of information in the HTTP Post header.

As we already know, whenever the Web server receives a request for an ASP.NET Web page, it hands off the request to the ASP.NET engine. Based on the data submitted in the form, the ASP.NET engine can ascertain that it was the button being clicked that caused the form to be submitted. (If there are multiple Button Web controls on the Web page, the ASP.NET engine can determine what button click caused the form submission.) Once it determines that the Button Web control was clicked, it raises the Button's Click event.

The key thing to understand is that Web control events are fired on the Web server by the ASP.NET engine. The ASP.NET engine has a chance to run only when an ASP.NET Web page is requested by a Web browser. Therefore, for an event to fire, the form on the ASP.NET Web page must be submitted. Because the form is a postback form, it is commonly said that the ASP.NET Web page is *posted back*.

Given this, you can see that the Button Web control's Click event does not fire immediately when the user clicks the associated button in the Web page. Instead, when the user clicks the button, the ASP.NET Web page is posted back, the ASP.NET engine reexecutes the ASP.NET Web page, detecting that the button was clicked, and fires the Click event. Figure 4.1 graphically summarizes how Web control events are fired.

FIGURE 4.1

Web control events are fired by the ASP.NET engine.

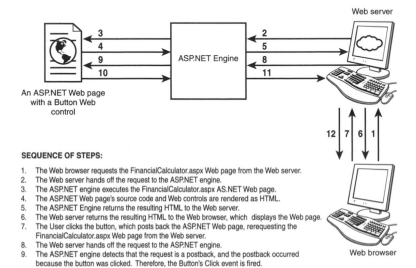

How Events Are Fired

SEQUENCE OF STEPS:

1. The Web browser requests the FinancialCalculator.aspx Web page from the Web server.
2. The Web server hands off the request to the ASP.NET engine.
3. The ASP.NET engine executes the FinancialCalculator.aspx AS.NET Web page.
4. The ASP.NET Web page's source code and Web controls are rendered as HTML.
5. The ASP.NET Engine returns the resulting HTML to the Web server.
6. The Web server returns the resulting HTML to the Web browser, which displays the Web page.
7. The User clicks the button, which posts back the ASP.NET Web page, rerequesting the FinancialCalculator.aspx Web page from the Web server.
8. The Web server hands off the request to the ASP.NET engine.
9. The ASP.NET engine detects that the request is a postback, and the postback occurred because the button was clicked. Therefore, the Button's Click event is fired.
10. The ASP.NET Web page is converted into HTML markup, just like in step 4.
11. Same as step 5.
12. Same as step 6.

Adding an Event Handler for a Web Control's Event

As we saw in the last hour, to add the `Click` event handler for the Button Web control, all we need to do is double-click the button in the designer. This action will take us directly to the Code tab, where we can enter the source code for the event handler. Web controls can have more than one event, but all Web controls have what is known as the *default event*. When double-clicking a Web control in the designer, the event handler for its default event is created.

Since Web controls can have more than one event, you may be wondering how one would add another event handler for the Button Web control besides its `Click` event. To add an event handler for an event other than the default event, we must perform two steps:

1. Add the event handler to the ASP.NET Web page's source code portion.

2. Associate the Web control's event with the event handler created in step 1.

Let's examine each of these steps.

Creating the Event Handler

The first step involves going to the ASP.NET Web page's source code portion and entering the following code:

```
Sub EventHandlerName(sender as Object, e as EventArgsParameter)

End Sub
```

Here *EventHandlerName* can be any name, such as `doCalculation`, `performCheck`, `btnSubmit_Click`, and so on. The *EventArgsParameter* depends on what event you are creating an event handler for. On line 4 in Listing 4.1, you can see that the *EventArgsParameter* value for the event handler for the Button's `Click` event is `EventArgs`. Most event handlers use this *EventArgsParameter*, but some require a different parameter value here.

It's not time at this point to delve into the specifics of creating the event handler or the various types of *EventArgsParameters* for a couple of reasons. First, we've yet to discuss Visual Basic .NET syntax in detail, which is the focus of the next three hours. Without an understanding of VB.NET syntax and subroutines, the event handler code will likely look like gobbledygook. Second, in the vast majority of the examples we'll be examining throughout this book, we'll only need to create an event handler for the Web control's default event. This means that we can create the event handler by simply double-clicking the Web control. Starting in Hour 18, "Allowing the User to Sort the Data in a DataGrid," we will need to create a number of event handlers for nondefault events, but we'll cross this bridge when we get to it.

4

Associating the Event Handler with an Event

In addition to providing the event handler in the source code portion, we also have to associate the event with the event handler. Typically, this is referred to as *wiring up* the event and event handler. To accomplish this, we need to add something extra to the Web control's declaration. Specifically, we must add

```
OnEventName="EventHandlerName"
```

This needs to appear within the Web control declaration, just like all of its properties. That is, to wire up a Button Web control's Click event and an event handler named performCalc_Click, we'd need to adjust the Button Web control's declaration so that it appeared as

```
<asp:Button OnClick="performCalc_Click" id="performCalc" Text="Compute Monthly
Cost" runat="server"></asp:Button>
```

In fact, if you examine line 66 of Listing 4.1, you can see OnClick="performCalc_Click" in the Button Web control's declaration. Of course, when creating the FinancialCalculator.aspx ASP.NET Web page, we did not need to add this in ourselves; rather, it was added for us automatically when creating the Click event handler by double-clicking the Button Web control in the designer.

Editing the Web Control's Declaration

There are two ways to edit a Web control's declaration, which you need to do when associating an event with an event handler. The first way is to click the All tab or HTML tab, find the Web control's declaration, and make the needed edits. A simpler way, in my opinion, is to right-click the Web control in the designer. This will display a menu that contains an option titled Edit Tag.

If you choose the Edit Tag option, a Quick Tag Edit dialog box will appear, displaying the Web control's declaration. Figure 4.2 shows the Quick Edit Tag for the Button Web control in FinancialCalculator.aspx.

FIGURE 4.2

The Quick Edit Tag shows the Button Web control's declaration.

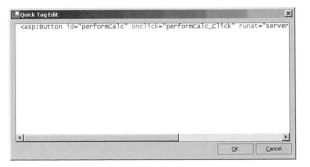

In Figure 4.2 you can see that the Click event has been wired to the performCalc_Click event handler. This was automatically added for us by the Web Matrix Project when we double-clicked the Button in the designer. If you are adding an event handler for an event other than the Web control's default event, however, you will need to add the following to the Web control's declaration in the Quick Tag Edit dialog box:

```
OnEventName="EventHandlerName"
```

Once you have made the necessary changes to the Web control's declaration via the Quick Tag Edit dialog box, you can simply click the OK button, which will save the changes you made and return you to the designer.

> Don't worry if you don't completely understand how to add event handlers for events other than a Web control's default event. For the next 14 hours, we won't need to add any such event handlers. When we reach Hour 18, where we need to create event handlers for nondefault events, we'll look at the process again in greater detail.

Summary

4

In this hour we examined in more detail the ASP.NET Web page created in the previous hour. Specifically, we examined the difference between the ASP.NET Web page's content and the HTML received by the Web browser requesting the ASP.NET Web page. Listing 4.1 shows the contents of the FinancialCalculator.aspx ASP.NET Web page, which includes source code and Web control syntax. When the FinancialCalculator.aspx ASP.NET Web page is requested by a user's Web browser, the ASP.NET engine executes the FinancialCalculator.aspx page, which produces the Web page's HTML output, which is then sent back to the user's browser (this HTML markup is shown in Listing 4.2).

We also examined when Web control events fire and how to create event handlers for Web control events other than the default event. Note that we did not delve into the specifics of the source code in the FinancialCalculator.aspx ASP.NET Web page, nor did we study the various Web controls. The reason these topics were omitted is that they are covered in detail in later hours.

The next three hours serve as a Visual Basic .NET primer. Recall that Visual Basic .NET, or VB.NET, is the programming language we will use to create the source code portions of our ASP.NET Web pages. Following these three hours, Hour 8, "ASP.NET Web Controls for Displaying Text," Hour 10, "Using Textboxes to Collect Input," and Hour 11, "Collecting Input by Using Drop-down Lists, Radio Buttons, and Checkboxes," focus on the Label Web control and Web controls for collecting user input. Hour 9 examines Web forms in detail.

Q&A

Q **Why is it important that an ASP.NET Web page, when requested by a Web browser, return only HTML?**

A As we saw in Listing 4.1, when creating an ASP.NET Web page, we can include source code, HTML markup, and Web controls. However, when an ASP.NET Web page is requested by a Web browser, the content returned to the Web browser is just HTML markup (refer back to Listing 4.2). You might wonder why this is so, since there are potential advantages for having an ASP.NET Web page return more than just plain HTML.

For example, imagine that an ASP.NET Web page could send the Web browser the Web control syntax, as opposed to the rendered HTML markup. That is, if an ASP.NET Web page contained a TextBox Web control, it would be sent to the user as

```
<asp:TextBox Text="Enter text here." ...></asp:TextBox>
```

as opposed to first being rendered into an `<input>` tag and then sent to the Web browser. The disadvantage of first rendering the HTML content is that the HTML produced might not be the optimal HTML for the user's browser. That is, if the user is using a PDA with Internet accessibility, the TextBox Web control might render to HTML markup that displays a large textbox, one that is wider than the PDA screen. If, on the other hand, the PDA's Web browser were to receive the actual Web control syntax, it could then decide on its own how best to display the textbox.

Although sending Web control syntax to the browser would be beneficial in such cases, it would have a very major disadvantage: Only those browsers that were designed to understand ASP.NET Web controls would be able to utilize ASP.NET Web pages. This would mean that users Web surfing with those browsers that chose not to support ASP.NET Web controls, and older browsers designed prior to ASP.NET's emergence, would not be able to visit ASP.NET Web pages.

Since all Web browsers know how to render HTML markup, ASP.NET Web pages return just HTML markup to ensure compatibility with all Web browsers. As mentioned earlier in this hour, when visiting an ASP.NET Web page, the Web browser does not know or care that the Web page is an ASP.NET Web page—all it cares about is the HTML content that is returned to it when the ASP.NET Web page is requested from the Web server.

Workshop

Quiz

1. ASP.NET Web pages consist of two portions. What is the name of each of these portions?

2. True or False: A Web browser requesting an ASP.NET Web page receives back both the HTML markup for the page and the code in the ASP.NET Web page's source code portion.

3. What does the term *wire up* mean with respect to events and event handlers?

4. How can a Web control's default event be easily wired up to an event handler?

5. What steps must be taken to wire up a Web control's nondefault event to an event handler?

Answers

1. The ASP.NET Web pages consist of a source code portion and an HTML portion. The source code portion contains source code, while the HTML portion contains HTML markup and Web controls.

2. False. The Web browser receives *only* HTML markup. No source code or Web control syntax is passed back to the browser.

3. A Web control's event can be wired up to an event handler by adding the following line in the Web control's declaration:

```
OnEventName="EventHandlerName"
```

Once an event handler is wired up to an event, whenever the event fires, the code in the event handler will be executed.

4. To wire up a Web control's default event to an event handler, all you need to do is double-click the Web control in the designer. This will automatically wire up the event to the event handler, create the event handler in the source code portion, and take you to the Code tab to add the event handler's code.

5. To wire up an event other than the Web control's default event, two steps must be taken. First the event needs to be created in the source code portion of the ASP.NET Web page. This is typically done by using the following syntax:

```
Sub EventHandlerName(sender as Object, e as EventArgs)
  ' ... insert code here ...
End If
```

4

Next the event must be wired up to the event handler *EventHandlerName*. This is accomplished by editing the Web control's declaration and adding the following line:

```
OnEventName="EventHandlerName"
```

Note that the Web control's declaration can be edited by right-clicking the Web control in the designer and selecting the Edit Tag menu option.

Exercise

1. This exercise is designed to illustrate the difference in the content of an ASP.NET Web page and the HTML markup received by the Web browser when requesting the same ASP.NET Web page.

   Start by creating a new ASP.NET Web page in the Web Matrix Project named `Exercise1.aspx`. First type in **Your name:** and then add a TextBox Web control following this text. After the TextBox hit Enter and type in **Your age:** and add another TextBox Web control after this text. Finally, add a Button Web control.

   Now, to examine the content of the ASP.NET Web page, click the All tab. Note that there exists an empty server-side script block, some HTML markup, and three Web controls (two TextBox Web controls and a Button Web control). Next visit the ASP.NET Web page through a browser. (Recall that if you are serving the ASP.NET Web pages locally, you can visit the ASP.NET Web page by hitting F5 or going to the View menu and selecting Start. If you are using a Web hosting company, you will need to enter the URL of the ASP.NET Web page in your Web browser.)

   Once you have loaded the ASP.NET Web page in your browser, opt to view the Web page's HTML source. You can accomplish this by going to the View menu and selecting Source. Notice that the HTML markup received by the Web browser does not contain any Web control syntax or server-side script blocks. Rather, the TextBox and Button Web controls have been converted into `<input>` tags.

HOUR 5

Visual Basic .NET Variables and Operators

ASP.NET Web pages are composed of two portions: an HTML portion, which contains HTML markup and Web controls, and a source code portion, which contains the ASP.NET Web page's server-side source code. Using the Web Matrix Project, this source code section can be written in one of two programming languages: Visual Basic .NET (often abbreviated as VB.NET) and C#.

Most beginning developers find Visual Basic .NET a much easier language to pick up than C#, mainly because Visual Basic .NET's syntax and structure is much closer to everyday English than C#'s. Therefore, all of the source code portions of ASP.NET Web pages discussed throughout this book use Visual Basic .NET as the programming language.

If you are new to programming, you likely found the source code portion of the example in Hour 3, "Creating Our First ASP.NET Web Page," to be a bit daunting. Don't worry; in this hour and the next two, we'll take an in-depth look at Visual Basic .NET. By the end of these three hours, you'll not only be able to make sense of source similar to that in Hour 3; you'll also be able to write similar code on your own.

If you've had programming experience with Visual Basic .NET in the past, you may want to just skim the contents of the next three hours, as they are geared toward those who have had limited programming experience. If you have had experience with Visual Basic 6.0 or VBScript but not Visual Basic .NET, I would encourage you to read these three hours, as there have been some important changes in the syntax and semantics from Visual Basic 6.0 and VBScript to VB.NET.

In this hour we will cover

- What a programming language is
- What variables are and how to declare them
- How to assign values to variables
- What data types are and why they are important
- VB.NET's operators and how to use them
- Typing rules

The Purpose of Programming Languages

When computers were first designed in the early twentieth century, they were created to carry out mathematical computations that at the time were performed by humans. Computers were preferred over man because they could perform the calculations faster, could work round the clock, and were not susceptible to error. That is, a computer doesn't forget to carry the one when subtracting two numbers, an error every human has likely made at some point.

Computers then, as computers today, were built to accept a sequence of *instructions* and to carry out these instructions in the order in which they arrived. This made computers ideal for solving problems that could be broken down into a sequence of simple steps. For example, addition of large numbers can be broken down into simpler addition problems by first adding together the ones place in both numbers, then the tens place, and so on, carrying over a digit into the proceeding column if needed.

To have a computer solve a problem, though, it first needs to be told the sequence of steps to perform. Think of a computer as a very obedient young child, one who can understand only simple words and commands and will always do whatever you instruct. If you want this child to, say, go to sleep, you would have to tell him first to go to his bedroom, which might require that you first tell him to start walking toward the stairs. Then you would need to talk him up the first step, then the second, and so on. After that you might need to tell him to walk down the hall to his room. You would then need to tell him to open his door, to walk into his room, to lie down in bed, and finally, to fall asleep.

The verbal commands you give must be fairly simple ones the child can understand. That is, if you said, "I implore that you acquiesce to slumber," the child would wonder what in the world you were saying.

Similarly, when providing instructions to a computer, the instructions must conform to a specific syntax and structure. Specifically, computers understand commands only from particular *programming languages*. A programming language is a language with a well-defined syntax and semantics. There are multitudes of programming languages. When creating ASP.NET Web pages, however, we are restricted to using .NET-compatible programming languages, such as VB.NET and C#.

 There are many .NET-compatible programming languages, among them JScript.NET, COBOL.NET, and C++.NET. However, ASP.NET Web pages are most typically created with either Visual Basic .NET or C#. In fact, the Web Matrix Project provides support for using one of only these two languages.

Concepts Common to All Programming Languages

Although there are many programming languages in existence, they all share some common features. These features include

- A means to store data temporarily—In VB.NET *variables* are used to store data. We'll be discussing variables in an upcoming section, "Declaring and Using Variables."

- A set of operators that can be applied to the data stored in variables—One such operator is +, which sums the values of two variables. We'll look at the operators available in VB.NET in the "Visual Basic .NET Operators" section.

- A variety of control structures that can alter the flow of instructions, based on the value of variables—The control structures in VB.NET are covered in the next hour, "Visual Basic .NET Control Structures."

- A way to modularize source code into reusable units—In Visual Basic .NET, code can be compartmentalized into subroutines and functions, as we'll see in the next hour.

In this hour we will look at how these two features are implemented in Visual Basic .NET.

The Importance of Knowing How to Program

Whenever learning something new, it is common to ask yourself, "How important is it that I learn this?" If you have had experience with HTML editors like Microsoft FrontPage or Macromedia DreamWeaver, you know that creating Web sites by using

5

these tools requires almost no knowledge of HTML syntax. The reason is that these tools allow developers to build Web sites by dragging and dropping Web page elements, as opposed to having to type in the actual HTML by hand. Since the Web Matrix Project is an editor designed for creating ASP.NET Web pages, it should come as no surprise that the Web Matrix Project contains a number of features that make creating ASP.NET Web pages, including the source code portion, as easy as clicking a few buttons.

Commonly, developers creating dynamic Web pages are creating *data-driven dynamic Web pages,* which are ones that interface with a *database,* either displaying data or allowing users to update, delete, or insert data. A database is a piece of highly specialized software that is designed for efficiently storing and retrieving structured data.

> We will begin discussing how to create data-driven ASP.NET Web pages in Hour 13, "An Introduction to Databases."

For data-driven ASP.NET Web pages, typically only a scant amount of source code is needed. For example, to display data from a database, the only source code that is required is code that interfaces with the database, retrieves the data to display, and indicates the Web control that should display the data. This can be accomplished oftentimes in fewer than 10 lines of code.

These 10 or so lines of code—which, again, interface with the database, retrieve the proper data, and specify what Web control is responsible for displaying the data—will be used over and over again in virtually any data-driven ASP.NET Web page that is designed to display data from a database. Of course, this common source code might differ slightly from page to page, but the majority of the code will be identical on many data-driven ASP.NET Web pages.

Because data-driven ASP.NET Web pages are commonly used, the Web Matrix Project provides *Code Builders,* which we'll start examining in Hour 15, "Displaying Data with the DataGrid Web Control." Code Builders are wizards that assist in producing the source code needed to accomplish common tasks, such as displaying data from a database.

Why Learning Visual Basic .NET Is Important

Given that the Web Matrix Project provides Code Builders that will write the source code for common cases, it might seem that learning Visual Basic .NET is not essential to creating a fully working ASP.NET Web application. Although you may be able to create a working Web application strictly through the use of the Web Matrix Project's Code Builders, without learning VB.NET, I would discourage such a shortcut for a few reasons.

First, learning Visual Basic .NET will enable you to create ASP.NET Web pages that provide functionality that is not supported by Code Builders. For example, in Hour 3 we examined how to create a financial calculator ASP.NET Web page. There is no Code Builder for building such a Web page.

Second, if you rely on Code Builders alone and do not learn Visual Basic .NET, what happens if you need to make a change to the source code produced by the Code Builder? For example, when using the Code Builder to display database information, there is no way to specify how the database data should be sorted. As we will see in Hour 23, "Displaying the Guestbook's Contents," if we want to specify how the database data should be ordered, we need to edit the source code produced by the Code Builder.

Finally, learning Visual Basic .NET will make you a better ASP.NET developer and will teach you the fundamentals of programming, which are lessons that will benefit you whenever you are dealing with computers.

Code Builders are great tools to use when creating data-driven ASP.NET Web pages, and we'll take advantage of them in future hours. However, it is important first to understand programming and to be familiar with Visual Basic .NET, so that the source code produced by the Code Builders is understandable.

Declaring and Using Variables

A *variable* is a location in the computer's memory where you can temporarily store information, such as a number or a string.

In a programming language, a *string* is a sequence of characters and is delimited by double quotes. An example of a string would be

`"Hello, World!"`

Variables have three components to them:

- A *value,* such as 5, or "Hello, World!"
- A *name,* which is used to refer to the value of the variable.
- A *type,* which indicates what type of values can be stored. For example, a variable whose value is 5 would have the type *Integer*. A variable whose value is "Hello, World!" would have the type *string*.

5

Because a variable's type dictates what data can be stored in the variable, a variable's type commonly is referred to as its *data type*.

Think of a variable as a specific type of box into which you can place things of a certain type. Each box has a name that you give it, which you can use to reference the value in a particular box. For example, as Figure 5.1 shows, there is a box named age that can accept an integer value. Inside this box we can place values like 24, 97, –3829294, or any other valid integer value.

FIGURE 5.1
Think of a variable as a named box that can contain a certain type of value.

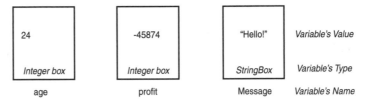

24	-45874	"Hello!"	Variable's Value
Integer box	Integer box	StringBox	Variable's Type
age	profit	Message	Variable's Name

Assigning Values to Variables

The name and data type of a variable are *immutable*. That is, once the variable's name and type have been specified, they cannot change during the program's execution. The variable's value, on the other hand, is *mutable,* meaning that it can change over the course of the program's execution.

Variables alter their value through an *assignment statement,* which assigns a value to a variable by using the = operator and has the following form:

variableName = value

This statement assigns *value* to the value of the variable *variableName*.

 We will discuss the = operator (often referred to as the assignment operator) in the "Visual Basic .NET Assignment Operators" section.

Declaring a Variable

In order to use a variable, you must first *declare* the variable by using the VB.NET Dim statement. When declaring a variable, you must provide both the name and data type of the variable and optionally may include the value. For example, to create a variable named age that accepts values of type integer, you would use the following Dim statement:

```
Dim age as Integer
```

More generally, the `Dim` statement has the following form:

```
Dim variableName as type
```

We'll examine the `Dim` statement in much greater detail in the "Examining the `Dim` Statement" section. First, though, we need to look at the rules for naming variables, as well as the available variable types.

Rules for Naming Variables

Each programming language imposes its own set of rules for naming variables. For Visual Basic .NET, variable names can start with an alphabetic character or an underscore character, followed by zero to many underscores, alphabetic characters, or numeric characters.

> Variable names in VB.NET may be anywhere from one character long to 16,383 characters long.

> Variable names in VB.NET are not case sensitive, meaning that the casing does not matter. Therefore, the variable name Age is equivalent to the variable names AGE, age, aGe, and so on.

Some examples of valid variable names are

- Age
- message2
- _xyz123abc
- __
- txtPassword

> If a variable name begins with an underscore, it *must* be followed by at least one other character. That is, you cannot have a variable simply named _.

5

Some examples of *invalid* variable names are

- 3Age—invalid because a variable name cannot start with a numeric character.
- _—invalid because if a variable name begins with an underscore, it must be followed by at least one other character.
- 234—invalid because a variable name cannot start with a numeric character.

When naming your variables, it is important to choose names that make sense given the information the variable will store. For example, if you are going to use a variable to store the product of two numbers, you might want to name that variable product or some other descriptive name, rather than using something ambiguous, like x or variable3.

Examining Variable Data Types

Recall that the data type of a variable dictates what type of values can be stored in the variable. For example, a variable of type integer can store only values that are integers (negative and positive whole numbers).

If you have worked with ASP, ASP.NET's predecessor, you've likely had experience with VBScript, a watered-down version of Visual Basic 6.0, which was Visual Basic .NET's predecessor. With VBScript, variables were *loosely typed*.

Loosely typed variables are variables that are declared without an explicit data type. Their type is inferred by the value assigned to the variable. For example, in VBScript you could write code that looked like

```
1: Dim x
2: x = "Hello, World!"
3: x = 4
```

Note that the Dim statement on line 1 does not contain a type (that is, it does not read: Dim x as String). The type of x is dynamically inferred by the value assigned to it. Therefore, on line 2, when x is assigned the value "Hello, World!", which is a string, x's type is considered to be of type string. On line 3, however, x is assigned the value 4, which is an integer. After line 3, x's type is considered to now be of type integer.

The opposite of loosely typed is *strongly typed*. In strongly typed languages, *all* variables must be declared to be of a certain type. Once a variable has been declared to be a certain type, it can be assigned only values that correspond to that type.

> With loosely typed languages, any value can be assigned to any variable, and the value being assigned determines the variable's type. With strongly typed languages, a variable's type is explicitly specified, and only values corresponding to the variable's type may be assigned to the variable.

Visual Basic .NET is a strongly typed language. Therefore, all variables must be given an explicit data type, and the set of values that can be assigned to a given variable is limited by the variable's type.

Because each type has a predefined set of values that can be assigned, it is important to give your variable the proper type. For example, in Hour 3 we looked at an ASP.NET Web page that calculated the monthly cost of a home loan. The variables used to hold the intermediary computations were of type `Double`, which is a numeric type that stores numbers with decimal places. Had we chosen to use integer variables, the calculation would have come out incorrectly because we were dealing with decimal numbers.

Specifically, the interest rate involved in the calculation, which might be 0.065 (for a 6.5% interest rate), could not be expressed as an integer. Rather, we would have to use 0 or 1 (or some other whole number), which would clearly produce an incorrect answer. For this reason, using the correct type is important.

In general, when declaring a variable, the following syntax is used:

```
Dim variableName as type
```

Integer Types

Integers are whole numbers that can be either positive or negative. For example, 34, 76, –3,432, and 234,124 are all valid integers, whereas 12.4 and –3.14159 are not.

There are three types of integer data types, each differing in the range of integers it can contain. The most common integer type is type `Integer`, which can accept values ranging from –2,147,483,648 to 2,147,483,647. To create a variable of type `Integer`, use the following syntax:

```
Dim variableName as Integer
```

If you need to store larger or smaller integer values, you can use the `Long` data type, which accepts integer values ranging from –9,223,372,036,854,775,808 to 9,223,372,036,854,775,807. To create a variable of type Long, use the following syntax:

```
Dim variableName as Long
```

5

If you need to store much smaller integer values, you can use the Short data type, which can store integers ranging from –32,768 to 32,767. To create a variable of type Short, use

```
Dim variableName as Short
```

Floating-Point Types

Integer variables cannot store numbers that have decimals. However, very often calculations involving numbers with decimals need to be performed. To provide for this, Visual Basic .NET provides three *floating-point data types*.

A floating-point data type is a data type that has a specific number of significant digits but can have the decimal place moved to improve the accuracy of the decimal portion.

The first floating-point data type is Single, which can accept values ranging from –3.4028235E+38 through –1.401298E–45 for negative values and from 1.401298E–45 through 3.4028235E+38 for positive values.

In scientific notation the number following the E represents the number's *magnitude*. The magnitude specifies the number of decimal places in the number. For example, 6.45E+8 is equal to 6.45 * 10^8, or 645,000,000. 6.45E-8 is equal to 6.45 * 10^-8, or 0.0000000645. Therefore, 3.4028235E+38 is a *very big* number!

To create a variable of type Single, use the following syntax:

```
Dim variableName as Single
```

A more precise floating-point data type that also allows for larger numbers is Double, which can accept values ranging from –1.79769313486231570E+308 through –4.94065645841246544E–324 for negative values and from 4.94065645841246544E–324 through 1.79769313486231570E+308 for positive values. To create a variable of type Double, use the following syntax:

```
Dim variableName as Double
```

The third and final floating-point data type is Decimal, which scales the decimal place by powers of 10. Decimals can have anywhere from 0 to 28 decimal places. With zero decimal places, the largest number a Decimal can have is 79,228,162,514,264,337,593,543,950,335 (the smallest being –79,228,162,514,264,337,593,543,950,335). The Decimal can have, at most, 28 decimal digits. Hence, the largest number with 28 decimal digits is 7.9228162514264337593543950335. To create a variable of type Decimal, use the following syntax:

```
Dim variableName as Decimal
```

Boolean Data Types

A Boolean variable is a variable that can be assigned only one of two values: either True or False. To create a Boolean variable, use the Boolean variable type. The following syntax demonstrates how to create a variable of type Boolean:

```
Dim variableName as Boolean
```

String Types

A string is a sequence of characters. For example, "ASP.NET is fun!" is a string comprised of 15 characters, the first being "A," the second being "S," and so on, with the 15th one being "!". To create a variable that can store string values, use the type String. To create a variable of type String, use the following syntax:

```
Dim variableName as String
```

Date Types

To allow for a variable to store dates, specify the variable's data type as Date using the following syntax:

```
Dim variableName as Date
```

The Object Type

Visual Basic .NET contains a catchall type, a data type that can be assigned *any* value. This base type is the Object type. The object type is, by its nature, extremely flexible because you can assign a variable of any type to it. For example, as the following code shows, you can assign a string to an Object type, and then an integer, and then a floating-point number:

```
Dim catchall as Object
catchall = "Jisun"
catchall = 4
catchall = 3.14159
```

Despite its flexibility, you should rarely, if ever, create a variable of type Object. The benefit of using more specific types like Integer, String, and Double is that if you accidentally try to assign an inappropriate value to one of these variables, an error message will be displayed.

5

Examining the `Dim` Statement

As we discussed earlier, before using a variable, you must declare the variable. When declaring a variable in a strongly typed programming language, you must specify not only the name of the variable but also the variable's type. In VB.NET this is accomplished using the `Dim` statement.

In its simplest form, the `Dim` statement simply specifies the variable's name and type, as follows:

```
Dim variableName as type
```

If you want to declare three variables of type `Integer`, you can use three separate `Dim` statements, such as

```
Dim a as Integer
Dim b as Integer
Dim c as Integer
```

Or you can use one `Dim` statement, separating each variable name and type with a comma, such as

```
Dim a as Integer, b as Integer, c as Integer
```

You can also supply a comma-delimited list of variable names and just one type. In this instance, all of the variable names appearing before the one type will have the same type. That is, we can declare three variables, a, b, and c, all to be of type `Integer` by using the following syntax:

```
Dim a, b, c as Integer
```

Performing Assignment when Declaring a Variable

As we've seen thus far, the `Dim` statement is used for declaring a variable but not for assigning the variable a value. That is, if we wanted to create a variable named a of type `Integer` and have it assigned the value 6, we'd use the following code:

```
Dim a as Integer
a = 6
```

This syntax is fine as is, but we can save ourselves a line of code by combining the assignment with the variable declaration on one line. To do this, use the following syntax:

```
Dim a as Integer = 6
```

Or, more generally, use

```
Dim variableName as type = value
```

Performing an assignment when declaring a variable is purely optional. We will use this variant of the `Dim` statement in many examples in this book in the interest of saving space.

Examining Visual Basic .NET's Operators

Simply having a variable with some value in it is not very interesting. Typically, we'd like to be able to perform some sort of operation on that variable or on multiple variables in tandem. For example, in mathematics there are numbers and operators. Numbers are things like 4, 17.5, pi, and so on, whereas operators are things like negate, add, subtract, divide, and so on.

Many of the traditional mathematical operators are operators in Visual Basic .NET. For example, to add together two numeric variables in VB.NET, the + operator is used. To multiply two numeric variables, the * operator is used.

There are different classes of operators, the most important being arithmetic operators, comparison operators, the concatenation operator, and assignment operators. We'll examine these four classes of operators in the following four sections.

Arithmetic Operators

The four most used arithmetic operators in VB.NET are +, -, *, and /, which perform addition, subtraction, multiplication, and division, respectively. These operators are referred to as *binary operators* because they operate on two variables.

For example, to add together two integer variables and store the result in an integer variable, you could use the following code:

```
Dim a, b, c as Integer
b = 15
c = 20
a = b + c
```

Here a will be assigned a value equal to the value of b plus the value of c, which is 35.

The - operator can be used both as a binary operator and as a *unary operator*. A unary operator is an operator that operates on just one variable. When the - operator is used as a unary operator, it performs the negation of a number. That is, if we had the code

```
Dim a, b, c as Integer
b = 15
c = 20
a = -(b + c)
```

a would be assigned the value –35. Here the - operator is used as a unary operator on the expression b + c, thereby negating the value returned by b + c.

5

Note that parentheses can be used to determine the order of operations. If, in the last code snippet, instead of

```
a = -(b + c)
```

we had used

```
a = -b + c
```

a would have been assigned the value 5 because negation has precedence over addition. That is, when the expression -b + c is evaluated, b is negated first, and then its negated value is added to c. With -(b + c), first b and c are summed, and then the resulting sum is negated.

The arithmetic precedence rules in Visual Basic .NET mirror the standard precedence rules of mathematics. If you ever need to alter the order of operations, simply use parentheses to group those expressions that should be evaluated first.

The / operator always returns a floating-point value, even if the resulting quotient does not have a remainder. That is, the value returned by 4 / 2 is the floating-point value 2.0, not the integer value 2. Of course the / operator can also have a quotient with a decimal remainder; for example, the value returned by 3 / 4 is 0.75.

Exploring the Comparison Operators

Comparison operators are binary operators that compare the value of two variables. There are six comparison operators, which are listed in Table 5.1. Comparison operators always return a Boolean value—True or False—depending on the value of the two variables being compared.

TABLE 5.1 Visual Basic .NET's Comparison Operators

Operator	Description
<	Less than
<=	Less than or equal
>	Greater than
>=	Greater than or equal
=	Equal
<>	Not equal

The following statements evaluate to True:

- 4 < 8
- 3.14159 >= 2
- "Bob" <> "Sue"
- (10/2) = (20/4)
- 4 <= 4

The following statements evaluate to False:

- 7 > 100
- "Bob" = "Frank"
- (10/2) = 7.5
- 4 < 4

Usually, comparison operators are used in control structures, which we'll look at in detail in the next hour.

Understanding the Concatenation Operator

The concatenation operator *concatenates* two string variables. Concatenating two strings produces a string that consists of the content of the first string with the content of the second string appended. The string concatenation operator in Visual Basic .NET is the ampersand, &.

Let's look at a quick code snippet to see how the concatenation operator works. Given the following code:

```
Dim firstWord as String = "ASP.NET"
Dim secondWord as String = "is"
Dim thirdWord as String = "neat"

Dim sentence as String
sentence = firstWord & " " & secondWord & " " & thirdWord & "."
```

The variable sentence will end up with the value "ASP.NET is neat." Note that first three string variables—firstWord, secondWord, and thirdWord—are created, where each variable holds a word in a sentence. Next the string variable sentence is declared. We wish to assign to sentence the value of each of the three words concatenated together, with a space between each word and a period at the end.

5

To accomplish this, we use the & operator to join together six strings. First the string `firstWord` and `" "` are concatenated, resulting in the temporary string "ASP.NET ". I use the word temporary here, because this string is immediately concatenated with `secondWord`, resulting in "ASP.NET is ", which is then concatenated with `" "`, resulting in "ASP.NET is ". Next this is concatenated with `thirdWord`, resulting in "ASP.NET is fun", and finally this is concatenated with `"."`, resulting in "ASP.NET is fun.", which is then assigned to the variable `sentence`.

Inserting the Value of a Variable into a String

There arise many situations in which we want to insert the value of a string variable into another string. For example, imagine that we have a variable called `firstName` that contains the user's first name, and we want to display a message on the Web page that reads "Hello, *FirstName*," where *FirstName* is the value of the variable `firstName`. That is, if the value of `firstName` is Scott, we want the message "Hello, Scott" to appear.

First we might want to create a string variable named `output` that would contain the final string that we wish to display. To accomplish this, we would use code like

```
Dim output as String
output = "Hello, " & firstName
```

It is important to realize that after these two lines of code execute, the variable `output` will contain the value "Hello, *FirstName*," where *FirstName* is the value of `firstName`. Note that we did *not* use

```
Dim output as String
output = "Hello, firstName"
```

Had we used this syntax, the value of `output` would be precisely as we indicated: "Hello, firstname". To insert the value of `firstName` into the string `output`, we need to concatenate the string "Hello " with the string value of `firstName`. This is done using the concatenation operator, *not* by simply inserting the variable name into the string.

Visual Basic .NET's Assignment Operators

The most common assignment operator is the = operator, which takes the form

```
variableName = value
```

For example, to assign the value 5 to an integer variable, you can use the following code:

```
Dim age as Integer
age = 5
```

The *value* assigned to a variable can be more complex than simple values like 5. The value can be an expression involving other operators. For example, we might want to sum two numbers and store this sum in a variable. To accomplish this, we could use code like

```
'Create three integer variables
Dim sum, number1, number2 as Integer
number1 = 15
number2 = 20

'Assign the sum of number1 and number2 to sum
sum = number1 + number2
```

Shorthand Versions for Common Assignments

In many situations we might have a variable that is routinely updated in some fashion. We'll see some concrete examples of this in the "Examining Control Structures" section, but for now take my word for it that commonly we will be interested in incrementing an integer variable by one.

To accomplish this, we could use the following code:

```
Dim someIntegerVariable as Integer = 0

...
someIntegerVariable = someIntegerVariable + 1
...
```

Initially, someIntegerVariable is declared with an initial value of 0. Later on we want to increment the value of someIntegerVariable. To do this, we add one to the current value of someIntegerVariable and then store the new value into someIntegerVariable. So, if someIntegerVariable equals 0,

```
someIntegerVariable = someIntegerVariable + 1
```

will take the value of someIntegerVariable (0), add 1 to it (yielding 1), and store 1 into someIntegerVariable. The next time the line

```
someIntegerVariable = someIntegerVariable + 1
```

is encountered, someIntegerVariable will equal 1. Hence, this line of code will first evaluate someIntegerVariable + 1, which is the value of someIntegerVariable (1) plus 1. It will then assign this value (2) back into someIntegerVariable. As you can see, this line of code increments the value of someIntegerVariable by 1 regardless of what the current value of someIntegerVariable is.

5

Because this is a very common line of code, Visual Basic .NET provides an alternate assignment operator to reduce the amount of code we need to write. This shorthand operator, +=, has the following form:

```
variableName += value
```

and has the effect of adding *value* to the current value of *variableName* and then storing the resulting value of this addition back into *variableName*. The following two lines have exactly the same meaning and produce exactly the same results—incrementing someIntegerVariable by 1:

```
someIntegerVariable = someIntegerVariable + 1
```

and

```
someIntegerVariable += 1
```

In addition to +=, there are a number of other shorthand assignment operators, as shown in Table 5.2. Along with the shorthand arithmetic operators, you'll notice the shorthand concatenation operator, &=. This and the += operator are the two shorthand assignment operators we'll use most often.

TABLE 5.2   The Shorthand Assignment Operators

Operator	Description
+=	`variable += value` adds `value` to the value of `variable` and then stores this resulting value back into `variable`.
-=	`variable -= value` subtracts `value` from the value of `variable` and then stores this resulting value back into `variable`.
*=	`variable *= value` multiplies `value` with the value of `variable` and then stores this resulting value back into `variable`.
/=	`variable /= value` divides `value` by the value of `variable` and then stores this resulting value back into `variable`. Recall that the / operator returns a floating-point value.
&=	`variable &= value` concatenates `value` to the value of `variable` and then stores this resulting value back into `variable`.

Learning Visual Basic .NET's Type Rules

Recall that Visual Basic .NET is a strongly typed language. This implies that all variables declared in a VB.NET program be given an explicit data type. Furthermore, the set of values that can be assigned to a variable are limited by the variable's type. That is, a variable that is of type Integer can be assigned only positive or negative whole number values that range between, approximately, positive two billion and negative two billion.

What happens, though, when you try to assign a floating-point number to an integer variable or when you try to assign an integer to a floating-point number? What about when you try to assign a string variable to a floating-point variable, or an integer variable to a string variable?

Because VB.NET is strongly typed, a value of one type cannot be assigned to a variable of a different type. That means you should not be able to assign an integer to a floating-point value. However, the following code will work fine, even though it assigns an integer value to a floating-point variable:

```
Dim fpVariable as Single
fpVariable = 5
```

Why does the preceding code snippet not produce an error? After all, doesn't it violate the typing rules of VB.NET by assigning an integer to a floating-point variable?

Such an assignment is legal because behind the scenes Visual Basic .NET *casts* the integer value 5 into a floating-point value (5.0) and *then* assigns it to the floating-point variable.

Understanding Casting

Casting is the process of changing the type of a variable or value from one type to another. There are two types of casting: implicit casting and explicit casting. *Implicit casting* occurs when the casting occurs without any needed intervention by the programmer. In the code snippet we looked at last, implicit casting is utilized because the integer variable 5 is cast to a floating-point representation of 5.0 without any extra code provided by us, the programmers.

The documentation accompanying the .NET Framework SDK refers to implicit casting as *coercion*.

5

Explicit casting, on the other hand, requires that we, the programmers, explicitly indicate that a cast from one type to another should occur. To cast a variable explicitly from one type to another, we use VB.NET's built-in CType() function, which has the following syntax:

```
CType(variableName, typeToCastTo)
```

The CType() function casts the variable *variableName* from its current type to the type specified by *typeToCastTo*. For example, imagine that the code snippet we looked at earlier implicitly cast an integer to a Single. We can make this cast explicit by using the following code:

```
Dim fpVariable as Single
fpVariable = CType(5, Single)
```

Here the `CType()` function is used to cast the integer value 5 explicitly to a `Single`, which is then assigned to the `Single` variable `fpVariable`.

> In addition to Visual Basic .NET's `CType` function, there is a `Convert` class in the .NET Framework, which contains methods of the form `ToDataType()`. For example, to cast the integer 5 explicitly to a `Single` type, you could use
>
> `fpVariable = Convert.ToSingle(5)`

Widening and Narrowing Casts

Visual Basic .NET can be run in one of two modes: strict and nonstrict. In the strict mode, implicit casting is allowed only for *widening casts*. A widening cast is when the set of legal values for one data type is a subset of the set of legal values for the data type the variable is being cast to. For example, a cast from an integer to a floating-point number is a widening cast because every possible integer value can be expressed as a floating-point value.

Another example of a widening cast is casting a variable of type `Integer` to a variable of type `Long`. This is a widening cast because any legal value for an `Integer` is included in the legal values for a `Long`.

The opposite of a widening cast is a *narrowing cast*. Consider casting a floating-point variable to an integer. If the floating-point variable has the value 5.0, we can safely cast this to the integer 5. But what if the floating-point variable has the value 3.14? There is no integer value that can represent 3.14 precisely. When casting 3.14 to an integer, the resulting integer value is 3; the remainder is dropped.

> In a narrowing cast there is the potential for lost information. When casting 3.14 to an integer, the 0.14 portion of the number is lost in the narrowing cast.

Rules for Implicit Casting

Considering that narrowing casts can result in a loss of data, should VB.NET allow for implicit narrow casts, or would it be prudent for the language to require that an explicit cast be used if a narrowing cast is required?

Truly strongly typed programming languages would require that all narrowing casts be explicit. In this case, if you tried to use code that would invoke an implicit narrowing cast, an error would result. That is, in a truly strongly typed programming language, the following code would produce an error:

```
Dim x as Integer
x = 8 / 4
```

The reason this would result in an error is because the / operator returns a floating-point number (2.0), which must be cast to an integer in order to assign it to x. However, this cast is a narrowing cast. In a truly strongly typed language, one would have to provide an implicit cast, like so:

```
Dim x as Integer
x = CType(8 / 4, Integer)
```

or

```
Dim x as Integer
x = Convert.ToInteger(8 / 4)
```

The disadvantage of requiring explicit casting for narrowing casting is that older versions of Visual Basic allowed for implicit narrowing casts, meaning that old Visual Basic code could not be reused as-is in a Visual Basic .NET program; rather, the programmer would have to alter the code to include explicit casting.

The designers of Visual Basic .NET decided to take a middle-of-the-road approach. By default, implicit narrowing casts are permitted, meaning that the code

```
Dim x as Integer
x = 8 / 4
```

will run without error, assigning the integer value 2 to the variable x.

Keep in mind that casting a floating-point number to an integer drops the remainder portion of the floating-point number. That is, after the following code is executed, the value of x will be 0:

```
Dim x as Integer
x = 3 / 4
```

5

You can configure VB.NET to disallow implicit narrow casting. To accomplish this, you will need to alter the first line in your ASP.NET Web page. Recall that the Web Matrix Project adds the following line of code:

```
<%@ Page Language="VB" %>
```

To this add `Strict="True"`, like so:

```
<%@ Page Language="VB" Strict="True" %>
```

If you do this, Visual Basic .NET will not allow implicit narrowing casts. With the `Strict="True"` option set, you will get a compile-time error message if you try to perform an implicit narrowing cast. For example, say you create an ASP.NET Web page whose source code content contains the following code:

```
<%@ Page Language="VB" Strict="True"%>
<script runat="server">
  Sub Page_Load(sender as Object, e as EventArgs)
    Dim a as Integer
    a = 8/4     'An implicit narrowing cast will occur here!
  End Sub
</script>
```

You will get the error shown in Figure 5.2 when viewing the ASP.NET Web page through a browser.

FIGURE 5.2

A compile-time error occurs if `Strict="True"` is set and an implicit narrowing cast is found.

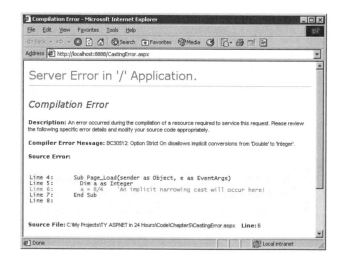

For this book I am *not* going to be adding Strict="True". In some code examples there may be implicit narrow casting. If you choose to add Strict="True", you will have to add the appropriate explicit casting for such code examples.

Summary

In this hour we examined the syntax and semantics for variables and operators in VB.NET. A variable is defined by three properties: its name, its data type, and its value. The name and data type of a variable are specified when the variable is declared and are immutable. Variables are declared in VB.NET via the Dim statement in the following fashion:

```
Dim variableName as type
```

The type of a variable dictates what values the variable can contain. Each type has a subset of legal values. For example, a variable of type Integer can store negative or positive whole numbers that range from –2,147,483,648 to 2,147,483,647.

A variable is assigned a value via an assignment statement, which is = in VB.NET. Along with the assignment operator, there are a number of other operators in VB.NET, including arithmetic operators, like +, –, *, and /; comparison operators, like <, <=, >, >=, =, and <>; and the string concatenation operator, &.

When assigning a value to a variable, it is vital that the type of the value match the type of the variable. If the types do not match, VB.NET may be able to cast the value's type implicitly into the needed type.

Casts can be implicit or explicit, narrowing or widening. An explicit cast can be declared by using Visual Basic .NET's built-in CType() function or by using the Convert class's methods. VB.NET, by default, allows for implicit, narrowing casts. However, by setting the Strict="True" option in the @Page directive of your ASP.NET Web page, implicit narrowing casts are not allowed.

In the next hour we will look at control structures in Visual Basic .NET. Control structures allow for changes in the program's instruction execution. Commonly, this is translated into having specified portions of code executed repeatedly until some condition is met, or encapsulating a series of related instructions in a subroutine or function, which can then be invoked in a single line of code.

5

Q&A

Q Are the shorthand assignment operators used often in practice?

A Visual Basic .NET contains a number of shorthand assignment operators, such as +=, -=, *=, and so on. These operators first perform a mathematical computation (such as addition, in the case of +=) and then an assignment. They are used in the form

```
variable += expression
```

and have the effect of adding the value of *expression* to the current value of *variable,* and then storing this summation as the new value of *variable*.

In Visual Basic 6.0, VB.NET's predecessor, the shorthand assignment operators did not exist. Therefore, a developer who wanted to increment a variable by one would have to use the more verbose code

```
variable = variable + 1
```

as opposed to the more succinct option that is available in VB.NET,

```
variable += 1
```

Shorthand assignment operators are used quite often in practice due to this succinctness. In fact, in a number of examples throughout this book, we'll see these shorthand assignment operators in use.

Q Are there any advantages to using the `Strict="True"` option?

A Recall that the `Strict="True"` option configures VB.NET so that implicit casting is not allowed. Omitting `Strict="True"` from the `@Page` directive configures VB.NET to allow implicit castings that are widening.

Personally, I prefer to enable implicit widening casts since I find that it leaves the code less cluttered. However, implicit casting is more error prone because a variable may be automatically cast from one type to another without your knowledge. For example, the / operator returns a floating-point result. The following code, however, will not produce an error message unless the `Strict="True"` option is specified:

```
Dim x as Integer
x = 10/3
```

Here the value of 10/3 will be 3.3333333. However, since the result is assigned to x, an Integer, the value is implicitly cast to an Integer, meaning that the decimal portion is truncated.

To see why implicit casting can potentially lead to errors, imagine that at some point later in your code, you display a particular message: if x is greater than 3. This conditional code will never execute, since x is equal to 3, not greater than 3. However, this may baffle you, since, in examining the code, you might mistakenly think that x has the value 3.3333333 and, therefore, the conditional code should execute.

Workshop

Quiz

1. What is the one mutable property of a variable, and how is it changed throughout the execution of the program?

2. If you wanted a variable to store the values from 0 up to a value no greater than 10,000, what data type should you use?

3. Does the following code contain an implicit narrowing cast?

```
Dim a, b as Integer
b = 10
a = b / 2
```

4. Does the following statement evaluate to True or False?

```
(4 / 3) = 1
```

5. Does the following statement evaluate to True or False?

```
CType(4 / 3, Integer) = 1
```

Answers

1. The value of a variable is the only mutable property; the name and data type are immutable. The value of a variable is changed via the assignment statement, which assigns a new value to a variable.

2. You could use the Short data type, although in the examples throughout this book, the default integer data type used will be Integer.

3. Yes. The / operator always produces a floating-point result, so b / 2 will return the value 5.0. Because this value must be cast to an integer to be assigned to a, a narrowing cast must be performed. The cast is implicit because there is no CType() function call there explicitly indicating that a cast should occur.

4. It evaluates to false. The division 4 / 3 will produce the value 1.3333333333..., which is not equal to 1.

5

5. It evaluates to True. 4 / 3 will produce the value 1.3333333333..., but when this is cast to type Integer, the remainder will be truncated, resulting in the value 1. Because 1 = 1, this will return True.

Exercises

There are no exercises for this hour, mainly because all that we know how to do in Visual Basic .NET at this point is declare typed variables and assign the values of expressions to these variables.

In the next hour we will be covering Visual Basic .NET control structures, which allow for code to be executed repeatedly or conditionally. Once we have covered this material, we'll be able to examine a number of germane coding examples.

HOUR 6

Visual Basic .NET Control Structures

In the last hour we looked at variables and operators in Visual Basic .NET, two important concepts in any programming language. In this hour we will examine an equally important aspect of all programming languages—*control structures*.

Control structures are constructs that alter the control flow during a program's execution. Without control structures, programs are executed by running the first line of code, then the second, and so on, where each line of code is executed precisely once in the order in which it appears.

Control structures, however, alter the order of instruction execution and can allow for a group of instructions to execute more than once. The control structures that we'll be examining in this hour are conditionals, loops, subroutines, and functions.

In this hour, we will cover these issues:

- Using conditional statements
- What types of looping constructs Visual Basic .NET supports
- Using For loops
- Using Do loops
- The differences between subroutines and functions
- Using subroutines and functions

Understand Control Structures

A computer is good at doing one thing and one thing only—executing a series of instructions. From the computer's point of view, it is simply handed a sequence of instructions to execute, and it does so accurately and quickly.

The instructions executed by the computer are spelled out using a programming language, such as Visual Basic .NET. For example, if you want the computer to create an integer variable, assign the value 4 to it, and then multiply the variable's value by 2, you could use the following code:

```
'Create a variable of type Integer and assign it the value 4
Dim someVariable as Integer = 4

'Multiply the value of someVariable by 2 and assign the product
'back to the variable someVariable (this is equivalent to using
'    someVariable = someVariable * 2)
someVariable *= 2
```

When this program is executed, the first line of code is executed (the Dim statement), which declares a variable of type Integer and assigns the value 4 to this variable. Next the code someVariable *= 2 is executed, which multiplies the value of someVariable by 2 and then assigns the result (8) to someVariable.

 Note that the lines of code in this snippet executed exactly once, with the first line of code executing before the second. This style of code execution is known as *sequential flow*.

What if we don't necessarily want to have someVariable assigned twice its value? Perhaps we want to execute the someVariable *= 2 line of code only if someVariable is less than 5. Or perhaps we want to continue to double the value of someVariable until the value is greater than 100.

In order to alter the flow of instructions, control structures are used. There are three primary classes of control structures:

- The conditional control structure, which executes a set of instructions only if some condition is met
- Looping control structures, which repeatedly execute a set of instructions until some condition is met
- Modularizing control structures, which group sets of instructions into modules that can be invoked at various places in the program

In this hour we will examine the syntax and semantics of all three classes of control structures.

Exploring the Conditional Control Structure

The conditional control structure is used to conditionally execute a set of instructions. The syntax for the condition control structure, in its simplest form, is given as

```
If condition Then
    Instruction1
    Instruction2
    ...
    InstructionN
End If
```

Here *condition* is a Boolean expression, one that evaluates to either True or False. If *condition* evaluates to True, instructions *Instruction1* through *InstructionN* are executed. If *condition* evaluates to False, *Instruction1* through *InstructionN* are skipped and therefore are *not* executed.

 Conditional statements are commonly referred to as If statements.

Recall from the previous hour, "Visual Basic .NET Variables and Operators," that the comparison operators always return a Boolean value. These operators are commonly used to compare the values of two variables or the value of a variable with a literal. For example, with VB.NET the current hour can be determined via the following code:

```
DateTime.Now.Hour
```

This returns an integer value between 0 and 23, where 0 is midnight, 9 is 9 in the morning, 12 is noon, and so on. We could create a simple ASP.NET Web page that uses a conditional statement to determine the current hour and display an appropriate message based on the hour of the day ("Good morning" versus "Good afternoon" versus "Good evening").

6

Let's create such an ASP.NET Web page. To start, create a new ASP.NET Web page named `TimeAppropriateMessage.aspx`. First, let's add a Label Web control that will display the message. To accomplish this, first make sure that the Web Control tab is selected from the Toolbox and then drag and drop the Label Web control onto the designer. Next, from the Properties pane, change the Label's `ID` property to `lblMessage` and clear out the Label's `Text` property. Your screen should look similar to the screenshot in Figure 6.1.

FIGURE 6.1

A Label control has been added.

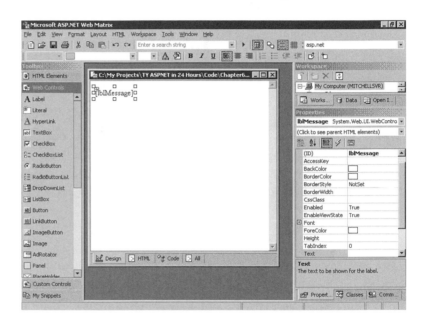

Now click the Code tab. Enter the code shown in Listing 6.1 into the code section.

LISTING 6.1   A Different Message Is Displayed Based on the Current Hour

```
 1: Sub Page_Load(sender as Object, e as EventArgs)
 2:   If DateTime.Now.Hour >= 6 And DateTime.Now.Hour < 12 then
 3:     lblMessage.Text = "Good morning."
 4:   End If
 5:
 6:   If DateTime.Now.Hour >= 12 And DateTime.Now.Hour <= 17 then
 7:     lblMessage.Text = "Good afternoon."
 8:   End If
 9:
10:   If DateTime.Now.Hour > 17 Or DateTime.Now.Hour < 6 then
11:     lblMessage.Text = "Good evening."
12:   End If
13: End Sub
```

Once you enter the code in Listing 6.1 into your ASP.NET Web page's Code tab section, save the ASP.NET Web page and then view it through a browser. You should see the message "Good morning" if the current hour is between 6 a.m. and 11 a.m., "Good afternoon" if it's between noon and 5 p.m., and "Good evening" if it's after 5 p.m. or before 6 a.m.

> Notice that the message you are displaying is based upon the current time of the machine that the Web server is running on. This means that if your ASP.NET Web page is being hosted by a Web hosting company that is in another time zone, the output you see may not be reflective of the current time in your time zone.

The code in Listing 6.1 works by using three If statements. The first If statement (lines 2–4) checks to see whether the current hour is greater than or equal to 6 and less than 12.

Note that the condition on line 2 contains two conditional statements: DateTime.Now.Hour >= 6 and DateTime.Now.Hour < 12. These two conditions are joined by the keyword And. VB.NET contains two keywords for joining conditional statements: And and Or. The semantics of And and Or are just like their English counterparts. That is, the expression *condition1* And *condition2* will return True if and only if both *condition1* and *condition2* are True, whereas the expression *condition1* Or *condition2* will return True if either *condition1* is True or *condition2* is True (or if both *condition1* and *condition2* are True).

> Parentheses can specify order of operations and help make compound conditionals more readable. For example, if we wanted to run a sequence of instructions if the hour either was between 9 and 12 or was 17, then we could use a statement like this:
>
> ```
> If (DateTime.Now.Hour >= 9 AND DateTime.Now.Hour <= 12) OR
>     (DateTime.Now.Hour = 17) then
>   ' ... Instructions ...
> End If
> ```

6

So, if the current hour is both (1) greater than or equal to 6 and (2) less than 12, then the condition on line 2 is True, and line 3 will be executed, which causes the message "Good morning" to be displayed.

Another conditional statement is found on line 6. This one checks to see whether the current hour is between noon and 5 p.m. (Because the hour is returned as a value between 0 and 23, 5 p.m. is returned as 17.) If the hour is both greater than or equal to 12 and less than or equal to 17, then line 7 is executed, and the message "Good afternoon" is displayed.

A third condition on line 10 checks to see whether the hour is greater than 17 or whether the hour is less than 6. If either of these conditions is true, then the code on line 11 is executed, which displays the message "Good evening."

Note that all three of these conditional statements are executed, but only one of the three conditionals will return True, meaning only one of the three messages will be displayed.

Executing Instructions if the Conditional Is False

As we have seen, the If statement executes a set of instructions if the supplied conditional is True. But what if we want to execute some instructions and the condition is false? For example, say that there is some string variable named password that contains the password for the user visiting our Web site. If the password variable is equal to the string "shazaam," we want to display some sensitive information; if, however, the password is *not* "shazaam," then the user has an incorrect password, and we want to display a warning message.

In this scenario we want to use an If statement because we want to execute one piece of code if the password is correct and another piece of code if the password is incorrect. We can accomplish this using the If statement as we saw earlier, like so:

```
If password = "shazaam" then
   'Display sensitive information
End If

If password <> "shazaam" then
   'Display message informing the user they've entered an
   'incorrect password
End If
```

However, there is an easier way to accomplish this. An If statement can contain an optional Else clause. The source code that appears within the Else portion is executed when the condition evaluates to False. The general form of an If statement with an Else clause is

```
If condition Then
    Instruction1
    Instruction2
```

```
   ...
   InstructionN
Else
   ElseInstruction1
   ElseInstruction2
   ...
   ElseInstructionN
End If
```

Here, if *condition* is True, then *Instruction1* through *InstructionN* are executed, and *ElseInstruction1* through *ElseInstructionN* are skipped. If, however, *condition* is False, then *ElseInstruction1* through *ElseInstructionN* are executed, and *Instruction1* through *InstructionN* are skipped.

Using the Else statement, we can rewrite the password checking code from two conditionals to one, as in the following code:

```
If password = "shazaam" then
   'Display sensitive information
Else
   'Display message informing the user they've entered an
   'incorrect password
End If
```

> An If statement can have either no Else clause or precisely one Else clause. There cannot be multiple Else clauses for a single If statement.

Performing Another If Statement when the Condition Is False

In addition to the Else statement, If statements can have zero to many optional ElseIf statements. An ElseIf clause follows an If statement, much like the Else. The ElseIf clause has a condition statement like the If statement. The instructions directly following the ElseIf are executed only if the If statement's condition as well as all of the preceding ElseIf conditions are False and the ElseIf in question's condition is True.

This description may sound a bit confusing. An example should help clear things up. First note that the general form of an If statement with ElseIf clauses is as follows:

```
If condition Then
   Instruction1
   Instruction2
   ...
   InstructionN
```

6

```
ElseIf elseIf1Condition
    ElseIf1Instruction1
    ElseIf1Instruction2
    ...
    ElseIf1InstructionN
ElseIf elseIf2Condition
    ElseIf2Instruction1
    ElseIf2Instruction2
    ...
    ElseIf2InstructionN
...
ElseIf elseIfNCondition
    ElseIfNInstruction1
    ElseIfNInstruction2
    ...
    ElseIfNInstructionN
Else
    ElseInstruction1
    ElseInstruction2
    ...
    ElseInstructionN
End If
```

If the condition *condition* is True, then the instructions *Instruction1* through *InstructionN* are executed, and the other instructions are skipped. If, however, *condition* is False, then the first `ElseIf` condition, *elseIf1Condition*, is evaluated. If this condition is True, then instructions *ElseIf1Intruction1* through *ElseIf1InstructionN* are executed. If, however, *elseIf1Condition* is False, then the second `ElseIf` condition, *elseIf2Condition*, is evaluated. Again, if it is True, then instructions *ElseIf2Intruction1* through *ElseIf2InstructionN* are executed. If, however, *elseIf2Condition* is False, then the third `ElseIf` condition is evaluated, and so on. If *all* `ElseIf` conditions are False, then the Else's instructions (*ElseInstruction1* through *ElseInstructionN*) are executed.

Let's return to the `TimeAppropriateMessage.aspx` example, whose source code was displayed in Listing 6.1. Take a moment to look back over that code listing; notice that we used three conditions: one to check whether the time was between 6 a.m. and 11 a.m., one to check whether the time was between noon and 5 p.m., and one to check whether the time was after 5 p.m. or before 6 a.m.

We can accomplish this with a single `If` statement using either two `ElseIf`s or one `ElseIf` and an `Else`. The code for using two `ElseIf`s is as follows:

```
If DateTime.Now.Hour >= 6 And DateTime.Now.Hour < 12 then
  lblMessage.Text = "Good morning."
ElseIf DateTime.Now.Hour >= 12 And DateTime.Now.Hour <= 17 then
  lblMessage.Text = "Good afternoon."
ElseIf DateTime.Now.Hour > 17 Or DateTime.Now.Hour < 6 then
  lblMessage.Text = "Good evening."
End If
```

The code for using an `ElseIf` and an `Else` looks like

```
If DateTime.Now.Hour >= 6 And DateTime.Now.Hour < 12 then
  lblMessage.Text = "Good morning."
ElseIf DateTime.Now.Hour >= 12 And DateTime.Now.Hour <= 17 then
  lblMessage.Text = "Good afternoon."
Else
  lblMessage.Text = "Good evening."
End If
```

Working with Visual Basic .NET's Looping Control Structures

Looping control structures allow for a set of instructions to be executed a repeated number of times. The number of times the code is repeated can be a fixed number of times, such as with `For ... Next` loops, or repeated until some condition is met, such as with `Do ... Loop` loops.

In the next three sections, we'll be looking at two of Visual Basic .NET's looping constructs: `For ... Next` loops and `Do ... Loop` loops. These two constructs are, at a high-level, equivalent, though they have differing syntax. That is, they accomplish essentially the same task—repeating a set of instructions a certain number of times. In fact, either one of the two looping structures we'll be examining can be implemented with any one of the other looping structures.

Using For ... Next Loops

If you have code that you want to execute a specific number of times, the `For ... Next` looping control structure is likely the looping structure best suited for your needs. The `For ... Next` loop has the following syntax:

```
For integerVariable = start to stop
  Instruction1
  Instruction2
  ...
  InstructionN
Next integerVariable
```

For ... Next loops are often referred to as For loops.

The semantics of the `For` loop are as follows: The variable *integerVariable*, which should be an integer variable type (`Short`, `Integer`, or `Long`), is assigned the value *start*. This variable is often referred to as the *looping variable*.

The looping variable does not necessarily need to be an integer—it can be any numeric type. However, in practice the overwhelmingly vast majority of For ... Next loops use an integer looping variable since For ... Next loops are designed to iterate a sequence of instructions an integral number of times.

After the looping variable is initially assigned to the *start* value, *Instruction1* through *InstructionN* are executed. After these instructions are executed, the value of the looping variable is incremented by one. If, at this point, the value of the looping variable is less than or equal to *stop*, instructions *Instruction1* through *InstructionN* are executed again, the value of the looping variable is incremented by one, and again, the looping variable's value is checked against *stop*. The loop continues to execute, with the value of the looping variable being incremented at each loop iteration, until the value of the looping variable is greater than *stop*.

Instructions *Instruction1* through *InstructionN* are commonly referred to as the body of the loop.

So, to display the message "Hello, World!" in the user's browser three times, you could put the following For ... Next loop in the ASP.NET Web page's Page_Load event handler:

```
Dim i as Integer
For i = 1 to 3
  Response.Write("Hello, World!")
Next i
```

The first thing we do is create an integer variable named i. This variable can have any name, but it needs to be an integer type. When the For loop executes, i is initially assigned the value 1. Then the body of the loop is executed, which outputs the message "Hello, World!" (Remember that the Response.Write(*string*) sends *string* to the user's browser along with the HTML portion of the ASP.NET Web page.)

After the body finishes executing, the value of i is incremented by one. A check is then made to see whether i's current value is less than or equal to 3. It is because i equals 2. Therefore, the loop body is executed again, which will output "Hello, World!" Again, i is incremented and compared to see whether it is less than or equal to 3. Being equal to 3, i is indeed less than or equal to 3, so the loop body executes again. After displaying "Hello, World!" i is (again) incremented, equaling 4. At this point, i is *not* less than or equal to 3, so the For loop body does not execute. Instead, the line of code immediately following the Next i executes.

Incrementing the Looping Variable by More than One Each Loop Iteration

The standard For loop syntax increments the looping variable by one with each iteration of the loop body. But what if you want to increment the looping variable by more than one, or what if you want to decrement the looping variable?

To accommodate for different looping variable increments per loop iteration, VB.NET's For loop can have an optional Step portion that indicates specifically the amount that the looping variable should be incremented per loop. The syntax of the For loop with a Step clause is as follows:

```
For integerVariable = start to stop Step stepAmount
  Instruction1
  Instruction2
  ...
  InstructionN
Next integerVariable
```

stepAmount should be an integer value.

Imagine that you wanted to perform a loop that iterated through the even numbers between 0 and 10. This could be accomplished using a For ... Next loop that started at 0 and went to 10, incrementing by 2 at each iteration. The syntax for such a For loop would be

```
Dim evens as Integer
For evens = 0 to 10 Step 2
  Response.Write(evens & " is an even number.<br>")
Next evens
```

This For loop, if added to an ASP.NET Web page's Page_Load event handler, will display

```
0 is an even number.
2 is an even number.
4 is an even number.
...
10 is an even number.
```

6

If you want a For loop that has its looping variable decremented at each iteration, you need to set the step amount to a negative value. For example, to display the even numbers between 0 and 10, but starting with 10 and working down to 0, you would need to use the following For loop:

```
Dim evens as Integer
For evens = 10 to 0 Step -2
  Response.Write(evens & "is an even number.<br>")
Next evens
```

Do ... Loop Loops

The Do ... Loop loop, often referred to simply as a Do loop, executes the loop body either while a condition holds or until a condition is met, depending on the syntax.

First let's consider the Do loop that iterates while a condition holds. The syntax for such a loop is as follows:

```
Do While condition
  Instruction1
  Instruction2
  ...
  InstructionN
Loop
```

condition is an expression that evaluates to a Boolean value. When the Do loop is encountered, the *condition* is checked. If it evaluates to True, the loop body—instructions *Instruction1* through *InstructionN*—is executed. After the loop body has executed, the *condition* is checked again. If it is still True, the loop body is executed again. This process repeats until *condition* evaluates to False after the execution of the loop body.

A Do loop can also be constructed so that its loop body is executed repeatedly until a condition is met. The syntax for this form of the Do loop is

```
Do Until condition
  Instruction1
  Instruction2
  ...
  InstructionN
Loop
```

Here the semantics of the Do loop are as follows: When the Do loop is encountered, the *condition* is checked. If it evaluates to False, the loop body—instructions *Instruction1* through *InstructionN*—is executed. After the loop body has executed, the *condition* is checked again. If it is still False, the loop body is executed again. This process repeats until *condition* evaluates to True after the execution of the loop body.

Like with the For loop, the Do loop can be used to display the even numbers between 0 and 10. To accomplish this, we could use the following syntax:

```
Dim number as Integer = 0
Do While number <= 10
  Response.Write(number & " is an even number.<br>")

  number += 2
Loop
```

Here an `Integer` number is created and assigned the value 0. The `Do` loop then iterates while the value of number is less than or equal to 10. Because 0 (number's initial value) is less than or equal to 10, the loop body executes. In the loop body a message is output ("0 is an even number"), and then the value of number is incremented by 2. This loop will continue to be executed until the end of the sixth iteration, after which number will have the value 12.

> The loop bodies of `Do` loops typically have a line of code that updates some variable that is used in the `Do` loop's *condition*. In such cases, if you forget to add this line of code, your loop will become an infinite loop, one that never ends. For example, imagine what would happen if we removed the number += 2 line of code from the previous `Do` loop example. Clearly the value of number would remain 0, meaning that the loop body would continually execute, never ending.

Exploring the Modularizing Control Structures: Subroutines and Functions

The code examples we looked at in this hour and the previous one have all been a few simple lines of code designed to illustrate the concept being discussed. In examining the execution of these code samples, we discussed how Visual Basic .NET interprets one line of code at a time, starting with the first line and working down. With control structures, however, this sequential flow of instructions can be altered, such as with loops or conditional statements.

In addition to altering the flow control with loops and conditionals, Visual Basic .NET allows for *modularizing control structures*. A modularizing control structure is a control structure that can be used to create a module of source code. This module may contain many lines of source code, can accept zero to many input parameters, and can optionally return a value. These modules can then be called from any location in the VB.NET source code.

There are two flavors of modularization control structures: *subroutines* and *functions*. Subroutines are modularization control structures that do not return any value, whereas functions always return a value. Subroutines and functions are handy for encapsulating programming logic.

6

To understand subroutines and functions, let's look at a somewhat contrived example that utilizes a subroutine to encapsulate the logic behind displaying a repeated text message. Start by creating a new ASP.NET Web page named `SubroutineLesson1.aspx`. Once the file is created, click the Code tab. Now we want this ASP.NET Web page to send the string "Welcome to my Web site" precisely four times to the user's browser by using the `Response.Write()` method. To accomplish this, we can either use four `Response.Write()` statements, or we can use a simple `For` loop with one `Response.Write()` statement in the loop body. Let's use the latter approach.

Listing 6.2 contains the source code that you should enter into the Code tab. Note that the code that emits the "Welcome to my Web site" message appears in the `Page_Load` event handler. This is because we want this message to be displayed every time the page is visited.

LISTING 6.2 The `Page_Load` Event Handler Displays a Message Four Times

```
1: Sub Page_Load(sender as Object, e as EventArgs)
2:   'Display the message, "Welcome to my Web site" 4 times
3:   Dim i as Integer
4:   For i = 1 to 4
5:     Response.Write("Welcome to my Web site<br>")
6:   Next i
7: End Sub
```

Once you have entered this code, save the ASP.NET Web page and view it through a browser. Notice that this Web page displays the message "Welcome to my Web site" four times, as shown in Figure 6.2.

FIGURE 6.2

The "Welcome to my Web site" message is displayed four times.

Now imagine that we also wanted a Button Web control on the Web page that, when clicked, would display the message "Welcome to my Web site" four times, as well.

To accomplish this, we first need to add a Button Web control. To do this, click the Design tab and take a moment to ensure that glyphs are on, so that you see the starting and closing `<form>` tags. (To turn on glyphs, go to the View menu and select Glyphs.)

Drag a Button Web control from the Toolbox and drop it between the `<form>` tags. At this point your screen should look similar to Figure 6.3.

FIGURE **6.3**

A Button Web control has been added.

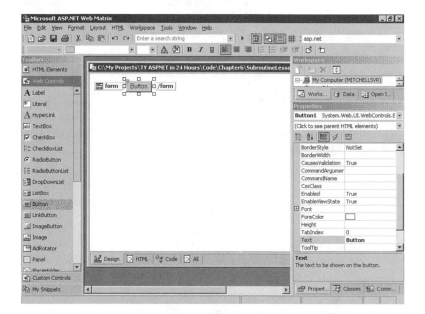

To add an event handler for the Button's `Click` event, double-click the Button Web control in the Designer. This will automatically take you to the Code tab with the appropriate event handler syntax already added. Recall from our discussions in Hours 3 and 4, ("Creating" and "Dissecting Our First ASP.NET Web Page," respectively) that when the Button is clicked, the Button's `Click` event handler is executed. Therefore, to have the message "Welcome to my Web site" displayed four times when the Button is clicked, we want to place the same code that appears in the `Page_Load` event handler in the Button's `Click` event handler.

Listing 6.3 contains the source code for the Button's `Click` event handler, which you should enter into the Code tab.

LISTING 6.3 The Message Is Displayed Four Times when the Button Web Control Is Clicked

```
1: Sub Button1_Click(sender As Object, e As EventArgs)
2:   'Display the message, "Welcome to my Web site" 4 times
3:   Dim i as Integer
4:   For i = 1 to 4
5:     Response.Write("Welcome to my Web site<br>")
6:   Next i
7: End Sub
```

With this addition to the ASP.NET Web page, when you first visit the Web page, the message "Welcome to my Web site" is displayed four times (from the Page_Load event handler). Additionally, a Button is displayed. Figure 6.4 contains a screenshot of SubroutineLesson1.aspx after the code from both Listing 6.2 and Listing 6.3 has been added to the source code portion of the ASP.NET Web page.

FIGURE 6.4

A Button Web control is displayed after the message.

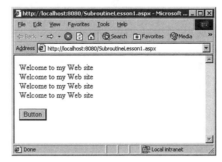

When the Button Web control is clicked, the ASP.NET Web page is posted back, which causes the Button's Click event handler to fire. In addition to the Button's Click event handler being executed, the Page_Load event handler is executed as well because the page is being loaded again. This causes the message "Welcome to my Web site" to be displayed eight times, as shown in Figure 6.5.

Recall that in Hour 4 we briefly discussed the series of actions that happen when a Button Web control is clicked. If you are still a bit confused or unclear, don't worry; we'll be covering this topic in much greater detail in Hour 9, "Web Form Basics."

FIGURE 6.5

The "Welcome to my Web site" message is displayed eight times after the button is clicked.

Reducing Code Redundancy by Using Subroutines and Functions

Although the code for our ASP.NET Web page is fairly simple, it contains redundancies. The code to display the "Welcome to my Web site" message is repeated twice: once in the Page_Load event handler and once in the Button's Click event handler. We can use a subroutine to reduce this redundancy.

A subroutine can be created using the following syntax:

```
Sub SubroutineName()
  Instruction1
  Instruction2
  ...
  InstructionN
End Sub
```

The code that appears between the Sub and End Sub lines is referred to as the *body* of the subroutine and is executed whenever the subroutine is *called*. A subroutine is called using the following syntax:

```
SubroutineName()
```

For our ASP.NET Web page, we can create a subroutine named DisplayMessage() that has as its body the code to display the "Welcome to my Web site" message four times. Then, in the Page_Load and the Button's Click event handlers, we can replace the code that displays the message four times with a call to the DisplayMessage() subroutine.

To employ a subroutine to display the message, replace the source code contents entered from Listings 6.2 and 6.3 with the source code provided in Listing 6.4. That is, go to the Code tab, remove all of the source code, and then enter the source code in Listing 6.4.

LISTING 6.4 The Code to Display the "Welcome to my Web site" Message Is Moved to a Subroutine

```
1: Sub Page_Load(sender as Object, e as EventArgs)
2:   DisplayMessage()
3: End Sub
4:
5: Sub Button1_Click(sender As Object, e As EventArgs)
6:   DisplayMessage()
7: End Sub
8:
9: Sub DisplayMessage()
```

6

continues

LISTING 6.4 Continued

```
10:   'Display the message, "Welcome to my Web site" 4 times
11:   Dim i as Integer
12:   For i = 1 to 4
13:     Response.Write("Welcome to my Web site<br>")
14:   Next i
15: End Sub
```

Listing 6.4 has encapsulated the code to display the "Welcome to my Web site" message four times in a subroutine (lines 9–15). The body of the subroutine can be invoked from anywhere else in the ASP.NET source code section by calling the subroutine (see lines 2 and 6).

Save the ASP.NET Web page and then view it through a browser. Upon first loading the page, you should see the same output shown in Figure 6.4: the message "Welcome to my Web site" displayed four times, followed by a Button. By clicking the Button, you should see the output shown in Figure 6.5: the message "Welcome to my Web site" displayed eight times, followed by a Button.

Strive to reduce code redundancy by modularizing repeated code into a subroutine or function. Redundant code has a number of disadvantages, such as making the code harder to read (due to its increased length), harder to update (because changes to the redundant code require updating the code in multiple places), and more prone to typos (because you have to reenter the code multiple times, the chances of making a mistake increase).

When we start working with databases, there are a number of lines of code that need to be executed to retrieve data from a database. On certain ASP.NET Web pages, we will need to retrieve data from a database in multiple places. Rather than repeating these lines of codes in our source code each time we need to access the database, we can package these lines of code into a subroutine. Then, whenever we need to access this database, we can just call the subroutine.

Passing in Parameters to a Subroutine or Function

In Listing 6.4 we used a subroutine to display a message four times. Specifically, the message "Welcome to my Web site" was displayed using a `Response.Write()` statement inside of a `For` loop. But what if we wanted to generalize the `DisplayMessage()` subroutine so that instead of always displaying the message "Welcome to my Web site," any message could be displayed four times?

Subroutines and functions can be generalized in this manner through the use of *parameters*. A parameter is a value that is passed into a subroutine or function when the subroutine or function is called. In order for a subroutine or function to utilize parameters, the syntax used differs in that a list of the parameters the subroutine or function accepts must be added, as in the following code:

```
Sub SubroutineName(Param1 as Type, Param2 as Type, ... ParamN as Type)
  Instruction1
  Instruction2
  ...
  InstructionN
End Sub
```

Param1 through *ParamN* are referred to as the subroutine's *parameters*. A subroutine may have zero to many parameters. Because VB.NET is a strongly typed language, each parameter must have a type. The instructions in the subroutine's body can access these parameters just like they would any other variable.

Let's take a moment to rewrite the `DisplayMessage()` subroutine from Listing 6.4 so that any message can be displayed four times. To accomplish this, the `DisplayMessage()` subroutine needs to accept a string parameter that indicates the message to display. This updated version of the `DisplayMessage()` subroutine can be seen below:

```
Sub DisplayMessage(message as String)
  'Display the message, "Welcome to my Web site" 4 times
  Dim i as Integer
  For i = 1 to 4
    Response.Write(message)
  Next i
End Sub
```

6

With this change, the `DisplayMessage()` subroutine accepts a parameter `message` of type `String`. In the subroutine's body, instead of using `Response.Write("Welcome to my Web site")`, which would display the message "Welcome to my Web site", we'll use `Response.Write(message)`, which emits the value of the `message` variable.

To call this updated version of the `DisplayMessage()` subroutine, we use the following code:

```
DisplayMessage(messageToDisplay)
```

So, if we want to display the message "Welcome to my Web site," we would call the subroutine like this:

```
DisplayMessage("Welcome to my Web site<br>")
```

Let's use this updated version of the `DisplayMessage()` subroutine to create a page whose output is exactly identical to that of Listing 6.4. Start by creating a new ASP.NET Web page named `SubroutineLesson2.aspx`. As with `SubroutineLesson1.aspx`, from the Design tab be sure to add a Button Web control between the Web form tags. Once you have done this, click the Code tab and enter the source code in Listing 6.5.

LISTING 6.5   The `DisplayMessage()` Subroutine Accepts a Parameter

```
 1: Sub Page_Load(sender as Object, e as EventArgs)
 2:   DisplayMessage("Welcome to my Web site<br>")
 3: End Sub
 4:
 5: Sub Button1_Click(sender As Object, e As EventArgs)
 6:   DisplayMessage("Welcome to my Web site<br>")
 7: End Sub
 8:
 9: Sub DisplayMessage(message as String)
10:   'Display the message, "Welcome to my Web site" 4 times
11:   Dim i as Integer
12:   For i = 1 to 4
13:     Response.Write(message)
14:   Next i
15: End Sub
```

Save the ASP.NET Web page and then view it through a browser. Upon first loading the page, you should see the same output shown in Figure 6.4: the message "Welcome to my Web site" displayed four times, followed by a Button. By clicking on the Button, you should see the output shown in Figure 6.5: the message "Welcome to my Web site" displayed eight times, followed by a Button.

> A subroutine or function may have more than one parameter. To create a subroutine with multiple parameters, simply list the parameters and their types, using a comma to separate each parameter.

Returning Values with Functions

At this point we've looked at only subroutines, so you may be wondering what, exactly, the difference between subroutines and functions is! Subroutines and functions actually have quite a bit in common. Both are modularization control structures, and both can have zero to many parameters. Both are used to reduce code redundancy and to enhance encapsulation of programming logic.

The main difference between subroutines and functions is that a function returns a resulting value, whereas a subroutine does not. In Listing 6.5 we looked at creating a `DisplayMessage()` subroutine that used a `Response.Write()` call in a `For` loop to display a string parameter four times. Because no resulting value is returned, we used a subroutine. But what if we wanted to modularize some programming logic that performed some sort of calculation?

In Hour 3 we created a financial calculator ASP.NET Web page. This page accepted some inputs—the user's home loan amount, the interest rate, and so on—and determined the monthly cost. This was accomplished in a little under 20 lines of code and was coded directly in the `Click` event handler for the Web page's Button Web control.

A more modular approach would be to place this logic in a function and then have the `Click` event handler call the function.

When creating a function, realize that a function's syntax differs from a subroutine's syntax in a few ways. First, instead of using the `Sub ... End Sub` keywords, `Function` and `End Function` are used. Second, because a function returns a value, we must specify the type of the value returned by the function. Finally, in the function body we need to actually return some value. This is accomplished via the `Return` keyword.

The general syntax of a function is as follows:

```
Function FunctionName(Param1 as Type, ..., ParamN as Type) as ReturnType
    Instruction1
    Instruction2
    ...
    InstructionN
End Function
```

The *ReturnType* specifies the type of the value returned by the function. As with subroutines, functions can have zero to many parameters. Functions are called in an identical fashion to subroutines, except that because functions return a value, oftentimes you will be using a function call in an expression, like the following:

```
Dim costPerMonth as Double
costPerMonth = ComputeCostPerMonth(P, r, t)
```

Here `ComputeCostPerMonth()` is a function that accepts three inputs and returns a `Double` value. Typically, you will assign the result of a function to a variable, although you can call a function and disregard its result, as in

```
ComputeCostPerMonth(P, r, t)   'disregards the return value
```

Let's create a function to compute the monthly cost of a mortgage. If you created the `FinancialCalculator.aspx` Web page from Hour 3, you can cut and paste the source code from the `performCalc_Click` event handler into the new function, `ComputeCostPerMonth()`. The code for the new function is given in Listing 6.6.

LISTING 6.6   The `ComputeCostPerMonth()` Computes the Monthly Cost of a Mortgage

```
 1: Function ComputeMonthlyCost(P as Double, r as Double, t as Double) as Double
 2:    'Specify constant values
 3:    Const INTEREST_CALCS_PER_YEAR as Integer = 12
 4:    Const PAYMENTS_PER_YEAR as Integer = 12
 5:
 6:    Dim ratePerPeriod as Double
 7:    ratePerPeriod = r/INTEREST_CALCS_PER_YEAR
 8:
 9:    Dim payPeriods as Integer
10:    payPeriods = t * PAYMENTS_PER_YEAR
11:
12:    Dim annualRate as Double
13:    annualRate = Math.Exp(INTEREST_CALCS_PER_YEAR * Math.Log(1+ratePerPeriod))
       - 1
14:
15:    Dim intPerPayment as Double
16:    intPerPayment = (Math.Exp(Math.Log(annualRate+1)/payPeriods) - 1) *
       payPeriods
17:
18:    'Now, compute the total cost of the loan
19:    Dim intPerMonth as Double = intPerPayment / PAYMENTS_PER_YEAR
20:
21:    Dim costPerMonth as Double
22:    costPerMonth = P * intPerMonth/(1-Math.Pow(intPerMonth+1,-payPeriods))
23:
24:    Return costPerMonth
25: End Function
```

The `ComputeMonthlyCost()` function accepts three parameters, all of type `Double`, and returns a value of type `Double`. Recall from Hour 3 that in order to compute the monthly cost of a mortgage, three bits of information are needed: the mortgage principal (`P`), the interest rate (`r`), and the duration of the mortgage (`t`). The `ComputeMonthlyCost()` function receives these three values and uses them to compute the monthly mortgage cost. It then returns this final value using the `Return` statement (line 24).

The code in Listing 6.6 from lines 2 through 22 was taken directly from the `performCalc_Click` event handler in the `FinancialCalculator.aspx` page created in Hour 3.

Now that we have the `ComputeMonthlyCost()` function written, we can call it from the `performCalc_Click` event handler, which is the event handler that fires whenever the page's Button Web control is clicked. The event handler's code replaces the computation with a call to `ComputeMonthlyCost()`, as shown in Listing 6.7:

LISTING 6.7 The `performCalc_Click` Event Handler Calls the `ComputeMonthlyCost()` Function

```
1: Sub performCalc_Click(sender As Object, e As EventArgs)
2:    'Create variables to hold the values entered by the user
3:    Dim P as Double = loanAmount.Text
4:    Dim r as Double = rate.Text / 100
5:    Dim t as Double = mortgageLength.Text
6:
7:    results.Text = "Your mortgage payment per month is $" &
       ComputeMonthlyCost(P, r, t)
8: End Sub
```

On lines 3–5, the values entered by the user into the loan amount, interest rate, and mortgage length TextBox Web controls are read and stored into local variables P, r, and t. Then, on line 7, the `Text` property of the `results` Label is assigned the string "Your mortgage payment per month is $," concatenated with the `Double` value returned by `ComputeMonthlyCost()`.

If you have the `Strict="True"` setting specified, the code in Listing 6.7 will generate an error, since lines 3, 4, and 5 use implicit casting to cast a `String` (`loanAmount.Text`, `rate.Text`, and `mortgageAmount.Text`) into a `Double`. If you are using `Strict="True"` you will need to use the `Convert.ToDouble()` method to convert the `String`s to `Double`s, like so:

`Dim P as Double = Convert.ToDouble(loanAmount.Text)`

6

Where Do Event Handlers Fit In?

As we discussed in the "Exploring the Modularizing Control Structures: Subroutines and Functions" section, VB.NET has two forms of modularization control structures: subroutines and events. In this hour we looked at an example of using a subroutine in an ASP.NET Web page, as well as an example using a function. However, one thing that we have been using in virtually all of our ASP.NET Web page examples throughout this entire book is an *event handler*. You may be wondering where, exactly, event handlers fit into the picture of subroutines and functions. To understand, let's first look at the form of the Page_Load event handler in the following code:

```
Sub Page_Load(sender as Object, e as EventArgs)
   ...
End Sub
```

As you can tell by the syntax of the Page_Load event handler, an event handler is a subroutine. Event handlers were designed as subroutines because event handlers never return a value. In addition, the event handlers we have looked at thus far—the Page_Load event handler and the Click event handler for Button Web controls—accept two parameters, the first of type Object and the second of type EventArgs. The details of these parameters are unimportant for now; in later hours we'll be examining their meaning in more depth.

The important information to grasp here is that an event handler is a subroutine. An event handler provides a modularized chunk of code that is executed whenever its corresponding event fires.

Summary

In this hour we looked at Visual Basic .NET's control structures. Control structures alter the program flow from a sequential, one line after the other model, to one where lines of code can be conditionally executed and can be executed repeatedly until some specified set of criteria is met.

VB.NET supports conditional control structures through the If statement. The If statement evaluates a condition and, if it is True, executes the instructions following the Then. In addition to the If ... Then portion of an If statement, ElseIf and Else clauses can be included.

Visual Basic .NET has a number of looping constructs, the two most common ones being the For loop and the Do loop. The For loop works with an integer variable that it assigns an initial starting value to. It then executes the loop body, incrementing the looping variable at the end of each execution of the loop body. The For loop executes until the looping variable has surpassed the specified bounds.

The Do loop is more general. Rather than having a looping variable, it simply executes the loop body until a specified condition is met. There are two flavors of Do loop: a Do loop that executes the loop body while the condition is True, and a Do loop that executes the loop body until a condition is True.

We also looked at modularization controls structures—the subroutine and function. Both the subroutine and the function allow for programming logic to be encapsulated, both can accept zero to many parameters, and both are called using the same syntax. The difference between the two is that a function always returns a value, whereas a subroutine never does.

The next hour, "Working with Objects in Visual Basic .NET," will be our last hour focusing specifically on VB.NET. After that we'll turn our attention back to the HTML portion of ASP.NET Web pages.

Q&A

Q What is the difference between a subroutine and a function?

A Subroutines and functions both are modularization control structures that can accept zero or more input parameters. However, a function returns a value, whereas a subroutine does not.

Q When calling a function, must its return value be assigned to a variable?

A Recall that functions always return a value. Typically, the return value of a function is either used in an expression or stored in a variable. However, it is not required that the return value of a function be used at all. Imagine that we had a function called SaveCustomerInformation(*name, age*), which took as input parameters the name and age of the customer and saved this information in a database. The return value of this function might be a DateTime variable that indicated the last time the customer's information was updated. In certain situations we might not care about when the customer's information was last updated—all we want to do is update the customer's information. In such a case, we could call the function and just disregard its return value. This is accomplished by calling a function just like you would a subroutine, as in

```
SaveCustomerInformation("Scott", 24)
```

6

Workshop

Quiz

1. True or False: Conditional control structures alter the control flow of a program.
2. If we wanted to print out a message five times if the current hour was past 12, what control structures would we need to use?

3. Is the following `For ... Next` loop an example of an infinite loop?

```
Dim i as Integer
For i = 10 to 20 STEP -1
  ' Instructions
Next i
```

4. True or False: Functions and subroutines must always have at least one input parameter.

Answers

1. True. Computer programs execute sequentially by default; however, control structures allow for more flexible control flow scenarios.

2. We'd need two control structures—a conditional control structure to evaluate whether the hour is past 12 and a looping control structure to output the message five times. The code for this could look like

```
Dim i as Integer
If DateTime.Now.Hour = 12 then
  For i = 1 to 5
    Response.Write("This is my message to you.<br>")
  Next i
End If
```

3. Yes. It is an infinite loop because at each loop iteration the looping variable is decreased by 1 (due to the `STEP -1`). Therefore, the looping variable, which starts at 10, will never read the loop termination value, 20. This means that this loop is an infinite loop and will run forever.

4. False. Subroutines and functions can have zero or more input parameters. It is not required that they have more than zero.

Exercise

1. A common mathematical function is the *factorial function*. The factorial function takes an integer input n that is greater than or equal to 1, and computes $n * (n-1) * ... * 2 * 1$. In mathematical texts, factorial is denoted with an exclamation point, as in $n!$.

   For this exercise write a function called `Factorial()` that takes a single `Integer` input and returns an `Integer` corresponding to the factorial of the inputted parameter. To help get you started, your function will look like this:

```
Function Factorial(n as Integer) as Integer
  ' Write code here to compute n!
  ' Return the value n!
End Function
```

Note that

```
1! = 1
2! = 2 * 1 = 2
3! = 3 * 2 * 1 = 6
4! = 4 * 3 * 2 * 1 = 24
5! = 5 * 4 * 3 * 2 * 1 = 120
```

Once you have this Factorial() function written, add a Page_Load event handler that calls the function, displaying on the ASP.NET Web page the values of 1! through 5!.

Hint: The Factorial() function will need to contain a looping construct from 1 to n, where at each iteration a variable is multiplied by the value of the looping variable.

6

HOUR 7

Working with Objects in Visual Basic .NET

In Hour 5 we looked at using variables and operators in Visual Basic .NET. In Hour 6 we looked at control structures, such as If statements, looping constructs, and subroutines and functions. There's one more important topic we need to discuss regarding Visual Basic .NET before moving on to future topics. Specifically, we need to examine how to use objects in Visual Basic .NET.

Recall from our discussion of object-oriented programming in Hour 2, "Understanding the ASP.NET Programming Model," that the key component of an object-oriented programming language is an object, which is an instance of a class. In this hour we'll reexamine the relationship between an object and a class, and we'll discuss the role of classes and objects in Visual Basic .NET, the .NET Framework, and ASP.NET Web pages.

One of the biggest challenges of using the .NET Framework is its sheer size. The .NET Framework contains literally hundreds of classes, each class containing a number of properties and methods. Fortunately, there exists extensive documentation for the .NET Framework that is easily accessible from the Web Matrix Project. In addition, there are numerous online sources with tutorials and documentation. This hour will conclude with a discussion on using the built-in .NET Framework documentation and searching for information online.

In this hour we will cover

- The difference between objects and classes
- Creating an object
- Setting an object's properties
- Calling an object's methods
- The .NET Framework documentation
- Examples of creating objects from classes in the .NET Framework

Reexamining the Role of Classes and Objects

In Hour 2 we discussed the ideas behind object-oriented programming. To refresh your memory, object-oriented programming is a programming paradigm in which the object is a key construct of the programming language. Objects contain methods and properties, the properties defining the state of the object, and the methods being called to have the object perform various actions.

Recall that in Hour 2 we described object-oriented programming using a car as an analogy. The properties of the car were such things as make, model, and color, while its methods were drive, reverse, turn, and so on.

The list of properties and methods that describe a car is referred to as a *class*, while an actual, concrete instance of a car, such as a green 2002 Honda Accord, is referred to as an *object*.

Classes are the abstractions from which objects are created. To understand the relationship between a class and an object, think of a calculator. The calculator may have properties like current battery power, current value on the screen, last operation entered, and others. It might have methods like add, subtract, and so on. If you were to sit down and list all of the properties and methods that a calculator has, this list would be equivalent to a class. This list is an abstract idea of what a calculator is and what it does. It clearly is not a concrete representation of a calculator; you cannot use this list of calculator properties and methods to compute the sum of two numbers.

An object, on the other hand, is a concrete representation of the class. The actual calculator that supports the properties and methods outlined by the class is an object and is said to be an instance of the class it represents.

To summarize, a class is an abstract definition, a simple list of properties and methods that are supported. An object, however, is an instance of the class, a concrete "thing" whose properties we can set and whose methods we can call.

The Role of Objects in an ASP.NET Web Application

Recall from our earlier discussions that the .NET Framework contains a plethora of classes that allow for a variety of functionality. For example, in the .NET Framework there is a class for each of the Web controls that we have seen and will be examining throughout this book.

There are also classes in the .NET Framework that allow for an e-mail to be sent from a Web page, for data to be retrieved from a database, for an image to be created, and so on. The source code portion of your ASP.NET Web page can utilize the variety of functionality present in the .NET Framework. For example, starting with Hour 13, "An Introduction to Databases," we'll be looking at how to retrieve information from a database through an ASP.NET Web page.

In order to use a class in the .NET Framework, the first thing we must do is create an object from the particular class whose functionality we are interested in. Once we have an object, we may need to set some of the object's properties. Additionally, we may need to call some of the object's methods.

For example, as we will see later in this book, to retrieve data from a database, we must first create an instance of the `OleDbCommand` object. Next we must set its `Connection` property, which indicates from what database to retrieve the information. After that we need to set its `CommandText` property, which indicates what data we want to have returned. Finally, we call the object's `ExecuteReader()` method to retrieve the results from the database.

The Three Common Tasks Performed with Objects

When using objects, there will be three tasks that we'll perform again and again. The first task is creating an instance of the object from the desired class. This is a required step that we must always do once when working with an object.

The second task is setting the object's properties. Not all objects have properties, and we do not always need to use the properties of those that do. However, most of the time we'll find ourselves setting the properties of an object. Remember that properties are values that describe the state of the object. For example, a class that sends an e-mail message might have properties like Body, Subject, To, From, Cc, and so on.

7

Finally, when using objects, we will always call one or more of the object's methods. A class that sends e-mail messages might have a method called `Send()`, which would send the e-mail. Therefore, to send an e-mail from an ASP.NET Web page by using this class, we'd first create an instance of the class, then set its body, subject, to, from, and other pertinent properties, and then call its `Send()` method.

In the remainder of this hour, we will look at the Visual Basic .NET syntax required to accomplish these three tasks.

Creating an Object

Recall that a class is an abstract definition listing the functionality that is provided. In addition to properties and methods, classes contain *constructors*. A constructor is a special method that is used to create an instance of the class.

> In a later section, "Calling an Object's Methods," we'll discuss what, exactly, methods are. For now you can think of a method as a function or subroutine. Like functions and subroutines, a method is a means of encapsulating a number of program instructions and, again like functions and subroutines, can have zero or more parameters.

Constructors always have the same name as the class. For example, the class that we will be using to work with databases is the `OleDbCommand` class. Therefore, the constructor for this class is a method named `OleDbCommand()`.

To create an instance of an object, the following syntax is used:

```
Variable = New Constructor()
```

The constructor `Constructor` returns an object of the class `Constructor`. Because VB.NET is a strongly typed language, the type of `Variable` must be of the class whose constructor is being called. For example, to create an instance of the `OleDbCommand` class, we'd first create a variable whose type was of `OleDbCommand` as follows:

```
Dim myCommand as OleDbCommand
```

Then we'd assign to this variable the object returned by the constructor:

```
myCommand = New OleDbCommand()
```

The first line of code creates a variable named `myCommand` of type `OleDbCommand`; the second line of code assigns to `myCommand` the object returned by the constructor `OleDbCommand()`.

Recall that to use an object, we must first create an instance of the object. This process is commonly called *instantiation*. In addition to instantiating an object using

```
Dim variable as type
variable = New Constructor()
```

an object can also be instantiated via the following line of code:

```
Dim variableName as type = New Constructor()
```

With the OleDbCommand example we examined, we could have rewritten it as

```
Dim myCommand as OleDbCommand = New OleDbCommand()
```

Constructors with Parameters

Constructors, like functions and subroutines, can have zero or more parameters. Additionally, classes may have more than one constructor. When constructors accept one or more parameters, the parameters are typically for initial values of various properties. For example, the OleDbCommand class has a constructor that accepts zero parameters as well as one that accepts a string parameter. The constructor that accepts zero parameters does not assign any initial value to any of its properties. The constructor that accepts a string parameter, however, assigns the passed-in parameter value to the object's CommandText property.

In general, any class method (such as the constructor) can have multiple versions, each accepting a different number of input parameters. For example, the OleDbCommand constructor can accept zero parameters as well as a string parameter. Class methods with versions that accept a different number of parameters are referred to as *overloaded*.

Constructors that accept more than one parameter are used frequently for reducing the amount of code that needs to be written. For example, in order to create an OleDbCommand object and set its CommandText property, we'd need to use the following two lines of code:

```
Dim myCommand as OleDbCommand = New OleDbCommand()
myCommand.CommandText = "some value"
```

However, by using the OleDbCommand() constructor that accepts a string parameter, we can condense these two lines into one as follows:

```
Dim myCommand as OleDbCommand = New OleDbCommand("some value")
```

7

Most classes have more than one constructor—one that accepts zero
parameters and also a myriad of others that accept one, two, three, four, or
even more parameters. The constructor that accepts zero parameters is
typically referred to as the *default constructor*.

Setting an Object's Properties

Once we have created an object, oftentimes we want to set some of the object's properties.
To reference an object's properties, the following syntax is used:

```
objectVariable.PropertyName
```

Here *objectVariable* is the object variable. That is, in the code

```
Dim myCommand as OleDbCommand
myCommand = New OleDbCommand()
```

the *objectVariable* is myCommand. The *PropertyName* is the name of the property that
you wish to access. Properties are used just like variables; they can be assigned values,
they have types, and they can be used in expressions just like variables.

Typically, you will assign a value to a variable just once and then will call one of the
object's methods, which uses the value of the property in some manner. For example, to
send an e-mail message from an ASP.NET Web page, the MailMessage class is used.
Once an instance of this class is created, a number of properties need to be set, such as
From, To, Subject, and others. The following code snippet demonstrates how to create an
instance of this class and set its properties:

```
'Create an instance of the MailMessage class
Dim myMailMessage As MailMessage = New MailMessage()

'Set the From, To, Subject, and Body properties
myMailMessage.From = "someone@example.com"
myMailMessage.To = "someone@example.com"
myMailMessage.Subject = "Email Subject"
myMailMessage.Body = "Hello!"
```

In Hour 24, "Sending E-mail when a New Guestbook Entry Is Added," we
will examine how to send an e-mail message from an ASP.NET Web page in
much greater detail.

Calling an Object's Methods

An object's methods are called just like other subroutines and functions, except that the name of the object whose method you wish to call must precede the method being called. That is, the syntax for calling an object's method is as follows:

```
objectVariable.MethodName(param1, param2, ..., paramN)
```

 Methods in classes are semantically just like subroutines and functions, since methods in classes can accept zero to many input parameters and can optionally provide a return value.

As we discussed earlier, the OleDbCommand class is used for retrieving information from a database. In using the OleDbCommand class, we must specify the database to retrieve the data from, as well as what data to retrieve. These two bits of information are specified via the Connection and CommandText properties. The OleDbCommand class contains an ExecuteReader() method, which returns the data specified by the CommandText property from the database specified by the Connection property.

In order to call this method, we first must create an instance of the OleDbCommand class and set its Connection and CommandText properties. Once these two steps have been accomplished, we can call the ExecuteReader() method. The following code snippet demonstrates the syntax for calling a method:

```
'Create an instance of the OleDbCommand class
Dim myCommand as OleDbCommand = New OleDbCommand()

'Set the Connection and CommandText properties
myCommand.Connection = ...
myCommand.CommandText = "..."

'Call the ExecuteReader() method
Dim myReader as OleDbDataReader
myReader = myCommand.ExecuteReader()
```

As you can see in this code snippet, the ExecuteReader() method returns an object of type OleDbDataReader.

 The OleDbDataReader class, which we'll examine in much greater detail once we start discussing databases with Hour 13, is a class designed for holding data retrieved from a database.

7

Methods that return a value are similar to functions; some methods do not return a value, making them similar to subroutines. Also, methods—both ones that do and ones that do not return a value—can have zero to many input parameters.

Examining the .NET Framework Documentation

While examining how to set properties and call methods of objects, our discussion has referred to two classes in the .NET Framework: OleDbCommand and MailMessage. I've listed some of the properties of these two classes and have mentioned the ExecuteReader() method of the OleDbCommand class. You may be wondering how in the world I knew about these classes and how I found out about their particular properties and methods.

The .NET Framework contains literally hundreds of classes, each of which contains numerous properties and methods, so trying to commit to memory the various classes, properties, and methods is out of the question. Fortunately, there is extensive documentation for the .NET Framework, available both locally, installed with the ASP.NET Web Matrix Project, and online.

Before we examine the Web Matrix Project's tools for examining the .NET Framework documentation, it is important to understand how the classes in the .NET Framework are organized. Rather than just having a long listing of classes, the .NET Framework uses *namespaces* to create a hierarchy of classes. Each namespace contains classes that share a common attribute or theme, as well as other namespaces.

 Namespaces are a tool used in object-oriented programming languages to group related classes.

For example, the .NET Framework hierarchy starts with the System namespace, which contains classes that describe the various data types available to .NET programming languages. In addition to these classes, the System namespace contains a number of other namespaces, such as System.Data, System.Web, and System.Drawing, to name a few. Inside the System.Data namespace are classes and namespaces that relate to accessing database data. The classes and namespaces inside the System.Drawing namespace are used for creating images and graphics. The classes that represent the various ASP.NET Web controls are found within the System.Web namespace.

Figure 7.1 shows a graphical representation of the .NET Framework's namespace hierarchy. The purpose of this hierarchy is to group related classes.

FIGURE 7.1

The classes of the .NET Framework are partitioned into a hierarchy.

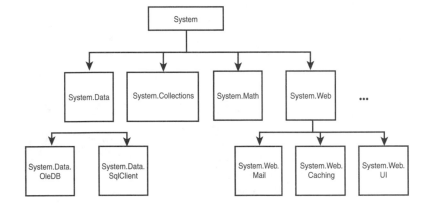

The Web Matrix Project's .NET Framework Class Browser

The Web Matrix Project allows you to examine the classes of the .NET Framework—along with their properties and methods—through the *Class Browser*. The Class Browser lists the various namespaces found within the .NET Framework and the classes underneath each namespace. The constructors, methods, and properties for a particular class can be viewed from the Class Browser.

The Class Browser can be used in one of two ways: as a standalone application or through the Web Matrix Project editor. There are only trivial differences between using the Class Browser as a standalone application and using it as an integrated part of the Web Matrix Project.

Personally, I prefer using the Class Browser that is integrated in the Web Matrix Project, because it saves one from having to switch from one window to another when examining the .NET Framework documentation. However, you may prefer using the Class Browser as a standalone application, so we will examine both approaches.

Running the Class Browser as a Standalone Application

7

To launch the Class Browser as a standalone application, go to Start, Programs, Microsoft ASP.NET Web Matrix, ClassBrowser. The Class Browser, when launched as a standalone application, lists the various namespaces of the .NET Framework. To view the classes in a particular namespace, simply click the plus to the left of the namespace name. To view a particular class in the namespace, double-click the class name, which will bring up a window displaying information about the class.

Figure 7.2 shows a screenshot of the Class Browser when it is started as a standalone application. To the left of the screenshot, you can see that the System.Data.OleDb namespace has been expanded, and the OleDbCommand class has been double-clicked. To the right you can see the constructors, properties, and methods of the OleDbCommand class listed.

FIGURE 7.2
The Class Browser can be started as a standalone application.

Using the Class Browser as an Integrated Component of the Web Matrix Project

The Class Browser can also be used directly through the Web Matrix Project editor. If you look down near the Properties pane in the lower right-hand corner, you will find three tabs: Properties, Classes, and Community, with the Properties tab selected. If you click the Classes tab, the Properties pane is replaced by the Classes pane, and the list of .NET Framework namespaces are shown just as they were in the standalone Class Browser application.

As you could with the standalone Class Browser application, you can expand a namespace with the integrated Class Browser by clicking the plus next to the namespace's name, which will list the classes belonging to that namespace. To view the details for a class, simply double-click the class name, which will create a window in the Web Matrix Project editor.

Figure 7.3 contains a screenshot of the Web Matrix Project with the Classes tab selected, the System.Data.OleDb namespace expanded, and the details for the OleDbCommand class displayed.

FIGURE 7.3

The Class Browser can be used within the Web Matrix Project.

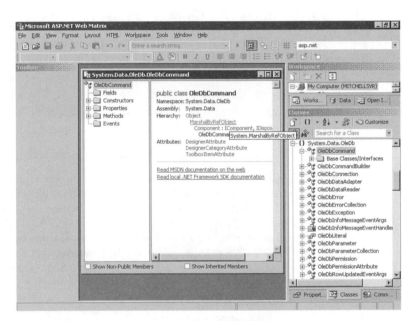

Getting Straight to the Classes Commonly Used by ASP.NET Developers

The Class Browser that is integrated into the Web Matrix Project has one advantage over the standalone Class Browser. Along with listing the various .NET Framework namespaces, the integrated Class Browser also has four shortcut folders to classes commonly used by ASP.NET developers.

Figure 7.4 contains a look at the top of the Classes pane in the Web Matrix Project. The four folder icons expand to list classes commonly used by ASP.NET developers.

7

FIGURE 7.4

*The integrated Class
Browser lists four
shortcut folders to
commonly used
classes.*

We will discuss the classes found in these folder shortcuts throughout the duration of this book.

The Show Inherited Members Checkbox

When viewing details about a class in either the standalone or the integrated Class Browser, you will find a checkbox labeled "Show Inherited Members." If you check the Show Inherited Members checkbox, a number of properties and methods are shown for each class that are not shown when the checkbox is empty. The specifics as to why this is the case are beyond the scope of this book. Be sure to check this checkbox, as it will show all of the properties and methods that you can set and call for the class.

By checking the Show Inherited Members checkbox, you will see the properties and methods that are *inherited* by the class. *Inheritance* is a key concept of object-oriented programming, but it is beyond the scope of this book. If you are interested in learning more about inheritance and object-oriented programming in general, I would encourage you to read Ian Stalling's article "Using Object-Orientation in ASP.NET: Inheritance," online at http://www.4guysfromrolla.com/webtech/022001-1.shtml

Viewing the Class Details

One of the downsides of the Class Browser is that it does not provide any explanation or English description of the classes or their properties or methods. For example, take a moment to click the Classes tab in the Web Matrix Project, expand the ASP.NET Web Controls shortcut folder, and then double-click the <asp:Label> item. This will bring up the details for the <asp:Label> Web control class.

The details window lists five folders: Fields, Constructors, Properties, Methods, and Events. The three we are interested in are Constructors, Properties, and Methods. Expand the Properties folder, and you should see one Property listed, Text. (If you have the Show Inherited Members checkbox checked, which I recommend, you will see a number of other properties, as well.) Clicking the Text property loads information about the property in the right pane of the window, as shown in Figure 7.5.

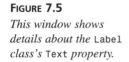

FIGURE 7.5

This window shows details about the Label *class's* Text *property.*

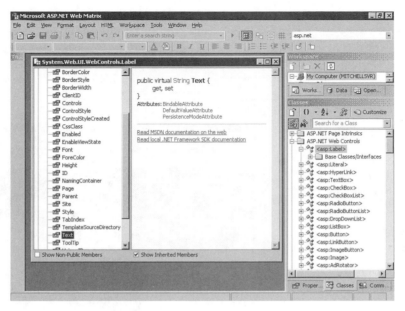

The description of the Text property isn't very helpful; in fact, you may find it a bit confusing. The right-hand side of the window shown in Figure 7.5 starts off with the following text:

```
public virtual String Text {
    set, get
}
```

If you are familiar with the programming language C#, this syntax should look familiar. This information essentially informs us of the data type of the Text property—String. Note that in C# the data type of a variable always immediately precedes the variable name. So, Text is the property name, and String is its data type. The other information, like public, virtual, set, and get, have various meanings, but a discussion of these is a bit beyond the scope of this book.

What is lacking from the details about the Label class's Text property is any sort of English description informing us what the property does. Also, wouldn't it be nice to have a code example and some syntax in VB.NET instead of just C#?

Unfortunately, such information is not available directly through the Class Browser. However, we're just one click away from such information. By clicking the "Read MSDN documentation on the web" hyperlink, you will be taken to a Web page that has the information about this class and property. Figure 7.6 shows a screenshot of this Web page. Note that it contains an English description of the property along with a code sample.

7

MSDN, which stands for Microsoft Developer Network, is accessible via the Web at `http://msdn.microsoft.com`. On that Web site you will find technical documentation on all of Microsoft's products and tools. This includes extensive documentation on the .NET Framework.

FIGURE 7.6
Microsoft's MSDN site contains more information about the class.

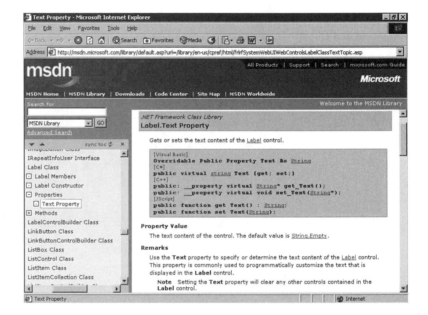

Beneath the "Read MSDN documentation on the web" hyperlink, you will find a "Read local .NET Framework SDK documentation" link. This link will not work if you do not have Visual Studio .NET installed. If you were click to the link without this installation, your browser would load a URL that would produce a "Cannot Find Server" error.

The Web Matrix Team is aware of this bug and will hopefully squash it in the next release.

The Local .NET Framework SDK Documentation

If you installed the .NET Framework SDK (as opposed to the .NET Redistributable), you can find all of the documentation available at Microsoft's MSDN Web site stored locally on your computer. To view the .NET Framework SDK documentation, go to Start, Programs, Microsoft .NET Framework SDK, Documentation. This will open up a documentation browser, as shown in Figure 7.7.

FIGURE 7.7

The .NET Framework documentation is installed on your computer along with the .NET Framework SDK.

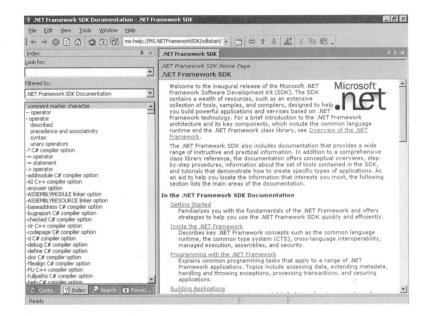

From here you can examine the contents of the documentation by drilling down into various categories. If you know the particular name of the class that you want details on, you can click the Index tab in the bottom left-hand corner. This will bring up a listing of all of the material in the .NET Framework SDK documentation, which you can search by entering text into a textbox at the top.

Using the Online Documentation

There is a wealth of information and documentation online. One of the most useful sites with this sort of information is Microsoft's MSDN site, which is accessible at http://msdn.microsoft.com. This is the site you are taken to when you click the "Read MSDN documentation on the web" hyperlink in the Class Browser.

Microsoft also has a Web site geared specifically for ASP.NET developers. This site, http://www.ASP.NET, contains articles, tutorials, and information about ASP.NET as well as an active online forum. If you have questions about ASP.NET that you cannot find an answer for, a good place to turn is the ASP.NET Forum, which can be reached at http://www.asp.net/forums.

In addition to Microsoft's MSDN and www.ASP.NET Web sites, there are a number of non–Microsoft-owned Web sites. These Web sites rarely boast the complete documentation,

7

as Microsoft's MSDN site does, but they do contain helpful tutorials and lessons that are lacking from MSDN. Some ASP.NET Web sites to consider visiting include

- `http://aspnet.4GuysFromRolla.com`
- `http://www.ASPAlliance.com`
- `http://www.ASPFree.com`
- `http://www.123aspx.com`

These Web sites, along with Microsoft's MSDN and `www.ASP.NET` Web sites, contain copious amounts of free information. Personally, I have always been quite impressed with the sheer amount of ASP.NET information available on the Web.

> Check out Google.com's Microsoft search engine. This page, available at `http://www.google.com/microsoft`, searches Microsoft-specific Web sites, such as MSDN, `www.ASP.NET`, and the community Web sites like ASPAlliance.com, 4GuysFromRolla.com, and others. This special Google page is one of the easiest and quickest ways to find specific ASP.NET information online.

Summary

In this hour we reexamined the concepts behind objects and classes. To use an object, it first must be created. This is accomplished using the VB.NET `New` keyword and a constructor. As we saw, a constructor is a function that has the same name as the class and returns an instance of the class. For example, to create an instance of the `OleDbCommand` class, we could use

```
Dim myCommand as OleDbCommand
myCommand = New OleDbCommand()
```

Once an object has been created, we can set its properties or call its methods. An object's property can be accessed by listing the object's name, followed by a period, followed by the property name. For example, to access the `CommandText` property of the `myCommand` object, we would use the following syntax:

```
myCommand.CommandText
```

Properties have the same semantics as ordinary variables; they have a type and can be used in expressions or assigned values.

An object's method is called by listing the object's name, followed by a period, followed by the method's name. Methods are like subroutines and functions in that they may accept zero or more input parameters and can optionally return a value.

Because the .NET Framework contains so many classes, and because each class contains a number of properties and methods, it is implausible to expect to remember all of the available classes, properties, and methods. In order to look up information about a particular class, the Web Matrix Project's Class Browser can be used. Additionally, the .NET Framework SDK Documentation can be used (if the .NET Framework SDK was installed), or the documentation can be looked up online at Microsoft's MSDN Web site.

This hour concludes our in-depth examination of VB.NET. In the next hour we will look at the two ASP.NET Web controls that are used for displaying text: the Label and Literal Web controls. Following that we will spend the next several hours examining how to collect and process user input.

Q&A

Q This hour showed us how to use classes in the .NET Framework, but is it possible to create our own classes?

A With object-oriented programming classes like Visual Basic .NET, you can create your own classes. However, this is far beyond the scope of this book. While we'll be using a number of the .NET Framework classes throughout the course of this book, we'll never need to create our own classes.

Q Is there an easy way to find ASP.NET information online?

A As discussed in the "Using the Online Documentation" section at the end of this chapter, there is a plethora of online ASP.NET resource Web sites. If you are looking for information on a particular topic, though, it can be frustrating to have to hop from one site to another searching for the particular topic. Thankfully, Google provides a special search engine page that searches only Microsoft-related Web sites. Using this special search page, you can search with a query like "send e-mail from ASP.NET Web page" and be returned results only from Web sites that publish information relating to Microsoft technologies. Google's special Microsoft search page can be accessed at: `http://www.google.com/microsoft`.

(As an aside, we will be discussing how to send e-mails from an ASP.NET Web page in Hour 24.)

Workshop

Quiz

1. What are the three actions commonly performed on objects?
2. True or False: The .NET Framework consists of classes that we will be using in our ASP.NET Web pages.

7

3. In the previous two hours, we examined a number of fundamental programming concepts. In this hour we have looked at objects, which have properties and methods. What programming concept is analogous to an object's properties?

4. What programming concept is analogous to an object's methods?

5. What is the purpose of the Class Browser?

Answers

1. Before objects can be used, they must first be instantiated. Once an object instance exists, often the properties of the object are then set, followed by calling the object's methods.

2. True.

3. Properties are analogous to variables.

4. Methods are analogous to subroutines and functions.

5. The Class Browser provides information about the properties and methods of the various .NET Framework classes. The Class Browser can be accessed in one of two ways: either as a standalone program or through the Web Matrix Project's Classes tab.

Exercises

There are no exercises for this hour.

Hour **8**

ASP.NET Web Controls for Displaying Text

In the past three hours, we examined the syntax and semantics for Visual Basic .NET, the programming language we'll be using in the source code portion of our ASP.NET Web pages. Prior to these three hours, we discussed ASP.NET fundamentals, such as how each ASP.NET Web page comprises a source code portion and an HTML portion. Recall that the HTML portion can contain HTML markup as well as Web controls.

Web controls, like regular HTML markup, are placed in the HTML portion. When a browser requests an ASP.NET Web page, the Web controls are converted into their associated HTML markup. However, Web controls can be accessed programmatically through the page's source code. In this manner Web controls serve as an intermediary between the source code and HTML portions of an ASP.NET Web page.

In the financial calculator example in Hour 3, "Creating Our First ASP.NET Web Page," our page had a number of Web controls. There were three TextBox Web controls, one for each of the inputs the user needed to enter; a

Button Web control, which the user would click upon having entered the information and wanting the result; and a Label Web control, where the output of the calculation was displayed.

There are a variety of Web controls that we'll be examining throughout this book. These various Web controls can be divided into a number of categories, such as Web controls used to display text, Web controls to collect user input, Web controls to display data from a database, and so on.

In this hour we will cover

- How to display text using the Literal and Label Web controls
- Using the Literal Web control
- Using the Label Web control
- Differences between the Literal and Label Web controls
- Altering the appearance of the Label Web control

Examining the Web Controls Designed for Displaying Text

There are two ASP.NET Web controls designed for displaying text: the Literal Web Control and the Label Web Control. These two controls differ in the HTML markup that is rendered by each when the ASP.NET Web page is executed. Recall from our discussions in Hour 4, "Dissecting Our First ASP.NET Web Page," that when an ASP.NET Web page is visited through a browser, the ASP.NET engine executes the page, producing HTML markup that is then sent back to the Web server. This HTML markup is then sent from the Web server back to the user's browser.

The HTML markup produced by an ASP.NET Web page comes from a number of sources. Specifically, HTML markup for a given page can come from

- `Response.Write()` statements in the source code portion
- HTML markup in the HTML portion
- HTML markup that is rendered by the Web controls

The HTML markup produced by a `Response.Write()` statement is precisely the string content that's passed into the method. That is, doing

```
Response.Write("<p>Hello!</p>")
```

will add the HTML markup

```
<p>Hello</p>
```

to the ASP.NET Web page. Similarly, the HTML markup in the HTML portion is passed on to the browser exactly as it's typed in. However, the HTML markup produced by Web controls is dependent upon the various property values of each Web control.

The differences between the Literal and Label Web controls are in the HTML markup produced by each control. The Literal Web control HTML markup is simply the value of its Text property. The Label Web control, on the other hand, has a number of formatting properties, such as BackColor, ForeColor, Font, and so on, that specify how the Label's Text property should be displayed.

In this hour we'll be examining how to use each of these two Web controls, including how to add them to an ASP.NET Web page's HTML portion and how to set their properties.

Using the Literal Web Control

The Literal Web control is one of the simplest Web controls. The HTML markup rendered by the Literal Web control is precisely the value of the Web control's Text property.

Let's create an ASP.NET Web page that has a Literal control. Start by creating a new ASP.NET Web page named LiteralControl.aspx. Once the new file has been created, verify that the Design tab is selected, and then drag and drop the Literal control from the Toolbox and onto the designer. Once you do this, you should see a screen similar to the screenshot shown in Figure 8.1.

FIGURE 8.1

A Literal Web control has been added to the designer.

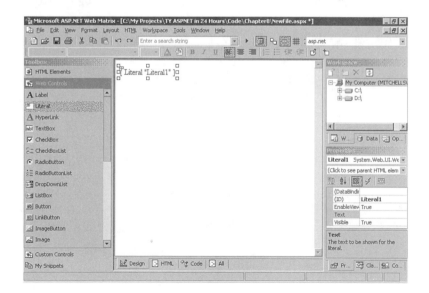

Make sure that the Literal Web control you just added is selected, and then examine the Properties pane in the lower right-hand corner. Note that the Literal Web control has only five properties. As displayed in the Properties pane, these five properties are

- (DataBindings)
- (ID)
- EnableViewState
- Text
- Visible

The only two properties that we will be working with in this hour are the ID and Text properties. As with the financial calculator example we examined in Hour 3, the ID property uniquely names the Web control so that its properties can be referenced in the source code portion of the ASP.NET Web page. The Text property of the Literal Web control is the value that is displayed in the ASP.NET Web page when the Literal Web control is rendered.

When the Literal Web control's Text property is not set, the Literal Web control is shown in the designer as

```
[Literal "ID"]
```

where ID is the value of the Literal Web control's ID property. In Figure 8.1 the Literal control is displayed as [Literal "Literal1"] because the ID property value is Literal1 and the Text property is not set.

If the Text property is set to some value, though, the designer displays the Literal Web control as this property value. For example, take a moment to change the Literal Web control's Text property to Hello, World! Figure 8.2 contains a screenshot of the designer after this change has been made. Note that the Literal Web control is displayed in the designer as the text "Hello, World!"

Now that we've added this Literal Web control and set its Text property, let's view this ASP.NET Web page through a browser. First save the ASP.NET Web page and then view it through your browser. Recall that if you are running the ASP.NET Web pages locally, you can just hit F5 or go to View, Start. If you are hosting the Web pages on a remote Web host, you will need to fire up your browser of choice and visit the appropriate URL. Figure 8.3 contains a screenshot of the LiteralControl.aspx

Web page when viewed through a browser. Note that the output is simply the value "Hello, World!"

FIGURE 8.2

The Literal Web control is displayed as "Hello, World!" in the designer.

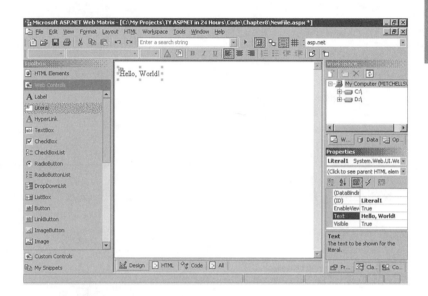

FIGURE 8.3

`LiteralControl.aspx`, *when viewed through a Web browser.*

Once you have loaded the Web page in your Web browser, view the HTML source code received by your browser. Listing 8.1 contains the HTML received by my browser when testing this page; the HTML markup your browser receives may be slightly different, depending on whether you added the Literal Web control before or after the Web Form.

LISTING 8.1   The HTML Markup Produced by the `LiteralControl.aspx` Web Page

```
 1: <html>
 2: <head>
 3: </head>
 4: <body>
 5:     <form name="_ctl0" method="post" action="LiteralControl.aspx"  id="_ctl0">
 6: <input type="hidden" name="_
            _VIEWSTATE" value="dDwtMjM2MzU3MjA2Ozs+Z8nvZp/1Z5tl5Opu/uvz/Dykgxg=" />
 7:
 8:         Hello, World!
 9:         <!-- Insert content here -->
10:     </form>
11: </body>
12: </html>
```

In Listing 8.1, line 8 contains the HTML markup produced by the Literal Web control. It is precisely the value of the Literal Web control's `Text` property. The remainder of the HTML markup is a by-product of the HTML content added when creating a new ASP.NET Web page with the Web Matrix Project.

Examining the Additional HTML Markup

In Listing 8.1 the `<html>`, `<head>`, and `<body>` tags on lines 1 through 4 and lines 11 and 12 were added by the Web Matrix Project when we created `LiteralControl.aspx` as a new HTML file. Additionally, the HTML comment on line 9 was inserted by the Web Matrix Project.

Lines 5, 6, and 10 contain a `<form>` tag and an `<input>` tag that has its `type` set to `hidden`. This HTML content is the markup that is produced by the Web form. Recall from our discussions in Hour 4 that a Web form is rendered as an HTML form with some extra information stored in a hidden `<input>` tag. The reason our ASP.NET Web page has a Web form in it is because the Web Matrix Project adds one in by default when creating a new ASP.NET Web page. We will be discussing the details of Web forms in the next hour, "Web Form Basics."

To see the exact content the Web Matrix Project enters when creating a new ASP.NET Web page, create a new ASP.NET Web page in the Web Matrix Project and then select the All tab.

Setting the Literal Control's `Text` Property Programmatically

As we just saw, the `Text` property of the Literal Web control can be set through the Properties pane in the Web Matrix Project. If you know what the `Text` property's value should be, there is nothing wrong with using this approach. However, if you want the value of the Text property to be dynamic, you will have to set the property value through the source code portion of your ASP.NET Web page.

For example, imagine that you wanted to use a Literal control to display the current date and time. Programmatically, the current date and time can be retrieved by the DateTime.Now property.

To set the Literal control's Text property programmatically, we can use the following syntax in our source code portion:

```
LiteralControlID.Text = value
```

LiteralControlID is the value of the Literal Web control's ID property, and value is a string value that we wish to assign to the Label Web control's Text property.

Let's create an ASP.NET Web page that uses a Label Web control to display the current date and time. Start by creating a new ASP.NET Web page named LiteralTime.aspx, and then drag and drop a Literal Web control onto the designer. There's no need to set the Text property through the Properties pane, because we will be setting this property programmatically. We should, however, rename the Literal Web control's ID property from the ambiguous Label1 to something more descriptive, such as currentTime.

After you have added the Label Web control and changed its ID property to currentTime, take a moment to compare what your screen looks like with Figure 8.4.

FIGURE 8.4

A screenshot of the designer after the Literal Web control has been added, and its ID property set.

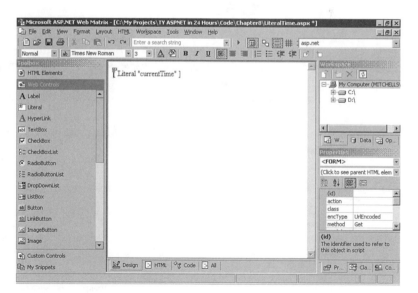

Once we've added the Literal Web control and set its ID property to currentTime, we're ready to add the needed source code. Start by clicking the Code tab, which will take you to the ASP.NET Web page's source code portion. For this ASP.NET Web page, we want to have the Literal Web control's Text property set to the current date and time whenever the page is visited. Therefore, we will do so in the Page_Load event handler.

Enter the following code into the Code tab:

```
Sub Page_Load(sender as Object, e as EventArgs)
  currentTime.Text = DateTime.Now
End Sub
```

Once you have entered this source code content, save the ASP.NET Web page and view it through a Web browser. Figure 8.5 contains a screenshot of the LiteralTime.aspx Web page when viewed through a browser.

FIGURE 8.5

The current date and time are displayed.

 To convince yourself that the current date and time are being shown, refresh your Web browser every few seconds, noting that the time displayed is updated accordingly.

Let's take a moment to examine the HTML markup received by the Web browser. Listing 8.2 contains this HTML content.

LISTING 8.2 The HTML Markup Produced by the LiteralTime.aspx Web Page

```
1: <html>
2: <head>
3: </head>
4: <body>
5:    <form name="_ctl0" method="post" action="LiteralTime.aspx" id="_ctl0">
6: <input type="hidden" name="__VIEWSTATE"
   value="dDwtMjM2MzU3MjA2O3Q8O2w8aTwxPjs+O2w8dDw7bDxpPDE+
           Oz47bDx0PHA8bDxUZXh0O0Oz47bDwxLzEvMjAwMyAxOjQOOjIwIwIFBNOz4+Ozs+Oz4+Oz4
           +Oz4ebPWHkSGGXdOYXFFrvvYHBhy5Xw==" />
```

LISTING 8.2   Continued

```
 7:
 8:        1/1/2003 1:44:20 PM
 9:        <!-- Insert content here -->
10:    </form>
11: </body>
12: </html>
```

The important line to pay attention to is line 8, which is the HTML markup produced by the Literal Web control. When the browser requests the `LiteralTime.apsx` Web page, the ASP.NET engine executes the page. The `Page_Load` event handler is fired, and the source code within that event handler is executed. This single line of code sets the `currentTime` Literal Web control's `Text` property to the current date and time.

After executing the `Page_Load` event handler, the ASP.NET engine renders the Web controls in the HTML portion. By this point the Literal Web control has had its `Text` property set to the current date and time. The Literal Web control renders as this current date and time, and it is this HTML, along with the additional HTML markup that was included by the Web Matrix Project, that is sent to the Web browser.

When refreshing your Web browser, the entire process is repeated, and the HTML sent back to your browser has the updated date and time.

What do you think the output of the `LiteralTime.aspx` Web page would be if we changed the code in the `Page_Load` event handler from

`currentTime.Text = DateTime.Now`

to

`currentTime.Text = "The current time is: " & DateTime.Now`

I encourage you to try this code change to see how the output changes.

Formatting the Output of the Literal Web Control

The Literal Web control, as we have seen, simply emits the contents of its `Text` property. So, if you want text in a Literal Web control to be bold, you must add the HTML `<b>` tags yourself to the Literal Web control's `Text` property.

For example, returning to the `LiteralControl.aspx` example we looked at earlier, recall that the Literal control's `Text` property was set to `Hello, World!` When this ASP.NET Web page was viewed through a browser, the words "Hello, World!" were displayed (see Figure 8.3).

What if we wanted to have the words "Hello, World!" displayed in a bold font? We'd have to change the Literal Web control's `Text` property from

```
Hello, World!
```

to

```
<b>Hello, World!</b>
```

 If you need to format the text displayed by a Literal Web control, you may want to consider using the Label Web control instead. As we will see in a bit, the Label Web control was designed to output formatted text.

Comparing the Literal Web Control
to `Response.Write()`

We've seen the `Response.Write()` method used in a few of the examples over past hours. `Response.Write()` accepts a single parameter—a string—and emits the string as is. This is quite similar to the Literal Web control, seeing as the Literal Web control, when rendered, emits the value of its `Text` property as is.

There is a rather important benefit in using the Literal Web control versus `Response.Write()`: With the Literal Web control, you can determine where, precisely, the output should appear within the HTML portion. With `Response.Write()` the output appears before any of the HTML output.

Using the Label Web Control

The Label Web control differs from the Literal Web control in that it contains a number of formatting properties that, when set, specify how the `Text` property should be displayed in the user's Web browser.

We saw that to display the `Text` property of the Literal Web control in a bold font, the `Text` property needed to include the appropriate HTML markup, such as `<b>` tags. With the Label Web control, however, we can display the text "Hello, World!" in a bold font by setting the Label Web control's `Text` property to `Hello, World!` and setting the `Font` property's `Bold` subproperty to True.

Let's create a new ASP.NET Web page to demonstrate using a Label Web control. Start by creating an ASP.NET Web page named `LabelControl.aspx`. From the Design tab, drag and drop a Label Web control onto the designer. Select the Label Web control and note its list of properties in the Properties pane. There are far more properties listed here than with the Literal Web control.

First let's set the Label Web control's `Text` property to `Hello, World!` Once you have done this, your screen should look like the screenshot in Figure 8.6.

FIGURE 8.6

A Label Web control has been added, and its Text *property has been set.*

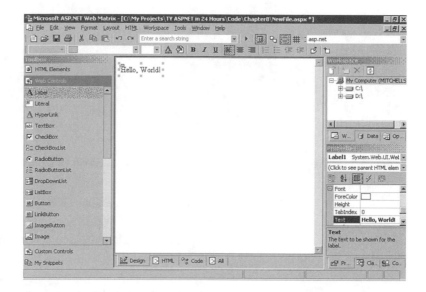

Once the `Text` property has been set, we need to set the Label Web control's `Font` property accordingly. Again, click the Label Web control, which will load the control's properties in the Properties pane. One of the properties listed is `Font`. To the left of this property name, you'll find a plus sign, which indicates that there are subproperties belonging to this property. Click the plus to expand these subproperties.

The subproperties of the `Font` property are listed in Table 8.1. One of these subproperties is `Bold`, which defaults to a value of False. Go ahead and select True from the drop-down list. This has the effect of making the Label Web control's text in the designer appear bold, as can be seen Figure 8.7, which is a screenshot after the `Bold` subproperty has been set to True.

Figure 8.7

The Label Web control's Bold *subproperty has been set to True.*

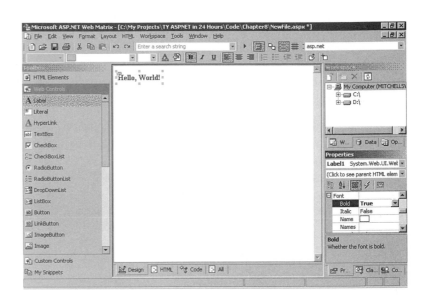

Table 8.1 The Subproperties of the Label Web Control's Font Property

Subproperty Name	Description
Bold	A Boolean value indicating whether the Text property will be displayed in a bold font.
Italic	A Boolean value indicating whether the Text property will be displayed in an italic font.
Name	The preferred font to use when displaying the text. Common font choices include Arial, Helvetica, and Verdana.
Names	A sequence of font names. If the browser visiting the page does not support one of the fonts, it will try using the next listed one.
Overline	A Boolean value indicating whether the Text property will be displayed with an overline.
Size	The size that the Text property will be displayed in. The Web Matrix Project allows you to choose settings such as Smaller, Medium, Larger, and so on. You can also enter a point value, like 14pt.
Strikeout	A Boolean value indicating whether the Text property will be displayed with a strikeout.
Underline	A Boolean value indicating whether the Text property will be displayed underlined.

Go ahead and save the ASP.NET Web page and view it through a Web browser. When viewing the `LabelControl.aspx` Web page through a browser, you should see the message "Hello, World!" in a bold font, just like we saw in the designer.

Examining the HTML Markup Generated by the Label Web Control

With the Literal Web control, the HTML markup sent to the Web browser was the value of the Literal Web control's `Text` property. With the Label Web control, the `Text` property is sent in addition to extra HTML markup to provide the associated formatting.

But what HTML markup is sent to the Web browser? Interestingly, this depends on what Web browser visits the ASP.NET Web page! Whenever a Web browser makes a request for a Web page, it sends along a piece of information known as the *User-Agent header*. This bit of information specifies what browser is being used.

Recall from the "Examining the Web Controls Designed for Displaying Text" section that when the ASP.NET Web page is being executed by the ASP.NET engine, the various Web controls are rendered and converted into HTML markup. When these controls are rendered, they take into account the User-Agent header and render HTML appropriate for the particular browser.

For example, Listing 8.3 contains the HTML markup received when visiting the `LabelControl.aspx` Web page through Internet Explorer 6.0.

LISTING 8.3 Internet Explorer Receives the Following HTML Markup from `LabelControl.aspx`

```
 1: <html>
 2: <head>
 3: </head>
 4: <body>
 5:     <form name="_ctl0" method="post" action="LabelControl.aspx" id="_ctl0">
 6: <input type="hidden" name="__VIEWSTATE" value=
           "dDwtMTU3ODAzNTQ4MDs7PrAPNCvaTyI6obnIQUAL+nC2smsK" />
 7:
 8:         <span id="Label1" style="font-weight:bold;">Hello, World!</span>
 9:         <!-- Insert content here -->
10:     </form>
11: </body>
12: </html>
```

Line 8 contains the HTML markup produced by the Label Web control. Note that it uses a `<span>` HTML tag whose `id` attribute is equal to the `ID` property of the Label Web control. Also note that for Internet Explorer 6.0, the text "Hello, World!" is made bold through the `<span>` tag's `style` attribute.

Listing 8.4 contains the HTML markup produced by `LabelControl.aspx` when visited by Mozilla 1.2.1.

> Mozilla is a Web browser derived from Netscape. Both Mozilla and Netscape use the same underlying technology to power their respective Web browsers. See `http://www.mozilla.org` for more information.

LISTING 8.4 Mozilla Receives the Following HTML Markup from `LabelControl.aspx`

```
 1: <html>
 2: <head>
 3: </head>
 4: <body>
 5:     <form name="_ctl0" method="post" action="LabelControl.aspx" id="_ctl0">
 6: <input type="hidden" name="__VIEWSTATE"
            value="dDwtMTU3ODAzNTQ4MDs7PrAPNCvaTyI6obnIQUAL+nC2smsK" />
 7:
 8:         <span id="Label1"><b>Hello, World!</b></span>
 9:         <!-- Insert content here -->
10:     </form>
11: </body>
12: </html>
```

Line 8 in Listing 8.4 differs from line 8 in Listing 8.3. Instead of specifying that the text "Hello, World!" should be bold using the `<span>` tag's `style` attribute, the HTML markup produced for Mozilla uses a `<b>` tag to make the text bold.

> It is important to realize here that the HTML markup produced by one ASP.NET Web page—`LabelControl.aspx`—depended upon what browser requested the page. Because ASP.NET Web controls can alter their produced HTML markup based upon the browser that visits them, Web controls are said to be *adaptive*.
>
> Despite the fact that the Internet Explorer and Mozilla receive different HTML markup, both browsers display the same output—the message "Hello, World!" in a bold font.

What HTML Markup Is Produced for Each Browser?

Because ASP.NET Web controls base HTML markup rendering upon the browser that is visiting the page, you may be wondering what output is produced for any given browser.

What HTML markup is produced for Internet Explorer 5.5? What HTML markup is produced for Netscape 7.0? What HTML markup is produced for Opera?

ASP.NET divides all browsers into one of two categories: *uplevel* or *downlevel*. Uplevel browsers are defined to be browsers that are Internet Explorer version 4.0 and up. All other browsers are considered to be downlevel browsers. With uplevel browsers the ASP.NET Web controls render their HTML markup using style sheets where possible (via the `style` attribute). With downlevel browsers style sheets are not used; instead, equivalent HTML tags are used, such as the <b> tag in Listing 8.4.

Because ASP.NET classifies all non–Internet Explorer 4.0 and up browsers as downlevel, browsers like Netscape 7.0 and Mozilla, which can support style sheets and client-side JavaScript, are still detected as downlevel. Microsoft has stated that it plans on identifying more browsers as uplevel in future releases of the .NET Framework.

Examining the Formatting Properties of the Label Web Control

The Label Web control contains a number of formatting properties. We've already seen how to make the text of the Label Web control bold. There is a plethora of other Label Web control formatting properties worth examining. These formatting properties can be divided into the following classes: color properties, border properties, font properties, and miscellaneous properties. We'll examine these classes one by one in the next four sections.

Looking at the Color Properties

The Label Web control contains two properties for specifying the color of the outputted text: `ForeColor` and `BackColor`. If you couldn't guess, `ForeColor` specifies the text's foreground color, whereas `BackColor` specifies its background color.

Although the color properties would seemingly be straightforward and simple to understand, there are a number of caveats to pay heed to, as we'll discuss in this section.

Let's create a new ASP.NET Web page to try out these two color properties. Start by creating an ASP.NET Web page named `ColorLabel.aspx`, and drag and drop a Label

Web control onto the designer. Once the Label Web control has been added, change the `Text` property to

`This is a test of the color properties.`

Now let's set the `BackColor` to Navy and the `ForeColor` to White. To accomplish this, make sure that the Label Web control is selected so that its properties are displayed in the Properties pane. Then find the `BackColor` property in the Properties pane.

Selecting the `BackColor` property will display a palette with three tabs: Custom, Web, and System. As Figure 8.8 shows, the Custom tab contains 64 colors that you can choose from for setting the `BackColor` property.

FIGURE 8.8

The Custom tab displays various colors.

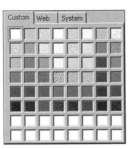

If you see a color that you want to set the `BackColor` to, simply click the color. If you do not see the color you want, you can right-click one of the 64 colors, which will cause the Define Color dialog box to appear (see Figure 8.9). From this you can choose a particular color from the color palette. Once you select a color and click the Add Color button, the color you right-clicked in the Custom tab will be replaced by the new color you defined. Additionally, the `BackColor` property will be set to this newly created color.

FIGURE 8.9

The Define Color dialog box allows you to create a custom color.

You can also choose a color by clicking the Web tab. The Web tab lists a number of colors you can select from.

Older versions of Netscape do not recognize the color names in the Web tab.

Finally, the System tab contains a list of Windows-specific color properties, such as ActiveCaption, Desktop, and WindowText. These names refer to various user-definable color settings in the Windows operating system. For example, the Desktop color is the background color of your Windows Desktop. If you choose to use one of these color names, the color displayed in the user's browser will depend on the color settings he or she has specified in Windows.

To change the color settings in Windows, right-click the Desktop and choose Properties. Then select the Appearances tab.

The color names in the System tab will work only for those Web visitors using Internet Explorer and running on the Windows operating system.

Let's go ahead and set the BackColor to Navy, which is a color listed in the Web tab.

The Label Web control's ForeColor property indicates the foreground color of the text displayed. When selecting the ForeColor property, the same three-tabbed palette appears. For this select the White color from the Web tab.

At this point we've set three of the Label Web control's properties. We set the Text property to This is a test of the color properties, the BackColor to Navy, and the ForeColor to White. The designer should show the text "This is a test of the color properties" in a white foreground color with a navy background color, as shown in Figure 8.10.

FIGURE 8.10

A Label with a white foreground and navy background is shown in the designer.

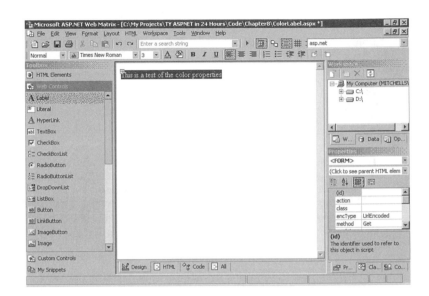

Now take a moment to save the ASP.NET Web page and view it through a browser. If you view the page through an uplevel browser (Internet Explorer 4.0 or higher), you see the same output shown in the designer—the text "This is a test of the color properties" in a white foreground color with a navy background color. However, if you view the Web page through a downlevel browser, such as Mozilla or Netscape, you will see. . . nothing! Figure 8.11 shows a screenshot of Mozilla when visiting `ColorLabel.aspx`.

FIGURE 8.11

When the page is viewed through a downlevel browser, no text appears on the screen.

To understand why we don't see anything in the latter case, let's take a look at the HTML markup received by the Mozilla (or any downlevel browser). Listing 8.5 contains this HTML.

LISTING 8.5   The HTML Markup Received by a Downlevel Browser

```
 1: <html>
 2: <head>
 3: </head>
 4: <body>
 5:     <form name="_ctl0" method="post" action="ColorLabel.aspx" id="_ctl0">
 6: <input type="hidden" name="__VIEWSTATE" value="
            dDwtMTU3ODAzNTQ4MDs7Pgir+5m8t+5uSNc0PJU0a6MGN/40" />
 7:
 8:         <span id="Label1"><font color="White">This is a test of
                  the color properties</font></span>
 9:         <!-- Insert content here -->
10:     </form>
11: </body>
12: </html>
```

As line 8 shows, the Label Web control's ForeColor property is rendered as a <font> tag, with its color attribute set accordingly. But how is the BackColor property rendered? As you can see from Listing 8.5, it isn't; at least it isn't for downlevel browsers. The reason is that without style sheets, the only way to give a background color to text is to place the text within an HTML <table> that has its bgcolor attribute set accordingly.

> To set the background color of text using style sheets, the background-color style sheet attribute can be used. This is how the BackColor property is rendered in uplevel browsers.

The short of it is that the BackColor of the Label Web control is not displayed in downlevel browsers. Keep this in mind when setting color properties for a Label Web control.

Examining the Border Properties

In uplevel browsers a border can be placed around the text displayed by a Label Web control. (In downlevel browsers, setting the border properties has no effect on the HTML markup rendered by the Label Web control.)

Let's create an ASP.NET Web page that displays a border around the text displayed by a Label Web control. Start by creating a new ASP.NET Web page titled BorderLabel.aspx. Drag and drop a Label Web control onto the designer and set the Label's Text property to Testing the border properties. Next click the Label Web control's BorderStyle property. This should cause the appearance of a drop-down list that contains various options for the style of border to be placed around the Label Web control. These options are enumerated in Table 8.2.

TABLE 8.2   The BorderStyle Property Can Be Set to Any One of the Following Values

Border Style	Description
NotSet	The default option. The border around the Label Web control depends upon external style sheet rules.
None	No border is displayed.
Dotted	A dotted border is displayed.
Dashed	A dashed border is displayed.
Solid	A solid border is displayed.
Double	A double border is displayed.
Groove	A grooved border is displayed.
Ridge	A ridged border is displayed.
Inset	An inset border is displayed.
Outset	An outset border is displayed.

Go ahead and select the Solid option for the BorderStyle property. In the designer you will see a border around only the vertical edges of the Label Web control. In order to see the entire border, you will need to click the Label Web control and enlarge it. To enlarge the Web control, click one of the squares around the corners of the Label Web control and, holding your mouse button down, drag the mouse until the appropriate size is achieved. To resize the Label Web control to this new size, simply release the mouse button. Go ahead and resize the Label Web control so that your screen looks similar to the screenshot in Figure 8.12.

Note that the border displayed in Figure 8.12 is black. We can change the border's color via the BorderColor property. Selecting the color for the BorderColor property is identical to selecting a color for the BackColor or ForeColor properties. Go ahead and opt to have our Label Web control's BorderColor property set to Red, a color from the Web tab.

FIGURE 8.12

The Label Web control has been resized and has a solid border.

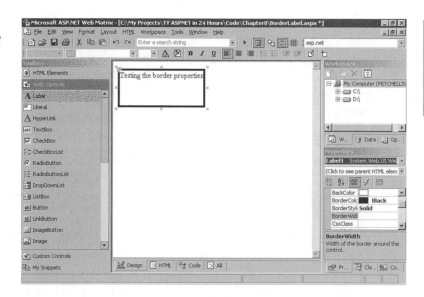

In addition to the `BorderStyle` and `BorderColor` properties, there's a `BorderWidth` property. Go ahead and enter a value of 2 as the `BorderWidth` property, which will create a border 2 pixels wide.

Figure 8.13 contains a screenshot of the Web Matrix Project designer with these property values set. Your screen should look similar.

FIGURE 8.13

The designer shows a Label Web control with a solid red border 2 pixels thick.

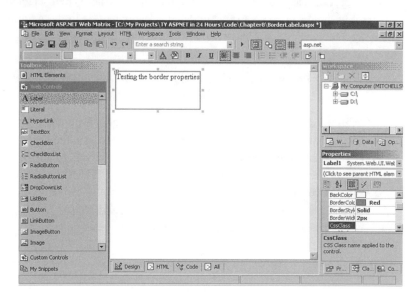

You should take a moment to view this ASP.NET Web page through a browser. If you view the page through Internet Explorer 4.0 or higher, the text "Testing the border properties" will be displayed with a red, solid border 2 pixels thick, just like in the designer. If you are viewing the ASP.NET Web page with a downlevel browser, just the text "Testing the border properties" will be displayed, without a border around it.

Delving into the Font Properties

As we saw earlier in this hour, the Label Web control has a Font property that contains a number of subproperties, such as Bold, Italic, Underline, and Name. We already examined how setting the Bold subproperty can make the text of a Label Web control appear in a bold font.

To further our examination of the other subproperties of the Font property, create a new ASP.NET Web page named LabelFont.aspx and drag and drop a Label Web control onto the designer. Set this Web control's Text property to Working with the Font properties. Next expand the Label Web control's Font property by clicking the plus sign to the left of the Font property name. This will expand the Font property, listing the subproperties. (A complete list of the Font property's subproperties can be found in Table 8.1.)

Let's set some of the Font property's subproperties. Start by setting the Italic subproperty to True, which should make the Label's text appear in an italic font in the designer. Next, under the Name property, choose the font name Arial. When selected, the Label Web control in the designer should be updated to show its text in the Arial font. Finally, set the Size subproperty to 22pt. This will cause the Label Web control's text in the designer to enlarge to a 22-point size.

Figure 8.14 contains a screenshot of the Web Matrix Project at this point. If you're following along, your screen should look similar.

Save the ASP.NET Web page and view it through a Web browser. If you visit the page with an uplevel browser (Internet Explorer 4.0 and up), the Label Web control's rendered HTML markup will specify its style settings via the style attribute. For example, with the Font property settings we used, the following HTML will be rendered by the Label Web control in an uplevel browser:

```
<span id="Label1" style="font-family:Arial;font-size:22pt;font-style:italic;
    ">Working with the Font properties</span>
```

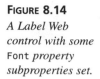

FIGURE 8.14

A Label Web control with some Font *property subproperties set.*

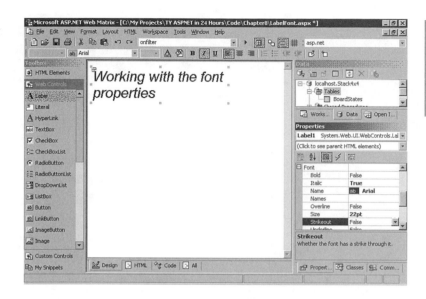

However, if you visit the Web page in a downlevel browser (any browser but Internet Explorer 4.0 and up), the HTML markup rendered by the Label Web control uses HTML tags to specify the style settings, as seen here:

```
<span id="Label1"><i><font face="Arial" size="6">Working with the Font
    properties</font></i></span>
```

The Miscellaneous Properties

The remaining Label Web control properties can be grouped as miscellaneous properties. For example, there is a Tooltip property, which can be set to a string value. If you specify a Tooltip, whenever the user hovers the mouse over the Label Web control, a floating light yellow box appears, displaying the value of the Tooltip property. Figure 8.15 shows a screenshot of an ASP.NET Web page being visited that has its Tooltip property set to

```
This is a tooltip.
```

FIGURE 8.15

*A tooltip is displayed
when the mouse hovers
over the Label Web
control.*

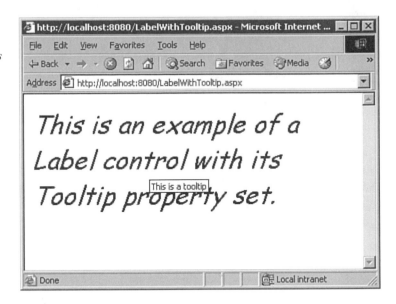

Two other miscellaneous Label Web control properties are `Height` and `Width`. These two properties can be set to specific values through the Properties pane. These values can also be set by resizing the Label Web control in the designer. To resize a Web control, simply select the Web control by left-clicking it. This will cause eight small, empty squares to appear around the Web control—one at each corner, one on the far left, one on the far right, one on the top, and one on the bottom. Then left-click one of the eight boxes and, while holding the mouse button down, move the mouse. Once you have resized the Web control appropriately, release the mouse button. The `Height` and `Width` properties will be updated accordingly.

The values of the `Height` and `Width` properties are rendered by the Label Web control when visited by a downlevel browser.

The `Visible` property, a Boolean property, determines whether the Label Web control appears in the browser. If the `Visible` property is set to True (the default), the Label Web control's rendered HTML markup is sent to the browser. If, however, the `Visible` property is set to False, the Label Web control is not rendered, and therefore, no HTML is sent to the browser for the Label Web control.

8

You may be wondering why in the world anyone would ever want to use this property. If someone didn't want to display the Label Web control, why create it and set its `Visible` property to False rather than simply not adding the Label Web control to an ASP.NET Web page?

In the next few hours, when we examine using Web forms to collect user input, we'll see scenarios where we just might want to create a Label Web control and initially set its `Visible` property to False. For example, imagine that we have an ASP.NET Web page that prompts the user for username and password. If the user provides an incorrect password, we want to display an appropriate message. Therefore, we can place a Label Web control on the Web page that has such a message and initially set its `Visible` property to False. Then, if the user enters an incorrect password, we can programmatically set the Label Web control's `Visible` property to True, thereby displaying the message.

The remaining Label Web control properties—`AccessKey`, `CssClass`, `Enabled`, `EnableViewState`, and `TabIndex`—are beyond the scope of this book. We will not be using these properties with Label Web controls in any of the examples in this book.

Summary

In this hour we looked at the two ASP.NET Web controls designed for displaying text output: the Literal Web control and the Label Web control. These two Web controls differ in the HTML markup they produce when being rendered.

When the Literal Web control is rendered, its `Text` property is returned as its HTML markup. No formatting is applied, and no extraneous HTML tags are added. The Literal Web control's rendered output is similar to that of the `Response.Write()` method, except that when using `Response.Write()`, the output is placed before any HTML content in the ASP.NET Web page's HTML portion. With the Literal Web control, you can place the Literal Web control anywhere within the HTML content, thereby having its output appear in a specific spot in the HTML output.

The Label Web control is useful for displayed formatted text—for example, if you want to display some text in a bold font or with a yellow background color. To accommodate this, the Label Web control has a number of display properties available, such as `BackColor`, `ForeColor`, `Font`, `BorderColor`, `BorderStyle`, and so on.

When a Label Web control is rendered, not only is the Text property displayed, but additional HTML tags are emitted, in order to provide the formatting specified by the various formatting property values.

Now that we've examined how to use the Literal and Label Web controls, we're ready to turn our attention to the Web controls that are designed to collect user input, such as the TextBox Web control, the DropDownList Web control, the RadioButton Web control, and others. Before we do, though, we need to examine how an ASP.NET Web page collects data from a Web visitor. We'll tackle this subject in the next hour, "Web Form Basics."

Q&A

Q Is there any difference in the HTML markup sent to the browser for Literal and Label Web controls?

A Recall from our discussions in this hour that when an ASP.NET Web page is executed by the ASP.NET engine, the Web controls are rendered into HTML markup. The precise HTML generated depends upon the Web control's properties.

In this hour we discussed two different Web controls: the Literal Web control and the Label Web control. If you create an ASP.NET Web page with Literal and Label Web controls and set the Text property of both to This is a test, it may appear, when visiting the ASP.NET Web page through a browser, as if both Web controls produce the same HTML output. However, it is important to note that the Label Web control produces slightly different HTML markup from the Literal Web control.

In such a Web page, the HTML markup produced by the Literal control is

```
This is a test
```

Note that the HTML markup produced by a Literal control is precisely the value of its Text property.

The Label Web control, however, actually uses a <span> HTML tag to display its Text property. That is, the HTML markup generated by the Label Web control in this example is

```
<span>This is a test</span>
```

The reason the Label Web control wraps its Text property in a <span> HTML tag is so that it can add formatting. For example, if the Label Web control's Font property's Bold subproperty were set to True, the following HTML markup would be produced in an uplevel browser:

```
<span style="font-weight:bold;">This is a test</span>
```

Note that slightly different HTML is produced for a downlevel browser:

```
<span><b>This is a test</b></span>
```

Q What properties would I want to set to change the color of a Label Web control?

A The Label Web control has color properties, ForeColor and BackColor. The ForeColor property specifies the foreground color, or the color of the actual text. The BackColor property indicates the background color. Note that downlevel browsers ignore the BackColor property.

8

Workshop

Quiz

1. What must you do to display formatted text with the Literal Web control?

2. What must you do to display formatted text with the Label Web control?

3. True or False: The Literal Web control contains only a single property, Text.

4. True or False: The Label Web control contains only a single property, Text.

5. Recall that when the ASP.NET engine executes an ASP.NET Web page, it renders the Web controls into their corresponding HTML markup. What factor(s) determine the HTML markup generated by a particular Web control?

6. What purpose do the Literal and Label Web controls serve?

7. Why is it said that Web controls are an intermediary between an ASP.NET Web page's HTML and source code portions?

8. True or False: The Label Web control's ForeColor property is ignored by downlevel browsers. (That is, all downlevel browsers display the Text of a Label control as black, regardless of the ForeColor property value.)

Answers

1. The Literal Web control does not have any formatting properties. Instead, its rendered HTML markup is precisely the value of its Text property. Therefore, if you want to display the Literal Web control with any kind of formatting, you must enter the appropriate HTML tags in the Text property.

2. The Label Web control contains a number of formatting properties that can specify the resulting text's formatting.

3. False. The Literal Web control contains, among others, an ID property.

4. False. In addition to its Text property, the Label Web control contains a plethora of formatting properties, an ID property, and several less germane properties.

5. The HTML markup generated by a Web control is dependent upon two factors: the value of the Web control's properties and the user's browser.

6. The Literal and Label Web controls are the two Web controls designed to display text.

7. Web controls are said to be intermediary between the HTML portion and source code portions of an ASP.NET Web page because they are placed in the HTML portion and generate HTML markup but can be programmatically accessed in the source code portion.

8. False. It is the Label's `BackColor` property that is ignored by downlevel browsers.

Exercises

1. Create an ASP.NET Web page that uses a Literal Web control to display the Web page's URL. Rather than hard-coding the URL into the Literal's `Text` property, set the `Text` property programmatically in the `Page_Load` event handler. Note that you can obtain the current page's URL via `Request.Url.ToString()`.

   That is, your ASP.NET Web page should contain a Literal Web control with its `ID` property set to some value (say, `urlDisplay`). Then, in the Code tab, enter the following source code:

   ```
   Sub Page_Load(sender as Object, e as EventArgs)
     urlDisplay.Text = Request.Url.ToString()
   End Sub
   ```

2. Create an ASP.NET Web page and add a Label Web control. Set its `Text` property to `What pretty text!` and then set a number of its formatting properties. Feel free to specify whatever formatting property values you'd like, but be sure to set at least five formatting properties.

3. For this exercise create an ASP.NET Web page that uses a Label Web control to display the IP address of the visitor visiting the Web page. (An IP address is a series of four numbers that identifies a computer on the Internet. If you are serving the ASP.NET Web pages from your own computer, your IP address will be 127.0.0.1.)

   The visiting user's IP address can be obtained via `Request.ServerVariables("REMOTE_ADDR")`. Therefore, to complete this exercise, you will need to create a Label Web control and set its `ID` property. Then you will need to create a `Page_Load` event handler in the ASP.NET Web page's source code portion that contains the following code:

   ```
   Sub Page_Load(sender as Object, e as EventArgs)
     LabelID.Text = Request.ServerVariables("REMOTE_ADDR")
   End Sub
   ```

PART II
Collecting and Processing User Input

Hour

Hour 9

Web Form Basics

In order to create a useful Web application, somehow we must be able to collect user input and return to the user a Web page customized to the input entered. For example, search engines like Google must be able to accept a user's search term and then display a Web page with the results based upon that search. Sites like Amazon.com must be able to read a shopper's credit card numbers so that they can correctly bill the shopper for purchases.

HTML was designed with such needs in mind, as evidenced by the various HTML tags designed to aid in collecting user input. The HTML `<input>` tag, for example, can be used to display a textbox, checkbox, radio button, or drop-down list. Once the user enters information, the HTML `<form>` tag specifies which Web page the input should be sent to.

With ASP.NET we do not need to enter such HTML tags. Rather, we use various Web controls, which, when rendered, produce the appropriate HTML tags. That is, if we want to have a textbox on our Web page, instead of adding an `<input>` tag, we add a TextBox Web control. Similarly, instead of using the HTML `<form>` tag, our ASP.NET Web pages need to use Web forms. We'll discuss what Web forms are and their semantics in this hour.

If you have worked with HTML forms and collecting user input in dynamic Web page technologies like ASP, PHP, or JSP, you'll find ASP.NET's model for collecting user input quite a bit different. By the end of this hour, though, you will likely find ASP.NET's way of collecting user input through Web forms to be much more intuitive and sensible than the techniques required for user input collection in older dynamic Web page technologies.

In this hour we will cover these topics:

- How user input is gathered through HTML
- What a Web form is
- Using a Web form in an ASP.NET Web page
- Properties of Web forms
- Collecting user input in an ASP.NET Web page
- Examining how the Web form persists the state of its Web controls

Gathering User Input in an HTML Web Page

Imagine that we wanted to create a Web page that calculated a user's Body Mass Index, or BMI.

The Body Mass Index, or BMI, is a ratio of a person's height to weight. BMI is commonly used as a quick determination of whether one is underweight, at a healthy weight, overweight, or obese. For more information about BMI, see `http://www.cdc.gov/nccdphp/dnpa/bmi/index.htm`.

In order to determine someone's BMI, we need to know his or her height and weight. For the time being, imagine that we want to create this Web page without using ASP.NET, instead using HTML markup to generate the two textboxes needed for the user's inputted height and weight.

When HTML was designed, two tags were created to facilitate collecting user input. These two HTML tags are the `<form>` tag and the `<input>` tag. Although a thorough understanding of these tags is not needed for collecting user input in an ASP.NET Web page, having a strong grasp of the concepts of how user input is collected from a Web page is important. Therefore, let's briefly examine the `<input>` and `<form>` tags as well as how they work in conjunction to allow a Web page to collect user input.

Examining the `<input>` Tag

The `<input>` tag can create a textbox, radio button, checkbox, or drop-down list. The `<input>` tag's type attribute specifies what type of user input control is displayed in the user's Web browser. For example, if you wanted to create an HTML Web page that contained a textbox, you could use the following HTML:

```
<input type="text">
```

To display a checkbox, you would use

```
<input type="checkbox">
```

 We will not delve into the HTML specifics for collecting user input in this book. For more information on this topic, check out http://www.w3schools.com/html/html_forms.asp, or consider picking up *Sams Teach Yourself HTML and XHTML in 24 Hours*.

Because our Web page will need two textboxes—one for the person's height in inches and one for the weight in pounds—we will use two `<input>` tags, both with `type="text"`.

Listing 9.1 contains the preliminary HTML Web page for our BMI calculator. Keep in mind that this page is far from complete!

LISTING 9.1 Our First Draft of the BMI Calculator

```
1: <html>
2: <body>
3:   <h1>BMI Calculator</h1>
4:   Your Height (in inches): <input type="text" name="height">
5:   <br>
6:   Your Weight (in pounds): <input type="text" name="weight">
7: </body>
8: </html>
```

Listing 9.1 simply displays two textboxes, one each for the user's height and weight. As you can see in lines 4 and 6, the `<input>` tags of Listing 9.1 each contains a name property. The name property is needed to uniquely identify each `<input>` tag. As we will see in the next section, "Passing the Input Back to the Web Server by Using the `<form>` Tag," the `<input>` tag's name attribute is used when sending the contents of the various `<input>` tags back to the Web server.

Figure 9.1 shows a screenshot of the code in Listing 9.1, when viewed through a browser.

FIGURE 9.1

The user is presented with two textboxes.

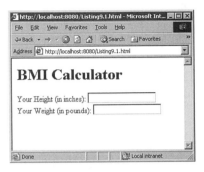

> If you are using an older version of Netscape, the textboxes in Figure 9.1 might not appear. Older versions of Netscape required that all <input> tags be placed within <form> tags.

In addition to the two textboxes, we need some way for the users to indicate to the Web browser that they've completed entering their data. To accomplish this, a *submit button* is used. A submit button is a button that, when clicked by the user, indicates to the Web browser that the user has finished entering the input. The HTML markup for a submit button is as follows:

```
<input type="submit" value="Text to Appear on Submit Button">
```

Listing 9.2 contains the HTML from Listing 9.1, but augmented with the submit button. Figure 9.2 shows the HTML from Listing 9.2 when viewed through a browser.

LISTING 9.2   Our Second Draft of the BMI Calculator

```
 1: <html>
 2: <body>
 3:   <h1>BMI Calculator</h1>
 4:   Your Height (in inches): <input type="text" name="height">
 5:   <br>
 6:   Your Weight (in pounds): <input type="text" name="weight">
 7:   <p>
 8:   <input type="submit" value="Calculate BMI">
 9: </body>
10: </html>
```

FIGURE 9.2

A submit button has been added.

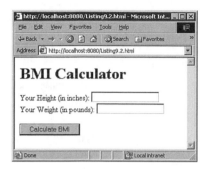

Passing the Input Back to the Web Server by Using the `<form>` Tag

Recall from our discussions in Hour 1, "Getting Started with ASP.NET," that when a user requests a Web page from a Web server, the Web server sends the Web page's HTML to the user's browser. This HTML is then rendered graphically in the user's browser. In order for the browser to receive this HTML, the Web browser and Web server must communicate with one another, but once the Web browser has received the HTML, the communication ends.

The most important point to take away from this discussion is that there is a clear disconnect between the Web server and the Web browser. The Web server has no idea what the user is entering into his or her browser. All the Web server ever does is wait for incoming Web requests and then return the appropriate HTML.

Due to this disconnect between the Web browser and the Web server, the Web browser needs some way to be able to let the Web server know the input entered by the user. This is accomplished via the HTML `<form>` tag.

The `<form>` tag must have, contained within it, the `<input>` tags used to collect the user input, as well as the submit button. When the `<form>` tag's submit button is clicked, the form is said to have been *submitted*. When a form is submitted, a specified Web page is called, and the data entered into the various `<input>` tags within the `<form>` tag are sent to this Web page.

This description of the `<form>` tag leaves two questions unanswered:

- When the `<form>` is submitted, how does it know what Web page to send the contents of its `<input>` tags to?
- How, exactly, are the contents of the `<input>` tags sent to this Web page?

These two questions can be answered by examining the `action` and `method` properties of the `<form>` tag. The `action` property specifies a URL that the browser is directed to once the `<form>`'s submit button is clicked. Therefore, it is the value of the `action` property that indicates the Web page that is visited once the `<form>` is submitted.

The contents of the `<input>` tags are compacted into a single string and are sent in a specific format. Precisely, the format used is as follows:

InputName1=InputValue1&InputName2=InputValue2&...&InputNameN=InputValueN

Here *InputName1* is the value of the first `<input>` tag's name attribute, and *InputValue1* is the value of the first `<input>` tag. *InputName2* is the value of the second `<input>` tag's name attribute, and *InputValue2* is the value of the second `<input>` tag, and so on. Note that each `<input>` tag's name and value are separated by an equals sign (=), and each pair of names and values is separated by an ampersand (&).

The `method` attribute determines how this string of `<input>` tag names and values is sent to the Web server. The `method` attribute can have one of two possible values: GET or POST. If `method` is set to GET, the contents of the `<input>` tags are sent through the *querystring*, which is an optional string that can be tacked on to the end of a Web page's URL. Specifically, if a Web site URL has a question mark in it (?), everything after the question mark is considered the querystring.

You have probably seen Web pages whose URL looks like

`http://www.someserver.com/somePage.aspx?Name=Scott&Age=21`

Here the contents after the question mark are considered the querystring.

If `method` is set to POST, the `<input>` tags' contents are sent through the *HTTP headers*, meaning there is no querystring tacked on to the end of the URL.

> Whenever a Web browser requests a Web page, it sends HTTP headers in addition to the requested URL. These are simple strings of text. One such HTTP header, as we discussed in the previous hour, "ASP.NET Web Controls for Displaying Text," is the User-Agent header, which sends information on the type of browser making the Web request.
>
> When the `method` attribute is set to POST, the Post HTTP header sends along the contents of the `<input>` tags. With this information placed in an HTTP header, the querystring is left uncluttered.

Let's augment Listing 9.2 to include a `<form>` tag that contains `action` and `method` attributes. Listing 9.3 is this augmented HTML page.

LISTING 9.3 A `<form>` Tag Has Been Added

```
 1: <html>
 2: <body>
 3:
 4:   <form method="GET" action="SomePage.aspx">
 5:     <h1>BMI Calculator</h1>
 6:     Your Height (in inches): <input type="text" name="height">
 7:     <br>
 8:     Your Weight (in pounds): <input type="text" name="weight">
 9:     <p>
10:     <input type="submit" value="Calculate BMI">
11:   </form>
12:
13: </body>
14: </html>
```

The `<form>` tag—spanning from line 4 to line 11—encloses the two `<input>` tags that generate the two textboxes as well as the submit button `<input>` tag. The `<form>`'s action attribute is set to `SomePage.aspx`, and the method attribute is set to GET.

A user visiting the HTML page shown in Listing 9.3 will be presented with two textboxes and a submit button, as was shown in Figure 9.2. After the user enters height and weight and clicks the submit button, the Web browser will request the Web page, as follows:

`SomePage.aspx?height=heightEnteredByUser&weight=widthEnteredByUser`

Figure 9.3 shows the Web browser's Address bar after the user has visited the HTML page generated by Listing 9.3 and has entered the value 72 for height and 155 for weight.

FIGURE 9.3

The querystring contains the values entered into the height and weight textboxes.

Address http://localhost:8080/SomePage.aspx?height=72&weight=155

> `SomePage.aspx` would need to read in the values passed in through the querystring, perform some calculation on these values, and then display the results to the user. We won't be examining the code for this fictional `SomePage.aspx` because the purpose of examining how the HTML `<form>` and `<input>` tags work is to help us gain an understanding of how ASP.NET's Web forms and Web controls manage to collect user input. We'll turn our attention to more ASP.NET-specific code shortly.

Postback Forms

If the `<form>`'s `method` attribute on line 4 in Listing 9.3 is changed to `POST`, then when users submit the form, they are still directed to `SomePage.aspx`. This time, though, no information will be passed through the querystring. Rather, this data will be hidden from sight from the users, passed through the HTTP headers instead.

As we saw, the `<form>`'s `action` attribute specifies the Web page that the browser requests once the `<form>` is submitted. In Listing 9.3 this Web page was `SomePage.aspx`. Such forms are typically called *redirect forms* because, when submitted, they redirect the user to a different Web page.

Imagine, though, what would happen if the `action` property were set to the same URL as the page that contains the `<form>` tag—that is, if we were to create an ASP.NET Web page called `PostbackFormExample.aspx` that has the following HTML:

```
<html>
<body>
  <form method="POST" action="PostbackFormExample.aspx">
    What is your age? <input type="text" name="age"><br>
    <input type="submit" value="Click to Continue">
  </form>
</body>
</html>
```

When users first visit `PostbackFormExample.aspx`, they will be shown a textbox labeled "What is your age?" Underneath this textbox they will see a submit button titled "Click to Continue." Once they enter some information into the textbox and submit the `<form>`, what will happen? Because the `method` attribute is set to `POST`, the `<input>` textbox's data will be sent via the HTTP Post header. Because the `action` attribute is set to `PostbackFormExample.aspx`, the user will be sent *back* to `PostbackFormExample.aspx` (but this time with information passed in through the HTTP Post header).

Such `<form>`s are called *postback forms* because they use the `POST` method and because when the `<form>` is submitted, the user is sent back to the same page. That is, the `<form>`'s `<input>` tag's data is posted back to the Web page.

Figure 9.4 is a pictorial representation of both a redirect form and a postback form. Note how the postback form sends the contents of its `<input>` tags back to itself, whereas a standard form forwards the contents to a different Web page.

FIGURE 9.4

Postback forms differ from redirect forms.

Postback Web Form Example

Page1.htm

A postback form is one whose ACTION property is set to the URL of the page the form appears on (i.e., Page1.htm). When the form is submitted, the user's browser requests the same page (Page1.htm), passing the form field inputs through either the querystring or HTTP Post headers.

Redirect Form Example

Page1.htm   Page2.htm

With a redirect form, Page1.htm has a form whose ACTION property is set to Page2.htm. When the form is submitted, the user requests the Page2.htm Web page, passing along the form field data in either the querystring or HTTP Post headers.

Dissecting Web Forms

In an ASP.NET Web page, collecting user input is much simpler than the techniques discussed in the previous section. In order to collect user input, the ASP.NET Web page must contain a *Web form*. A Web form is an HTML control that has the syntax

```
<form runat="server">
  ...
</form>
```

Recall that HTML controls are processed just like Web controls. Each available HTML control has a corresponding class in the .NET Framework. When an ASP.NET Web page is requested, the ASP.NET engine creates an object for each HTML control in the ASP.NET Web page's HTML section. These HTML controls can be programmatically referenced in the source code portion of the ASP.NET Web page. The ASP.NET engine calls the HTML control's `RenderControl()` method, which produces the HTML markup for the HTML control. The HTML markup produced depends on the type of the HTML control and its properties' values. In these ways, HTML controls are identical to Web controls.

HTML controls and Web controls differ in the syntax used to create them. HTML controls use the standard HTML tag with the `runat="server"` attribute, like

```
<input type="text" runat="server">
```

whereas Web controls use the syntax

```
<asp:WebControlName runat="server" ... />
```

When you create a new ASP.NET Web page in the Web Matrix Project, a Web form is automatically added. To demonstrate that this is the case, let's create a new ASP.NET Web page, one that we'll build upon throughout the remainder of this hour. Name this new ASP.NET Web page `BMICalculator.aspx`.

Once the new file is created, click the HTML tab, which will display the HTML portion of the `BMICalculator.aspx` page. As the screenshot in Figure 9.5 shows, the HTML portion already contains a Web form (the `<form runat="server">` on the fifth line down).

FIGURE 9.5

A Web form is automatically included in new ASP.NET Web pages created by the Web Matrix Project.

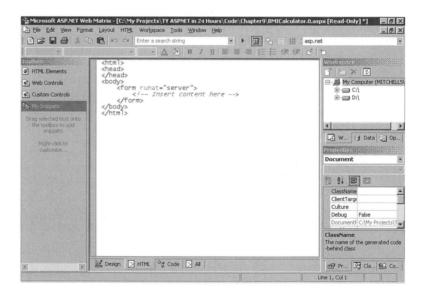

Now click back on the Design tab. You should see an empty designer because we've yet to add any Web controls to our ASP.NET Web page. By default the designer is a WYSIWYG editor, meaning that it displays only those Web controls and HTML controls that you would see when viewing the ASP.NET Web page through a browser. Because Web forms do not have any visual impact on a Web page, the designer does not show the Web form.

As we will see shortly, though, it is important that the Web controls used to collect user input (the TextBox Web controls and the Button Web control) be placed within the Web form. Therefore, it would be nice to see where, precisely, the Web form begins and where it ends in the designer. To accomplish this, you must go to the View menu and select Glyphs. This will display the start and close tag of the Web form, as can be seen in Figure 9.6.

9

FIGURE 9.6

Turning on Glyphs displays tags showing where the Web form begins and ends.

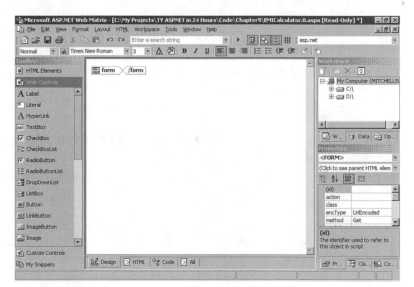

Adding Web Controls to Collect User Input

In an HTML Web page, user input is collected using a number of <input> tags, which can provide a variety of input mediums, such as textboxes, checkboxes, radio buttons, and so on. Additionally, a <form> must be placed around these <input> tags and have its method and action properties specified.

With an ASP.NET Web page, collecting user input is much simpler. As we've seen already, we need to have a Web form, which the Web Matrix Project has already kindly added for us. In addition to this Web form, we need to have a number of input Web controls into which the user will enter input.

For example, if we want to provide the user with a textbox to enter input, we would use a TextBox Web control. If we want to have the user enter input via a radio button, we'd use a RadioButton Web control. These various Web controls must be placed within the Web form.

Earlier in this hour we looked at creating an HTML Web page to collect user input for a BMI calculator. The BMI calculator needs to collect two bits of information from the user: height and weight. These two pieces of information can be provided via two textboxes. Therefore, let's add two TextBox Web controls to our `BMICalculator.aspx` ASP.NET Web page.

Before you add the first TextBox Web control, though, first type in the title to precede the TextBox Web control: **Your height (in inches):**. To enter this text into the designer, simply move your mouse cursor between the Web form's start and end tags and left-click. This should place the cursor between the Web form tags. Take a moment to hit the Enter key a few times to create some space. Now type in the text **Your height (in inches):**.

Next drag and drop a TextBox Web control from the Toolbox onto the designer, placing it immediately after the text you just added. Figure 9.7 shows a screenshot of the Web Matrix Project after adding this first TextBox Web control.

FIGURE 9.7

The first TextBox Web control has been added.

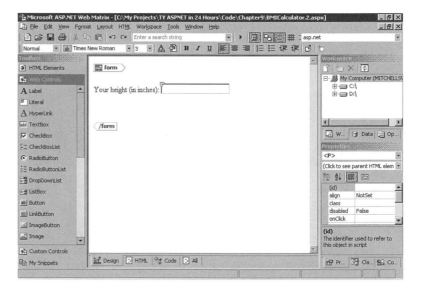

When dragging and dropping the TextBox Web control from the Toolbox onto the designer, make sure that the Toolbox's Web Controls tab is selected. If the Toolbox's HTML Elements tab were selected instead, you would be dragging and dropping an HTML `<input>` tag onto the designer.

To verify that you have indeed added the TextBox Web control and not the textbox HTML element, click the HTML tab. If you see in your HTML portion a TextBox Web control—`<asp:TextBox ...></asp:TextBox>`—then you have added the TextBox Web control. If, however, you see a textbox HTML element—`<input type="text">`—then you have accidentally added the textbox HTML element.

9

Now let's add the second TextBox Web control. Start by moving your mouse cursor after the TextBox Web control we just added and left-click. This will show the cursor in the designer. You can then type in the title for the TextBox Web control that we are about to enter. Specifically, enter the text **Weight (in pounds):**. As before, after entering this text, drag and drop a TextBox Web control from the Toolbox onto the designer, placing it immediately after the newly entered text. Take a moment to ensure that your screen looks similar to the screenshot in Figure 9.8.

FIGURE 9.8

The second TextBox Web control has been added.

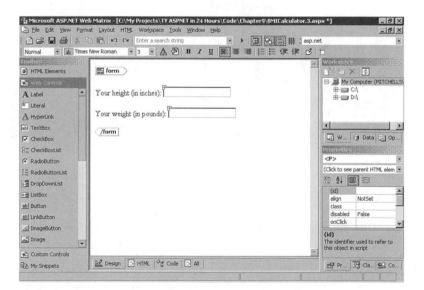

At this point we have added two TextBox Web controls to the ASP.NET Web page, both within the Web form. We are still missing one Web control, though. Recall from our earlier discussion that the browser needs to know when the user has completed entering his input. This was accomplished in the HTML Web page in Listing 9.2 by adding a submit button.

We need to add a submit button to our ASP.NET Web page, as well. To accomplish this, drag and drop the Button Web control from the Toolbox to the designer, placing it beneath the two TextBox Web controls. Like the two TextBox Web controls, the Button Web control must also be placed within the Web form.

Figure 9.9 shows a screenshot of the designer after the Button Web control has been added.

FIGURE 9.9

The final Web control—the Button Web control—has been added.

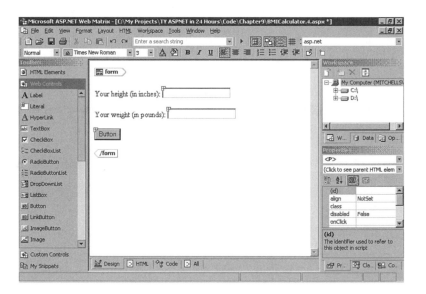

We have now added all of the Web controls that are needed to collect the user's input. The next step is to set the properties of these various Web controls. The Button Web control, for example, is currently displaying the text "Button," which we can change to a more descriptive message by changing the Button Web control's Text property. Also, the ID properties of the three Web controls are still set to their default values, which are not very descriptive, either.

Let's take a moment to change the properties of these Web controls. First click the Button Web control, which will load the Button's properties in the Properties pane. Take a moment to change the ID property to btnSubmit and the Text property to Calculate BMI. Once you change the Text property, the text appearing on the Button in the designer should change, as well.

Recall that the ID property is labeled (ID) in the Properties pane, making it appear near the top of the list of properties.

Next click the first TextBox Web control, the one appearing after the text "Your height (in inches):." Change the ID property to height. Finally, click the second TextBox Web control and change its ID property to weight.

Testing the `BMICalculator.aspx` ASP.NET Web Page

Now that we have added the needed Web controls, let's visit the BMICalculator.aspx Web page through a browser. Start by saving the ASP.NET Web page and then visiting it through a browser. The output you see should be identical to that shown in the designer in Figure 9.9.

Once you have visited the ASP.NET Web page through your browser of choice, take a moment to view the HTML source code that was sent to your browser. Listing 9.4 shows the source code received when visiting BMICalculator.aspx with Internet Explorer 6.0.

LISTING 9.4 The Browser Receives <form> and <input> Tags

```
 1: <html>
 2: <head>
 3: </head>
 4: <body>
 5:     <form name="_ctl0" method="post" action="BMICalculator.aspx" id="_ctl0">
 6: <input type="hidden" name="__VIEWSTATE" value=
                "dDwtMzg4MDA0NzA7Oz6cE9FHEXjV/MLWZSi/yH0JPOMcvA==" />
 7:
 8:         <p>
 9:         </p>
10:         <p>
11:         </p>
12:         <p>
13:             Your height (in inches):
14:             <input name="height" type="text" id="height" />
15:         </p>
16:         <p>
17:             Your weight (in pounds):
18:             <input name="weight" type="text" id="weight" />
19:         </p>
20:         <p>
21:             <input type="submit" name="btnSubmit" value="Calculate BMI"
                        id="btnSubmit" />
22:         </p>
23:         <p>
```

continues

LISTING 9.4 Continued

```
24:                   <!-- Insert content here -->
25:             </p>
26:         </form>
27: </body>
28: </html>
```

The first thing to notice from Listing 9.4 is that the Web form and Web controls produce roughly the same HTML markup that we crafted by hand in Listing 9.3. This is a powerful concept, because it pleases both us, the ASP.NET developers, and the Web browser requesting the ASP.NET Web page. It allows for us developers to not have to worry about HTML specifics. Rather, we can just drag and drop the Web controls needed from the Toolbox onto the designer. When the page is visited, the ASP.NET engine will convert the Web controls into the appropriate HTML markup, which is what the browser expects.

 ASP.NET's Web control model relieves developers from having to know HTML details. Rather, ASP.NET developers can focus on creating the user interface as they see fit (by dragging and dropping controls onto the designer) and working on the source code portion of the ASP.NET Web page.

There are three more important things in Listing 9.4 that you should take note of before we move on. First notice that the Button Web control is rendered as a submit button. That means when this button is clicked, the `<form>` tag contained within will be submitted.

Next note that the Web form in our ASP.NET Web page is rendered as a postback `<form>` tag (line 5). (Recall that a postback form is one that has its `method` set to `POST` and its `action` set to its own URL.) This means that when the Button Web control is clicked by the user, the `<form>` will submit, causing the page to be reloaded.

Finally, take note of the `<input>` tag on line 6. This `<input>` tag is a hidden `<input>` tag (note that its `type` attribute is set to `hidden`), meaning that it is not displayed in the browser. This hidden `<input>` tag, called the *ViewState*, is produced when the Web form is rendered. A thorough discussion of what the ViewState is and how it accomplishes its tasks is beyond the scope of this book.

Web Forms Remember the Values Entered By Users

While you have `BMICalculator.aspx` loaded into your browser, take a moment to fill some values into the two textboxes and then click the "Calculate BMI" button. What happens? Upon first glance it may have appeared that nothing happened. The same Web page is shown, and the textboxes contain the values you entered.

However, something *has* happened. Specifically, when you clicked the submit button, the <form> was submitted. Because this <form> is a postback form, the same Web page was reloaded, which is why you still see the same Web page. In fact, the HTML markup sent to your Web browser has changed, but ever so slightly. If you view the HTML received by your browser after entering some data into the textboxes and submitting the form, you'll see that the <input> tags now contain a value attribute, with the value equal to the value you entered into the textbox.

To better understand what has just happened, take a look at Figure 9.10. This is a screenshot of BMICalculator.aspx after the values 70 and 155 have been entered into the height and weight textboxes and the submit button has been clicked.

FIGURE 9.10

The textboxes have had values entered into them, and the form has been submitted.

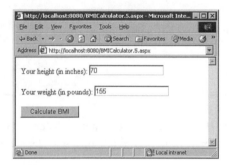

The HTML sent to the browser in Figure 9.10 is shown in Listing 9.5. Note that the HTML markup in Listings 9.4 and 9.5 is nearly identical, the only exception being that the <input> tags on lines 14 and 21 of Listing 9.5 differ from lines 14 and 21 of Listing 9.4. Specifically, the <input> tags in Listing 9.5 have a value attribute set to the value entered into each respective textbox (see Figure 9.10). The HTML markup rendered by the TextBox Web controls in Listing 9.5 is different from that in Listing 9.4.

LISTING 9.5 The HTML Received by the Browser after the Form Has Been Submitted

```
 1: <html>
 2: <head>
 3: </head>
 4: <body>
 5:     <form name="_ctl0" method="post" action="BMICalculator.aspx" id="_ctl0">
 6: <input type="hidden" name="__VIEWSTATE" value="
        dDwtMzg4MDA0NzA7Oz6cE9FHEXjV/MLWZSi/yH0JPOMcvA==" />
 7:
 8:         <p>
 9:         </p>
10:         <p>
```

continues

LISTING 9.5 Continued

```
11:          </p>
12:          <p>
13:              Your height (in inches):
14:              <input name="height" type="text" value="70" id="height" />
15:          </p>
16:          <p>
17:              Your weight (in pounds):
18:              <input name="weight" type="text" value="155" id="weight" />
19:          </p>
20:          <p>
21:              <input type="submit" name="btnSubmit" value="Calculate BMI"
                          id="btnSubmit" />
22:          </p>
23:          <p>
24:              <!-- Insert content here -->
25:          </p>
26:      </form>
27: </body>
28: </html>
```

To understand why the TextBox Web controls rendered different HTML markup after the form was submitted (Listing 9.5) from before (Listing 9.4), let's walk through this process in detail.

First realize that the TextBox Web control has a Text property. If this property is set to some value, the HTML markup rendered by the TextBox Web control is different from that if this property is not set at all. That is, if this property is not set, the HTML rendered by the TextBox Web control is simply

```
<input name="ValueOfIDProperty" type="text" id="ValueOfIDProperty" />
```

For example, on line 14 in Listing 9.4, you can see that the first TextBox Web control, whose ID property is set to height, produces the following HTML markup:

```
<input name="height" type="text" id="height" />
```

If, however, the Text property is set to some value, the value attribute is included in the rendering of the TextBox Web control like so:

```
<input name="ValueOfIDProperty" type="text" value="ValueOfTextProperty"
        id="ValueOfIDProperty" />
```

So, when the BMICalculator.aspx page was first visited, the Text property of the TextBox Web controls was not set, as evidenced by the HTML markup produced (see lines 14 and 21 in Listing 9.4). When the user enters some values into these two textboxes, such as 70 in the height textbox and 155 in the weight textbox, and then submits the form, the `Text` properties of the TextBox Web controls are set to the values entered by the user. Then, when the TextBox Web controls are rendered, they include the `value` attribute set to the value entered by the user (see lines 14 and 21 in Listing 9.5).

Writing the Source Code Portion
for `BMICalculator.aspx`

Note that when we enter values into the textboxes and submit the form, the Web page is reloaded (because the form is a postback form) and the values entered into the textboxes are persisted across the postback. Although this is fine and good, we still need to provide code to actually perform the Body Mass Index calculation, which is quite simple and is shown in Figure 9.11.

FIGURE 9.11

The BMI is a ratio of weight to height.

English Formula:

$$BMI = (\frac{WeightInPounds}{HeightInInches^2}) \cdot 703$$

Metric Formula:

$$BMI = \frac{WeightInKilograms}{HeightInMeters^2}$$

The code required for this calculation is fairly straightforward and is shown in Listing 9.6.

LISTING 9.6   The Code for the BMI Calculation

```
 1: 'Find out the person's height and weight
 2: Dim h as Integer = height.Text
 3: Dim w as Integer = weight.Text
 4:
 5: 'Calculate the person's BMI
 6: Dim BMI as Double
 7: BMI = (w / (h * h)) * 703
 8:
 9: 'Output the BMI value
10: Response.Write("Your BMI is " & BMI)
```

On line 2 an `Integer` variable named `h` is declared and assigned the value of the `height` TextBox Web control's `Text` property. On line 3 an `Integer` variable named `w` is declared and assigned the value of the `width` TextBox Web control's `Text` property. Next, on line 6 a

`Double` variable named `BMI` is created. On line 7 it is assigned the person's weight divided by the person's height squared; that quantity is then multiplied by 703.

Clearly, this code must appear in our ASP.NET Web page's source code portion, but where? One option would be to place the code in Listing 9.6 in the `Page_Load` event handler. Recall that the `Page_Load` event handler is executed every time the page is visited. This is not what we want, though. By placing the code in Listing 9.6, the code would execute every time the page was loaded, even when a user first visited the Web page and before having had a chance to enter height and weight.

> In fact, if you place the code in Listing 9.6 in the `Page_Load` event handler, you will get an "Input string was not in a correct format" error when visiting the page. This error results from line 2 of Listing 9.6. When the page is first loaded, the `Text` property of the `height` and `width` TextBox Web controls is a blank string. VB.NET cannot convert a blank string into an Integer, hence the error.

The `Page_Load` event handler is not a suitable place for the code in Listing 9.6 because we want this code to run whenever the user submits the form, not whenever the page is loaded. Fortunately, the Button Web control contains a `Click` event, which fires whenever the Web form is submitted. By adding this event handler to our ASP.NET Web page's source code section and placing the code in Listing 9.6 in this event handler, the code will execute whenever the Web form is submitted.

In order to add a `Click` event handler for the button, simply double-click the Button Web control in the designer. This will take you to the Code tab, with the following code automatically entered:

```
Sub btnSubmit_Click(sender As Object, e As EventArgs)

End Sub
```

Now simply add the code from Listing 9.6 between these two lines of code.

Once you have added this code, save the ASP.NET Web page and view it through a browser. When you first visit the page, you should see two empty textboxes and a button labeled "Calculate BMI"; Figure 9.12 shows a screenshot of the browser when the page is first visited.

FIGURE 9.12

The final
`BMICalculator.aspx`
ASP.NET Web page,
when first visited.

9

Now enter some appropriate values into the two textboxes and then click the "Calculate BMI" button. If you enter my height and weight—70 and 155—you should see the output shown in Figure 9.13.

FIGURE 9.13

The user's BMI is
displayed.

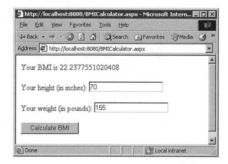

 To determine what the various BMI ratings mean, visit `http://nhlbisupport.com/bmi/bmicalc.htm`. Briefly, a healthy BMI range is between 18.5 and 24.9. Persons with a BMI of 25.0 to 29.9 are considered overweight, whereas a BMI over 30 indicates obesity. (BMI conclusions can be inaccurate for athletes and the elderly.)

 If you enter noninteger values into the textboxes in `BMICalculator.aspx`, you will get an error when submitting the page. Similarly, if you enter negative values for your height or weight, the computed BMI might be a negative number itself.

In Hour 12, "Validating User Input with Validation Controls," we'll examine how to use a special kind of Web control that ensures that a user's input is in an acceptable form and within acceptable boundaries.

> There are many ways the `BMICalculator.aspx` ASP.NET Web page can be improved. For example, rather than using a `Response.Write()` to output the value of the `BMI` variable, it would be more aesthetically pleasing to have the output placed in a Label Web control.

Summary

In this hour we examined how user input can be collected in an ASP.NET Web page. We started by examining the HTML tags needed to collect user input, which include a number of `<input>` tags for each textbox, checkbox, radio button, or drop-down list, and a `<form>` tag, inside which the `<input>` tags must be enclosed. Additionally, a submit button is needed.

With ASP.NET Web pages we do not need to worry about creating these HTML tags by hand. Rather, we can simply use appropriate Web controls, such as the TextBox Web control for displaying a textbox, a CheckBox Web control for displaying a checkbox, and so on. To collect a user's input, these Web controls must be placed inside a Web form. A Web form, as we saw, is an HTML control of the form, as follows:

```
<form runat="server">
  ...
</form>
```

A Web form is automatically entered by the Web Matrix Project when creating a new ASP.NET Web page.

In addition to the Web controls needed to collect the user's input, a Button Web control should be added in the Web form. The Button Web control is rendered as a submit button that, when clicked, submits the form, performing a postback. If you have source code that you want to execute whenever the Web form is submitted, you can place it in the Button Web control's `Click` event handler. To add a `Click` event handler to your ASP.NET Web page, simply double-click the Button Web control in the designer.

Now that we have seen how an ASP.NET Web page can collect user input and perform calculations on this input, we're ready to examine the Web controls for collecting user input in much finer detail. In the next hour, "Using Textboxes to Collect Input," we'll focus on examining the TextBox Web control. Following that hour, we'll look at collecting a user's input by using the DropDownList, RadioButton, and CheckBox Web controls.

Q&A

Q **Sometimes when I refresh my browser on a Web page with a form, a message-box appears that says, "This page cannot be refreshed without resending the form information" or "The page contains POSTDATA. Do you want to refresh?" What does this mean?**

A Recall that there are two ways that an HTML form can submit its values: through the querystring or through the HTTP Post headers. When a postback form is used, the HTML form uses the HTTP Post headers and submits the form to the same URL. (Refer back to Figure 9.4 for more on postback forms.)

When you ask your browser to refresh the Web page after you have submitted a postback form, the browser doesn't know whether you want to repost the Web page resubmitting the HTTP Post headers or not. Therefore, it asks you if you want to resend the form information.

Q **Why do ASP.NET Web forms use postback? Why not direct the user to another page or pass the information along in the querystring?**

A ASP.NET Web forms use postback forms over alternative methods for a number of reasons, the most important being that postback forms allow the ASP.NET Web controls to maintain their state across postbacks. Recall that when a user enters a value into a TextBox Web control and submits the form, the ASP.NET Web page is posted back, and the TextBox Web control's Text property is updated to the value entered by the user. In order for the TextBox Web control's Text property to be updated with the value entered by the user, the Web form must submit back to the same page that contains the TextBox Web control. (A lengthy discussion on *why* this is the case is far beyond the scope of this book.)

Additionally, the HTTP Post headers are used, as opposed to the querystring, because oftentimes a large amount of data is being passed back in the Post headers. Recall that some older browsers have a limit on the amount of information that can be passed through the querystring. Furthermore, it would be unsightly to have such mangled querystrings.

Workshop

Quiz

1. What are the germane differences between a form with its method property set to GET versus a form with its method property set to POST?

2. Imagine that you saw the following querystring:

   `SomePage.aspx?SSN=123-45-6789&age=24&gender=M`

   What does this tell you about the form that the user filled out?

3. What are the differences between a postback form and a redirect form?

4. What type of forms do ASP.NET Web forms use?

Answers

1. A form with its `method` property set to `GET` passes its form values through the querystring. A form with its `method` property set to `POST` passes its form values through the HTTP Post headers. When passing information through the querystring, it appears in the browser's Address bar (see Figure 9.3). With the HTTP Post headers, however, the information is hidden from sight. Realize that ASP.NET Web forms use the HTTP Post header to pass form value information.

2. Since the information is passed in the querystring, it is obvious that the form's `action` property was set to `GET`. Also, based on the values in the querystring, it can be determined that there were three form fields, with the names `SSN`, `age`, and `gender`, and that the user entered the values `123-45-6789`, `24`, and `M` for the three form fields.

3. A postback form is a form whose `method` property is set to `POST` *and* whose `action` property is set to the same URL that the form exists on. For instance, if the Web page `Page1.aspx` has a postback form, its form's `action` property will be set to `Page1.aspx`.

   A redirect form is a form whose `action` property is set to a URL other than the URL the form exists on. For instance, if the Web page `Page1.aspx` has a redirect form, its form's `action` property is set to some other Web page's URL, such as `Page2.aspx`.

   (Refer back to Figure 9.4 for more on the differences between postback forms and redirect forms.)

4. ASP.NET Web forms use postback forms.

Exercises

There are no exercises for this hour. Web forms by themselves are quite useless. To make Web forms useful, we need to add Web controls designed for collecting a user's input. In the next hour we'll see how to use the TextBox Web control to collect user input. At the end of this next hour, we'll work on a number of exercises that examine the use of Web forms.

HOUR 10

Using Textboxes to Collect Input

In the previous hour, "Web Form Basics," we examined how to collect user input through an ASP.NET Web page. To summarize, we saw that in order to retrieve user input, a Web form needs to be used. Inside the Web form, Web controls are placed to allow user input.

For example, in the last hour we looked at a BMI Calculator ASP.NET Web page. For this Web page, the user needed to enter two pieces of information: height and weight. To enter this information, two TextBox Web controls were used.

The TextBox Web control contains a number of properties that can be set to specify the appearance of the resulting textbox. The TextMode property of the TextBox Web control can be set to MultiLine, for example, which will create a textbox with multiple lines. The Columns property can be adjusted to specify how many columns wide the textbox should be.

In this hour we will look at the various TextBox Web control properties and the visual effects they have. Specifically, we will look at

- Creating multiline textboxes
- Creating password textboxes
- Specifying the number of columns in a textbox
- Indicating the maximum number of characters that can be entered into a textbox
- Changing the look and feel of the textbox by changing the font size, font name, and color of the textbox

Learning the TextBox Web Control Basics

As you already know, when an ASP.NET Web page is visited, its Web controls are rendered into HTML markup. The Label Web control, for example, is rendered as a `<span>` tag whose content is the Label's `Text` property. The TextBox Web control, as we saw in the previous hour, is rendered into an `<input>` tag whose `type` attribute is set to `text`.

TextBox Web controls are used when user input is needed. Textboxes arc ideal for collecting user input that is general text, such as a person's name, mailing address, or credit card number.

> For certain types of user input, a textbox might not be ideal. In the next hour we will examine other Web controls designed for collecting user input and why they are better suited than the TextBox Web control for some situations.

In this hour we will examine the various types of textboxes—such as password textboxes and multiline textboxes—as well as how to alter the aesthetics of a textbox. Before we begin this exploration, though, let's get a bit of practice adding a TextBox Web control to an ASP.NET Web page and displaying the value entered by the user.

To do this, start by creating a new ASP.NET Web page named `TextBoxPractice.aspx`. In this page we will add two TextBox Web controls to collect two bits of information from the user—name and age.

> It may be helpful to enable glyphs by opening the View menu and selecting the Glyphs option. Recall from the previous hour that enabling glyphs displays the start and closing tags of the Web form in the designer.

Start by entering the following title for the first TextBox Web control into the designer: **Your name:**. After entering this text, drag and drop a TextBox Web control from the Toolbox onto the designer. Next enter the text **Your age:** and, after this text, add another TextBox Web control. Finally, as with all Web forms, we will need a Button Web control. Add this below the two TextBox Web controls.

Figure 10.1 shows a screenshot of the Web Matrix Project after these three Web controls have been added. Take a moment to make sure that your screen looks similar.

FIGURE 10.1

Two TextBox Web controls and a Button Web control have been added to the designer.

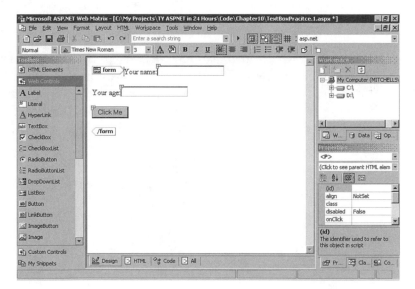

 For the ASP.NET Web page to collect user input correctly, the TextBox and Button Web controls must be placed within the Web form. By turning on Glyphs (go to the View menu and select Glyphs), you can ensure that the Web controls are within the Web form.

Now let's set the properties of our three Web controls. For the two TextBox Web controls, we'll be specifying only their ID properties at this time. (Later in the hour we will look at the other TextBox Web control properties.) The Button Web control will have both its ID property and its Text property set. Recall that the Button's Text property indicates the text that appears on the button.

Start with the first TextBox Web control. Because this Web control is used to collect the user's name, let's set its ID property to name. To accomplish this,

1. Click the TextBox Web control in the designer, which will load its properties into the Properties pane.

2. Next change its ID property to name.

3. Repeat the same process for the second TextBox Web control but set its ID property to age.

4. Finally, click the Button Web control to set its properties. Start by setting the ID property to btnSubmit and its Text property to **Click Me**.

Let's take a moment to test this ASP.NET Web page, so that we can observe the HTML markup generated by the TextBox Web controls. Save the ASP.NET Web page and then visit it via your Web browser. Figure 10.2 shows a screenshot of the ASP.NET Web page when visited through a browser. Note that the two TextBox Web controls and the Button Web control we added via the Web designer are present.

FIGURE 10.2
The ASP.NET Web page, when visited through a browser, displays two textboxes and a button.

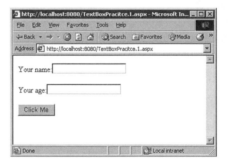

Listing 10.1 contains the HTML markup received by the Web browser when visiting the ASP.NET Web page.

LISTING 10.1   The TextBox Web Controls Are Rendered as <input> Tags

```
1: <html>
2: <head>
3: </head>
4: <body>
5:     <form name="_ctl0" method="post" action="TextBoxPractice.aspx" id="_ctl0">
6: <input type="hidden" name="__
          VIEWSTATE" value="dDwtMzg4MDA0NzA7Oz4rkFt/hCN2fbmjhx2X49AZ5kPBcQ==" />
7:
8:          <p>
```

LISTING 10.1   Continued

```
 9:            </p>
10:            <p>
11:                Your name:<input name="name" type="text" id="name" />
12:            </p>
13:            <p>
14:                Your age:<input name="age" type="text" id="age" />
15:                <!-- Insert content here -->
16:            </p>
17:            <p>
18:                <input type="submit" name="btnSubmit" value="Click Me"
                          id="btnSubmit" />
19:            </p>
20:            <p>
21:            </p>
22:        </form>
23: </body>
24: </html>
```

As you can see on lines 11 and 14, the TextBox Web controls are rendered as `<input>` tags with their `type` attribute set to `text`.

Performing an Action when the User Submits the Form

At this point the `TextBoxPractice.aspx` ASP.NET page will do nothing when the form is submitted. Typically, though, when the user submits information, you want to do something with it. Perhaps you want to perform a calculation on the data entered and present some computed value to the user. As we will see in later hours, you may want to display data from a database that matches the input provided by the user. In either case the input provided by the user is utilized in some fashion.

In order to access the values entered into the two textboxes, we need to add an event handler for the Button Web control's `Click` event. By doing so, we can provide source code that will run once the user has submitted the form (by clicking the button).

Adding an event handler for the Button's `Click` event is easy—simply double-click the Button Web control in the designer. This will add the event handler and automatically take you to the Code tab, where you can add the needed code. Now we have to decide what, specifically, we want to do with the input once the user submits the form. For this ASP.NET Web page, let's simply display the user's input in the browser.

In the previous hour we looked at a BMI calculator that used a `Response.Write()` method call to display the user's BMI. We discussed how this method of outputting information is not ideal, because it places the output prior to the HTML markup specified in the ASP.NET Web page's HTML portion. It's better to add a Label Web control to the

ASP.NET Web page's HTML section and then set this Web control's Text property programmatically in the source code portion.

Because using a Label Web control to display output is the preferred approach, let's do that here. Start by adding a Label Web control to the TextBoxPractice.aspx ASP.NET page. You can add this anywhere in the HTML portion; if you want to follow along with this book's example, though, please add the Label Web control after the Button Web control.

Remember from Hour 8, "ASP.NET Web Controls for Displaying Text," that to add a Label Web control, you simply need to drag and drop it from the Toolbox and onto the designer. Once you have done this, set the Label Web control's ID property to results and clear out the Text property. Figure 10.3 is a screenshot of the Web Matrix Project's designer after this Label Web control has been added and its properties set.

FIGURE 10.3

A Label Web control has been added to TextBoxPractice.aspx.

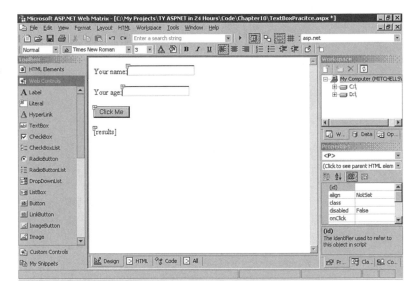

If you want to set some of the aesthetic properties of the results Label Web control at this time, feel free to do so. Recall that the aesthetic properties of the Label Web control include such properties as Font, BackColor, ForeColor, and so on.

Now that you have added the Label Web control, let's go ahead and add the source code for the Button Web control's Click event handler. To add the event handler, double-click the button in the designer. This will take you to the Code tab, as shown in Figure 10.4.

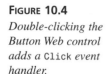

FIGURE 10.4

Double-clicking the Button Web control adds a Click *event handler.*

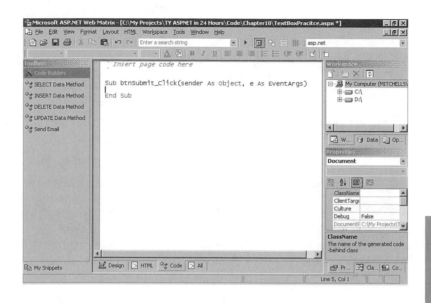

Add the needed code so that the Button Web control's Click event handler looks as follows:

```
Sub btnSubmit_Click(sender As Object, e As EventArgs)
  results.Text = "Hello, " & name.Text
  results.Text &= ". You are " & age.Text & " years old."
End Sub
```

The code in the event handler sets the results Label's Text property so that it displays the user's entered name and age. Recall that the ID of the TextBox Web control into which the user's name is entered is name, and the ID of the TextBox Web control into which the user's age is entered is age.

Figure 10.5 is a screenshot of TextBoxPractice.aspx when visited through a browser. The screenshot was taken after a user entered his name and age and submitted the form by clicking the "Click Me" button.

FIGURE 10.5

The user-supplied name and age are displayed.

The `TextBoxPractice.aspx` ASP.NET Web page we just created and tested demonstrates using TextBox Web controls in an ASP.NET Web page. For the remainder of this hour, we will focus on the various properties of the TextBox Web control and how these properties alter the appearance of the resulting textbox in the user's Web browser.

Creating Multiline and Password Textboxes

Take a moment to examine the textboxes in Figure 10.5. Note that these textboxes allow for a single line of text. As you likely know from your Internet surfing experience, textboxes come in other forms. The two variants of the textbox are multiline and password.

A multiline textbox contains more than one row of text. This type of textbox is commonly used when the user needs to input a large amount of text. For example, online message board sites are discussion Web sites where visitors can post questions or comments and reply to other comments. Typically, multiline textboxes are used when the user enters a comment. (See Figure 10.6 for an example of a multiline textbox.)

Password textboxes are textboxes whose input is masked by asterisks (*). Password textboxes are used to collect sensitive input from the user, such as his or her password. The masked input prevents an onlooker from being able to determine the user's password or other sensitive information by glancing over the user's shoulder. (Consult Figure 10.7 to see an example of a password textbox.)

The TextBox Web control contains a `TextMode` property that specifies how the resulting textbox is displayed: as a normal textbox, as a multiline textbox, or as a password textbox. As we have seen, the TextBox Web control displays a normal textbox by default. In the next two sections, we will examine how to get the TextBox Web control to render as a multiline textbox and then as a password textbox.

Using Multiline Textboxes

Creating a multiline textbox involves the following simple steps:

1. Add a TextBox Web control to the ASP.NET Web page by dragging and dropping the TextBox Web control from the Toolbox and onto the designer.
2. Set the TextBox Web control's `TextMode` property to `MultiLine`.
3. Set the TextBox Web control's `Columns` and `Rows` properties to specify the number of columns and rows the multiline TextBox should have.

Let's create an ASP.NET Web page with a multiline textbox. Start by creating a new ASP.NET Web page named `MultiLineTextBox.aspx`. (As with the previous example, you are encouraged to turn on glyphs.) Start by typing the following text into the designer inside the Web form: **Share your thoughts:**.

The first step in adding a multiline textbox is to add the TextBox Web control to the Web page. So, drag and drop a TextBox Web control from the Toolbox onto the designer after the "Share your thoughts:" text.

Next we need to set the TextBox Web control's `TextMode` property. To accomplish this, first click the TextBox Web control so that its properties are loaded in the Properties pane. Next scroll down through the list of properties until you reach the `TextMode` property.

By default the `TextMode` property is set to the value `SingleLine`, which creates a standard, single-line textbox like the one shown in Figure 10.5.

Clicking the `TextMode` property drops down a list of three options: `SingleLine`, `MultiLine`, and `Password`. Select the `MultiLine` option. Once you choose the `MultiLine` option, the TextBox Web control in the designer will automatically be displayed as a multiline textbox.

At this point we can adjust the number of columns and rows in the mutliline textbox by setting the TextBox Web control's `Columns` and `Rows` properties. Go ahead and set these two properties to values of 25 and 5, respectively. The columns and rows displayed by the TextBox Web control in the designer will be updated accordingly.

Figure 10.6 shows a screenshot of the Web Matrix Project after these steps have been completed.

FIGURE 10.6

A multiline textbox is displayed.

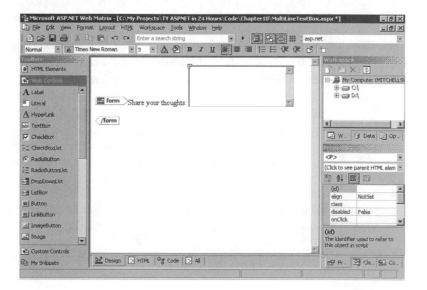

10

For practice you are encouraged to complete the `MultiLineTextBox.aspx` Web page by adding a Button Web control and providing source code in the Button's `Click` event handler. For now simply have the source code display the text entered by the user.

Using Password Textboxes

There are many Web applications that require the user to create an account and to log in before being able to enjoy the services of the site. For example, to check your e-mail at Hotmail.com, you must first sign in by providing your username and password.

The password textbox is a variant of the standard textbox created for hiding the text entered by a user. With a password textbox, each character entered by the user is displayed as an asterisk in the textbox. Figure 10.7 shows a password textbox that has had the text "This is a password" typed into it.

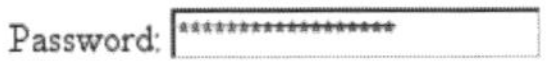

FIGURE 10.7

A password textbox masks the text entered by the user.

Password: [********************]

To create a password textbox in an ASP.NET Web page, we simply need to add a TextBox Web control and set its `TextMode` property to `Password`. Create an ASP.NET Web page named `PasswordTextBox.aspx` to try out creating a password textbox.

Start by typing the text **Username:** into the designer. After this, add a TextBox Web control. On the next line, type in the text **Password:** and, after this, add another TextBox Web control. Set the second TextBox Web control's `TextMode` property to `Password`.

Setting the TextBox Web control's `TextMode` property to `Password` will not change the display in the designer. Recall that setting the `TextMode` property to `MultiLine` had the effect of displaying a multiline textbox in the designer.

After these two TextBox Web controls, add a Button Web control. Set the Button Web control's `Text` property to `Login`.

After you perform these steps, your screen should look similar to the screenshot in Figure 10.8.

FIGURE 10.8

The ASP.NET Web page has two TextBox Web controls and a Button Web control.

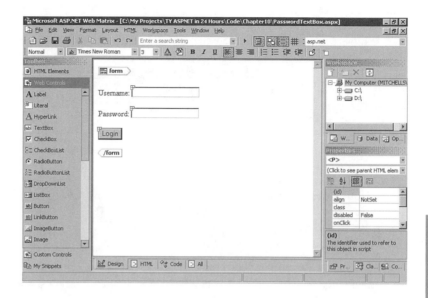

Password Textbox Values Are Not Continued across Postbacks

The password textbox has some potentially unexpected behavior when viewed through a Web page. To illustrate these subtleties, let's view the PasswordTextBox.aspx through a browser. When you first visit the page, take a moment to enter some text into the username and password textboxes. Note that the username textbox behaves like a normal textbox, but the password textbox has its input masked by asterisks. Figure 10.9 shows a screenshot of the PasswordTextBox.aspx ASP.NET Web page through a browser and with values entered into both textboxes.

FIGURE 10.9

The text in the password textbox is masked by asterisks.

Once you have entered information into both the two textboxes, submit the form by clicking the Login button. Clicking the button will cause the form to be submitted. Since Web forms, as we discussed in the previous hour, are postback forms, the Web page will be reloaded.

Upon reloading, though, the text entered into the password textbox will disappear, as Figure 10.10 illustrates. (Note that the text in the username textbox remains.)

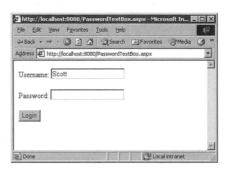

Why did the text in the username textbox remain, but the text in the password textbox disappear? Recall that when the button is clicked, the Web form is submitted, and the data entered by the user into the textboxes is sent back to the PasswordTextBox.aspx ASP.NET Web page.

When the request for the PasswordTextBox.aspx ASP.NET Web page arrives at the Web server, the ASP.NET engine is invoked to produce the proper HTML output for the ASP.NET Web page. The ASP.NET Web page can determine that the page has been posted back and sets the Text properties of the two TextBox Web controls to the values entered by the user.

With TextBox Web controls whose TextMode property is set to SingleLine or MultiLine, the value of the Text property is expressed in the HTML markup generated by the TextBox Web control when it is rendered. For example, a TextBox Web control whose Text property equals Scott and whose ID property equals TextBox1 will render the following HTML markup:

```
<input name="TextBox1" type="text" value="Scott" id="TextBox1" />
```

However, when a password textbox is rendered, the Text property is not expressed in the resulting HTML markup. Security reasons prevent the Text property from being expressed in the TextBox Web control's resulting HTML markup.

Imagine that a TextBox Web control with its TextMode property set to Password had its Text property set to password123 and its ID property set to TextBox2. Now, if the Text property were expressed in the resulting HTML markup, the TextBox Web control would produce the following HTML markup when rendered:

```
<input name="TextBox2" type="text" value="password123" id="TextBox2" />
```

Now imagine that a user visits a Web page is prompted for a username and a password, and imagine that once the correct username and password are entered, the ASP.NET Web page displays some information specific to the user account in a Label Web control on the same Web page. If the user gets up from the computer to get a quick drink of water, an unscrupulous coworker could view the HTML received by the Web browser. If the Text property of the password textbox were expressed in the rendered HTML, the HTML received by the browser, which our nefarious coworker is viewing, would contain the following HTML markup:

```
<input name="TextBox2" type="text" value="password123" id="TextBox2" />
```

(Assuming password123 was the person's password.)

At this point the coworker could learn the user's password. To help prevent this, Text properties for a TextBox Web control whose TextMode property is set to Password are not displayed.

Once a month or so, a person will ask the following question on one of the ASP.NET newsgroups: "Why is it that when I set a password TextBox Web control's Text property, it does not appear when I visit the ASP.NET Web page through a browser?" Now you can answer this type of question!

Examining the TextBox Web Control's Properties

So far in this hour, we have looked at one property in particular—the TextMode property, which is used to specify whether the TextBox Web control should be rendered as a standard textbox, a multiline textbox, or a password textbox. In addition to this property, there are a number of other TextBox Web control properties that we will examine for the remainder of this hour.

Specifying the Length of a Textbox

There may be times when you need to use the TextBox Web control to collect information from a user, such as age or the two-letter home state abbreviation. In such cases the user's input will be only a few characters long. However, as you can see with the age textbox in Figure 10.5, the textbox displayed in the Web browser is much larger than it has to be for such cases.

Fortunately, you can specify how many columns wide the textbox should be by setting the TextBox Web control's Columns property. To demonstrate this property, open the

ASP.NET Web page `TextBoxPractice.aspx`. Recall that this is the ASP.NET Web page we created in the first example in this hour (see Figure 10.5).

Now let's adjust the age TextBox Web control's `Columns` property so that the textbox into which the user enters his or her age is more appropriately sized. To accomplish this, click the age TextBox Web control so that its properties are loaded in the Properties pane. Then set this TextBox's `Columns` property to a value of 3.

Once you set the `Columns` property to 3, the textbox in the designer will shrink from its default width to a width of three columns. Refer to Figure 10.11 for a screenshot of the Web Matrix Project designer after this property has been set.

FIGURE 10.11

The age textbox is three columns wide.

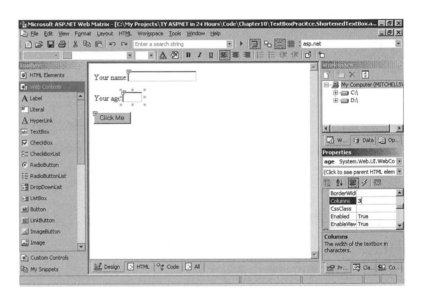

This shorter textbox is more appropriate for this situation than the longer one displayed in Figure 10.5.

Be sure to have your TextBox Web controls properly sized for the input you are expecting the user to enter. Properly sized textboxes help ensure that the user enters the data in the correct format. For example, if you want users to enter a *short* description about themselves, they will be more apt to enter shorter descriptions if you provide them with only a single-line textbox than if you were to provide a multiline textbox.

Limiting the Number of Characters a User Can Enter into a Textbox

Adjusting the size of the textbox by setting the TextBox Web control's Columns property does not regulate how much text the user can enter. Even if you create a TextBox Web control three columns wide, the user can still enter hundreds of characters of text.

There are times, however, when you may want to limit the amount of text a user may enter into a particular textbox. For example, sites like eBay allow only 80 characters to be entered when providing feedback about another buyer or seller.

Web sites typically limit the number of characters that can be entered into a textbox for two reasons. First, and most importantly, it is usually easier to format data for display at a later time by limiting the number of characters that can be supplied by the user. For example, the feedback entered by a user at eBay about a buyer or a seller is viewable by other eBay users in a feedback summary page. This summary page is clean and concise because no one user can enter more than 80 characters of feedback at a time. Due to this restriction in feedback input, the feedback summary page can be formatted so that it doesn't contain any lengthy blocks of feedback.

Second, sites like eBay use databases to store the information entered by their users. When setting up a database, the maximum number of characters for text fields must be specified in advance. Therefore, this feedback limit is in place because of the limit imposed by those who designed eBay's database tables. (We'll be examining how to create and use databases later in this book, starting with Hour 13, "An Introduction to Databases.")

To set a limit to the number of characters that can be entered into a TextBox Web control, set the MaxLength property accordingly. In our TextBoxPracitce.aspx example, we may wish to limit the age textbox to a maximum of three characters (because it would be impossible for a visitor to have an age greater than 999).

To do so, click the age TextBox Web control and set its MaxLength property to 3. Note that this change will not have any visual effect on the designer. Once you have made this change, take a moment to view the TextBoxPractice.aspx ASP.NET Web page through a browser. Try to type more than three characters into the age textbox—you can't!

While you might think that a MaxLength value of 0 would not permit the user to enter information into the textbox at all, it means quite the opposite. A MaxLength value of 0 means that there are no restrictions on the amount of information the user can enter into the textbox.

Advanced users can circumvent the textbox restrictions imposed by the MaxLength property. Therefore, the MaxLength property does not guarantee that the user's supplied value will indeed be less than the MaxLength setting. In Hour 12, "Validating User Input with Validation Controls," we will see how to ensure that a user has entered no more than a specified number of characters into a particular textbox.

Aesthetic Properties—Changing the Textbox's Font and Color

The Label Web control has a number of aesthetic properties, such as BackColor, ForeColor, Font, and so on. In Hour 8 we examined these various properties, how to specify them, and the visual effect they had on the text displayed by the Label Web control. The exact same aesthetic properties as the Label Web control, the TextBox Web control properties are summarized in Table 10.1.

TABLE 10.1 The Aesthetic Properties of the TextBox Web Control

Property	Description
BackColor	Specifies the background color of the textbox
BorderColor	Specifies the color of the textbox's border
BorderStyle	Specifies the style of the textbox's border
BorderWidth	Specifies the width of the textbox's border
Font	Specifies the font properties for the text entered by the user into the textbox; recall that the Font property has a number of subproperties, such as Name, Size, and Bold.
ForeColor	The color of the text entered into the textbox by the user

Let's create a new ASP.NET Web page called PrettyTextBox.aspx, in which we'll create a number of TextBox Web controls to determine the effects of various aesthetic properties. Once you create the ASP.NET Web page, add two TextBox Web controls to the designer by dragging and dropping them from the Toolbox.

Now let's set some aesthetic properties for these two TextBox Web controls. Let's first specify a BackColor property for the first TextBox. Recall that when you are selecting a color property, the Web Matrix Project provides three tabs: Custom, Web, and System.

Click the Web tab and set its BackColor property to Linen. Next choose the BorderColor property, click the Web tab, and select the color Maroon. Choose the Dashed option from the BorderStyle property and, finally, enter a value of 5px for the BorderWidth property.

For the second TextBox Web control, set the Font property's Bold subproperty to True, the Name subproperty to Comic Sans MS, and the Size subproperty to Large. Then, for the ForeColor property, select the Web tab and choose the color Red.

Figure 10.12 is a screenshot of the Web Matrix Project designer after these properties have been set. (Some of the color differences may not be noticeable in the figure.)

FIGURE 10.12

Both TextBox Web controls have had a number of their aesthetic properties set.

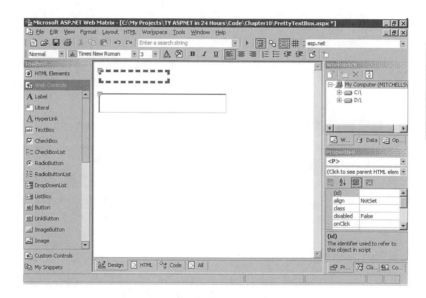

Take a moment to view the PrettyTextBox.aspx ASP.NET Web page through Internet Explorer. When viewing the page, type some text into the second textbox and note that it is red, large, and in the Comic Sans MS font. Figure 10.13 is a screenshot of the PrettyTextBox.aspx ASP.NET Web page when viewed through Internet Explorer.

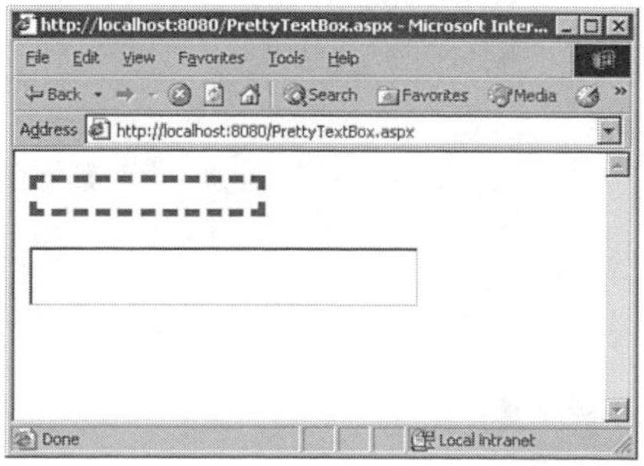

FIGURE 10.13

The PrettyTextBox.aspx ASP.NET Web page as viewed through Internet Explorer.

Unfortunately, the aesthetic properties of the TextBox Web control are reflected only in uplevel browsers (Internet Explorer 4.0 and up). That means that if you view the PrettyTextBox.aspx ASP.NET Web page using Netscape, Opera, Mozilla, or any other non-IE Web browser, you will be shown two plain textboxes, as shown in Figure 10.14.

FIGURE 10.14

The PrettyTextBox.aspx *ASP.NET Web page as viewed via Mozilla.*

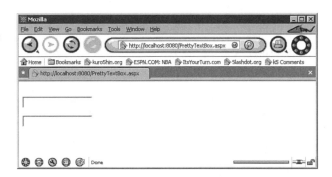

Summary

In this hour we looked at one of the most commonly used Web controls for collecting user input: the TextBox Web control. The TextBox Web control can create three types of textboxes: a single-line textbox, a multiline textbox, and a password textbox. To specify what kind of textbox should be rendered by the TextBox Web control, the TextMode property is used.

In addition to the TextMode property, the TextBox Web control contains a number of other properties. The Columns property, for example, specifies how wide the textbox is. The MaxLength property can indicate the maximum number of characters a user is allowed to enter into a textbox.

Like the Label Web control, the TextBox Web control also contains a number of aesthetic properties, such as BackColor, ForeColor, Font, and so on. However, these properties are displayed only in uplevel browsers, meaning that users visiting your Web page using a Web browser other than Internet Explorer will see only vanilla textboxes. For example, Figure 10.13 shows two TextBox Web controls that have various aesthetic properties when viewed through Internet Explorer 6.0; Figure 10.14 shows this same ASP.NET Web page when viewed through Mozilla.

In addition to the TextBox Web control, there are a number of other Web controls that can be used to collect user input, which is our topic for the next hour, "Collecting Input by Using Drop-down Lists, Radio Buttons, and Checkboxes."

Q&A

Q **I want to create a textbox that allows the user to enter only a certain type of input, such as numbers. How can I do this?**

A In the BMI calculator example we examined in the previous hour, the user was prompted for weight and height. Clearly, these inputs must be numeric ones. As we saw, if the user enters some input like "Fred" as weight, it breaks the BMI calculator.

Therefore, you might think that an ideal solution would be to create a textbox into which the user can enter numbers *only*. Such *masked textboxes*, as they are called, are rarely, if ever, used on Web pages for a number of reasons.

First, while a masked textbox would prevent the user from entering something like "Fred" as weight, it would not prevent the user from entering nothing into the weight textbox. Entering nothing will also break the BMI calculator.

Second, creating masked textboxes requires a bit of tricky client-side JavaScript programming. Users that have JavaScript disabled in their browsers would therefore be able to enter any values into a masked textbox.

Finally, and perhaps most importantly, users are not accustomed to masked textboxes on Web pages. Therefore, the inclusion of masked textboxes would likely irritate users and lead them to conclude that your Web site was fundamentally different from the plethora of other Web sites they're used to.

As we will see in Hour 12, it is quite easy to ensure that a user's textbox input conforms to a certain format. This is accomplished through validation Web controls, which we'll discuss in detail then.

Q **Is there any way to force an ASP.NET Web page to render its Web controls' aesthetic properties as if an uplevel browser were visiting even if the page is being visited by a downlevel browser?**

A Recall that the aesthetic properties of Web controls are rendered differently depending on whether the ASP.NET Web page is visited by an uplevel or downlevel browser. However, there may be times that you want your Web controls to render their aesthetic attributes as if the page were being visited by an uplevel browser even if it is being visited by a downlevel browser.

To accomplish this, you need to add the following to the @Page directive:

```
ClientTarget="Uplevel"
```

The @Page directive can be found by clicking the All tab. The first line at the top of the page should read

```
<% @Page Language="VB" %>
```

To have all Web controls render as if the page were being visited by an uplevel browser, change this line to

```
<% @Page Language="VB" ClientTarget="Uplevel" %>
```

Note that if you want all Web controls to render as if they were being visited by a downlevel browser, use

```
ClientTarget="Downlevel"
```

Workshop

Quiz

1. What are the possible values of the TextBox Web control's `TextMode` property?
2. If you wanted to create a multiline textbox, with 40 columns and 5 rows, that limited user input to 100 characters, what TextBox Web control properties would you need to set?
3. True or False: Aesthetic settings for textboxes will display the same in all Web browsers.
4. What TextBox Web control property contains the text that was entered by the user?
5. What Web control that we've examined in previous hours shares a number of properties with the TextBox Web control?
6. If you set the `Text` property of a TextBox Web control whose `TextMode` is set to `Password`, no text will appear in the textbox when viewed through a Web browser. Why is this the case?

Answers

1. The TextBox Web control supports three possible values for its `TextMode` property. These are: `MultiLine`, `Password`, and `SingleLine`. The default property value is `SingleLine`.
2. To create such a textbox, you would need to set the TextBox Web control's `TextMode` property to `MultiLine`, its `Columns` property to 40, its `Rows` property to 5, and its `MaxLength` property to 100.
3. False. ASP.NET Web controls are rendered differently depending on whether the page is visited by an uplevel or a downlevel browser.
4. The `Text` property.
5. The Label Web control shares a number of properties with the TextBox Web control. Both have a `Text` property, the same set of aesthetic properties, and the `ID` property, among others. In fact, as we'll see throughout the remainder of the book, *all* Web controls share a base set of properties.

6. Password textboxes cannot have their `Text` property programmatically set, nor do they continue their values across postbacks. This is because doing so would serve as a security risk, since a nefarious onlooker could simply examine the HTML received by the browser to determine the user's password.

Exercises

1. For this exercise we'll create an ASP.NET Web page that prompts the user for two integers and then computes and displays the integers' greatest common divisor. (The greatest common divisor of two integers a and b, commonly denoted `gcd(a,b)`, is the largest number that divides both a and b without a remainder. For example, `gcd(49, 21)` is 7.)

Since the user will need to provide two integers, you'll need two TextBox Web controls. Set the `ID` property of the first Web control to a and the second to b. You'll also need to add a Button Web control as well as a Label Web control. Set the `ID` property of the label Web control to `lblResults`.

As with the BMI calculator example from the previous hour, you'll need to create an event handler for the Button Web control's `Click` event. This event handler will need to compute the greatest common divisor of the values entered into the a and b TextBox Web controls.

The greatest common divisor of two integers can be quickly computed using the Euclidean algorithm. If you are not familiar with the details of this algorithm, don't worry—the needed source code is presented below:

```
'Assign the maximum of a and b to x and the minimum to y
If a.Text < b.Text then
  x = b.Text
  y = a.Text
Else
  x = a.Text
  y = b.Text
End If

'Compute the remainder of x / y
z = x mod y
While z <> 0
  x = y
  y = z

  z = x mod y
End While

gcd = y
```

For more information on the Euclidean Algorithm, check out `http://www.wikipedia.org/wiki/Euclidean_algorithm`.

10

2. Given two integers a and b, their least common multiple, commonly denoted `lcm(a,b)`, is the smallest integer that is a multiple of both a and b. For example, the least common multiple of 6 and 4 is 12, since 12 is both a multiple of 6 (6 times 2) and 4 (4 times 3) and is the smallest such multiple. For this exercise create an ASP.NET Web page that accepts two integer inputs from the user and computes the least common multiple.

Fortunately, computing the least common multiple of two numbers is quite simple once you compute the greatest common divisor of the two numbers. Specifically,

`lcm(a,b) = (a * b) / gcd(a,b)`

Therefore, for this exercise you should create a function named `GCD` that takes in two integer inputs and returns an integer value. You can cut and paste the greatest common divisor code that you entered for Exercise 1.

As with the previous Exercise, be sure to include two TextBox Web controls, a Button Web control, and a Label Web control. Through the `GCD()` function the Button Web control's `Click` event handler should compute the least common multiple of the two integers entered by the user.

HOUR 11

Collecting Input by Using Drop-down Lists, Radio Buttons, and Checkboxes

In the previous hour we saw how to collect user information through the TextBox Web control. There are often times, though, when the textbox is not the most suitable means for collecting a particular piece of input. For example, imagine that you wanted to create a Web page where the user answered a bunch of yes/no questions. Would it make sense to use a TextBox Web control for these yes/no questions?

Fortunately, there are alternative Web controls for collecting user input, such as the DropDownList Web control, the RadioButton Web control, and the CheckBox Web control. We will examine these three Web controls in this hour.

Specifically, in this hour we will discuss

- Ideal times for using Web controls other than the TextBox Web control
- Adding DropDownList Web controls to an ASP.NET Web page
- Programmatically accessing a selected value and text from a DropDownList Web control
- Using the RadioButton Web control
- Grouping related RadioButton Web controls
- Using the CheckBox Web control
- Programmatically determining whether a particular CheckBox Web control is checked or not

Examining the Different Types of User Input Classifications

So far we have worked with only one Web control that is used to gather user input, the TextBox Web control. As we have seen in the examples thus far in the book, the TextBox Web control presents users with a textbox into which they can type their input. For example, in the monthly mortgage cost calculator in Hour 3, "Creating Our First ASP.NET Web Page," the user inputted the amount, duration, and interest rate of a mortgage to determine its monthly cost. In the BMI Calculator in Hour 9, "Web Form Basics," the user supplied height and weight in textboxes. Additionally, there was a plethora of TextBox Web control examples in the previous hour, "Using Textboxes to Collect Input."

Textboxes, however, are not the only means by which user input can be collected. As we will see in this hour, other input collection Web controls include the DropDownList Web control, the CheckBox Web control, and the RadioButton Web control. The DropDownList Web control presents the user with a list of options, from which one may be chosen; the CheckBox Web control presents the user with a checkbox; and the RadioButton Web control presents the user with a radio button.

Given that there are a number of Web controls designed to collect user input, you may be wondering when you should use a TextBox Web control versus when you should use an alternative Web control. The type of Web control used should be determined by the kind of input that is being collected.

The input collected from a user can be classified into various types. The following classifications group input in terms of their restrictiveness, from the most restrictive form of input to the least:

1. Yes/No input
2. Input selected from a finite list of acceptable choices
3. General text input

The first classification, Yes/No input, is input that can be inputted in only one of two ways. For example, an online survey may ask you for your gender, which can obviously be only one of two values, male or female.

A slightly more general input classification is input selected from a list of acceptable choices. If you live in the United States and are filling out your address on an online form, the state you live in can be selected from a finite list of the 50 states. Another example of input that falls into this category is a list of shipping options that an e-commerce site might provide for you to select from.

General text input is the most lax of the three categories. Input that falls into this category includes filling in your name and address on an online form or entering your message on an online message board site.

Using an Appropriate Web Control

When collecting user input, you must decide what Web control to use. For example, if you are asking the user to specify gender, you could use a TextBox Web control, asking each person to type in whether he or she is male or female. But a less error-prone approach would be to use a DropDownList Web control with two options: Male or Female.

Other Yes/No inputs work well with checkboxes. For example, there are many Web sites that require you to create an account to access certain portions of the site. When filling in the account information, you will typically find a checkbox that says something like, "Send me the site newsletter" or "Keep me abreast of new products from your company."

This same account creation page may prompt the user to specify how he had learned about the Web site. Rather than requiring the user to type in an explanation, many Web sites will provide a drop-down list that contains a number of potential choices, such as "Read about it in print," or "Heard about it from a friend," and so on.

Input that falls into the general text input category, such as a person's name or mailing address, must be entered via TextBox Web controls.

11

The point of this discussion is to highlight that there are different classes of user input and that different Web controls work best with different classes of user input. Keep this in mind when learning about the DropDownList, CheckBox, and RadioButton Web controls in this hour. Table 11.1 summarizes the classifications of user input and what types of Web controls work best.

TABLE 11.1   Choose an Appropriate Web Control Based on the Data Being Collected

Class of User Input	Description	Web Control(s) to Use
Yes/No	The user can select only one of two potential values.	Drop-down list, checkbox, or two radio buttons
One selection from a list of acceptable answers	The user must select one option from a finite list of acceptable options.	Drop-down list or a series of radio buttons
General text	The user can provide text input in any form.	Textbox

Examining the DropDownList Web Control

There are certain forms of input in which the user must select precisely one option from a list of suitable choices. For example, a software company might want to create a support site where users can find answers to common questions about the company's various software products. When looking for answers to product questions, it would be helpful if, along with searching for certain keywords, the user could select the particular software product causing trouble.

In such a scenario, a suitable Web control for collecting this bit of input would be a DropDownList Web control. The DropDownList Web control creates a drop-down list of one to many options from which the user can choose. Figure 11.1 shows an example of a drop-down list in an HTML Web page.

FIGURE 11.1

With a drop-down list, the user can select one option from a list of options.

Adding Options to the DropDownList Web Control

When using the DropDownList Web control you must specify the drop-down list's various *list items*. The list items are the legal choices that the user can select from. Each individual option in the list of choices is a list item.

There are two ways to specify a DropDownList Web control's list items. The first method, which we'll be examining in this hour, is to enter the list items by typing them in, one after another. This approach works well if you know in advance what list items the user should be presented with. For example, if you are using a DropDownList Web control to present the user with a list of the 50 states in the U.S., this method is sufficient.

Imagine, however, that you wanted to populate the choices shown in the DropDownList Web control based on some external input. An online banking Web site, for example, might allow customers to have more than one account, such as a savings account, a checking account, a money market account, and so on. Some customers may have just a checking account, while others may have checking and savings accounts.

When the user first logs on to the Web site, you might want to have the user select which customer accounts (assuming the individual has multiple accounts) to start working with. These options could be presented in a DropDownList Web control. However, the accounts shown depend upon what accounts the customer has opened with the bank. So, the list items in the DropDownList Web control will depend on the user's accounts with the bank. Therefore, the list items shown in the DropDownList Web control are dependent upon external input—namely, the accounts that the user has opened with the bank.

In order to handle situations like this, you can store the list items in a database. Then, when using the DropDownList Web control, you can indicate that the list items to be displayed in the drop-down list should come from the database. We'll examine this mode of specifying list items in Hour 17, "Working with Data-Bound DropDownList, RadioButton, and CheckBox Web Controls."

Adding a DropDownList Web Control to an ASP.NET Web Page

To demonstrate using a DropDownList Web control and adding list items to it, let's create a new ASP.NET Web page named DropDownList.aspx. For this page start by turning on the glyphs by going to the View menu and selecting the Glyphs option. Next, within the Web form, type in the text **What is your favorite ice cream flavor?** After this text drag and drop a DropDownList Web control from the Toolbox.

11

> Be certain that you add a DropDownList Web control to the ASP.NET Web
> page, not a ListBox Web control. The DropDownList Web control allows the
> user to select precisely one list item from a list of acceptable ones. The
> ListBox Web control, on the other hand, allows the user to select zero or
> more list items. (We will not be covering the ListBox Web control in this
> book; for more information on this Web control, check out
> http://www.aspalliance.com/das/tutorial/listbox.aspx.)

Next add a Button Web control beneath the DropDownList Web control. Once you have
typed in the text prior to the DropDownList Web control and have added both the
DropDownList and Button Web controls, your screen should look similar to the screenshot
in Figure 11.2.

FIGURE **11.2**

*A DropDownList Web
control and Button
Web control have been
added to the designer.*

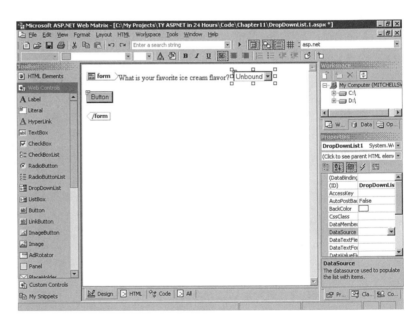

At this point we've yet to add any list items to the DropDownList Web control. If you
viewed the ASP.NET Web page through a browser now, you would be presented with an
empty drop-down list, as shown in Figure 11.3.

Figure 11.3

The drop-down list is empty—it contains no items for the user to choose from.

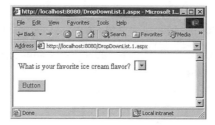

The Items property of the DropDownList Web control contains the list items that appear in the DropDownList Web control. So, to add list items to the DropDownList Web control, we will need to edit this property. Start by clicking the DropDownList Web control so that its properties are loaded in the Properties pane. Next scroll down to the Items property. You should see that the property value currently reads (Collection). If you click this property value, a button with an ellipsis (three periods) will appear to the right of (Collection) (see Figure 11.4).

Figure 11.4

Clicking the Items property reveals a button with an ellipsis.

Go ahead and click this button; upon doing so, a ListItem Collection Editor dialog box will appear. This dialog box, shown in Figure 11.5, allows you to add and remove list items from the DropDownList Web control.

Figure 11.5

The ListItem Collection Editor dialog is used to manage the options for a DropDownList Web control.

Since users will be using our Web page to specify their favorite ice cream flavors, let's add a few ice cream flavors as list items. To add a new list item, click the Add button.

Once you click the Add button, a new entry is added to the left-hand textbox in the ListItem Collection Editor dialog box. On the right-hand side, the properties of the newly added list item are displayed. As Figure 11.6 shows, list items have three properties: Selected, Text, and Value.

FIGURE 11.6

*Once you have added
a new list item, you
can specify its
properties.*

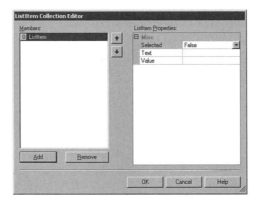

The first property, Selected, expects a Boolean value (either True or False) and indicates whether the list item is the item selected by default when the Web page loads. To elaborate, realize that there may be many list items in a drop-down list, and because only one item is shown at a time, the Selected property specifies what list item is selected when the Web page is first loaded. That is, imagine that the DropDownList Web control has the following list items in this order: Vanilla, Chocolate, and Strawberry. When visiting this ASP.NET Web page through a browser, the drop-down list will, by default, show the first option—Vanilla. However, what if you want the Strawberry option to be the selected item by default? One option is simply to make it the first list item. Another option is to set its Selected property to True.

The Text and Value properties expect string values. The Text property is the text that is displayed to the user in the drop-down list. For our flavors of ice cream, we'd want the Text property to be Vanilla for the first list item, Chocolate for the second, and Strawberry for the third. The Value property, on the other hand, is not seen by the user. It serves as a means to pass along, with each list item, additional information that you may not want the user to see.

The Value property is typically used when displaying list items from a database. In this hour we won't examine the Value property further; we will be setting only the Text property.

Now that you understand the roles of the three list item properties, go ahead and set the Text property for the list item just added to **Vanilla**. Next add another list item and set its Text property to **Chocolate**. Finally, add a third list item and set its Text property to **Strawberry**.

For the three list items added, there is no need to set the Value properties. If you don't specify a Value property for a list item, the ListItem Collection Editor will automatically set the Value property to the same value as the Text property.

After you have added the three list items, the ListItem Collection Editor should look similar to Figure 11.7.

FIGURE 11.7

Three list items have been added.

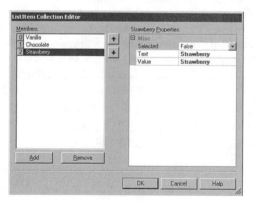

11

Note that you can rearrange the order of the list items through the ListItem Collection Editor. To do so, click the list item in the left-hand textbox whose position you wish to alter. Then click the up and down arrows in the middle of the ListItem Collection Editor dialog box to move that particular list item up or down with respect to the other list items.

Finally, click OK on the ListItem Collection Editor dialog box. Note that the DropDownList Web control in the designer has changed such that it shows the word Vanilla as its selected list item.

Now let's take a moment to check out our progress by visiting `DropDownList.aspx` through a Web browser. Figure 11.8 shows a screenshot of this ASP.NET Web page when viewed through a browser. Note that now listed are all three ice cream flavors, which weren't present before we added the three list items via the ListItem Collection Editor. (Refer back to Figure 11.3 to see the output prior to adding list items.)

FIGURE 11.8

The Web page presents the user with the three ice cream flavor options.

When visiting the `DropDownList.aspx` Web page, if you choose a list item from the drop-down list (say the Strawberry list item) and then submit the form by clicking the button, the ASP.NET Web page will be posted back, and the Strawberry item will remain the selected one. This indicates that the DropDownList Web control continues the selected item across postbacks, just like the TextBox Web control continues its `Text` property value across postbacks.

In order to have the ASP.NET Web page take some action when the form is submitted, we need to provide source code in the ASP.NET page's source code portion. Specifically, we must add some source code to the Button Web control's `Click` event handler.

For the time being, let's just have the Web page output equal the option selected by the user, placing the output in a Label Web control. To facilitate this, start by adding a Label Web control to the `DropDownList.aspx` Web page and then specify the Label Web control's `ID` property as `results`. Also, clear out the `Text` property.

Let's also take a moment to specify some properties for our other Web controls. Set the Button Web control's `ID` property to `btnSubmit` and its `Text` property to `Click Me`. Then set the DropDownList Web control's `ID` property to `flavors`.

Next double-click the Button Web control. This will, as you know, add an event handler for the Button's `Click` event. In this event handler we need to provide code that will set the `results` Label Web control's `Text` property to some message that indicates what option the user just selected. This can be accomplished with the following code:

```
Sub btnSubmit_Click(sender As Object, e As EventArgs)
  results.Text = "You like " & flavors.SelectedItem.Text
End Sub
```

As this source code illustrates, the DropDownList Web control's selected list item can be accessed using

DropDownListID.SelectedItem

Recall that each list item has three properties: `Selected`, `Text`, and `Value`. So, to retrieve the `Text` property, we use

DropDownListID.SelectedItem.Text

If we wanted to get the `Value` property, we could use

DropDownListID.SelectedItem.Value

Once you have added the needed source code to the Button Web control's `Click` event handler, go ahead and view the ASP.NET Web page through a browser. When the page loads up, select a particular flavor and click the "Click Me" button. This will cause the form to be posted back. Upon the ASP.NET Web page's reloading, you should see the message "You like *flavor*" (where *"flavor"* is the ice cream flavor you selected from the drop-down list). Figure 11.9 contains a screenshot of `DropDownList.aspx` after the Strawberry flavor has been selected and the "Click Me" button has been clicked.

11

FIGURE 11.9
The Web page has responded to the user's ice cream flavor selection.

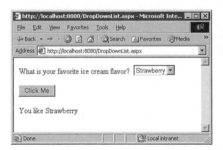

The DropDownList Web Control's Aesthetic Properties

Along with the `Items` property, the DropDownList Web control has a number of aesthetic properties. These aesthetic properties are the same as the aesthetic properties for the Label and TextBox Web controls and are listed in Table 11.2 for reference. These aesthetic properties are specified in the same manner as with the Label and TextBox Web controls, and they have the same limitations in downlevel browsers.

TABLE 11.2   The Aesthetic Properties of the DropDownList Web Control

Property	Description
BackColor	Specifies the background color of the drop-down list
Font	Specifies the font properties for the text entered by the user into the drop-down list; recall that the Font property has a number of subproperties, such as Name, Size, and Bold.
ForeColor	The color of the text in the drop-down list

Selecting One Option from a List of Suitable Choices with RadioButton Web Controls

Another means of collecting user input are radio buttons, which, like drop-down lists, are suited for choosing one option from a list of valid options. You have probably seen and used radio buttons on Web pages before. Radio buttons are small circles that, when selected, have a black circle displayed within them. See Figure 11.10.

FIGURE 11.10

Radio buttons allow the user to select one option from a list of options.

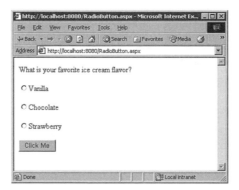

Radio buttons can be grouped into a series of related radio buttons. Given a related group of radio buttons, only one of the radio buttons from the group can be selected at a time. This means that if there are three related radio buttons and the first one is selected, neither the second nor the third can be selected; if the second is selected, neither the first nor the third one can be selected; and so on. Another way to put it is that related radio buttons are *mutually exclusive*.

In order to create a radio button in an ASP.NET Web page, we use the RadioButton Web control. The RadioButton Web control, when rendered, produces the HTML markup for creating a single radio button. Therefore, if we want the user to select one option from a list of, say, three, we must use three RadioButton Web controls.

Let's create a new ASP.NET Web page named `RadioButton.aspx` and examine how to use the RadioButton Web control. The `RadioButton.aspx` Web page will be similar in functionality to the `DropDownList.aspx` Web page, inasmuch as the user will be asked to pick the favorite of three ice cream flavors.

Once you create the new ASP.NET Web page, go ahead and type into the designer the text **What is your favorite ice cream flavor?** Beneath this text drag and drop a RadioButton Web control onto the designer. A radio button and the RadioButton Web control's `ID` property (in brackets) will be displayed in the designer.

> In the Toolbox you might have noticed that beneath the RadioButton Web control, there is a RadioButtonList Web control. The RadioButtonList Web control is used when the options for the radio buttons are stored in a database. We'll examine using the RadioButtonList Web control in Hour 17.

Figure 11.11 shows a screenshot of the designer after the first RadioButton Web control has been added.

FIGURE 11.11

A RadioButton Web control has been added to `RadioButton.aspx`.

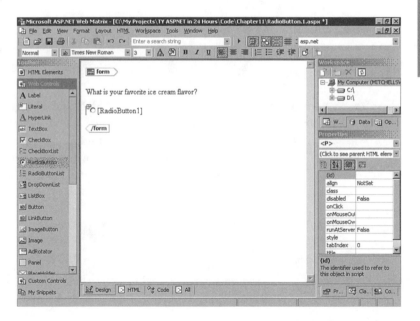

Now change the `ID` property of the just-added RadioButton Web control from the default `RadioButton1` to **vanilla**. Next add two more RadioButton Web controls, each beneath the previous, and set their `ID` properties to **chocolate** and **strawberry**, respectively.

Finally, add a Button Web control after all three RadioButton Web controls. Set the Button Web control's ID property to btnSubmit and its Text property to **Click Me**.

Figure 11.12 shows a screenshot of the Web Matrix Project designer after these two additional RadioButton Web controls and the Button Web control have been added.

FIGURE 11.12

The RadioButton.aspx *page now contains three RadioButton Web controls and a Button Web control.*

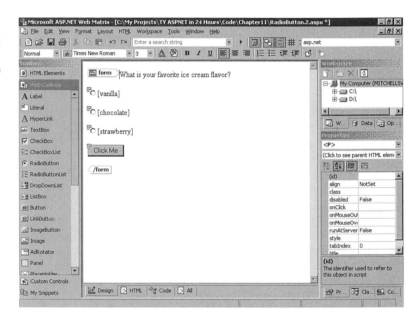

Take a moment to view the RadioButton.aspx ASP.NET Web page through a browser and take note of two things. First, there are only three radio buttons but no text explaining what each radio button represents. Second, you can select more than one radio button. (To see this, click the first radio button and then click the second—*both* radio buttons will be selected.) Figure 11.13 shows a screenshot of the RadioButton.aspx Web page when viewed through a browser, highlighting these two issues.

FIGURE 11.13

There is no text explaining what each radio button represents, and multiple radio buttons can be selected.

The `Text` and `GroupName` Properties

Notice that for each RadioButton Web control, you must add some text explaining what choice the resulting radio button represents. To accomplish this, simply set the RadioButton Web control's `Text` property to the appropriate text. For the `RadioButton.aspx` Web page, set the first RadioButton Web control's `Text` property to **Vanilla**, the second's to **Chocolate**, and the third's to **Strawberry**. Once you do this, your screen should look similar to the screenshot in Figure 11.14.

FIGURE 11.14

Text has been added next to each RadioButton Web control.

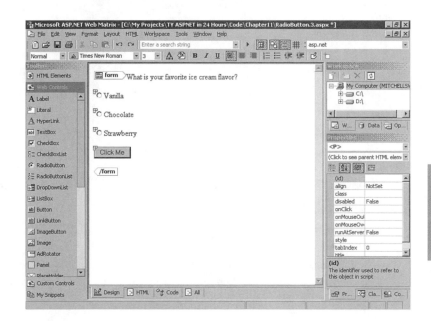

Now we need to be able to group the three RadioButton Web controls so that the user can select only one option from the three. The RadioButton Web control contains a string property named `GroupName`. Those RadioButton Web controls on a Web page that have the same value for their `GroupName` properties are considered to be related. Therefore, in order to make our three RadioButton Web controls relate (so that the user can select only one flavor of the three), set the `GroupName` property for the three RadioButton Web controls to the value `flavors`.

What value you set the `GroupName` property to doesn't matter; what is important is that all related RadioButton Web controls have the same `GroupName` value. That is, we could have set the `GroupName` property of all three RadioButton Web controls to `ScottMitchell`, and the results—the user now being able to select only one of the three radio buttons—would be the same.

Let's view the `RadioButton.aspx` Web page through a browser now that we've specified the `Text` and `GroupName` properties for each of the three RadioButton Web controls. Figure 11.15 shows a screenshot of the Web page when visited through a Web browser. Note that the three radio buttons are mutually exclusive, only one radio button being able to be selected at a time.

FIGURE 11.15

The radio buttons now have text explaining what they represent.

Determining What RadioButton Web Control Was Selected

Allowing the user to select a radio button from a list of radio button options is only half of the battle in collecting user input. The other half is determining what option the user selected in our ASP.NET Web page's source code portion. Each RadioButton Web control has a `Checked` property, which returns True if the RadioButton Web control's resulting radio button is selected, and False if not.

Therefore, to determine whether the `vanilla` RadioButton Web control was selected, we can use an `If` statement like this:

```
If vanilla.Checked then
  'The vanilla radio button was selected.
End If
```

Imagine that, by using a Label Web control, we simply wanted to display the flavor the user chose, much like we did with the DropDownList Web control example earlier in this hour. The first step would be to add a Label Web control after the Button Web control. Then clear out the Label Web control's `Text` property and set its `ID` property to `results`.

The code for setting the `results` Label Web control's `Text` property needs to appear in the Button Web control's `Click` event handler. To add the event handler, simply double-click the Button Web control in the designer. This, as you know by now, will take you to the Code tab, ready to enter the appropriate code. Into the Code tab, enter the code shown in Listing 11.1.

LISTING 11.1   The Code for the Button's Click Event Handler

```
1: Sub btnSubmit_Click(sender As Object, e As EventArgs)
2:   If vanilla.Checked then
3:     results.Text = "You like Vanilla"
4:   ElseIf chocolate.Checked Then
5:     results.Text = "You like Chocolate"
6:   ElseIf strawberry.Checked Then
7:     results.Text = "You like Strawberry"
8:   End If
9: End Sub
```

The code in Listing 11.1 starts by checking to see if the first RadioButton Web control, vanilla, was selected. If it was (that is, if vanilla.Checked is True), then the results Label Web control has its Text property set to You like Vanilla. If, however, vanilla was not selected, chocolate is checked. Similarly, if chocolate was the selected RadioButton Web control, then the results Label Web control's Text property is set to You like Chocolate. Finally, if the chocolate RadioButton Web control is not checked, strawberry is checked.

Realize that all three conditionals—vanilla.Checked, chocolate.Checked, and strawberry.Checked—may be False. This case occurs if the user does not select a radio button before clicking the "Click Me" button.

11

The Aesthetic Properties

The RadioButton Web control has the same aesthetic properties as the DropDownList, TextBox, and Label Web controls. As you might have already guessed, *all* Web controls contain these aesthetic properties.

Using the CheckBox Web Control

In the "User Input Classifications" section at the beginning of this hour, we examined three different classes of user input. The most restrictive class of user input was the Yes/No input class, which is Boolean input, which can be answered in only one of two ways, like Yes/No, Male/Female, and so on. The checkbox is an ideal candidate for collecting user input that falls into this category. The checkbox, as you've no doubt seen in use before, is a square box that can be checked or unchecked.

Checkboxes can also be used for presenting a list of options from which the user can select multiple choices. For example, in our previous two examples—DropDownList.aspx and RadioButton.aspx—a user can select only one of three flavors of ice cream as favorite. If we use three checkboxes, however, the user can select zero, one, two, or all three of the options.

The CheckBox Web control is used to add a checkbox to an ASP.NET Web page. Like the RadioButton Web control, a single CheckBox Web control displays a single checkbox, so to create a Web page with three checkboxes, for example, three CheckBox Web controls must be added.

Let's create an ASP.NET Web page to demonstrate using the CheckBox Web control. Start by creating a new ASP.NET Web page named CheckBox.aspx. This Web page will be similar to the previous two examples in that we will be prompting the users for their favorite ice cream flavors, except each user will be able to choose more than one flavor.

Once you have created the new ASP.NET Web page, type in the text **What are your favorite ice cream flavors?** Then drag and drop three CheckBox Web controls from the Toolbox onto the designer, one after another. Next place a Button Web control. Let's go ahead and also add a Label Web control after the button.

In the Toolbox you might have noticed that beneath the CheckBox Web control, there is a CheckBoxList Web control. The CheckBoxList Web control produces a list of checkboxes from data found in a database. We'll examine using the CheckBoxList in Hour 17.

Now let's set the properties for the Web controls we just added. First clear the Label Web control's Text property and set its ID to results. Next click the Button Web control and set its Text property to **Click Me** and its ID property to btnSubmit. For the three CheckBox Web controls, specify their Text and ID properties just like we did for the three RadioButton Web controls in our previous example: Set the first CheckBox Web control's Text property to **Vanilla** and its ID to **vanilla,** set the second CheckBox Web control's Text property to **Chocolate**, and so on. Once you have set these Web controls' properties, your screen should look similar to the screenshot in Figure 11.16.

FIGURE 11.16

The ASP.NET Web page has three CheckBox Web controls.

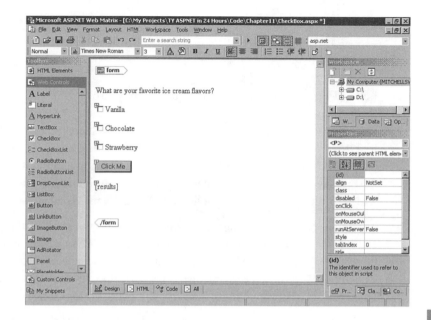

Take a moment to view the CheckBox.aspx Web page through a browser. In Figure 11.17 you can see that the page lists three checkboxes and that more than one of the three checkboxes can be checked.

FIGURE 11.17

The user can select zero to three ice cream flavors.

Determining Which Checkboxes Have Been Checked

In order to determine what CheckBox Web controls have been checked, we use the same syntax as with the RadioButton Web controls, which returns either a True or False value, namely,

```
CheckBoxID.Checked
```

So, to determine whether the `vanilla` checkbox is checked, the following code will suffice:

```
If vanilla.Checked then
  'The vanilla CheckBox is checked
End If
```

Let's add an event handler for the Button Web control's `Click` event, in which we'll add code that lists which checkboxes the user checked. You may be tempted to use the same code that was used in Listing 11.1 for the RadioButton Web controls example. However, if you look back over Listing 11.1, you will see that on lines 4 and 6, `ElseIf` statements are used, which means the conditional statements following them will be evaluated only if the previous conditional statement was False. To put it another way, line 4 in Listing 11.1 will be evaluated only if the condition on line 2—`vanilla.Checked`—is False.

Therefore, the code in Listing 11.1 will display only the name of the ice cream flavor that it first finds selected. This is not a problem for the RadioButton Web control example, because the user can select only one of the three radio buttons. However, with this CheckBox Web control example, we'll need to allow for multiple ice cream flavors to be listed in the Label Web control because multiple ice cream flavors may be selected.

Listing 11.2 contains the source code needed. Remember that to add a `Click` event handler, you first need to double-click the Button Web control in the designer.

LISTING 11.2   The User's Ice Cream Preferences Are Displayed

```
 1: Sub btnSubmit_Click(sender As Object, e As EventArgs)
 2:   'Clear out the value of the results Text property
 3:   results.Text = ""
 4:
 5:   If vanilla.Checked then
 6:     results.Text &= "You like Vanilla."
 7:   End If
 8:
 9:   If chocolate.Checked then
10:     results.Text &= "You like Chocolate."
11:   End If
12:
13:   If strawberry.Checked then
14:     results.Text &= "You like Strawberry."
15:   End If
16: End Sub
```

The first thing that happens in Listing 11.2 is that the `Text` value of the `results` Label Web control is cleared out (line 3). Next, on lines 5, 9, and 13, the `Checked` property is examined for each of the three CheckBox Web controls. If the checkbox is checked, an appropriate message is concatenated with the current value of the `results` Label Web control's `Text` property.

For example, on line 9 the `chocolate.Checked` property is examined. If this property returns True, this means that the Chocolate checkbox has been selected, and line 10 is executed. On line 10, the `results` Label Web control's `Text` property has its current value concatenated with the string `You like Chocolate.`

> Recall from Hour 5, "Visual Basic .NET Variables and Operators," that the &= operator takes the value of the variable on its left-hand side, concatenates it with the expression on the right-hand side, and then assigns the resulting concatenated value to the left-hand-side variable. Thus, the following two statements are equivalent:
>
> *Variable* = *Variable* & "Some string"
>
> and
>
> *Variable* &= "Some string"

The reason we concatenate the current value of the Label Web control's `Text` property with our message instead of just assigning our message to the Label Web control's `Text` property is because we do not want to overwrite the Label Web control's property. Why? Because if the Vanilla checkbox is checked, it will add the message `You like Vanilla.` to the Label Web control.

Figure 11.18 contains a screenshot of the `CheckBox.aspx` Web page when visited through a browser and after the user has selected multiple checkbox choices and submitted the form. Note that all of the user's checked choices are listed in the Label Web control at the bottom of the Web page.

FIGURE 11.18

The user can select multiple ice cream flavors as favorites.

11

Summary

In this hour we examined three Web controls commonly used to collect user input: the DropDownList, RadioButton, and CheckBox Web controls. These Web controls are typically used when the user's input is restricted to either a set of available options or just one of two options. For example, a DropDownList Web control can present all the time zones in the world, from which the user can choose only one. Another example is using a CheckBox Web control to ask a yes/no question, which is common in online surveys.

We saw that the DropDownList Web control has a number of list options out of which the user can select one. When adding a DropDownList Web control to an ASP.NET Web page, we need to explicitly specify those list items that should appear in the drop-down list. Fortunately, this is a simple task through the Web Matrix Project's ListItem Collection Editor dialog box (refer back to Figure 11.5). In the ASP.NET source code portion, the list item that was selected can be determined by the DropDownList Web control's SelectedItem property.

Like drop-down lists, radio buttons allow the user to select one from a series of options. A radio button is needed for each option, and a set of radio buttons must be made mutually exclusive with one another, so that the user can select only one at a time.

The RadioButton Web control creates a single radio button. To denote that a certain set of multiple RadioButton Web controls should be considered related (so that the user can select only one radio button from the set), the GroupName property is used. The RadioButton Web control's Checked property can determine whether a particular RadioButton Web control's corresponding radio button was selected by the user.

A list of checkboxes, unlike drop-down lists and radio buttons, permits the user to choose multiple options simultaneously. To create a checkbox, the CheckBox Web control is used. As with the RadioButton Web control, the CheckBox Web control has a Checked property, which indicates whether a checkbox was selected or not.

Now that we've examined the Web controls for collecting user input, we're ready to learn how to ensure that the input entered is valid, such as of a specified format. In the next hour we'll examine ASP.NET's validation Web controls, which are Web controls designed to validate input data.

Q&A

Q If I use a DropDownList or series of RadioButton Web controls to let the user choose one option from, say, 50 legal choices, does this mean I have to enter all 50 choices by hand?

A With what you know now, the answer is yes. In Hour 17 we will examine how to populate the DropDownList Web control with data from a database. Furthermore, we will see how to create a series of radio buttons from database data by using the RadioButtonList Web control.

Q **I have created a DropDownList with 10 list items on an ASP.NET Web page. Now I want to provide this exact same DropDownList Web control on a different ASP.NET Web page. Obviously, I can accomplish this by creating a new DropDownList Web control on the second page and reentering the 10 options by hand. Is there any easier or quicker way?**

A If you want to copy a DropDownList Web control and all of its list items from one ASP.NET Web page to another, start by loading up both ASP.NET Web pages. On the ASP.NET Web page that contains the DropDownList Web control, click the All tab and find the DropDownList Web control in the ASP.NET Web page's HTML section. This will contain Web control markup like

```
<asp:DropDownList id="DropDownListID" runat="server">
    <asp:ListItem Value="Value1">Text1</asp:ListItem>
    <asp:ListItem Value="Value2">Text2</asp:ListItem>
    ...
    <asp:ListItem Value="ValueN">TextN</asp:ListItem>
</asp:DropDownList>
```

Note that for each list item in the drop-down list, there will be an `<asp:ListItem>`. Copy all of the DropDownList Web control syntax and then paste it into the All tab portion of the ASP.NET Web page that you want to add this same drop-down list to. Using this technique, you will not have to reenter all of the DropDownList options by hand in the second page.

Workshop

Quiz

1. Imagine that you wanted to create an online multiple-choice quiz that presented the user with a question that had one correct answer. The user would be asked to choose from a list of five possible answers. What user input Web control would be best suited for this Web page?

2. Imagine that you wanted to have users specify the time zones they live in. What user input Web controls could be used for this task, and what ones could not be used? What user input Web control would be the *best* option?

3. True or False: The DropDownList Web control can be used to allow the user to select multiple items from a list of available options.

11

4. Imagine that you wanted to create a Web page where users could specify the countries they've visited from a list of 100 countries. Why would using a series of CheckBox Web controls make sense here?

5. For the example in Question 4, precisely how many CheckBox Web controls would you need to add to the ASP.NET Web page?

6. What CheckBox Web control property specifies whether a checkbox was checked?

7. What is the major difference between a series of RadioButton Web controls and a series of CheckBox Web controls?

8. If you wanted to add five RadioButton Web controls to an ASP.NET Web page such that the user could select only one of the five resulting radio buttons, what property of each of the radio buttons would you need to set?

Answers

1. Since the user can select precisely one option from a list of options, either a DropDownList Web control or a series of RadioButton Web controls would suffice. The best choice would likely be the latter, since virtually all existing online quizzes use radio buttons for the quiz-user interface.

2. This information could be provided via a textbox, a series of radio buttons, or a drop-down list. A series of checkboxes would not be suitable, since a user cannot live in multiple time zones. The best user input Web control for the job would likely be either a series of radio buttons or a drop-down list, because the user would be restricted to choosing one option from a list of possible options.

3. False. The DropDownList Web control allows the user to select only *one* item from a list of items.

4. A series of CheckBox Web controls would allow the user to select more than one option. Had we opted to use, say, RadioButton Web controls, the user would be able to select only *one* country from the list of 100.

5. A CheckBox Web control would need to be added for each option. Since there are 100 countries from which the user can select, there would need to be 100 CheckBox Web controls on the ASP.NET Web page.

6. The Checked property indicates whether a CheckBox Web control has been checked.

7. The RadioButton Web control is designed to allow the user to choose precisely one option from a list of available options. The CheckBox Web control, on the other hand, is designed so that the user can choose zero or more options. Therefore, a series of RadioButton Web controls would restrict the user to selecting just one

option from the array of options, while a series of CheckBox Web controls would allow the user the flexibility of choosing many of the available options.

8. Since all RadioButton Web controls that have the same value for their `GroupName` are considered grouped, and the user can select only *one* radio button from the group, each of the five RadioButton Web controls would need to have its `GroupName` property set to the same value as the other four.

Exercises

1. The book you have in your hands is my fifth book on ASP and ASP.NET. As a shameless plug for my other books, this exercise would like you to create an ASP.NET Web page that allows users to indicate what other books of mine they have read. Please create four CheckBox Web controls, each with its `Text` property set to the title of one of my four other books. In case you are not abreast of my other books, the four titles are (1) *Teach Yourself Active Server Pages 3.0 in 21 Days;* (2) *Designing Active Server Pages;* (3) *ASP.NET: Tips, Tutorials, and Code;* and (4) *ASP.NET Data Web Controls.*

   In addition to creating the four CheckBox Web controls, create a Button Web control and a Label Web control. In the Button Web control's event handler, count the number of books that the reader has read and emit an appropriate message. If I may so humbly suggest, if the user has read, say, 3 or more of my books, you might display the message "You are indeed a wonderful person!" If the user has yet to read any of my other books, you could emit a message like "It is absolutely imperative that you go to your nearest bookstore without delay and pick up one or more of Scott's books!"

2. For this Exercise create a short online quiz. Make sure the quiz has at least three questions and that each question has at least three options. Each question should have exactly one correct answer.

   After the questions there should be a Button Web control that, when clicked, will display the user's score. If you are interested in a more difficult additional challenge, list next to each *incorrect* answer the correct one.

11

Hour **12**

Validating User Input with Validation Controls

As we have examined in the previous hours, collecting user input via an ASP.NET Web page is a relatively easy task. Unfortunately, when collecting such input, there is no guarantee that the user has provided the desired input in an acceptable format. Imagine that you are asking the user to specify weight, much like we did with the BMI calculator a few hours ago. What should happen if, for weight, the user enters something like "Far too much"?

Ensuring that user input is in a proper format, a technique known as *input validation*, is the topic for this hour. If you have had experience with other dynamic Web page creation technologies, such as ASP, PHP, or JSP, you likely are more than familiar with input validation. Performing input validation in these older technologies was a real headache.

Fortunately, ASP.NET makes input validation a breeze with the help of *validation controls*, which are Web controls designed to do nothing else but perform input validation. We will examine how to use four validation controls in this hour: the RequiredFieldValidator, the CompareValidator, the RangeValidator, and the RegularExpressionValidator.

Specifically, in this hour we will examine

- The various classes of input validation
- How to use the RequiredFieldValidator to ensure that the user has provided input
- How to use the CompareValidator
- How to use the RangeValidator to ensure that the user's input falls between a range of values
- How to use the RegularExpressionValidator
- The aesthetic properties of the validation Web controls

Examining the Need for User Input Validation

In the past two hours, we've examined a number of ways to collect user input. In Hour 10, "Using Textboxes to Collect Input," we saw how to use the TextBox Web control to collect text input; in Hour 11, "Collecting Input by Using Drop-down Lists, Radio Buttons, and Checkboxes," we saw how to use DropDownList, RadioButton, and CheckBox Web controls to collect user input that was restricted to one or more items from a predefined list of items.

Typically, when collecting user input, we want the input to be in a certain format or conform to some set of guidelines. Input validation is the process of ensuring that the data entered by a user is in the proper format or meets certain constraints.

For example, imagine that you wanted to collect the following information from a user:

- Name
- Age
- Zip code

To collect this input, you would probably want to use three TextBox Web controls, one for each of the three inputs. When presented with a textbox, clearly, users can enter any value they choose, or they may enter no input at all. For example, when asked to input his age, the user could choose not to enter any value. On the other hand, the user may choose to enter "24." Instead of entering "24," the user may use an alternative representation for 24, like "twenty-four." The user might even enter something nonsensical, like "I am a Jisun."

More likely than not, we would want the age entered as a number, because a number is less ambiguous than a string. (In our example, 24 is unambiguous, because it's the only numerical way to specify the value 24; with text, however, 24 can be written as "twenty-four," "twenty four," "Twentyfour," "Twenty Four," and so on.) Furthermore, a number can be used in mathematical calculations, whereas a string like "twenty-four" cannot.

Even if we can ensure that a user will enter his age as a number, he can still enter bad input. For example, values like –3,456,354.14159, 250, and 0 are valid numbers but not valid ages.

Types of Input Validation

The validation requirements for age input show that there are different classes of input validation. Ensuring that a user enters a value for the age input and ensuring that the age is entered as a number are both considered forms of input validation, but they differ in that the former simply checks to see whether a value is entered, whereas the latter ensures that the entered data is in a predefined format.

Input validation can be broken down into five distinct classes. Let's take a moment to examine these five classes.

Required Field Input Validation

The first type of input validation is *required field validation*. Required field validation is used to ensure that the user has entered a value for a particular input. For example, when filling out shipping information at an e-commerce Web site, required fields would include the street address, city, state, and zip code the package was being shipped to; optional fields might include special shipping instructions.

A Web site that allows a visitor to sign up to create an account often has many required fields that the user must fill out in order to create an account. Typically, such required fields include e-mail address, age, gender, and other such information.

12

Data Type Validation

For numeric inputs it is often important that the input be entered as a number, not a string. That is, when a user is prompted for the year of birth, it is important that the year be entered as four digits, like 1978, as opposed to a string, like "Nineteen seventy eight." Data type validation can be used to ensure that a number has been entered, as opposed to a string.

Range Input Validation

For certain numeric inputs, it is important that the resulting input fall within a certain range of values. For example, if a user is prompted for age, we might want to ensure that it's between the values 0 and 150.

Comparison Validation

Another typical input validation for numeric inputs is a comparison validation. For example, if the user is asked to enter a salary figure or range, we might want to make sure that the number entered is greater than or equal to 0.

Alternately, we may wish to compare the value of one user input with the value of another user input. An example here might be if users are asked to enter their total income for a particular year and then are later asked to enter how much their income tax was for that same year. Clearly, one's income taxes can't amount to more than one's total income. Therefore, we may want to ensure that the number entered by a user for a particular year's income tax is less than the number entered for that same year's total income.

Pattern Validation

Certain types of string input must conform to a particular format. For example, if users are asked to enter their phone number, you might want to ensure that they enter it in the following format, where each X is a digit:

(XXX) XXX-XXXX

Clearly, there are alternate ways to provide a phone number, such as

XXX-XXX-XXXX

Typically, though, data that has numerous legal formats should always be recorded in one specific format. This makes it easier to search the data.

For example, imagine that you are storing the phone numbers entered by your Web visitors. If all phone numbers are required to be entered in the format (XXX) XXX-XXXX, it is much easier to search for all phone numbers in, say, a certain area code than it would be if phone numbers could be entered in a myriad of formats. (The area code is the first three digits of the phone number.)

Validating User Input in an ASP.NET Web Page

In ASP.NET, input validation is performed through the use of—you guessed it—Web controls. The Web controls that perform input validation are commonly called *validation Web controls* or just validation controls.

There are four kinds of validation controls we'll be examining in this hour. Each of these Web controls, as summarized in Table 12.1, is geared for providing one or more of the input validation classes we've just been discussing.

TABLE 12.1 The ASP.NET Validation Web Controls

Validation Control	Description
RequiredFieldValidator	Ensures that data has been entered into a specific input
CompareValidator	Ensures that a numeric value in one input is less than, less than or equal, equal, greater than, greater than or equal, or not equal to some constant value or some user-inputted value; can also be used to perform data-type validation
RangeValidator	Ensures that a numeric value in an input is between two constant numeric values
RegularExpressionValidator	Ensures that a string value matches some specified pattern

In the next few sections, we will examine each of these validation Web controls in detail. Specifically, we will look at how to add these Web controls to an ASP.NET Web page, how to specify what user input they are to validate, and how to determine whether the user's input meets the required validation.

After examining each of these four Web controls individually, we will see how to use multiple validation controls on a single ASP.NET Web page.

12

An ASP.NET Web Page for Examining the Validation Controls

Before examining how to use this Web control, let's first create an ASP.NET Web page that we can use throughout all of the hands-on learning. Specifically, we will create an ASP.NET Web page that collects the following information from users:

- Name, which is a required field
- Age, which is a numeric field that must be between 0 and 150
- Social security number (ssn), which is a string input with the following format: NNN-NN-NNNN, where N is a digit

- Number of children, which must be greater than or equal to 0
- Number of male children, which must be greater than or equal to 0 and less than or equal to the number of total children the person has

Start by creating a new ASP.NET Web page named ValidationControlTestBed.aspx and turning on glyphs. Now let's add five TextBox Web controls for the five user inputs. Before each TextBox enter a descriptive title with a colon, such as **Your name:**, **Your age:**, and **Social-security number:**. Figure 12.1 shows a screenshot of the Web Matrix Project designer after five TextBox Web controls have been added.

FIGURE 12.1

Five TextBox Web controls have been added, along with a title for each.

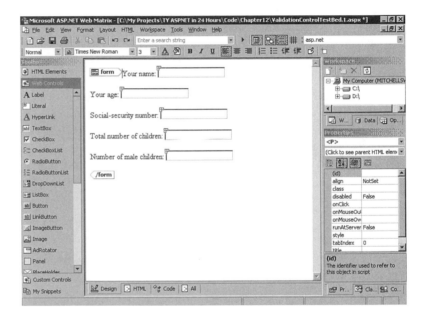

Now that we've added the needed TextBox Web controls, let's set the ID properties for them. Set the first TextBox Web control's ID property to **name**, the second's to **age**, the third's to **ssn**, the fourth's to **totalChildren**, and the fifth's to **maleChildren**. For the age, totalChildren, and maleChildren TextBox Web controls, also set the Columns property to 4.

Next add a Button Web control after the five TextBox Web controls. Set this Web control's ID property to btnSubmit and its Text property to Click Me. Your screen should now look similar to the screenshot in Figure 12.2.

12

FIGURE 12.2

The TextBox Web controls have had their properties set, and a Button Web control has been added.

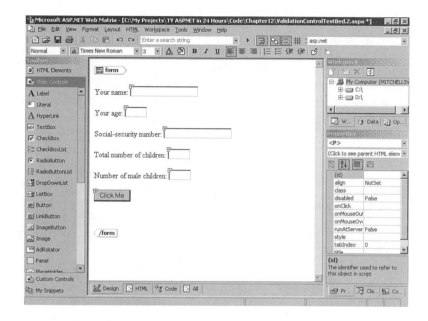

At this point, you may want to test out the `ValidationControlTestBed.aspx` ASP.NET Web page (you can see a screenshot in Figure 12.7). When you visit the ASP.NET Web page via a browser, go ahead and enter some test information into the various textboxes. Naturally, there is no input validation, meaning you can enter nonsensical text into any of these textboxes.

> As we will see shortly, with the ASP.NET validation controls, if you enter data that violates the validation control that is assigned to that particular input, a warning will immediately appear.

Now that we have created the ASP.NET Web page to which we will add the various ASP.NET validation controls, we are ready to begin our examination of these controls, starting with the RequiredFieldValidator Web control.

Examining the RequiredFieldValidator Validation Control

User input can be divided into two categories: required input and optional input. Required input is the set of inputs that the user *must* provide, whereas optional input is the set of inputs that the user may choose to provide or not to provide. In order to ensure

that the user provides a response for a particular input, we can use a RequiredFieldValidator
Web control.

To add a RequiredFieldValidator validation Web control to an ASP.NET Web page, all
that we have to do is drag and drop the control from the Toolbox and onto the designer,
just like we do with any other Web control. Go ahead and drag the
RequiredFieldValidator Web control from the Toolbox onto the designer; place the Web
control immediately to the right of the first TextBox Web control.

> You may have to scroll down through the Toolbox to find the
> RequiredFieldValidator Web control. The RequiredFieldValidator is the
> seventh Web control from the bottom of the Toolbox's Web Controls tab.

When you drag and drop the RequiredFieldValidator validation control onto the designer,
the text "RequiredFieldValidator" will appear in a red font, seen as light gray in the
screenshot in Figure 12.3.

FIGURE 12.3

*A RequiredFieldValidator
has been added to the
ASP.NET Web page.*

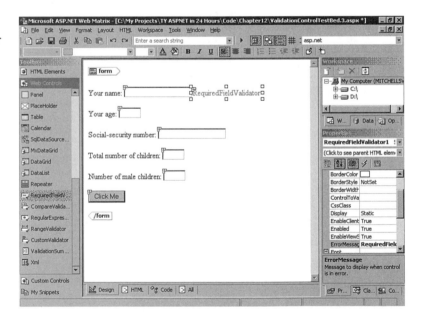

Specifying Which Web Control the Validation Web Control Is Validating

Realize that the validation Web controls are designed to validate input for a particular *input Web control*. By "input Web control" is meant a Web control used to collect user input, such as the TextBox Web control.

All validation Web controls contain a `ControlToValidate` property, which specifies which input Web control the validation Web control is validating. For example, if in the `ValidationControlTestBed.aspx` ASP.NET Web page, we want to require users to provide their names, we need to add a RequiredFieldValidator and set the RequiredFieldValidator's `ControlToValidate` property to `name`, the `ID` of the Web control that has a required field.

Note that each validation Web control that you add to your ASP.NET Web page can validate only a single input Web control. Therefore, if in our `ValidationControlTestBed.aspx` ASP.NET Web page, we had three required input fields (say, name, age, and social security number), we would need three RequiredFieldValidator validation controls on the Web page.

For the time being let's assume that the only required field on the ASP.NET Web page is the `name` input. Therefore, we need to set the `ControlToValidate` property of the RequiredFieldValidator that we just added to the ASP.NET Web page to `name`. To do this, click the RequiredFieldValidator, which will load its properties in the Properties pane.

Next click the `ControlToValidate` property, which will show a drop-down list of the various Web controls on the page (see Figure 12.4). Go ahead and select the `name` option from the list.

FIGURE 12.4

Select the Web control you want the RequiredFieldValidator to validate.

12

One important word of warning: If you set the `ControlToValidate` property to a specific Web control and then change that Web control's `ID` property, you will get an error when visiting the ASP.NET Web page through a browser (see Figure 12.5). This is because the validation Web control's `ControlToValidate` property is not automatically updated when the Web control it is to validate has its `ID` property changed. Therefore, if you change a Web control's `ID` property after you have added validation controls to the page, make sure to double-check that the `ControlToValidate` properties for your validation controls map to the correct, current value of the `ID` property of the Web control it is set to validate.

FIGURE 12.5

An error will occur if the validation Web control's `ControlToValidate` *property is incorrectly set.*

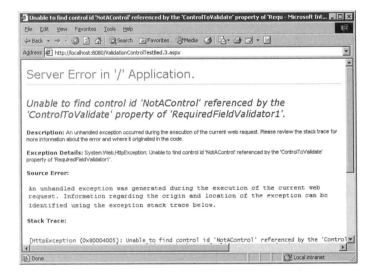

Specifying What Error Message to Display for Invalid Input

Along with a `ControlToValidate` property, all validation Web controls contain an `ErrorMessage` property. This string property contains the text that is displayed when the user's input fails to meet the validation requirements. Typically, this text should provide a brief explanation as to the problem with the input and what the user needs to do to fix it.

For example, for a RequiredFieldValidator, you might want to set the `ErrorMessage` to "You must provide a value for *input*" (where in place of *"input,"* you put the particular name of the input that the user is required to provide). Another common `ErrorMessage` value for RequiredFieldValidators is an asterisk. As you probably know from firsthand experience, many Web sites place asterisks next to required form fields.

For the `ValidationControlTestBed.aspx` ASP.NET Web page, go ahead and set the RequiredFieldValidator's `ErrorMessage` to **You must provide your name.** Once you enter this value, the text for the RequiredFieldValidator in the designer will change to the new `ErrorMessage` value (see Figure 12.6).

FIGURE 12.6

The designer after the RequiredFieldValidator's ErrorMessage *property has been set.*

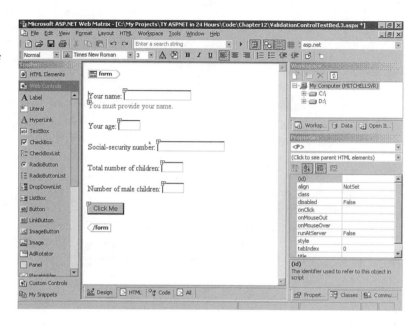

Testing Out the ASP.NET Web Page

Now that we have specified the ControlToValidate and ErrorMessage properties, the RequiredFieldValidator will inform users if they forget to provide a value for the name textbox. To test this out, be sure to save the ValidationControlTestBed.aspx ASP.NET Web page and then view it through a browser. Figure 12.7 shows a screenshot of this Web page when first visited.

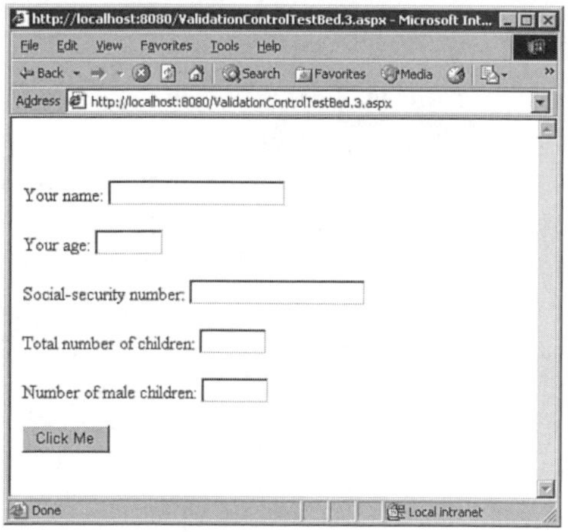

FIGURE 12.7

The ValidationControl TestBed.aspx *ASP.NET Web page, viewed through an uplevel browser.*

Note that there is a slight difference in the appearance of the Web page when viewed through a browser versus when shown in the designer. Namely, the RequiredFieldValidator is not displayed.

Now go ahead and click the "Click Me" button *without* entering any text into the name textbox. What happens? If you are using an uplevel browser (Internet Explorer 4.0 or higher), clicking the button did not cause the form to be submitted but instead caused the message "You must provide your name." to appear next to the name textbox. If you are using a downlevel browser (a browser other than Internet Explorer), clicking the button caused the form to submit, but upon postback the message "You must provide your name." was displayed next to the name textbox. Figure 12.8 shows a screenshot of the `ValidationControlTestBed.aspx` ASP.NET Web page after the "Click Me" button has been clicked when there was no input entered into the name textbox.

FIGURE 12.8

The message "You must provide your name." appears next to the name textbox.

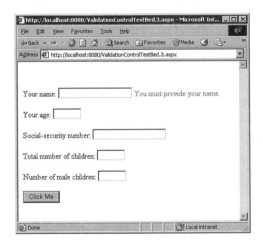

Now enter some text into the name textbox. Once you have done this, click a different textbox so that some other textbox receives the focus. If you are using an uplevel browser, clicking out of the name textbox after entering text into the name textbox caused the "You must provide your name." message to magically disappear! If you are using a downlevel Web browser, the message will still be present; however, if you submit the form by clicking the "Click Me" button, upon postback the message will have disappeared.

Client-side and Server-side Validation

What's going on here? Why does the validation error message behave differently depending on what browser is being used? The differences arise due to the fact that validation Web controls, when rendered on uplevel browsers, include *client-side validation*, which is client-side JavaScript code that runs on the user's Web browser. When the user tabs or clicks out of a textbox, a piece of JavaScript code that determines whether the input provided is valid is run on the user's Web browser. If the input is not valid, the browser automatically displays the validation Web control's `ErrorMessage` property value. If a user is visiting the Web page with an uplevel browser, client-side validation will be used.

Downlevel browsers, on the other hand, employ just *server-side validation*, which, as the name implies, occurs in code that is executed on the Web server. This is the reason why with a downlevel browser the "You must provide your name." message does not disappear, even after text has been entered into the name textbox, until the user submits the form. In order for the message to disappear, the ASP.NET Web page must be posted back, which, as you already know, causes the ASP.NET Web page to be fetched from the Web server again. When this page is requested from the Web server, the user's input can be checked there, and it can be determined whether the user's input meets the validation criteria.

All validation controls, regardless of whether the visitor is using an uplevel or downlevel browser, perform server-side validation checks. That means that for uplevel browsers both client-side and server-side checks are performed. The rationale behind this is that client-side validation can be circumvented by simply disabling JavaScript in an uplevel browser.

Client-side validation's main advantage over server-side validation is that it provides immediate feedback to the user without requiring a postback to the Web server. This has the advantage of saving the user time, especially if on a slow connection, because it does not require a round-trip to the Web server.

To learn more about client-side validation, check out the article "Form Validation on the Client Side" at http://www.webmasterbase.com/ article/862.

Programmatically Determining whether the User's Input Is Valid

As we have seen, simply by setting the `ControlToValidate` and `ErrorMessage` properties of the validation Web controls, these controls will automatically alert users if their input is in an improper format. But how can we determine whether all of the user's input is valid programmatically?

12

Typically, we will want to process the user's input in some fashion; for example, in previous hours we have seen how to create a mortgage cost calculator and a BMI calculator. In both examples we needed to perform some mathematical computations on the user's input. Of course, we don't want to perform these calculations unless the data entered by the user is valid.

To determine programmatically whether the user's input is valid, we can check the `Page.IsValid` property. The `Page.IsValid` property returns True only if all validation Web controls on the ASP.NET Web page have indicated that the input entered into their respective input Web controls has been entered in the proper format. Put another way, if any one user's input is not valid, `Page.IsValid` will be False.

To demonstrate using this property, let's create an event handler for the Button Web control's `Click` event. Recall that by creating an event handler for the `Click` event, the event handler's code will be executed every time the Web form is posted back. To create an event handler for the `Click` event, simply double-click the button in the designer.

This will take you to the Code tab, where you enter the following code:

```
Sub btnSubmit_Click(sender As Object, e As EventArgs)
  If Page.IsValid then
    'User input is valid
    Response.Write("Input is valid...")
  Else
    'There is at least some invalid input
    Response.Write("Input is <b>not</b> valid...")
  End If
End Sub
```

A quick examination of the code reveals that if the `Page.IsValid` property is True, then the string "Input is valid..." will be displayed. If there is any invalid input, however, the string "Input is **not** valid..." will be displayed.

This behavior can be seen in Figures 12.9 and 12.10. Figure 12.9 shows a screenshot of the `ValidationControlTestBed.aspx` ASP.NET Web page when no input has been entered into the name textbox and the form has been submitted. Note that the message "Input is **not** valid..." is displayed at the top of the Web page. Figure 12.10 shows the same ASP.NET Web page after the user has entered some value into the name textbox and has submitted the form. Here the message "Input is valid..." is displayed.

If you are visiting the page with an uplevel browser, you will not be able to submit the form without entering a value into the name textbox (unless you have JavaScript disabled in your browser). Therefore, you will need to use a downlevel browser to see the output displayed in Figure 12.9.

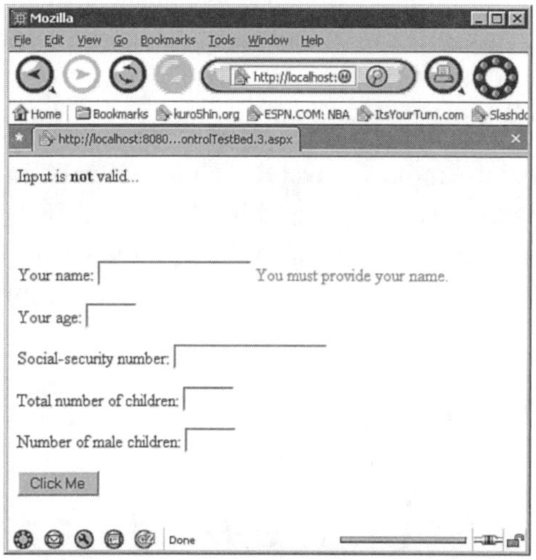

FIGURE 12.9
The form has been submitted with invalid user input.

FIGURE 12.10
The form has been submitted, and all of the user input is valid.

12

Summarizing the Basic Validation Control Features

This section started with a discussion of the RequiredFieldValidator and quickly turned into a talk about the common properties, features, and semantics of the validation Web controls in general. Before we move on to examining the other validation Web controls, let's take a moment to summarize the common features of validation controls.

First, all validation Web controls are designed to validate a single input Web control. The input Web control a given validation Web control validates is specified via the validation control's `ControlToValidate` property.

All validation controls also contain an `ErrorMessage` property, which specifies the text that is displayed if the input is invalid. The actual validation behaves differently depending on the Web browser being used by the visitor. If the user has an uplevel browser, the user's experience is enhanced through the use of client-side validation as well as server-side validation. For downlevel browsers, however, only server-side validation occurs.

Finally, to determine programmatically whether the input entered by a user is valid, we can refer to the `Page.IsValid` property.

Examining the CompareValidator

The CompareValidator validation control is useful for comparing the value of a user's input to a constant value or to the value of a different user input. For example, on the `ValidationControlTestBed.aspx` ASP.NET Web page, the last two inputs, which ask users for the total number of children they have and the number of male children, are prime candidates for the CompareValidator.

The input that prompts users for their total number of children, for example, must be a value that is greater than or equal to 0. The input for the number of male children must be both greater than or equal to 0 and less than or equal to the value the user entered into the total number of children textbox.

Let's first provide this validation check for the total number of children input. Start by dragging and dropping a CompareValidator from the Toolbox and onto the designer, placing the CompareValidator immediately after the `totalChildren` TextBox Web control, as shown in Figure 12.11.

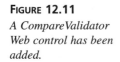

FIGURE 12.11

A CompareValidator Web control has been added.

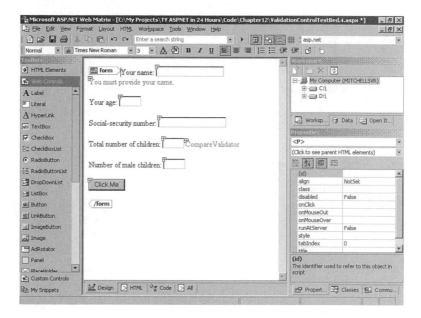

The CompareValidator is capable of performing a number of comparisons. For example, the CompareValidator can compare an input to ensure that it's less than some value, greater than or equal to a value, or not equal to some value. The Operator property specifies what comparison the CompareValidator should perform.

To set the Operator property, click the CompareValidator whose property you wish to set; this will load the CompareValidator's properties in the Properties pane. Scroll down to the Operator property. When you click this property, a drop-down list box will appear that shows the valid settings for this property. Specifically, the Operator property can be set to one of the following comparisons:

- Equal
- NotEqual
- GreaterThan
- GreaterThanEqual
- LessThan

12

- LessThanEqual
- DataTypeCheck

Since we want to ensure that the number of total children entered by users is greater than or equal to zero, we will set the Operator property to GreaterThanEqual.

In addition to the operator property, we need to set the Type property, which indicates which data type the user's input should be provided in. The Type property, which can be accessed via the Properties pane just like the Operator property, can be set to one of the following data types:

- String
- Integer
- Double
- Date
- Currency

Since we want the user to enter the total number of children input as a numeric value without a decimal, set the Type property to Integer.

At this point we have specified what comparison should be performed and which data type the user's input should appear as. We must now specify the value we want to compare the user's input to. The value to compare the user's input to can be either a constant value or the value entered by the user in some other input. Since we want to ensure that the user's input is greater than or equal to 0, the comparison is being performed against a constant value, namely 0. To specify this, set the CompareValidator's ValueToCompare property to 0.

All that remains now is to set the ControlToValidate and ErrorMessage properties. Because the CompareValidator is validating the user's input for the totalChildren TextBox Web control, set the ControlToValidate property to **totalChildren**. Then set the ErrorMessage property to a descriptive message, such as **The total number of children must be a whole number greater than or equal to 0**. Once you have set all of these properties, your screen should look similar to the screenshot in Figure 12.12.

FIGURE **12.12**

The CompareValidator will ensure that the input is greater than or equal to 0.

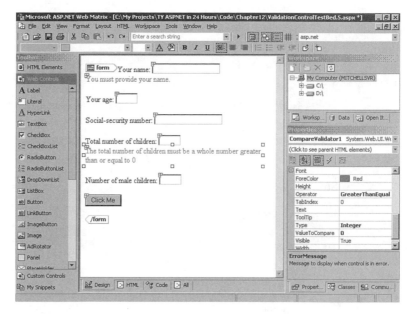

At this point we can test the functionality of the CompareValidator by visiting the `ValidationControlTestBed.aspx` ASP.NET Web page through a browser. If you enter invalid input into the total number of children textbox, you will get the error message "The total number of children must be a whole number greater than or equal to 0," as can be seen in Figure 12.13.

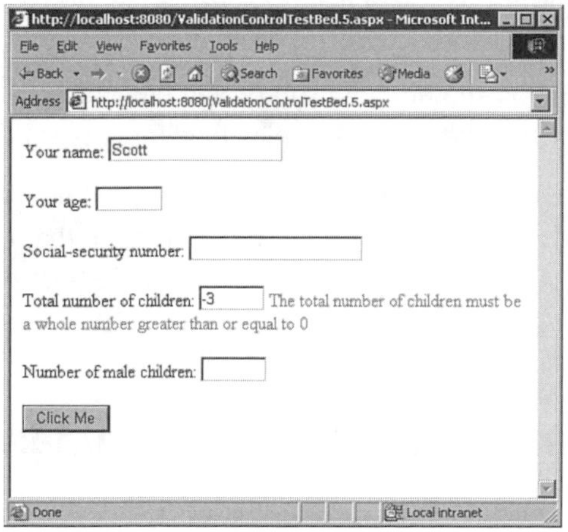

FIGURE **12.13**

An invalid input produces an appropriate error message.

12

Invalid input is input that is not an integer and not greater than or equal to zero. Some examples of invalid input are

- Scott
- −4
- 3,456 (the presence of the comma makes this an illegal input)
- 3.14159

Some examples of legal input include

- 0
- 2
- 3456
- 45533

> It might make sense to put an upper bound on the total number of children input. For example, we can safely assume that no one will have more than 50 children. In order to place such an upper bound, we could add an additional CompareValidator and set its Operator property to LessThanEqual and its ValueToCompare property to 50. Alternately, instead of having to use two CompareValidators, we could use a single RangeValidator, which we will examine in an upcoming section.

One very important thing to notice is that you can provide no value for the total number of children input. For instance, if you were to enter a value into the name textbox but no value into the total number of children textbox, and then click the "Click Me" button, the ASP.NET Web page will post back and display the "Input is valid..." message.

The lesson to take away from this is that only the RequiredFieldValidator ensures that input is provided. With our example, if you want to require that the user enter a value into the total number of children input, you must add a RequiredFieldValidator for this input as well as a CompareValidator. (Coming up we will see how to have multiple validation controls validating a single input Web control.)

Using the CompareValidator to Compare One Input to Another

In the previous example we used a CompareValidator to compare the total number of children input with a constant value—0. In addition to comparing the value of a user input with a constant value, CompareValidators can also compare the value of one user input with the value of another user input. For example, the value entered into the number of male children input must be less than or equal to the value the user entered into the total number of children input.

The only difference between a CompareValidator that performs a comparison against a constant value and one that performs a comparison against the value in another input is that in the former case the CompareValidator's `ValueToCompare` property is set to the constant value to compare the user's input to. In the latter case, instead of setting the `ValueToCompare` property, we set the `ControlToValidate` property, specifying the `ID` property of the input Web control whose value we wish to compare.

To add a CompareValidator that ensures that the value entered into the number of male children input is less than or equal to the total number of children input, start by dragging and dropping a CompareValidator from the Toolbox and onto the designer, placing the CompareValidator after the `maleChildren` TextBox Web control. Next set the CompareValidator's `ControlToValidate` property to **maleChildren**, its `Operator` to `LessThanEqual`, its `Type` to `Integer`, its `ErrorMessage` to **The number of male children must be less than or equal to the number of total children**, and its `ControlToCompare` property to **totalChildren**. Once you have set these five properties, your screen should look similar to the screenshot shown in Figure 12.14.

FIGURE 12.14

A CompareValidator has been added after the maleChildren *TextBox Web control.*

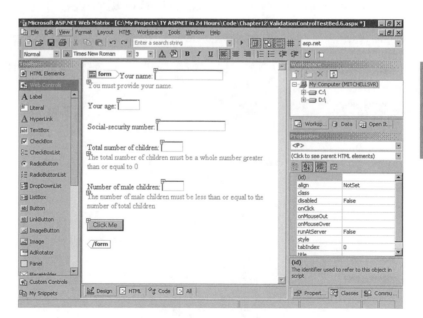

12

Now take a moment to visit the ASP.NET Web page through a browser. If you enter a value of, say, 4 into the total number of children textbox and a value of 8 into the number of male children textbox, you will be shown the error message "The number of male children must be less than or equal to the number of total children." Similarly, if you enter a non-integer value into the number of male children textbox (such as "Scott" or 4.5), you will get the same error message.

What will happen, though, if you enter a value of 5 into the total number of children textbox and a value of –2 into the number of male children textbox? No error message is displayed, because –2 is less than 5, and –2 is an integer. In order to protect against this, we must do what we did for the total number of children input—add a CompareValidator. This one must check to ensure that the value entered into the number of male children input is greater than or equal to 0.

To accomplish this, drag and drop another CompareValidator, placing it after the `maleChildren` TextBox Web control's existing CompareValidator. Next set this CompareValidator's `ControlToValidate` property to **maleChildren**, its `Type` property to `Integer`, its `Operator` property to `GreaterThanEqual`, its `ErrorMessage` property to **The number of male children must be greater than or equal to 0**, and its `ValueToCompare` property to `0`. Figure 12.15 shows a screenshot of the Web Matrix Project designer after this CompareValidator has been added and its properties have been set.

FIGURE 12.15
An additional CompareValidator has been added to help validate the number of male children input.

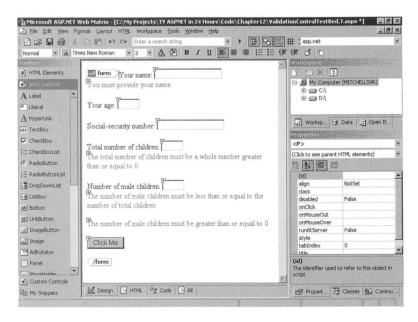

With this additional CompareValidator, an error message is displayed on the ASP.NET Web page if the user enters a negative value for the number of male children input.

Using the RangeValidator

As we saw in the previous section, the CompareValidator can ensure that an input maintains some relation with either a constant value or the value in another user input. However, what if we wanted to ensure that an input was between a range of values? If we were to use the CompareValidator, we'd need to use two CompareValidators, one that did a `GreaterThanEqual` comparison on the lower bound of the range and one that did a `LessThanEqual` comparison on the upper bound of the range.

If the upper and lower bounds of the range are constant values, we can use a single RangeValidator instead of two CompareValidators. For the `ValidationControlTestBed.aspx` ASP.NET Web page, the age input is a suitable candidate for a RangeValidator, since the input must fall within a sensible range (such as 0–150).

> The RangeValidator can be used only when both the upper and lower bounds of the range are constant values. Therefore, a RangeValidator could not be used for the number of male children input because the upper bound of the range is the value the user entered in the total number of children input.

Add a RangeValidator immediately following the age TextBox Web control, as shown in Figure 12.16.

FIGURE 12.16

A RangeValidator has been added to the ASP.NET Web page.

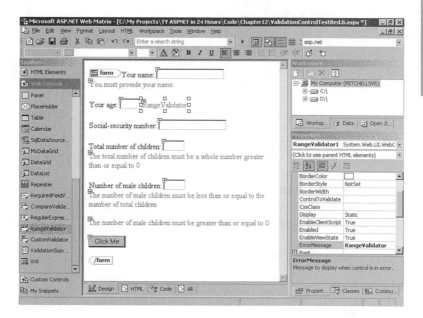

12

As with all validation controls, we need to set the `ControlToValidate` and `ErrorMessage` properties. Since we want to validate the input from the age TextBox Web control, set the `ControlToValidate` property to **age**. Set the `ErrorMessage` property to **Age must be between 0 and 150**.

The RangeValidator, like the CompareValidator, has a `Type` property that specifies the data type the input must be provided in. Since we want the user to enter his or her age as a number without decimals, set the `Type` property to `Integer`.

All that remains is to specify the upper and lower bounds of the acceptable range of values for the age input. The RangeValidator's `MaximumValue` and `MinimumValue` properties specify the upper and lower bounds, respectively. Since we want to force the user to enter an age between 0 and 150, set the `MaximumValue` property to **150** and the `MinimumValue` property to **0**. After you have set these properties, your screen should look similar to the screenshot in Figure 12.17.

FIGURE 12.17

The properties of the RangeValidator have been set.

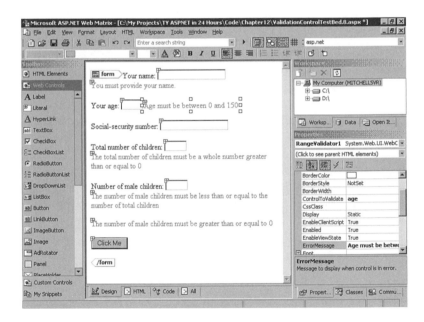

If you take a moment to view the `ValidationControlTestBed.aspx` ASP.NET Web page through a browser, you can see that an error message is displayed unless either no input is provided into the age textbox or the input provided is an integer value between 0 and 150.

Validating Input with the RegularExpressionValidator

Many forms of user input must be entered in very particular formats. For example, when asking for a user's e-mail address, the provided address must follow the following format: one to many alphanumeric characters, @, one to many alphanumeric characters, period, top-level domain name, such as com, net, org, edu, us, uk, fr, and so on.

For the ValidationControlTestBed.aspx ASP.NET Web page, the user is asked for a social security number. In the United States, every citizen is given a social security number, which contains nine digits and is typically written in the form

XXX-XX-XXXX

In order to ensure that a string input meets some specified format, we can use a RegularExpressionValidator, which uses *regular expressions* to determine whether the user's input matches the accepted pattern. A regular expression is a string that contains characters and special symbols and specifies a general pattern. Fortunately, you do not need to be well versed in regular expression syntax in order to use the RegularExpressionValidator.

> Regular expressions are commonly used in a number of program domains and are definitely worth learning. However, an extensive examination of the topic is far beyond the scope of this book, especially because the Web Matrix Project provides a number of built-in regular expression patterns that you can use in the RegularExpressionValidator without knowing a thing about regular expression syntax.
>
> If you are interested in learning about regular expressions, I encourage you to read "An Introduction to Regular Expressions" at http://www.4guysfromrolla.com/webtech/090199-1.shtml and "Common Applications of Regular Expressions" at http://www.4guysfromrolla.com/webtech/120400-1.shtml.

12

In order to ensure that the social security number is inputted in a proper format, let's add a RegularExpressionValidator Web control to the ASP.NET Web page. Drag and drop this Web control from the Toolbox and onto the designer, placing it immediately after the ssn TextBox Web control, as shown in Figure 12.18.

FIGURE 12.18

A RegularExpression Validator has been added to the ASP.NET Web page.

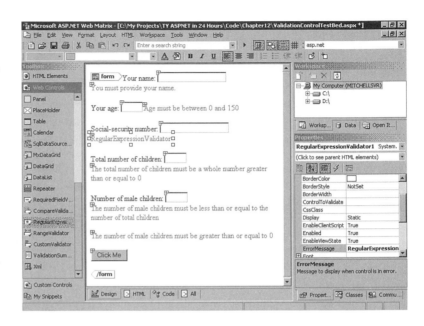

Set the RegularExpressionValidator's `ControlToValidate` property to **ssn** and its `ErrorMessage` property to **Your social security number must be in the format XXX-XX-XXXX**. The only other property you need to specify is the `ValidationExpression` property, which specifies the regular expression pattern that the user's input must conform to. To edit this property, click the RegularExpressionValidator in the designer, thereby loading its properties in the Properties pane. Scroll down and click the `ValidationExpression` property.

To the right you will see an ellipsis, which, when clicked, will display the Regular Expression Editor dialog box (see Figure 12.19). The Regular Expression Editor dialog box contains a list of standard regular expression patterns that you can choose from. Alternately, you can type a custom regular expression pattern into the Validation Expression textbox. Since we need validation for a social security number, scroll down to the U.S. Social Security Number option.

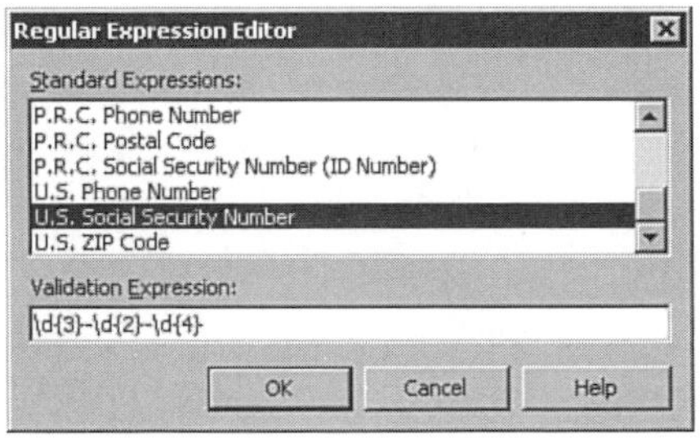

FIGURE 12.19

The Regular Expression Editor dialog box allows you to choose a predefined regular expression pattern.

Once you have selected the U.S. Social Security Number option, the regular expression pattern will be displayed in the Validation Expression textbox. Click the OK button to set the RegularExpressionValidator's `ValidationExpression`.

Once you have done this, take a moment to view the `ValidationControlTestBed.aspx` ASP.NET Web page through a browser. Note that an error message is displayed if you provide a social security number that doesn't follow the correct format: three digits, hyphen, two digits, hyphen, four digits. A legal social security number would follow the following format: `123-45-6789`.

> If you need to provide a regular expression pattern for a format not listed in the Regular Expression Editor dialog box, you can visit the Regular Expression Library at `http://www.regexlib.com`. There you will find the regular expression patterns for a large number of formats. (At the time of this writing, there were over 200 regular expressions provided at the Regular Expression Library.)

Aesthetic Properties for the Validation Web Controls

As we have seen numerous times in this hour, when a user enters invalid input, the appropriate validation control's `ErrorMessage` is displayed. In all of the examples, this error message has been displayed in a red font. However, the look and feel of the error message can be specified by setting the various aesthetic properties of the validation Web controls.

As with all Web controls, the validation Web controls contain the typical aesthetic properties—`BackColor`, `BorderColor`, `BorderStyle`, `Font`, and so on. In addition to these standard aesthetic properties, the validation controls also contain a `Display` property, which specifies how the `ErrorMessage` property is displayed when the user provides invalid input. The `Display` property can accept one of three values:

- None
- Static (the default)
- Dynamic

Setting `Display` to `None` causes the `ErrorMessage` property not to be displayed ever, even if a user's input is invalid. When `Display` is set to `Static`, the error message takes up the same amount of space on the Web page when it isn't displayed as when it is displayed. On the other hand, when `Display` is set to `Dynamic`, the validation control's error message does not take up space when not being displayed.

12

The differences between the Static and Dynamic settings is observable only from uplevel browsers.

To illustrate the difference between the Static and Dynamic settings, create a new ASP.NET Web page named DynamicVsStatic.aspx. In the Web page, add two TextBox Web controls, one right beneath the other. After each TextBox Web control, type in the text **This appears right after a textbox.** Figure 12.20 shows a screenshot of the Web Matrix Project designer at this point.

FIGURE 12.20

Two TextBox Web controls have been added to the designer.

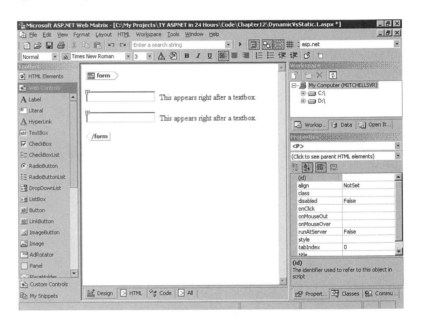

Next, between each of the TextBox Web controls and its entered text, drop a RequiredFieldValidator control. Set the RequiredFieldValidator controls' ControlToValidate properties to the ID values of the two TextBox Web controls. Set the ErrorMessage property to the value **This demonstrates the differences between Static and Dynamic Display**. Next set one of the two RequiredFieldValidator's Display properties to Dynamic, leaving the other's as Static.

Finally, add a Button Web control beneath the second TextBox Web control. Take a moment to make sure your screen looks similar to Figure 12.21.

FIGURE 12.21

Two RequiredFieldValidators have been added to the mix.

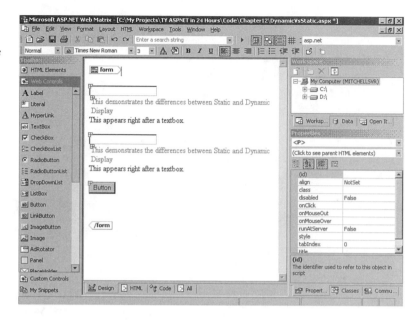

Now view the DynamicVsStatic.aspx ASP.NET Web page through an uplevel browser. Notice that for the RequiredFieldValidator whose Display property was left as Static, the text "This appears right after a textbox." is far from the right side of the textbox. This gap represents the space where the RequiredFieldValidator's error message will be displayed.

For the RequiredFieldValidator whose Display property was set to Dynamic, however, the text "This appears right after a textbox." appears immediately after the textbox. Figure 12.22 shows a screenshot of the DynamicVsStatic.aspx ASP.NET Web when viewed through an uplevel browser.

12

FIGURE 12.22

The apparent gap is due to the RequiredFieldValidator whose Display property is set to Static.

Now click the button on the Web page without entering any input into either of the textboxes. This will cause the error message to display for each of the RequiredFieldValidators. Figure 12.23 shows a screenshot after both error messages are displayed. For the RequiredFieldValidator whose Display property was set to Dynamic, the text "This appears right after a textbox." was dynamically moved to the right to accommodate the error message.

FIGURE 12.23

The screenshot after the button has been clicked.

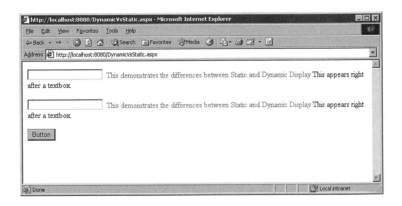

Table 12.2 contains a summary of the validation Web controls' aesthetic properties.

TABLE 12.2   The Aesthetic Properties of the Validation Web Controls

Property	Specification
BackColor	Background color of the error message
BorderColor	Color of the error message's border
BorderStyle	Style of the error message's border
BorderWidth	Width of the error message's border
Display	How the error message should be displayed
Font	Font properties for the error message; the Font property has a number of subproperties, such as Name, Size, Bold, and so on
ForeColor	Color of the error message (defaults to red)

A Look at the Remaining Validation Controls

In addition to the four validation controls we have examined in this hour, there are two additional validation controls. The first is the CustomValidator, which is, as its name implies, a validation control that is customizable. The CustomValidator can be used to validate user input in a way that is not handled by one of the four validation controls we've looked at.

However, in my experience, rarely will you find that you need to use a CustomValidator. More often than not, one of the four main validation controls will suffice. If, however, you find that you do need the power of a CustomValidator, I encourage you to read "Using the CustomValidator Control" at http://aspnet.4guysfromrolla.com/articles/073102-1.aspx.

The other validation control is the ValidationSummary control, which lists the ErrorMessage properties for all of the validation controls on a Web page that have indicated invalid user input data.

> To learn more about the ValidationSummary control, refer to http://www.w3schools.com/aspnet/control_validationsummary.asp.

Summary

Typically, when collecting user input, it is important that the user input conform to some set of guidelines. Perhaps certain input is required or must be numeric. Maybe the input needs to be lower than a certain value or between two constant values. Or perhaps the input needs to conform to some pattern, such as a United States zip code, which needs to be in the form XXXXX or XXXXX-XXXX (where each X is a digit).

The process of ensuring that a user's input is in the correct format is referred to as input validation. In previous technologies, such as ASP and PHP, input validation was a real bear, requiring developers to create source code to validate user input. With ASP.NET, however, input validation is a breeze because of its various validation Web controls.

In this hour we examined four such controls: the RequiredFieldValidator, the CompareValidator, the RangeValidator, and the RegularExpressionValidator. The RequiredFieldValidator is used for required fields and ensures that a particular input Web control has a value entered into it.

The CompareValidator ensures that the input it validates holds a certain defined relation with some value, which can be either a constant value or the values of other input Web controls. The CompareValidator can work with such relations as less than, equal, not equal, and so on. In addition to ensuring that the value conforms to some relation, the CompareValidator can also ensure that the input is in the format required for a particular data type.

The RangeValidator ensures that the input it validates is between two constant values. The RegularExpressionValidator demands that an input conform to a specified pattern. As we

12

saw, you can specify your own pattern by using the regular expression syntax or choose from a list of common patterns via the Web Matrix Project.

This concludes our four-hour examination of collecting user input. Starting with the next hour, "An Introduction to Databases," we'll be turning our attention to working with databases. While there are no more hours dedicated to collecting user input, a number of the examples throughout the remainder of the book will require user input, so be certain that you have a firm grasp on this material before continuing.

Q&A

Q I noticed that the `Display` property can have one of three settings: `None`, `Static`, and `Dynamic`. I understand the `Static` and `Dynamic` settings, but why on Earth would anyone ever want to use the `None` setting?

A When a validation Web control's `Display` property is set to `None`, the `ErrorMessage` property is *never* displayed, regardless of whether or not the data being validated is valid. It may seem confounding as to why anyone would ever want to do this.

One of the validation Web controls that we didn't discuss in length in this hour is the ValidationSummary control, which lists all of the validation errors on a Web page. If each validation Web control displays its error message *and* the ValidationSummary Web control displays each error message, each error message is displayed twice on the page. For this reason, when using the ValidationSummary Web control, developers typically set the various validation Web controls' `Display` properties to `None` so that the `ErrorMessage` property is displayed only once—in the ValidationSummary control.

Workshop

Quiz

1. To have a validation Web control display a particular error message when the data is invalid, what property would you set?

2. How does the `Display` property affect the display of the validation Web control's error message?

3. Many Web sites allow users to create accounts. When creating an account, the user oftentimes must choose a password and enter the desired password twice to ensure that there were no typos the first time. Now imagine that you are asked to create

such a Web page. What validation Web control would you use to ensure that the text entered into these two textboxes was identical?

4. True or False: A CompareValidator can be used to ensure that a user's input is a certain data type.

5. What are regular expressions, and why is it worthwhile to have a RegularExpressionValidator validation Web control?

6. True or False: Each user input Web control can have at most one validation Web control associated with it.

7. How do validation Web controls differ between uplevel and downlevel browsers?

Answers

1. The `ErrorMessage` property.

2. The `Display` property can be set to one of three values: `None`, `Static`, and `Dynamic`. If `Display` is set to `None`, then the `ErrorMessage` property is never shown, regardless of whether the input data is valid. A value of `Static` allocates space on the Web page for the validation Web control's error message, regardless of whether the error message is displayed. A value of `Dynamic` does *not* pre-allocate space for the error message. See Figures 12.22 and 12.23.

3. You would use a CompareValidator with its `ControlToValidate` and `ControlToCompare` properties set to the two TextBox Web controls. The CompareValidator's `Operator` property should be set to `Equal`. (Exercise 3 asks you to implement this scenario.

4. True.

5. A regular expression is a string that contains characters and special symbols and specifies a general pattern. A RegularExpressionValidator is a validation Web control that validates user input by using a regular expression. Such a validation control is worthwhile because it can validate that a user's input is in a certain pattern. For example, you may want to ensure that the user provides a phone number as three digits, followed by a hyphen, followed by three digits, followed by a hyphen, followed by four digits. This can be easily accomplished with a RegularExpressionValidator but not with any of the other validation Web controls.

6. False. Web controls may have an arbitrary number of associated validation Web controls. For example, if you had a TextBox Web control where the user needed to enter a social security number, you'd want to use both a RegularExpressionValidator, to ensure that the data entered was entered in the proper format, and a RequiredFieldValidator, to ensure that the user supplied a value and did not leave the textbox blank.

12

7. Validation Web controls in uplevel browsers display their `ErrorMessage` property immediately after invalid data is entered. Imagine that you have created an ASP.NET Web page that contains a TextBox Web control with a RequiredFieldValidator. Now, if a user visiting this ASP.NET Web page with an uplevel browser tried to submit the form before entering a value into the textbox, an error message would be immediately displayed. Furthermore, as soon as the user provides a value, the error message will disappear.

If a user visits this page with a downlevel browser and fails to enter a value into the textbox, no error message will be displayed until the user submits the Web form and a complete postback occurs. Furthermore, after entering a value into the textbox, the error message will still be present until the user submits the form. In essence, the validation Web controls lose their client-side validation capabilities when visited by a downlevel browser.

Exercises

1. In this exercise you will build a simple ASP.NET Web page that uses a CompareValidator and two RequiredFieldValidators. Specifically, create an ASP.NET Web page that prompts the user for two favorite ice cream flavors. There should be two TextBox Web controls, one for each of the user's two favorite flavors. Add the needed validation Web controls to ensure that the user provides input for both of these TextBoxes and that the values for the two TextBoxes are different from one another.

2. For this exercise create an ASP.NET Web page that prompts the user to provide an e-mail address and the URL to a homepage. Add the necessary validation Web controls to ensure that the user supplies an email address and that both the e-mail address and the homepage URL are in the proper format. (Hint: The RegularExpressionValidator Regular Expression Editor contains predefined regular expressions for both Internet e-mail addresses and Internet URLs.)

3. Many Web sites allow users to create accounts. The account creation process usually prompts the user, at minimum, to provide a desired username, a password, and an e-mail address. Please create an ASP.NET Web page that has a TextBox Web control for the user's desired username, two TextBox Web controls for the user's password, and one TextBox Web control for the user's email address.

   For the user input to be valid, all TextBoxes must have a value entered. The user's e-mail address must conform to the standard e-mail address format, and the values entered into the two password TextBoxes must be equal. (Be sure to set the password TextBox Web controls' `TextMode` property to `Password`.)

PART III

Working with Databases

Hour

Hour 13

An Introduction to Databases

One of the most powerful and useful features of ASP.NET is the ability for ASP.NET Web pages to interact seamlessly with database systems. Databases, as we'll discuss in detail in this hour, are software applications designed to serve as repositories of data. For example, Amazon.com's product information is stored in a database.

In this hour we will look at what databases are and how data is stored in databases. We'll also quickly examine a number of popular commercial and free database systems, focusing specifically on Microsoft SQL Server 2000 Desktop Engine, a free database system from Microsoft that is included in this book's accompanying CD.

By the end of this hour we will have installed MSDE 2000, created a database, and populated this database with some data. Specifically, we will examine

- What databases are
- How data is stored in a database

- What database tables, columns, fields, rows, and records are and how they pertain to storing data

- The types of data that can be stored in a table column

- Some of the popular, commercially available database systems, as well as some of the free database systems

- How to install and configure Microsoft SQL Server 2000 Desktop Engine (MSDE 2000, or just MSDE)

- How to create a new database and new database tables with MSDE

Examining Database Fundamentals

You might have heard the term *database* used before without being completely clear about what a database is or what it is used for. In the simplest terms, a database is a collection of structured information that can be efficiently accessed and modified.

Databases contain data and allow four operations to be performed on that data: retrieval, insertion, modification, and deletion. Most commonly, databases are used as a means to retrieve already inserted data. Therefore, we will spend the bulk of our study of databases examining how to retrieve the database's data.

Before you can insert, update, delete, or query a database, you must first set up and install a database. We will start this hour by examining the basic concepts of a database. After this we will look at installing and configuring Microsoft SQL Server 2000 Desktop Engine, a free database system available on the book's accompanying CD.

There are a number of ways to access a database. Typically, database systems provide some sort of application to insert, delete, update, and access the database's data.

More interestingly from our perspective, databases can be accessed via an ASP.NET Web page. This means that we can create an ASP.NET Web page that reads data from a database and displays its contents to the Web visitor. This approach is common in a vast number of real-world Web sites. For example, when you search for a book at Amazon.com, the search query Web page retrieves matching records from a database and then displays these matching records in a resulting Web page.

Over the next several hours, we will examine how to display data from a database in an ASP.NET Web page.

Once we've examined the fundamental properties and aspects of a database and looked at installing a database system, we'll turn our attention to the syntax databases use for inserting, updating, deleting, and retrieving data. This language, referred to as *structured query language*, or *SQL*, is the topic of the next hour, "Understanding SQL, the Language of Databases."

Following that hour we'll be focusing on using various ASP.NET Web controls that are designed to display data from a database. For example, in Hour 15, "Displaying Data with the DataGrid Web Control," we'll look at the DataGrid Web control and how it can easily display information stored in a database. In Hour 17, "Working with Data-Bound DropDownList, RadioButton, and CheckBox Web Controls," we'll look at how to populate the contents of Drop-down lists, radio buttons, and checkboxes from data residing in a database. (Recall from Hour 11, "Collecting Input by Using Drop-down Lists, Radio Buttons, and Checkboxes," that these Web controls, along with the TextBox Web control, are designed for collecting user input.)

Current Database Systems

There are a slew of commercial and free database systems available that will run on a variety of platforms. Some of the more popular commercial database systems include

- Microsoft SQL Server—`http://www.microsoft.com/sql/`
- Oracle—`http://www.oracle.com/`
- IBM's DB2—`http://www-3.ibm.com/software/data/db2/`
- Microsoft Access—`http://www.microsoft.com/office/access/`
- IBM's Informix—`http://www-3.ibm.com/software/data/informix/`

These commercial database products are industrial-strength, suited for large companies with demanding data needs. Because these are such high-grade database systems, the costs can be quite high, in the tens of thousands of dollars.

Fortunately for us amateur developers, there are also a number of free database systems. These database systems are still impressive software accomplishments, but they lack the features and high performance that the commercial-grade database systems have. However, since we are just using these databases to test our ASP.NET Web pages, they more than meet our needs. Some of the more popular free databases include

- PostgreSQL—`http://www.postgresql.com/`
- MySQL—`http://www.mysql.com/`
- Microsoft SQL Server 2000 Desktop Engine (MSDE)—`http://asp.net/msde/`

13

With the book's accompanying CD, you will find the Microsoft SQL Server 2000 Desktop Engine database system (or MSDE for short), which is what we'll be using to test our ASP.NET Web pages. We'll be examining how to install locally and configure this database system in the "Installing and Setting Up Microsoft SQL Server 2000 Desktop Engine (MSDE)" section.

> If you are running your ASP.NET Web pages from a Web hosting company, you will not be able to install Microsoft SQL Server 2000 Desktop Engine on the computers hosting your Web site. Rather, you will have to rely on the database system that's likely already installed at the Web hosting company. We'll discuss database options for you readers using Web hosting companies later in this hour, in the "Installing and Setting Up Microsoft SQL Server Desktop Engine (MSDE)" section.

Storing Structured Data

Recall from our earlier definition that a database is a collection of *structured* information that can be efficiently accessed and modified. Databases structure their data by storing it into *tables*. A two-dimensional grid, a table is a combination of columns and rows. Each column corresponds to an attribute of the data, whereas each row corresponds to an actual data item. Furthermore, each table is assigned a unique identifier to differentiate it from other tables in the database.

To clarify this concept, imagine that we wanted to use a database to store information about customers. Let's name the table Customers. In order to decide how to store the customer information, we must first decide what information, specifically, describes a customer. For this example, assume that we need to store the customer's name, phone number, and zip code, as well as the date of the customer's first purchase from our fictitious company.

These customer attributes make up the columns of the Customers table. In database terminology, these attributes are commonly called either *columns* or *fields*. Figure 13.1 shows a graphical representation of a table designed to store information about customers.

FIGURE 13.1

The Customers *table's columns represent attributes of the customer.*

The Customers Database Table

Name	Phone	ZipCode	DateBecameCustomer

Now imagine that our company had five customers (it's amazing it stays in business!). These five customers and their associated data might be:

- Jisun Lee, 858-321-1234, 92109, January 27, 2001.
- Dave Yates, 619-123-4321, 92101, October 10, 2000.
- Todd Callister, 630-555-9898, 60126, August 27, 1989.
- Marie Vogan, 314-555-1111, 65401, September 8, 1997.
- Kate Wiseman, 858-555-4343, 92108, November 24, 2000.

Each of these five customers would be represented by one row in the Customers table. In database terminology the rows of a database table (not including the row of column heads) are commonly referred to as either *rows* or *records*. Figure 13.2 graphically represents the Customers table after these five rows have been added to the table.

FIGURE 13.2

The Customers *table contains five rows, one row for each customer record.*

The Customers Database Table

Name	Phone	ZipCode	DateBecameCustomer
Jisun Lee	858-321-1234	92109	January 27, 2001
Dave Yates	619-123-4321	92101	October 10, 2000
Todd Callister	630-555-9898	60126	August 27, 1989
Marie Vogan	314-555-1111	65401	September 8, 1997
Kate Wiseman	858-555-4343	92108	November 24, 2000

You may be wondering how one inserts data into a database table. We'll examine how to accomplish this in the next hour.

Examining a Table's Columns

As we saw in Figures 13.1 and 13.2, a database table is a two-dimensional grid for storing structured data. Each attribute-specifying column of a database table, like a variable in Visual Basic .NET, has a name and a type. In our Customers table example, the names of the four database columns might be Name, Phone, ZipCode, and DateBecameCustomer. In addition to its name, each column has a type, which specifies the type of data that can be stored in the column.

For example, the Name column would likely have a type of varchar(50), the Phone column a type of varchar(12), the ZipCode column a type of varchar(5), and the DateBecameCustomer column a type of datetime. Despite the type name differences, table columns can have types quite similar to the types that Visual Basic .NET variables

13

can have. The type varchar(50) is akin to a String type in Visual Basic .NET, where the string can have, at most, 50 characters. The datetime table column type is synonymous to Visual Basic .NET's DateTime type.

In addition to the varchar(*n*) and datetime types, there are a number of other types. Table 13.1 summarizes some of the more common table column types and their Visual Basic .NET parallels.

TABLE 13.1 Commonly Used Table Column Types

Table Column Type	Description	Visual Basic .NET Parallel
varchar(n)	String up to *n* characters in length	String
int	Integer	Integer
bit	0 or 1—a Boolean	Boolean
datetime	Date and time	DateTime
float	Floating-point number	Single

When we create a database table later in this hour, you will see that there are many more column types than those listed in Table 13.1. However, the types presented in Table 13.1 are the ones you'll find yourself using most of the time.

Primary Key Columns

In addition to the various table columns that store pertinent data, database tables often contain a *primary key column,* which is typically a column of type int that has some special flags set. (We'll see how, specifically, to add a primary key column to a database table in the "Creating Database Tables" section.)

Primary key columns of type int can be marked as *auto-increment* columns. An auto-increment primary key column uniquely identifies successive rows in the table with increasing integer values. Auto-increment primary keys, then, can uniquely identify each row. Furthermore, primary key columns are oftentimes given the name *TableName*ID.

When inserting data into a database, you cannot explicitly specify the value of an auto-increment primary key column; instead, it is up to the database system to determine the primary key value for a newly inserted row. This responsibility is delegated to the database system so that it can ensure that each and every row in a database table has a unique value in its auto-increment primary key field.

In order to make sense of this information, let's return to our Customers table example and add a primary key. Since primary key columns are usually named *TableName*ID, let's call the Customers primary key **CustomerID**. With the addition of this new field, the Customers table would have the structure shown in Figure 13.3.

FIGURE **13.3**

A primary key field has been added to the Customers *table.*

The Customers Database Table with a Primary Key Column Added

CustomerID	Name	Phone	ZipCode	DateBecameCustomer

Now, if we were to insert the five records examined earlier, the table's rows would have the data shown in Figure 13.4. Note that the value in the auto-increment primary key column is unique and increasing for each successive row in the Customers table. Furthermore, realize that when inserting data, we would not specify the value for the CustomerID field; rather, the database system would automatically do this for us.

FIGURE **13.4**

Each row contains a unique CustomerID value.

The Customers Database Table with a Primary Key Column Added

CustomerID	Name	Phone	ZipCode	DateBecameCustomer
1	Jisun Lee	858-321-1234	92109	January 27, 2001
2	Dave Yates	619-123-4321	92101	October 10, 2000
3	Todd Callister	630-555-9898	60126	August 27, 1989
4	Marie Vogan	314-555-1111	65401	September 8, 1997
5	Kate Wiseman	858-555-4343	92108	November 24, 2000

Installing and Setting Up Microsoft SQL Server Desktop Engine (MSDE)

In order to access a database through our ASP.NET Web pages, we must first install a database system that is accessible from the Web server where the ASP.NET Web pages are hosted. If you have been serving the ASP.NET Web pages from your own computer, then you will need to install the Web server on this same computer.

If you are hosting your ASP.NET Web pages with a remote Web hosting company, then you will likely be unable to install a database system. More likely than not, a professional, commercial-grade database system is already installed for your use at your Web hosting company. Contact your Web hosting company for details.

13

> Those readers who are hosting their ASP.NET Web pages on a remote Web host and therefore cannot install a database system may skip this section, although they are invited to read it to learn more about MSDE. Regardless of whether you read this section, make sure that you do start reading the section "Creating a New Database."

Before we begin installing MSDE, let's first take a moment to discuss what exactly MSDE is. MSDE, which stands for Microsoft SQL Server 2000 Desktop Engine, is a free version of Microsoft's SQL Server geared for developers.

MSDE does not provide the professional-grade strength that commercial database systems, such as Oracle and Microsoft SQL Server, do. Although under the hood MSDE uses the same technology as Microsoft's professional-grade database system, Microsoft SQL Server, MSDE is purposely handicapped so that its performance is limited.

Installing MSDE

Before we can install MSDE, we must first obtain the file necessary for installation. This file, `SQL2KDeskSP3.exe`, can be found on the book's accompanying CD. Alternately, if you do not have the CD or if you wish to obtain the latest version of MSDE, you can download the installation file from `http://asp.net/msde/`.

To install MSDE, follow these steps:

1. Double-click the `SQL2KDeskSP3.exe` file, which will bring up an installation wizard.
2. The first screen is a license agreement screen for the installation process. After reading the license, click I Agree to advance to the second screen.
3. Now you are asked to specify where the files in the `SQL2KDeskSP3.exe` should be unpacked. Leave the default value, `C:\sql2ksp3`. (A screenshot of this second screen can be seen in Figure 13.5.)

FIGURE 13.5

You can specify where to install MSDE.

4. Once you have selected a directory to unpack the files, click Continue. This will unpack the files in the specified directory. Once this step is complete, the installation wizard will quit.

5. Now here's where the installation process gets a little hairy. In order to install MSDE, you must drop to the command line. To do this in Windows 2000 or Windows XP, click the Start button and then select Run.

6. This will display a dialog box asking you to type in the name of the program you want to run. Type **cmd** and then click the OK button (see Figure 13.6).

FIGURE 13.6

Run the program cmd.

This will display a command line dialog box (see Figure 13.7). From here you can enter commands.

13

FIGURE 13.7

The command line dialog box allows you to type commands to execute.

7. First we must navigate to the directory created by the first installation program. Recall that this directory was `C:\sql2ksp3`. To get to this directory, type in **cd \sql2ksp3** and hit Enter.

8. To see the directories and files in `C:\sql2ksp3`, type in **dir** and hit Enter. As Figure 13.8 shows, the `C:\sql2ksp3` directory contains only a single directory, `MSDE`.

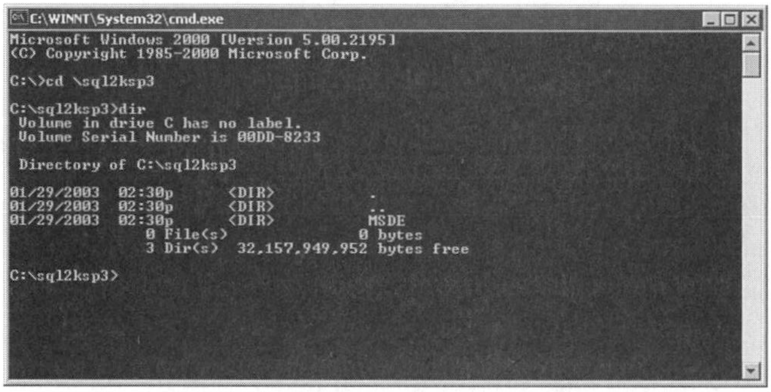

FIGURE 13.8

There are one directory, `MSDE`, and no files in the `C:\sql2ksp3` directory.

9. To navigate to the `MSDE` directory, type **cd MSDE** and hit Enter.

10. To see a list of files in this directory, type **dir** and hit Enter. As Figure 13.9 shows, one of the files in this directory is `setup.exe`.

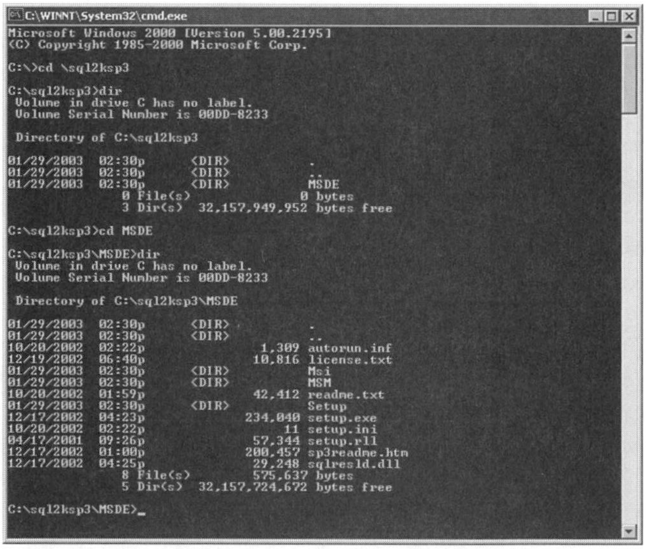

FIGURE 13.9

The `MSDE` directory contains the installation file `setup.exe`.

11. To install MSDE, you must type in the following text: **setup SAPWD=*password***
    SECURITYMODE=SQL, where *"password"* is the password you want for the
    administrative MSDE account.

> Make sure that you write down and remember your password. You will
> need to provide this supplied password when working with MSDE.

12. After you type the command in step 11, hit Enter; this will start the installation
    process. The installation process is marked by the dialog box shown in Figure
    13.10. The installation may take a few minutes.

FIGURE 13.10
The dialog box for the
final installation
process.

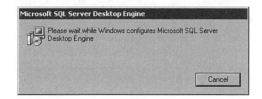

> If you are having troubles installing MSDE, consider reading the installation
> tutorial available online at http://asp.net/msde/. If, after reading this tutorial,
> you are still experiencing errors or problems of one sort or another, consider
> asking a question on the MSDE Forum at http://asp.net/Forums/
> ShowForum.aspx?ForumID=54.

13. After the MSDE configuration is done, you will be prompted to restart your computer—
    do so. Upon returning to Windows, you should see a new icon in your system tray.
    The icon should look like a computer tower with a green arrow in a white circle
    (see Figure 13.11).

13

FIGURE 13.11
A new icon should
be present in
your computer's
system tray.

MSDE icon

If you see a computer tower icon with a red square in a white circle, right-click the icon and select the MSSQLServer, Start option. This should, after a few moments, change the red square to a green arrow. The green arrow indicates that the MSDE service is running. It is vital that this service be running in order to use the database system.

If an error message appears when clicking the MSSQLServer, Start option, something has gone awry. Try uninstalling MSDE and then reinstalling it. If that fails to work, consider posting a question explaining your problem to the MSDE Forum at http://asp.net/Forums/ShowForum.aspx?ForumID=54.

At this point we have successfully installed Microsoft SQL Server 2000 Desktop Engine. Congratulations! We can now connect to the MSDE database through the Web Matrix Project. We'll examine how to do this, as well as create our first database, in the next section.

Creating a New Database

Before you can start using a database system like MSDE, the first thing you will need to do is create a new database. Each database contains a group of one or more database tables. Realize that database systems can contain many databases. For example, if you are hosting your ASP.NET Web pages at a remote Web hosting company, chances are they use a single database system like Microsoft SQL Server but have a database for each customer.

We will need to use the Web Matrix Project in order to work with MSDE. Let's start by creating a new database.

If you are hosting your ASP.NET Web pages at a remote Web host, chances are you cannot create a new database. Rather, you must ask the Web hosting company to create a new database for you.

To create a new database through the Web Matrix Project, follow these steps:

1. Start by clicking the Data tab in the Workspace pane. (The Workspace pane, which is shown as clicked over to Data in Figure 13.12, is located in the top right-hand corner of the Web Matrix Project.)

FIGURE 13.12

To access MSDE, start by selecting the Data tab from the Workspace pane.

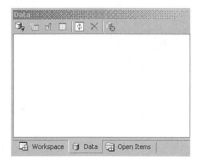

2. With the Data tab selected, click the New Connection icon in the upper left corner of the Data tab (see Figure 13.13). This will raise a Connect to Database dialog box, which can be seen in Figure 13.14.

FIGURE 13.13

There are a number of clickable icons in the Data tab.

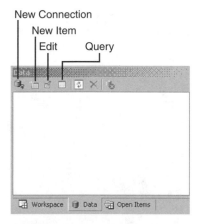

FIGURE 13.14

The Connect to Database dialog box is displayed after clicking the New Connection icon.

13

3. Leave "localhost" as the Server name but be certain to check the "SQL Server authentication" radio button. This will activate the User name and Password textboxes.

4. In the User name textbox enter the value **sa**, and in the Password textbox enter the password you specified when installing MSDE.

5. In the lower left corner of the Connect to Database dialog box, you will find a link titled "Create a new database." Click this link.

6. You will next be prompted to enter the name for your new database—choose the name **ASPExamples** (see Figure 13.15). Once you enter this name and click the OK button, a new MSDE database will be created behind the scenes.

This process can take a few moments, but once it's complete, the Connect to Database dialog box will disappear, and the Data tab will show the new database.

FIGURE 13.15
The ASPExamples database will be accessible from the Data tab.

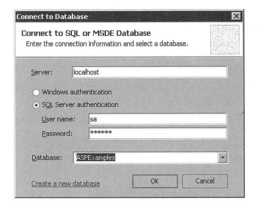

Connecting to an Existing Database

One *major* annoyance of the Web Matrix Project is that it doesn't save the connection preferences in the Data tab. If you close down the Web Matrix Project, the next time you start the Web Matrix Project, the Data tab will not have the ASPExamples icon present. This does not mean that the database has been lost—the database still exists. The reason you don't see it in the Data tab is because the Web Matrix Project does not save the Data tab preferences.

If you have shut down the Web Matrix Project and later restart it to work with an existing database, you need to connect to the database via the Connect to Database dialog box. To accomplish this, perform the following steps:

1. Click the New Connection button, which will display the dialog box seen in Figure 13.14.

2. Next choose which database you want to reconnect to. For this example let's reconnect to the ASPExamples database. Realize that we just want to connect to the ASPExamples database, which already exists, not to create a whole new database. Therefore, in the Connect to Database dialog box, instead of clicking the "Create a new database" link, as we did to create the ASPExamples database, click the Database drop-down list. This will display a list of databases for the server specified in the Server textbox. (You should have left this as localhost.)

3. From the drop-down list of available databases, one of the options should be the ASPExamples database. Select this option and then click the OK button. You should now see the ASPExamples database icon in the Data tab.

If your Web site is hosted by a remote Web hosting company, you should follow the instructions in the next section for connecting to the proper database.

If You Are Using a Remote Web Hosting Company

If you are using a remote Web hosting company you will likely not need to create a new database. Rather, you will need to connect to the database that has already been created for you at your Web hosting company.

To find out how to connect to this database, contact the Web hosting company. It should provide you with the following information:

- The database server's name, which will be either an IP address, such as 203.45.33.10, or a name, such as sql.webhostingcompany.com
- A username
- A password

In order to connect to this database, click the New Connection icon (see Figure 13.13), which will display the Connect to Database dialog box (see Figure 13.14). In this dialog box first enter the database server's name into the Server textbox. Next select the SQL Server authentication radio button. Finally, enter your username and password into the User name and Password textboxes. Finally, click OK.

13

Assuming you have entered the correct database server, username, and password, after you click the OK button, you should see icons in the Data tab similar to those shown in Figure 13.15. If you get any error messages when trying to connect to your Web hosting company's database system, contact your Web hosting company for further assistance.

> If your Web hosting company uses a database system other than Microsoft SQL Server, you will not be able to connect to it via the Web Matrix Project.

Creating Database Tables

Now that we have created a database, we're ready to create our first database table. Recall that database tables are two-dimensional grids, with the columns specifying the attributes of the data stored in the table, the rows of the table specifying the data. Additionally, tables have names that uniquely identify them.

When creating a new database table, we do not specify any of the data. Rather, we name the table as well as specify its structure—the name and type of each of the table's columns.

Creating database tables through the Web Matrix Project is quite easy. Just proceed as follows:

1. Start by clicking the Tables icon in the Data tab.

2. Next click the New Item icon, which is the second icon in the Data tab (the icon immediately to the right of the New Connection icon; refer back to Figure 13.13). The Create New Table dialog box will now appear (see Figure 13.16).

FIGURE 13.16
The Create New Table dialog box is displayed after clicking the New Item icon.

3. From the Create New Table dialog box, you can specify the new table's name as well as all of the table's columns. Let's create a database table that will store the customer information we discussed earlier in this hour. Start by entering into the Table Name textbox the name of our table, **Customers**.

4. Before we start creating the columns of the Customers table, realize that the Web Matrix Project will not let you create a database table without a primary key column. This is a bit restrictive, because there are common cases when we might want to create a database without a primary key. Unfortunately, this is not possible when using the Web Matrix Project's data tools.

   To add the primary key column (which you must add before any other columns), click the New button. This will activate the inputs on the right half of the dialog box under the Column Properties heading.

5. In the Name textbox enter the name **CustomerID** and select the Int option from the Data Type drop-down list.

6. Next click the Required checkbox, which will activate the Primary Key and Auto-increment checkboxes—check both of these checkboxes. Figure 13.17 contains a screenshot of the Create New Table dialog box after adding the CustomerID primary key field.

FIGURE 13.17

The CustomerID primary key column has been added.

13

7. Now that we have added the primary key column, we're ready to add our four other columns. Let's start by adding the Name column. Click the New button to add a new column; this will add a new column to the list of columns. Now enter into the Name textbox the value **Name**. Select the Data Type as Varchar and ensure that the Field Size textbox is set to **50**.

8. Next let's add the Phone column. Again, click the New button. In the Name textbox enter the column's name, **Phone**. Select Varchar from the Data Type drop-down list and set the Field Size to **12**.

9. To add the ZipCode column, click the New button. Enter **ZipCode** into the Name textbox and select Varchar as the Data Type and **5** as the Field Size.

10. Finally, add the DateBecameCustomer column by clicking the New button and entering **DateBecameCustomer** in the Name textbox.

11. Now that we have added all of the needed columns to the Customers table, click the OK button. This should cause the Create New Table dialog box to disappear. In the Data tab you should now see an icon labeled Customers nested beneath the Tables icon (see Figure 13.18).

FIGURE 13.18
The Customers *table has been added to the* ASPExamples *database.*

We have successfully added our first database table. Just as a database system can have multiple databases, each database can have multiple tables.

Adding Data to the Customers Table

At this point we have installed MSDE, created a database (or, if you're hosting your ASP.NET Web pages on a remote Web host, connected to a remote database), and created a Customers table. The next step is to add data to the Customers table. This can be accomplished through the Web Matrix Project.

To edit or add data to a database table via the Web Matrix Project, either double-click the Table icon in the Data tab or single-click the icon and then click the Edit icon, which is located after the New Connection and New Item icons we've already examined (refer back to Figure 13.13). This action will display the Edit Table dialog box, from which you can add or edit data. Figure 13.19 shows a screenshot of the Edit Table dialog box.

FIGURE 13.19

Add data to a database table by using the Edit Data dialog box.

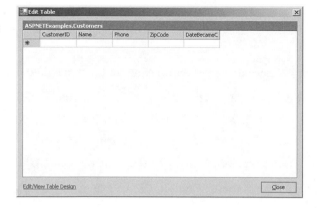

To add a new record to the Customers table, simply click the textbox beneath the Name column. Doing so will place the value (null) in the Name, Phone, ZipCode, and DateBecameCustomer columns and a value of –1 in the CustomerID column (see Figure 13.20).

FIGURE 13.20

Clicking a blank row allows you to add a new record to the table.

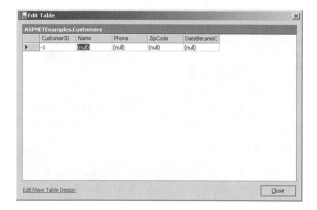

13

At this point we can enter values into the Name, Phone, ZipCode, and DateBecameCustomer columns. For the first record, add the value **Jisun Lee** into the Name column. Hit the Tab key, which will allow you to start entering the value for the Phone column; type in the value **858-321-1234**. Again, hit Tab to move to the ZipCode column and enter **92109**. Hit Tab once again to move to the DateBecameCustomer column and enter the value **January 27, 2001**. (Alternately, you can enter the value **1/27/2001**.)

Once you have completed the DateBecameCustomer column, hit Tab again. This will move you to the next row, where you can enter the next customer's information. Note that in hitting Tab, the CustomerID column changed from a value of –1 to 1; also, if you entered the DateBecameCustomer column as January 27, 2001, hitting Tab changed this to 1/27/2001.

At this point go ahead and enter information for the remaining four customers:

- Dave Yates, 619-123-4321, 92101, October 10, 2000
- Todd Callister, 630-555-9898, 60126, August 27, 1989
- Marie Vogan, 314-555-1111, 65401, September 8, 1997
- Kate Wiseman, 858-555-4343, 92108, November 24, 2000

After you have entered these values, the Edit Table dialog box should look similar to Figure 13.21.

FIGURE 13.21

*Five customers have
been added to the*
Customers *table.*

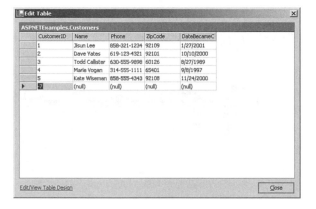

> Notice that the primary key column, CustomerID, contains unique increasing values for each row in the Customers table.

Recall from the beginning of this hour that a database is a collection of structured information that can be efficiently accessed and modified. We've seen how to create the structures to hold information (database tables), and we've looked at how to add data to a table (via the Edit Table dialog box), but we've yet to examine the most useful aspect of databases: efficiently accessing the data stored within. This topic, though, will have to wait until the next hour.

The Edit Table dialog box can also be used to edit existing table data. To change the value of an existing record, simply click the record's column(s) that you want to edit and type in the new values.

Summary

In this hour we learned that databases are software systems designed for storing structured data that can be efficiently accessed and modified. Data in a database is structured by means of tables. A table is described by its columns (sometimes referred to as fields), each of which has a name and a type.

Database tables can have a special kind of column known as a primary key column, a column of type `int` whose value is automatically provided by the database system when adding a new record. The primary key column's purpose is to identify as unique each record in a table.

In addition to columns, database tables contain rows. The rows of a table make up the table's data. For example, in Figure 13.17, the `Customers` table has five rows, which indicates that there is information about five customers. The Edit Table dialog box, which is displayed by double-clicking a table name in the Data tab, can be used to add a row. In addition to adding new records to a database table, the Edit Table dialog box also permits us to edit existing records.

Of course, to be able to work with a database, a database system must be present. In this hour we examined how to install Microsoft SQL Server Desktop Engine (MSDE), how to create a database, and how to create a table. Keep in mind that if you are hosting your ASP.NET Web pages on a remote Web hosting company there is no need to install MSDE locally on your computer. Rather, you should contact your Web hosting provider about how to connect to whatever databases they provide to their customers.

Now that we've examined the structure of databases, how to create databases and database tables, and how to add data to a database table, we're ready to read the data from a table. In the next hour we will be examining a query language specifically designed for accessing database data.

13

Q&A

Q **In this hour you mentioned that MSDE is not an appropriate database choice for a production Web server. What database systems *are* appropriate?**

A If you are creating a production Web server, you will need to use a production-grade database server, such as Microsoft SQL Server 2000. Unfortunately, Microsoft SQL Server is an expensive piece of software, ranging in price from several thousand dollars to tens of thousands of dollars, depending on how many licenses are needed. Typically, though, you can find a Web hosting company that will offer Microsoft SQL Server support for under $50 per month.

Interestingly, MSDE 2000 is simply a watered-down version of Microsoft SQL Server 2000. MSDE has had some of SQL Server 2000's bells and whistles stripped from it and has been modified to allow only a small number of concurrent connections. Since MSDE is free, the MSDE license prohibits use of MSDE in production settings.

Workshop

Quiz

1. How are columns, tables, and databases related to one another?

2. A particular column for a particular row in a database table is a lot like a variable in a programming language in that it can be completely described by what three attributes?

3. True or False: MSDE is a good option for a production Web site database.

4. How does an auto-increment primary key column guarantee that it will uniquely identify each row?

5. True or False: When you're creating a database table via the Web Matrix Project, the database table must have a primary key column.

Answers

1. A table contains one or more columns. A database contains one or more tables.

2. The column name, the column data type, and the value of the column for the specific row.

3. False. MSDE is designed to handle only a small amount of concurrent connections. In fact, it is a violation of the MSDE license to use MSDE in a production setting.

4. When inserting a new row into a column with an auto-increment primary key column, the database server decides the value of the auto-increment primary key column. Since the database server gets to determine this value, it can ensure that the value is unique relative to all other rows. This is accomplished by incrementing the auto-increment primary key column value from the last-inserted row.

5. True.

Exercise

To familiarize yourself with MSDE and creating databases and database tables through the Web Matrix Project, for this Exercise create a new database named TestDB. Once the database has been created, create a new database table called Albums. Imagine that you want to use this database table to hold information about the music recordings you own. Add columns with appropriate types and names. Some suggested columns include: an auto-increment primary key column named AlbumID; a varchar(50) column titled Name; a varchar(75) column titled Artist; and a date/time column titled DatePurchased. (Please take the time to add additional pertinent columns.)

13

Hour 14

Understanding SQL, the Language of Databases

In the previous hour, "An Introduction to Databases," we examined, from a high-level perspective, what databases are and their purpose. We looked at installing MSDE and creating a database. We also saw how to create a database table and populate it with data via the Web Matrix Project.

Often we will want to retrieve information from a database and display it on an ASP.NET Web page. To be able to do this, we need to learn how to retrieve data from a database. In this hour we will examine *Structured Query Language*, or *SQL* (pronounced either "S-Q-L" or "see-quell"), the language used by all modern database systems for retrieving data. In addition to learning the general syntax of SQL, we'll examine the tools the Web Matrix Project provides to assist in data retrieval.

Specifically, this hour will cover

- An overview of SQL
- Retrieving data from specific database tables
- Retrieving specific columns from a database table

- Using WHERE clauses to get data that meets a certain criterion
- Using the ORDER BY clause to order the results of a database query
- Using the Web Matrix Project's Code Builder tools to retrieve data

An Overview of SQL

In the last hour we saw that all modern database systems have several things in common. For example, all databases use tables to store their structured data. For all database systems, tables contain columns, each of which have a name and data type associated with it. In addition, modern database systems also use similar syntax to query the data residing in the database.

Structured Query Language, or SQL, is the syntax used by database systems to retrieve and modify data. Do not think of SQL as a programming language like Visual Basic .NET. Rather, think of SQL as syntax for requesting data. SQL is not designed to work with variables, data types, operators, and so on. Instead, SQL is designed to retrieve and modify data.

To retrieve data from a database, a *SQL SELECT statement* is used. The SELECT statement, in its simplest form, specifies from which database table to retrieve data. For example, in the previous hour we created a database table called Customers, which had the columns CustomerID, Name, Phone, Zip, and DateBecameCustomer. The following SQL SELECT statement returns the values in the Name column for each customer in the Customers table:

```
SELECT Name
FROM Customers
```

We will examine the SQL SELECT clause in great detail in the next section.

Although SQL is used primarily for retrieving database data, it can also insert new data and update or delete existing data. In addition to the SELECT statment, SQL contains three other statements: INSERT, UPDATE, and DELETE. As you can probably guess, these three statements are used for inserting, updating, and deleting database data.

In this hour we will focus strictly on using SQL to retrieve data. However, starting in Hour 21, "Devising a Plan for the Guestbook Application," we will examine how to build an online guestbook application, where we'll need to be able to insert data via SQL statements. Therefore, we'll examine how to use SQL to insert data in later hours.

Using the SQL SELECT Statement

As we have already seen, the SQL SELECT statement is used to retrieve the values of a particular database table's columns via the following syntax:

```
SELECT Column1, Column2, ..., ColumnN
FROM TableName
```

where *Column1 ... ColumnN* are columns from the database table *TableName*. For example, to retrieve the values from the Name and Phone columns from the Customers table, the following SQL statement would be used:

```
SELECT Name, Phone
FROM Customers
```

Note that this SELECT statement contains two *clauses*: the SELECT clause and the FROM clause. Clauses are keywords in the SQL SELECT statement that precede the data they operate on. The two required clauses in a SELECT statement are the SELECT and FROM clauses. As you have probably already ascertained, the SELECT clause specifies the columns whose values are to be returned, and the FROM clause specifies what database table to retrieve data from.

There are a number of optional clauses that can be found in the SELECT statement, many of which we will examine in this section. For example, the WHERE clause can be used to return only those rows that meet a certain criteria. The ORDER BY clause can be used to sort the results of the SELECT statement by a particular column.

The SELECT clause contains a comma-delimited list of the columns whose values you are interested in. If you want to retrieve the values of *all* columns for a specific table, you can use the asterisk (*) instead of having to enter each column name. For instance, if you wanted to display all of the columns of the Customers table, either of the following two SQL SELECT statements would suffice:

```
SELECT *
FROM Customers
```

or

```
SELECT CustomerID, Name, Phone, Zip, DateBecameCustomer
FROM Customers
```

14

Viewing SQL Queries Results through the Web Matrix Project

When learning SQL, it helps to be able to run a SQL query against a database so that you can see the specific results returned by the SQL query. Fortunately, the Web Matrix

Project makes this task quite simple. As we saw in the last hour, we can connect to a database system via the Web Matrix Project by first clicking the Data tab in the Workspaces pane and then clicking the New Connection icon.

In the previous hour we studied the Web Matrix Project's data features by creating a new database called ASPExamples, which contained a database table called Customers. In this hour we will run SQL queries against this database table. If you'd like to follow along by running the SQL queries on your computer, start by opening the Web Matrix Project and connecting to the ASPExamples database. You should see a list of the database's tables in the Data tab, as shown in Figure 14.1.

FIGURE 14.1

The Customers *table is shown in the Data tab.*

Single-click the Customers table and then click the Query icon. Doing so will display the Test Query dialog box. This dialog box, which is shown in Figure 14.2, contains a textbox into which you can enter a SQL SELECT statement and a Results pane, which shows the results of the query.

FIGURE 14.2

The Test Query dialog box allows you to view the results of a SQL query.

As Figure 14.2 shows, the Test Query dialog box displays the following SQL SELECT statement by default:

```
SELECT * FROM Customers
```

Recall that the asterisk in the SELECT clause will return all of the columns from the table in the FROM clause. That is, the preceding SQL statement will return the values in all of the columns for all of the data in the Customers table.

To see the results of a SQL query, you can click the Test Query button in the lower right corner of the Test Query dialog box. The results of the SQL query will appear in the Results pane of the Test Query dialog box. As Figure 14.3 shows, the SELECT * FROM Customers SQL query returns every row in the Customers table, displaying the values for all of the columns.

FIGURE 14.3

The results of the SQL query are displayed.

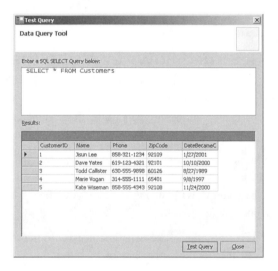

Let's try a new SELECT statement. Change the SQL query in the textbox from SELECT * FROM Customers to

```
SELECT Name, Phone
FROM Customers
```

This SQL query will return all of the rows from the Customers table, displaying the values for the Name and Phone columns. Once you have entered this query into the textbox, click the Test Query button to see the results, which are shown in Figure 14.4.

14

FIGURE **14.4**

The SQL query returns the values for two columns.

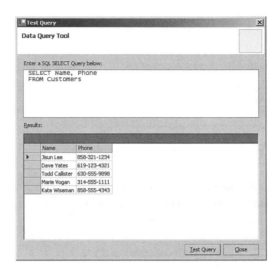

Results shown in dialog box:

	Name	Phone
▶	Jisun Lee	858-321-1234
	Dave Yates	619-123-4321
	Todd Callister	630-555-9898
	Marie Vogan	314-555-1111
	Kate Wiseman	858-555-4343

Restricting Returned Rows by Using the WHERE Clause

The SELECT statement, when composed of just the SELECT and FROM clauses, returns all of the rows of the specified database table. For example, the SQL query results shown in Figures 14.3 and 14.4 display all of the rows in the Customers table, the only difference between the two results being the columns whose values are returned.

Often, when querying database data, we are not interested in all of the data in a table, but only a subset. For example, when searching Amazon.com for books on ASP.NET, the search result page lists only those books that match your search criteria, rather than all of the books in Amazon.com's database.

To limit the rows returned by the SELECT statement, we use the WHERE clause, which specifies conditions that a row must match in order to be returned by the SELECT statement. For example, the following SQL SELECT statement returns only those rows in which the Name column's value equals Jisun Lee:

```
SELECT *
FROM Customers
WHERE Name = 'Jisun Lee'
```

Go ahead and enter this query into the textbox of the Test Query dialog box and click the Test Query button. The results should show all of the columns of the Customers table but only one row—the customer information for Jisun Lee.

Note that there are single quote marks around the string `Jisun Lee` in the `WHERE` clause. If you accidentally enter double quote marks instead of single quote marks, you will get the following error message when you click the Test Query button: `Invalid Query: Invalid column name 'Jisun Lee'.`

As you can see, the `WHERE` clause has a Boolean condition preceding it—`Name = 'Jisun Lee'`. The = operator here is synonymous with the = operator in Visual Basic .NET, which we examined in Hour 5, "Visual Basic .NET Variables and Operators." In addition to the = operator, other comparison operators, such as <, <=, >, and >=, can be used. Table 14.1 summarizes these other comparison operators.

TABLE 14.1 Comparison Operators That Can Be Used in the `WHERE` Clause

Operator	Example	Description
=	`Name = 'Jisun Lee'`	Compares two values, returning True if they are equal
<>	`Name <> 'Jisun Lee'`	Compares two values, returning True if they are *not* equal
<	`Price < 14.95`	Compares two values, returning True if the left value is less than the right value
<=	`Price <= 14.95`	Compares two values, returning True if the left value is less than or equal to the right value.
>	`Price > 14.95`	Compares two values, returning True if the left value is greater than the right value.
>=	`Price >= 14.95`	Compares two values, returning True if the left value is greater than or equal to the right value.

In addition to the comparison operators, the Boolean operators `AND` and `OR` can be used to string together multiple Boolean expressions. The Boolean `AND` and `OR` are synonymous with the VB.NET `And` and `Or` keywords. For example, the following SQL `SELECT` statement returns the `Name`, `Phone`, and `ZipCode` columns of customers whose `ZipCode` equals `92101` or whose `Name` equals `Jisun Lee`:

```
SELECT Name, Phone, ZipCode
FROM Customers
WHERE Name = 'Jisun Lee' OR ZipCode = '92101'
```

This query returns the `Name`, `Phone`, and `ZipCode` columns for customers Jisun Lee and Dave Yates.

14

When comparing a column's value to a string constant, such as WHERE Name = 'Jisun Lee', the string constant (Jisun Lee, in this example) must be enclosed by single quote marks. If, however, you are comparing a numeric column to a numeric constant, the numeric constant should not be surrounded by single quote marks. For example, if we had a column called Age, which was of type int, and we wanted to list all Customers whose Age was less than 30, we would use

```
WHERE Age < 30
```

and not

```
WHERE Age < '30'
```

WHERE Clauses That Return No Records

You can easily construct SQL queries that end up returning no records. For example, if we were to use the following SQL query, no records would be returned:

```
SELECT Name, Phone, ZipCode
FROM Customers
WHERE Name = 'Scott Mitchell'
```

No records are returned because there is no customer in the Customers table whose Name column has the value Scott Mitchell. If you run a query in the Test Query dialog box that returns no records, the messagebox shown in Figure 14.5 will be displayed.

FIGURE 14.5
This messagebox indicates that the query returned no matching results.

Understanding What Happens When a WHERE Clause Is Present

When a WHERE clause is used, the following sequence of steps happens behind the scenes. Each record in the Customers table is enumerated. The condition in the WHERE clause is checked for each record. If the condition returns the value True, the record is included in the output; otherwise, it is discarded.

For example, consider the following query:

```
SELECT Name, Phone
FROM Customers
WHERE Name <> 'Dave Yates' AND CustomerID <= 3
```

For each row in the `Customers` table that is visited, the `WHERE` clause's condition is analyzed. Starting with the first customer, Jisun Lee, we see that this customer's name doesn't equal `Dave Yates` and her `CustomerID` is indeed less than or equal to 3; therefore, the customer Jisun Lee will be returned by the `SELECT` statement.

The next customer is Dave Yates. Clearly, this customer won't be returned because the `Name <> 'Dave Yates'` condition will return False. The next customer evaluated is Todd Callister; because this customer's name is not `Dave Yates` and his `CustomerID` is less than or equal to 3, he will be returned. The remaining customers (Marie Vogan and Kate Wiseman) will be evaluated one at a time as well, but neither will pass the `WHERE` clause criteria because the `CustomerID` field of each of them is greater than 3.

Therefore, the aforementioned SQL statement will return the Name and Phone columns for two customers: Jisun Lee and Todd Callister.

Ordering the Results through the `ORDER BY` Clause

You might have noticed that the results returned by the SQL queries we have examined so far have all been ordered by the `ColumnID` value. To see this point illustrated, refer back to Figure 14.3, which shows the results of the query `SELECT * FROM Customers`.

What if we want the results ordered by some other column value, though? Perhaps we want to list the customers and have the list of customers ordered alphabetically by the customers' names.

The `SELECT` statement can include an optional `ORDER BY` clause, which specifies the column to sort the results by. To retrieve customer information for all customers, sorted alphabetically, we could use the following `SELECT` query:

```
SELECT *
FROM Customers
ORDER BY Name
```

Figure 14.6 shows a screenshot of the Test Query dialog box when this SQL query is used. The customers are ordered by the values in the `Name` column (where, it should be noted, first name precedes surname), instead of the values in the `CustomerID` column.

14

FIGURE **14.6**

*The customers are
ordered alphabetically
by the* Name *column
value.*

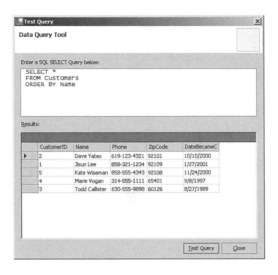

If you want to construct a query that has both a WHERE clause and an ORDER
BY clause, it is vital that the ORDER BY clause appear *after* the WHERE clause.
The following is a legal SQL query:

```
SELECT *
FROM Customers
WHERE Name <> 'Dave Yates'
ORDER BY Phone
```

The following is not:

```
SELECT *
FROM Customers
ORDER BY Phone
WHERE Name <> 'Dave Yates'
```

Sorting in Ascending and Descending Order

By default the ORDER BY clause sorts the results of a query by a specified column in
ascending order. You can specify that the sort ordering should be in descending order by
using the following syntax:

```
ORDER BY ColumnName DESC
```

Notice that sorting the results by a column that contains alphabetic characters
in ascending order, such as the Name column, has the effect of sorting the results in
alphabetical order. If you want to sort the results in reverse alphabetical order, use
the DESC keyword.

Figure 14.7 shows a screenshot of the Test Query dialog box when the following SQL query is used:

```
SELECT *
FROM Customers
ORDER BY Name DESC
```

Due to the DESC keyword at the end of the ORDER BY clause, this has the effect of sorting the results in reverse alphabetical order by the Name column.

FIGURE 14.7

The customers are ordered in reverse alphabetical order by the Name *column value.*

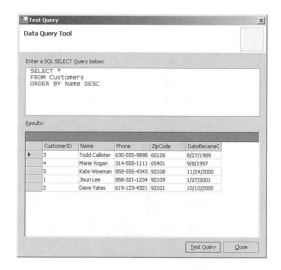

Accessing Database Data from an ASP.NET Web Page

In the examples we've looked at so far, we've been accessing the data in our database through the Web Matrix Project tools. However, our end goal is to have this data displayed on an ASP.NET Web page. This means our ASP.NET Web pages will have to be able to access the data from a database. How is this accomplished? We need to perform the following tasks in our ASP.NET Web page's source code portion:

1. Connect to the database whose data we are interested in.
2. Issue a SELECT SQL query.
3. Retrieve the results from the database.
4. Display the results.

Realize that before we can work with any database's data, we must first establish what is called a *connection*, a link between the program that requests data and the database system.

14

To connect to a specific database, you must provide a *connection string*, which specifies information about the database you want to connect to.

> The concept of a database connection might become clearer if you draw an analogy to a phone connection. To have a telephone conversation with a friend, you must first dial his number. Your friend's telephone number is akin to the connection string—they both provide information on how to make the connection. After entering the telephone number, the telephone system makes a connection between your telephone and your friend's. Then you can have a conversation.

The next step involves issuing the SQL query. Here we must specify the SQL SELECT query we are interested in executing. Once this SQL statement is specified, the query is performed on the database, and the results are returned to the ASP.NET Web page. We can choose to have these results passed back in one of two ways: either as a DataSet or a DataReader.

Comparing the DataSet and DataReader

The DataReader lacks some of the functionality that the DataSet has, but it requires fewer resources and can parse the data quicker. The DataReader limits the ASP.NET Web page to accessing the resulting data in order, one record at a time, from the first record to the last. The DataSet, on the other hand, permits the ASP.NET Web page to access the data in random order.

Because we will typically want to display the resulting data in the precise order it is returned, the DataReader is usually the optimal choice. However, for some features, such as allowing the user to sort the database data interactively, a task we'll examine in Hour 18, "Allowing the User to Sort the Data in a DataGrid," a DataSet is needed.

At this point, our ASP.NET Web page has the correct database data residing in either a DataSet or a DataReader. All that's left to do is display the data. This can be accomplished in a number of ways. Typically, we'll use one of a number of Web controls specifically designed to display data. In the next three hours, we'll see how to use a number of these controls.

These four steps are all that are needed to display database data on an ASP.NET Web page. While they may seem like four short, simple steps, they involve a good deal of required source code. Fortunately, the Web Matrix Project provides a Code Builder wizard that will literally write all of this needed code for you! We'll examine this Code Builder in the next section.

Constructing SQL Queries by Using the Web Matrix Project's Code Builder Wizards

Some of the most useful and time-saving features of the Web Matrix Project that we've yet to examine in detail are the Code Builders. The Code Builders are wizards that can be launched from the Web Matrix Project and are designed to produce source code for commonly performed programming tasks. These wizards operate by writing source code based on the answers to a number of questions put to the ASP.NET Web page developer or the settings the developer has specified.

To use one of the Code Builders, you first need to have an ASP.NET Web page open for editing in the Web Matrix Project. To demonstrate the utility of these Code Builders, let's create a new ASP.NET Web page named **DataTools.aspx**. Because you must be viewing the ASP.NET Web page's Code tab to use the Code Builders, take a moment to click the Code tab, if you haven't already. Once we enter the Code tab, the Toolbox lists the Code Builders (see Figure 14.8).

FIGURE 14.8

The Toolbox lists the Code Builders.

In the Toolbox you should see five Code Builders:

- SELECT Data Method
- INSERT Data Method
- DELETE Data Method
- UPDATE Data Method
- Send Email

The SELECT Data Method is the only Code Builder we will be examining in this hour. As its name implies, it is useful for retrieving data from a database table via a SELECT query. The INSERT, DELETE, and UPDATE Data Methods can be used to produce source code to insert, delete, or update data from a database. Finally, the Send Email Code Builder is useful for creating source code to send an e-mail message from an ASP.NET Web page.

14

We will examine using the INSERT Data Method and Send Email Code Builders later in this book. Hour 22, "Allowing Users to Add Guestbook Entries," will include a look at the INSERT Data Method, whereas Hour 24, "Sending E-Mail when a New Guestbook Entry Is Added," will examine how to send an e-mail from an ASP.NET Web page by using the Email Code Builder.

To launch a Code Builder wizard, simply click the Code Builder you want to run and drag it from the Toolbox to the place in the Code tab where you want the source code to appear. Since we are interested in accessing database data from an ASP.NET Web page, drag and drop the SELECT Data Method Code from the Toolbox to the Code tab, just beneath the default VB.NET comments

```
' Insert page code here
'
```

This will display a Connect to Database dialog box (see Figure 14.9). Note that this is the exact same dialog box that is displaycd when the New Connection icon is clicked in the Data tab.

FIGURE 14.9

The SELECT *Data Method Code Builder displays the Connect to Database dialog box.*

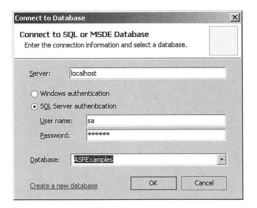

To connect to the ASPExamples database that we created in the previous hour, select the SQL Server authentication radio button. Enter **sa** into the User name textbox, and then the password you chose when installing MSDE into the Password textbox. Next click the Database drop-down list and select the ASPExamples database. Then click the OK button.

If you are using a remote Web hosting company as a server for your ASP.NET Web pages, you will need to provide the SQL Server's location in the Server dialog box and the values for the "User name" and "Password" textboxes.

The next dialog shown is the Query Builder dialog. This dialog box allows you to construct a SQL SELECT query graphically. As you can see in Figure 14.10, the Query Builder contains Tables and Columns listboxes. The Tables listbox lists the tables in the database, and the Columns listbox lists the columns for the selected table.

FIGURE 14.10

You can graphically construct a query.

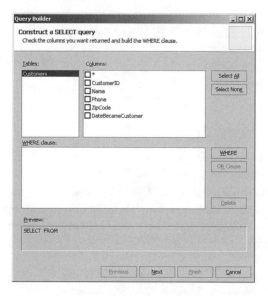

To build your SQL query, start by clicking the Table whose data you are interested in, and then check the columns whose values you want returned. For example, if we wanted to build a query that returns the Name and Phone columns from the Customers table, we would select the Customers table from the list of tables (this is already done for us, because Customers is the only table currently in our database) and then check the Name and Phone columns.

As you are building your query, you can see the resulting SQL syntax in the Preview area at the bottom of the Query Builder. Figure 14.11, which has the Name and Phone columns checked, illustrates this.

14

FIGURE **14.11**

The Name *and* Phone
*columns have been
selected.*

Creating a WHERE Clause

The Query Builder dialog box can also add a WHERE clause. To do this, click the WHERE button. This will display the WHERE Clause Builder dialog box (shown in Figure 14.12). On the left side you can choose the database table and column that you want to have in the WHERE clause. In the middle you can choose the comparison operator. (See Table 14.1 for a review of the comparison operators valid in the WHERE clause's conditions.) On the right side you can specify the value that the WHERE clause condition might meet.

FIGURE **14.12**

WHERE *clauses are
constructed via the*
WHERE *Clause Builder
dialog box.*

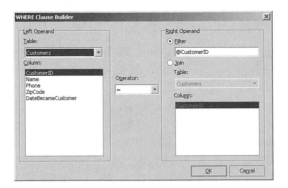

The right side of the WHERE Clause Builder has two radio buttons: one for
Filter and one for Join. For this book we will be using just the Filter option.
A Join is used in cases where two database tables contain related data via a
shared column. Joins, while an integral concept of databases, are beyond
the scope of this book. For more on joins, consider picking up a copy of
Sams Teach Yourself SQL in 21 Days.

Note that the value in the Filter textbox in Figure 14.12 reads @CustomerID. If you click a
different column name from the Column listbox, the filter changes to *@ColumnName*, which
is referred to as a *parameter*. A parameter can be thought of as a placeholder that can have
some value plugged into it at a later time, such as a value entered by the user. Compare this
to the WHERE clause examples we saw earlier in this hour. In these earlier examples we saw
how to compare the column to a constant value, such as WHERE ColumnName = 4.

For example, imagine that we wanted to create an ASP.NET Web page that displayed
information about one particular customer. If we were interested in showing information about
Marie Vogan, we could use the following SQL query to retrieve Marie Vogan's information:

```
SELECT *
FROM Customers
WHERE Name = 'Marie Vogan'
```

In this example our ASP.NET Web page will always display information about customer
Marie Vogan. A more useful ASP.NET Web page would be one in which the user could
enter the name of a customer, and then that customer's information would be displayed.
We will examine precisely how to build such an ASP.NET Web page in the next hour.
For now, realize that if you want to construct a query whose WHERE clause is dependent
on some yet unknown value, leave the *@ColumnName* value in the Filter textbox.

If you want the WHERE clause to compare a column to a constant value,
you can enter the constant value in the Filter textbox. For example, if you
wanted the SQL SELECT query to return only customers who lived in zip code
92109, you could select the ZipCode column from the Column listbox and
specify '92109' in the Filter textbox.

Using Multiple Conditions in the WHERE Clause

The WHERE Clause Builder allows you to specify only a single condition; that is, it
allows for only a single table's column to be compared to either a constant value or

14

the value of a parameter. If you want to have multiple conditions in the WHERE clause, such as

```
WHERE Name = @Name AND ZipCode = '92101'
```

you can do so via the Query Builder. To see how to do this, let's work through an example that lists the Name and Phone number for all customers who live in some specified zip code and have a CustomerID less than some specified number. (By "some specified zip code" is meant a zip code value that will be selected at a later point, perhaps by the user; this, then, implies that we will need to use parameters for the conditions.)

In Figure 4.11 the Query Builder was used to select the Name and Phone columns from the Customers table. Let's extend this example to include a suitable WHERE clause. Start by clicking the WHERE button, which will display the WHERE Clause Builder. (Refer back to Figure 14.12 for a screenshot of this dialog box.)

Let's first specify the condition involving the ZipCode field. In the WHERE Clause Builder dialog box, select the ZipCode column from the Column listbox and leave its Operator as = and its Filter textbox value as @ZipCode. Figure 14.13 shows a screenshot of what the WHERE Clause Builder should look like.

FIGURE 14.13

A WHERE condition that checks whether the ZipCode column equals some parameter value has been added.

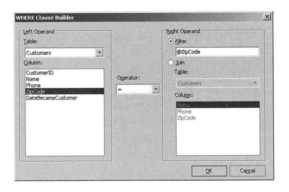

Save this WHERE condition by clicking the OK button, which will return you to the Query Builder dialog box, shown in Figure 14.14. Note that the ZipCode WHERE condition that we just added is now displayed.

FIGURE **14.14**

The Query Builder after a WHERE *condition has been added.*

As Figure 14.14 shows, once a WHERE condition has been added to the query, two buttons, AND and OR, are displayed in place of the WHERE button. You can click these buttons to add additional WHERE conditions.

Immediately after returning from the WHERE Clause Builder dialog box, you may find the AND button disabled (grayed out). If this is the case, simply shift your focus to the WHERE Clause portion of the Query Builder dialog box by clicking the WHERE condition. This will activate the AND button, making it clickable.

To add the condition on the CustomerID column, click the AND button. This will display the WHERE Clause Builder dialog box again. This time choose the CustomerID from the Column listbox, select the < operator from the Operator drop-down list, and leave the parameter @ColumnID as the Filter textbox value. After you have added this WHERE condition, click OK, which will take you back to the Query Builder dialog box, which should look like Figure 14.15.

14

FIGURE 14.15
The Query Builder after a second WHERE *condition has been added.*

At this point we have completed building our SQL query and are ready to progress to the next step in the SELECT Data Method Code Builder wizard. Click the Next button, which can be found in the bottom right corner of the Query Builder dialog box.

To remove a WHERE condition from the query in the Query Builder dialog box, simply click the WHERE condition you wish to remove and then click the Delete button.

Examining the SQL SELECT Statement with the Query Viewer

After building a SELECT query in the Query Builder portion of the wizard, you can test the results of your query through the Query Preview. Shown in Figure 14.16, this Query Preview tool is displayed after clicking the Next button from the Query Builder dialog box.

FIGURE 14.16

The Query Preview allows you to view the results of the query constructed in the Query Builder dialog box.

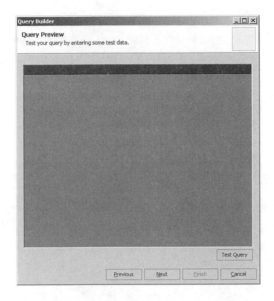

To test the query, click the Test Query button, which will display a Preview dialog box that shows the SQL syntax that will be executed. If your query contains any WHERE clause parameters, the Preview dialog box prompts you to enter values to use for the query. Figure 14.17 shows a screenshot of the Preview dialog box for our SQL query. Note the two textboxes for the @ZipCode and @CustomerID parameters.

FIGURE 14.17

You can specify parameter values in the Preview dialog box.

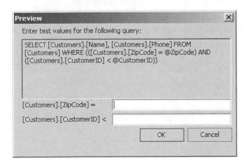

14

To see what results will be returned when the values 92109 and 4 are entered for the
@ZipCode and @CustomerID parameters, enter the value **92109** into the ZipCode textbox
and **4** into the CustomerID textbox. Click the OK button to view the results of the query,
which are shown in Figure 14.18.

FIGURE **14.18**

*The results for the
specified parameter
values are displayed.*

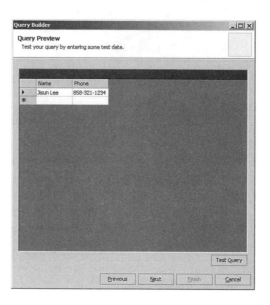

When entering a value into the ZipCode textbox, notice that we entered the
value 92109 and that we did *not* surround this value with single quote
marks. When supplying values to parameters, we never need to surround
the values with single quote marks.

After viewing the query results, you can rerun a test query by clicking the Test Query
button again. If you need to change the query, you can click the Previous button to return
to the Query Builder screen.

Completing the Wizard

Once you have completed testing the query to your satisfaction, click the Next button.
This will take you to the final stage of the SELECT Data Method Code Builder (shown in
Figure 14.19).

FIGURE 14.19

The last stage of the Code Builder wizard.

Keep in mind that the whole purpose of the Code Builder is to write the source code needed to connect to a database, execute a SQL SELECT statement, and return the results. The source code produced by the Code Builder is placed in a function that is named, by default, MyQueryMethod. You can—and are recommended to—change the name of this function. Simply type the function name you would like to use into the textbox on this final wizard stage. A good, albeit verbose, function name for this query might be GetCustomersByZipAndCustomerID.

Next we have to specify whether we want the data returned from the database to be returned as a DataSet or as a DataReader. Recall that more often than not we'll want to have a DataReader returned. Therefore, for this example, click the DataReader radio button. Now go ahead and click the Finish button. This will cause about 15 lines of code to be automatically added to your ASP.NET Web page, as seen in Figure 14.20.

If you are following along at your computer right now, you may be a bit intimidated by the code produced by the Code Builder. I'll agree that the code may look a bit over-whelming, but you don't need to concern yourself with the details—the Code Builder can produce the needed code for you.

14

FIGURE 14.20

The Code Builder automatically writes the needed source code.

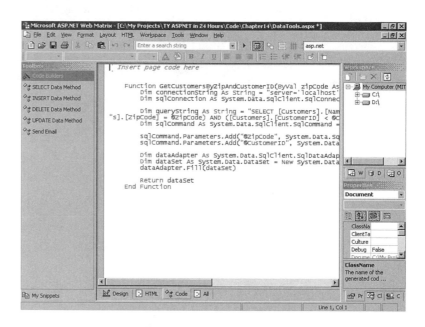

We are not going to delve into the code produced by the Code Builder in this book. Instead, over the next few hours, we'll examine how to display the results returned by the function the Code Builder creates for us automatically. If, however, you would like to learn more about the source code needed to access database data and how to provide this code in an ASP.NET Web page, consider picking up a copy of *ASP.NET Unleashed*, which covers this, and a myriad of other ASP.NET topics, in much greater detail than we can here.

Summary

In this hour we examined Structured Query Language, or SQL, which is the language used by all modern databases for retrieving, inserting, updating, and deleting data. This hour focused on retrieving database data by using both SQL and the data tools provided by the Web Matrix Project.

To retrieve rows from a database table, a SELECT statement is used, with the syntax

```
SELECT Column1, Column2, ..., ColumnN
FROM TableName
WHERE whereConditions
ORDER BY ColumnName
```

where the WHERE and ORDER BY clauses are optional.

Fortunately, we do not have to be SQL aficionados to retrieve database data in an ASP.NET Web page. As we saw in the "Constructing SQL Queries by Using the Web Matrix Project's Code Wizards" section, the Web Matrix Project provides a set of data tools that allow us to construct our SELECT queries graphically. In the following hours, we will use these tools to display database data in a variety of Web controls!

Q&A

Q Can SQL be used to retrieve data from multiple database tables?

A Yes. Although in this book we will only be studying examples that involve a single database table, database tables commonly share relationships. For example, imagine that we were working on a Web site for an e-commerce site, like Amazon.com. There might be a database table called Orders, which would contain a row for each order. Each order, of course, could have one or more items. Therefore, we might also have a table called OrderItems, which would contain a row for each item placed in each order.

These two tables obviously share a relationship with one another. Each row in the OrderItems table "belongs" to a particular row in the Orders table. This relationship can be expressed using *foreign keys,* which are special column types that relate a row in one table to a row in another. The topic of foreign keys is beyond the scope of this book.

Once a relationship has been established between two tables, oftentimes you will want to retrieve results from both tables. For example, using the Orders and OrderItems example, we might want to issue a query that returns the list of orders placed in the past 24 hours. Along with each order, we might want to also retrieve its particular items. Such multitable SQL queries are beyond the scope of this book, but realize they are quite common in practice.

For more information on multitable relationships and more advanced SQL queries, consider picking up a copy of *Sams Teach Yourself SQL in 24 Hours*.

Workshop

Quiz

1. Imagine that you had a database table named Albums that contained the following columns: AlbumID, Name, Artist, and DatePurchased. Write a SQL query to retrieve the Name of the albums, ordered alphabetically.

14

2. Write a SQL query to retrieve, in this order, the artist, the name, and the date every album was purchased, ordered alphabetically by the artist.

3. Write a SQL query that retrieves the names of all of the albums by the artist Nirvana, ordered by the dates the albums were purchased, starting with the most recently purchased.

4. True or False: The following two SQL queries would return the exact same data:
```
SELECT AlbumID, Name, Artist, DatePurchased
FROM Albums
```
and
```
SELECT *
FROM Albums
```

5. Describe the steps you would take to create the source code necessary to retrieve the name and purchase date of every album recorded by the artist Pavement whose AlbumID is greater than 5. The function created should be named GetPavementAlbums() and return a DataReader.

Answers

1. The following SQL query would suffice:
```
SELECT Name
FROM Albums
ORDER BY Name
```

2. The following SQL query would suffice:
```
SELECT Artist, Name, DatePurchased
FROM Albums
ORDER BY Artist
```

3. The following SQL query would suffice:
```
SELECT Name
FROM Albums
WHERE Artist = "Nirvana"
ORDER BY DatePurchased DESC
```

4. True.

5. Start by dragging the SELECT Data Method Code Builder from the Toolbox and onto the code portion of the ASP.NET Web page. Next choose the database that the Albums table resides in and enter the logon credentials.

   In the Query Builder screen, select the Albums table from the Tables listbox and check the Name and DatePurchased columns from the Columns listbox. Next click the WHERE button—this will display the WHERE Clause Builder dialog box.

From the WHERE Clause Builder dialog box, select the column AlbumID, the Operator >, and the Filter 5. Click the OK button. This will add the WHERE clause portion that filters the records returned to those whose AlbumID is greater than 5. Next click the AND button to add another WHERE clause component. This time choose the Artist column, the Operator =, and type into the Filter textbox the value **Pavement**. Click the OK button.

This completes the Query Building stage. Click the Next button until you reach the final screen, where you are prompted to enter the function name and choose whether the function should return a DataSet or a DataReader. Name the function **GetPavementAlbums** and select the DataReader option.

Exercise

This exercise is intended to improve your proficiency with SQL SELECT queries and the Web Matrix Project's Test Query tool. Start by clicking the Query icon in the Data tab in the Web Matrix Project. This will display the Test Query dialog box. (If you are not connected to a database, first connect to the database that contains the Customers table.)

In the Test Query dialog box, write the SQL query to retrieve those customers whose CustomerID is less than or equal to 3. Note the list of customers you see when testing the query. Now run another query, this time retrieving those customers whose zip code equals 92109. (You are encouraged to experiment with the Test Query tool further.)

14

HOUR 15

Displaying Data with the DataGrid Web Control

In the past two hours, we examined what databases are, their importance, and how to retrieve data from them. As ASP.NET developers, what we are really interested in is being able to display data in an ASP.NET Web page; that's the topic of this hour and the next two.

In this hour we will examine the DataGrid Web control. As you will see, this Web control is designed for displaying two-dimensional data, such as the data in the results of a SQL SELECT query, by using an HTML <table> tag. The DataGrid is an incredibly powerful Web control that provides impressive functionality. In this hour we focus on the fundamentals of the DataGrid, looking at how to add a DataGrid to an ASP.NET Web page, how to display data in a DataGrid, and how to format the appearance of the DataGrid.

Be sure to read and comprehend this hour before moving on. A number of future hours will explore the DataGrid in more detail, building on the material covered in this hour.

Specifically, in this hour we will cover

- What the DataGrid Web control is
- How to add a DataGrid to an ASP.NET Web page
- How to specify what data the DataGrid should display
- Customizing the data displayed by the DataGrid
- Setting the DataGrid's aesthetic properties
- Using the Web Matrix Project's Auto Format tool to generate visually pleasing DataGrids

Displaying Database Data in an ASP.NET Web Page

In the last hour we looked at the four things that need to be done to display database information in an ASP.NET Web page, as follows:

1. Connect to the database whose data interests you.
2. Issue a SELECT SQL query.
3. Retrieve the results from the database.
4. Display the results.

The last hour examined using the Web Matrix Project's SELECT Data Method Code Builder to have the source code for steps 1 through 3 performed automatically. That is, the function created by the Code Builder contains the source code to connect to the specified database, issue the proper SQL SELECT statement, and retrieve the database results, storing them in either a DataSet or a DataReader. Step 4, displaying the database query results, is all that remains.

Displaying Database Data with ASP.NET Web Controls

As we saw in Hour 8, "ASP.NET Web Controls for Displaying Text," the Label and Literal Web controls are designed for displaying text. In Hours 9 through 11 we examined the TextBox, DropDownList, RadioButton, and CheckBox Web controls, which are used for retrieving user input.

Not surprisingly, there are a number of Web controls designed for displaying database data. The Web controls for displaying data, referred to as the *data Web controls,* include the following:

- DataGrid
- DataList

15

- Repeater
- DropDownList
- RadioButtonList
- CheckBoxList
- ListBox

We will not be examining all of these Web controls in this book but will instead focus on the most salient ones, namely, the DataGrid, DropDownList, RadioButtonList, and CheckBoxList. This hour focuses on the DataGrid Web control.

If you are interested in a more in-depth look at the ASP.NET data Web controls, including an examination of the DataList and Repeater controls, consider picking up a copy of my book *ASP.NET Data Web Controls Kick Start*, from Sams Publishing.

Getting Started with the DataGrid Web Control

Recall that a database table can be thought of as a two-dimensional grid. The columns of the table specify the attributes for the data stored in the table, whereas each row represents a particular instance of information. For example, in the Customers table, there are columns for each of the customer attributes: Name, ZipCode, Phone, and so on. Each customer is represented by a single row in the table.

Furthermore, when executing a SELECT query, a two-dimensional grid is returned. For example, the query

```
SELECT Name, Phone
FROM Customers
```

returns a two-dimensional grid with two columns (one for Name and one for Phone) with a row for each row in the Customers table.

A natural way to display the two-dimensional data from a SELECT statement on a Web page is with an HTML <table> tag. The HTML <table> tag creates a two-dimensional table with a specified number of columns and rows. The syntax for an HTML <table> tag uses a <tr> tag for each row and a <td> tag for each column in the row. A 3 × 2 grid could be displayed in a Web page like so:

```
<table>
  <tr>  <!-- This <tr> tag marks the first row -->
```

```
     <td>This text will appear in the first column of the first row.</td>
     <td> This text will appear in the second column of the first row.</td>
   </tr>
   <tr>  <!-- This <tr> tag marks the second row -->
     <td>This text will appear in the first column of the second row.</td>
     <td> This text will appear in the second column of the second row.</td>
   </tr>
   <tr>  <!-- This <tr> tag marks the third row -->
     <td>This text will appear in the first column of the third row.</td>
     <td> This text will appear in the second column of the third row.</td>
   </tr>
</table>
```

Often you will want to display the contents of an SQL SELECT query by using an HTML
<table> tag, with one column in the table for each column returned in the SELECT query
and one row in the <table> for each row returned by the query.

The DataGrid Web control provides precisely this functionality. When the DataGrid is
rendered, it produces an HTML <table> tag, with a <table> row for each row in the
database data it is displaying, and a <table> column for each column of the database data.

Our First DataGrid Example

Using a DataGrid Web control to display database data involves the following steps:

1. Add the DataGrid Web control to the ASP.NET Web page.
2. Use the SELECT Data Method Code Builder to generate the needed source code to
   connect to the database and retrieve the SELECT query results.
3. Display the database results to the DataGrid Web control.

In the next three subsections, we will examine how to perform these three steps. In the
process you'll be creating an ASP.NET Web page that displays the contents of the
Customers database table in a DataGrid Web control.

Adding the DataGrid to an ASP.NET Web Page

To add the DataGrid to an ASP.NET Web page, we simply need to drag and drop the
DataGrid Web control from the Toolbox onto the designer. To accomplish this, let's create a
new ASP.NET Web page called SimpleDataGrid.aspx. Once this page has been created,
add a DataGrid Web control. In the designer the DataGrid Web control will appear as a
3 × 6 grid. Figure 15.1 contains a screenshot of the designer after a DataGrid has been
added.

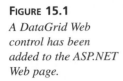

FIGURE 15.1
A DataGrid Web control has been added to the ASP.NET Web page.

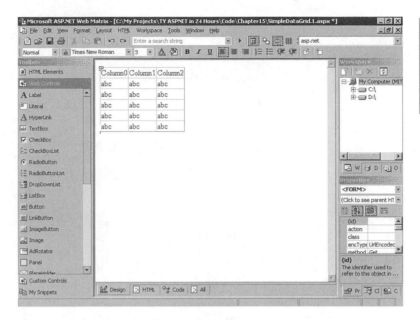

Next set the ID property of the DataGrid to **dgCustomers**.

Using the SELECT Data Method Code Builder

The next step is to create the source code needed to connect to the database, perform the appropriate SQL query, and retrieve the database results as a DataReader. To accomplish this, we will use the SELECT Data Method Code Builder.

Recall that to use the Code Builders, you must be in the Code tab, so take a moment to visit this tab. Next run the SELECT Data Method Code Builder by dragging and dropping the SELECT Data Method Code Builder from the Toolbox onto the Code tab.

As we saw in the previous section, the first step prompts you to specify database information. Start by selecting the ASPExamples database (assuming you have installed MSDE locally and are running ASP.NET Web pages from your computer) as we did previously and click Next. In the Query Builder, choose the * option from the Columns listbox and click Next (see Figure 15.2 for a screenshot of what the Query Builder dialog box should look like prior to clicking Next).

FIGURE 15.2

Construct the SELECT *query to retrieve all columns.*

The next screen is the Test Query screen; feel free to bypass this stage if you'd like. However, if you want, you can click the Test Query button, and you will see the data returned by the SQL query. On the final screen of the Code Builder wizard, you will be prompted for the function name and whether you want the data returned as a DataSet or DataReader. Specify the function name as **GetCustomers** and have the data returned via a DataReader. After specifying these values, click Finish.

Upon completion of the Code Builder wizard, you should see a new function in the code section. This function, when called, will return a DataReader that contains the complete information of each and every customer in the Customers table.

Displaying the Database Query Results in the DataGrid

At this point we have a DataGrid Web control in our ASP.NET Web page and a function, GetCustomers(), that returns a DataReader containing the data in the Customers database table.

The task ahead of us now is to have the DataReader's contents displayed in the DataGrid. This task is accomplished via *data binding*. Data binding is the process of associating data from some object that contains data, such as a DataReader or DataSet, to a Web control that is designed to display data, such as the DataGrid, DropDownList, and so on.

All Web controls that can participate in data binding have a property called DataSource and a method called DataBind(). To bind data to a Web control, two lines of source code are needed. The first must be used to set the Web control's DataSource property to the

15

object that contains the data to display, and the second line of code must call the Web control's `DataBind()` method. In the general case this code looks as follows:

```
WebControlID.DataSource = someObject
WebControlID.DataBind()
```

Typically *someObject* is a DataReader or DataSet.

Recall that our ASP.NET Web page's DataGrid's ID property was set to dgCustomers. Furthermore, the function `GetCustomers()` returns a DataReader object that contains the data we want to display. Therefore, these two general lines of code, for the `SimpleDataGrid.aspx` ASP.NET Web page, become

```
dgCustomers.DataSource = GetCustomers()
dgCustomers.DataBind()
```

Now the only question is where this code should be placed. Since we want the DataGrid to display the database's data when the page is first loaded, we'll place this code in the Page_Load event handler. Recall that code in the Page_Load event handler is executed every time the ASP.NET Web page is visited.

To add this, click the Code tab and enter the following code:

```
Sub Page_Load(sender as object, e as EventArgs)
  dgCustomers.DataSource = GetCustomers()
  dgCustomers.DataBind()
End Sub
```

After adding this, the Code tab should contain both the code for the `GetCustomers()` function and the code for the Page_Load event handler.

Once you have added this code, save the ASP.NET Web page and view it through a browser. As Figure 15.3 shows, the Web page, when viewed through a browser, displays the contents of the Customers table using an HTML <table>.

FIGURE 15.3
The contents of the Customers *table are displayed.*

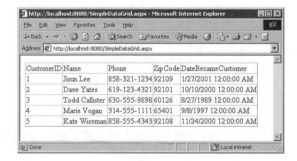

From the `SimpleDataGrid.aspx` example, you can see that displaying database data in the form of an HTML <table> is quite easy and straightforward. We needed to perform

only three steps: First we added a DataGrid Web control to the ASP.NET Web; next we used the SELECT Data Method Code Builder to automatically produce source code required to query the database for us; and finally, we added two lines of source code to bind the database data to the DataGrid.

In Hour 17, "Working with Data-Bound DropDownList, RadioButton, and Checkbox Web Controls," we will see that these same three steps are used with those Web controls.

Specifying the Columns That Appear in the DataGrid

As previously discussed, the DataGrid displays the data that has been bound to it using an HTML <table> tag, where each field in its *DataSource* is rendered as a column in the HTML <table>, and each row in the DataSource is rendered as a row in the HTML <table>. (The data the DataGrid is bound to is commonly referred to as the DataSource because the data is bound to the DataGrid by setting the DataGrid's DataSource property.)

Recall from Hour 13, "An Introduction to Databases," that "field" is a synonym for "columns" when talking about database table columns. Since the DataGrid produces HTML <table> columns, it can quickly become confusing as to whether the word "column" pertains to a database table column or a column generated by the DataGrid. Therefore, for the remainder of this hour, I will refer to database table columns as fields.

What is important to realize is that *every* field in the DataSource is displayed as a column in the DataGrid's resulting HTML <table>; moreover, the columns in the HTML <table> are displayed in the precise order they are contained in the DataSource. For example, if the SQL query used in the SimpleDataGrid.aspx example was changed from

```
SELECT *
FROM Customers
```

to

```
SELECT Phone, Name, ZipCode
FROM Customers
```

the resulting DataGrid would contain three columns displaying the DataSource field values for Phone, Name, and ZipCode, in that order. Furthermore, note that the DataGrid displays header text for each column. For example, in Figure 15.3 you can see that above the first DataGrid column, it reads CustomerID. Such headers are precisely the names of the DataSource fields.

Fortunately, the DataGrid allows the developer to specify what columns from the DataSource it should display and in what order. To illustrate this, let's create a new ASP.NET Web page and add a DataGrid that will show only a subset of the columns in its DataSource.

Start by creating a new ASP.NET Web page named ColumnsSpecified.aspx. Next drag and drop a DataGrid Web control from the Toolbox and onto the designer and set the DataGrid's ID property to **dgCustomers**. Note that when the DataGrid's properties are displayed in the Property pane, there are two blue hyperlinks beneath the list of properties. The first is titled Auto Format..., and the second Property Builder... (see Figure 15.4).

FIGURE 15.4

The DataGrid's Properties pane contains Auto Format *and* Property Builder *hyperlinks.*

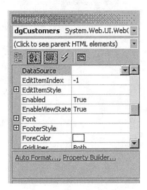

In order to specify what columns should appear in the DataGrid, we need to enter the DataGrid's Property Builder. To do this, simply click the Property Builder... hyperlink. Doing so will display a dialog box titled dgCustomers Properties. This dialog box is shown in Figure 15.5.

FIGURE 15.5

The DataGrid's Property Builder *dialog box.*

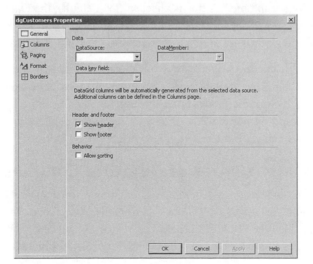

The dgColumns Properties dialog box has five "screens" that contain various DataGrid settings. You can toggle between these screens by clicking the appropriate screen name in the upper-left corner. The default screen is the General screen; the other four are Columns, Paging, Format, and Borders.

To set the DataGrid's columns, we need to specify some properties in the Columns screen. To get to this screen, simply click the Columns label in the upper-left corner. Doing so will display the screen shown in Figure 15.6.

FIGURE 15.6
The Columns screen.

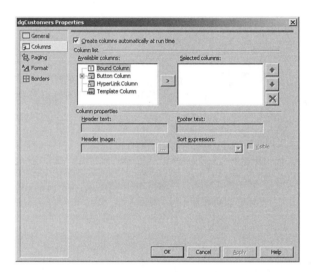

The first thing to notice in the Columns screen is the checkbox titled "Create columns automatically at run time." If this is checked (the default), the DataGrid will automatically create a column for each field in the DataSource. To specify what columns should appear in the DataGrid, as in this discussion, you'll want to uncheck this checkbox.

Underneath this checkbox there are two listboxes. The one on the left, titled "Available columns," contains the various types of columns that can be placed in a DataGrid. The right listbox, "Selected columns," lists the columns that have been explicitly added to the DataGrid. To add a column to the DataGrid, select the column type you want to add from the left listbox and click the > button between the two listboxes.

The Different Types of DataGrid Columns

Each column type creates a different kind of column for the DataGrid. For example, the Bound Column displays the value of a field from the DataSource. This is the type of column that is used when the DataGrid is set to create its columns automatically from the DataSource, as was the case with the DataGrid shown in Figure 15.3.

15

Other column types provide alternate functionality. The HyperLink Column, for example, displays a hyperlink to a URL. The hyperlink URL or text can be set to the value of a DataSource field.

A DataGrid can consist of a mix of column types. We could create a DataGrid with a HyperLink Column followed by a Bound Column. Each row in the DataGrid would have its first column containing a hyperlink and its last column containing the value of the specified DataSource field for that row.

In this hour we will examine only the Bound Column. In Hour 16, "Examining Further DataGrid Examples," we will continue our examination of the Bound Column and also explore the HyperLink Column.

Adding a Bound Column to the DataGrid

At this point we have created an ASP.NET Web page named ColumnsSpecified.aspx and added a DataGrid Web control. We then clicked the Property Builder... hyperlink from the DataGrid's properties displayed in the Properties pane, and selected the Columns screen. Then we unchecked the "Create columns automatically at run time" checkbox, which informs the DataGrid that it should not automatically create a column for each field in the DataSource.

Now we can specify what columns we want to be displayed in the DataGrid. In Figure 15.3 we saw how to display all of the fields from the Customers database table. Now imagine that we wanted to display only the Name and Phone fields. To accomplish this, we would need to explicitly add two Bound Columns.

Let's first add the Bound Column for the Name field. Start by clicking the Bound Column from the "Available columns" listbox and then click the > button. This will add a Bound Column list item to the "Selected columns" listbox. Once this Bound Column item has been copied to the "Selected columns" listbox, a number of textboxes will appear in the section titled "BoundColumn properties." Figure 15.7 shows a screenshot of the Property Builder's Columns screen after a Bound Column has been added.

Once you have added a column to the DataGrid, you can remove it by selecting the column from the "Selected columns" listbox and then clicking the delete icon (the black X next to the lower-right corner of the "Selected columns" listbox). Furthermore, you can alter the order of the columns in the DataGrid by selecting a column from the "Selected columns" listbox and clicking the up and down arrow icons.

FIGURE **15.7**

A Bound Column has been added to the DataGrid's list of columns.

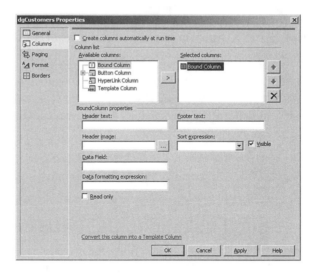

Recall that the Bound Column displays the value of a particular `DataSource` field. For this Bound Column we want to display the value of the `Name` field. To specify the `DataSource` field displayed by the Bound Column, all we have to do is enter the name of the field (**Name**) in the Data Field textbox.

Next we can supply a value for the text that will appear in this column's header. Recall that by default the actual name of the field is what is displayed in the column's header. This means that if we don't specify the header, the value "Name" will be displayed. However, let's set the column's header text to the value "Customer Name." To do this, enter the value **Customer Name** into the Header text textbox. Once you have entered these values, your screen should look similar to the screenshot in Figure 15.8.

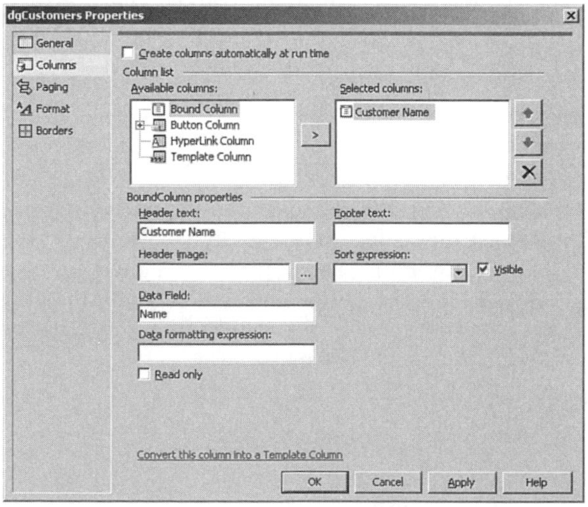

FIGURE **15.8**

The first Bound Column has been added.

Now that we have added a Bound Column for the Name field, all that remains is to add a Bound Column for the Phone field. Simply click the Bound Column column type from the "Available columns" listbox and then click the > button. This will add a new Bound Column list item to the "Selected columns" listbox. For this Bound Column, enter **Phone** into the Data Field textbox and **Phone Number** into the Header text textbox.

Once you have completed these steps, click the OK button. This will close the Property Builder dialog box. You will notice that the DataGrid displayed in the designer has changed its appearance. As Figure 15.9 shows, the DataGrid has two columns, each with the text we specified in the Header text textboxes. Also, the "abc" value that was previously displayed in each cell of the DataGrid has been replaced by the value "Databound."

FIGURE 15.9

The DataGrid in the designer's appearance has changed to reflect the two columns added.

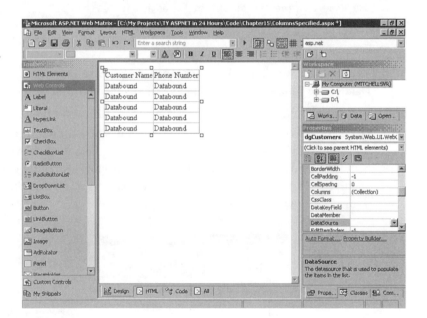

If in the designer you see the two columns shown in Figure 15.9, plus some additional columns, you may have forgotten to uncheck the "Create columns automatically at run time" checkbox in the Columns screen of the Property Builder. If this is the case, take a moment to go back to the Property Builder and uncheck this option.

Binding Data to the DataGrid and Testing the ASP.NET Web Page

Now that we have added the DataGrid to the ASP.NET Web page and specified its settings, we need to specify what data is to be bound to the DataGrid. Recall that this is accomplished by first using the SELECT Data Method Code Builder wizard to generate a function that returns a DataReader with the database data we're interested in displaying. Let's use the same function as in the SimpleDataGrid.aspx example we looked at earlier in this hour. That is, when using the Code Builder, specify that the query should return all columns and have no WHERE clause. Name this function **GetCustomers**, just as we did before.

Then add a Page_Load event handler with the following code:

```
Sub Page_Load(sender as Object, e as EventArgs)
    dgCustomers.DataSource = GetCustomers()
    dgCustomers.DataBind()
End Sub
```

This code, as we discussed earlier, sets the DataGrid's DataSource property to the DataReader returned by the GetCustomers() function and then binds the data to the DataGrid via a call to the DataGrid's DataBind() method.

Once you have provided these source code changes, test out the ASP.NET Web page by visiting it through a browser. You should see the output shown in Figure 15.10. Note that the DataGrid displayed shows two columns (even though the DataSource has five fields), and the columns have the text we specified in the headers, as opposed to the fields' names.

FIGURE 15.10

The DataGrid now shows just two columns.

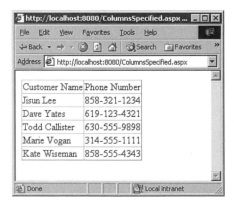

Examining the DataGrid's Aesthetic Properties

Recall that when we examined the Label Web control, the TextBox Web control, the DropDownList Web control, and so on, we noted that these controls had what are called *aesthetic properties*, which affect the visual appearance of the rendered Web control in the Web page. For example, with the Label Web control, we could set the ForeColor property to specify the color for the Label's text.

The DataGrid Web control, like all Web controls, has a number of aesthetic properties as well, such as ForeColor, BackColor, Font, and so on. Setting the DataGrid's aesthetic properties affects the entire DataGrid. For example, if you set the DataGrid's Font properties Name subproperty to Verdana, all text displayed in the DataGrid will be displayed in the Verdana font.

You will typically want different parts of the DataGrid to be formatted differently. For example, you may want the DataGrid's column header text to be displayed in a larger, bold font and the text in the rows of the DataGrid to be displayed in a smaller font.

Specifying aesthetic properties for various portions of the DataGrid is a breeze with the Property Builder. Let's extend our previous example, ColumnsSpecified.aspx, to include aesthetic formatting. (For this example, it is recommended that you work with a copy of the ColumnsSpecified.aspx, naming the copy AestheticProperties.aspx.) To tweak a DataGrid's aesthetic properties, perform the following steps:

1. Launch the Property Builder and visit the Format screen. Recall that to display the Property Builder, you click the DataGrid Web control so its properties are loaded in the Properties pane.

2. Next click the Property Builder... hyperlink at the bottom of the Properties pane. This will display the Property Builder (refer back to Figure 15.5).

3. Finally, click the Format label listed in the upper left corner of the Property Builder dialog box.

Figure 15.11 shows a screenshot of the Format screen. Note that in the screenshot the Items and Columns options from the Objects listbox have been expanded.

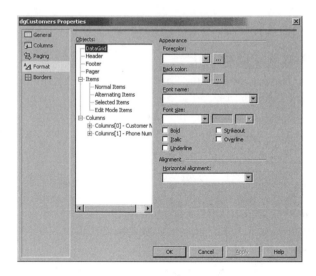

The Format screen lists the various components of the DataGrid Web control in the
Objects listbox. These are the components that can have aesthetic properties specified for
their content. For example, the aesthetic properties specified for the DataGrid object
apply to all the content in the DataGrid; the aesthetic properties set for the Header object,
however, apply only to the headers of each column.

To familiarize ourselves with specifying aesthetic properties for the DataGrid and its
components, let's perform the steps necessary to produce the following visual specifications:

- Display all of the text in the DataGrid in the Verdana font.
- Center the header columns' text and display them in a bold font of size 16pt. Also,
  make the header's foreground color white and its background color navy.
- Display the text in the items of the DataGrid with a nonbold font of size 10pt. Also,
  create alternating rows of a lighter background color.
- Italicize the text in the Phone Number column and center the phone number.

To provide these visual effects, we will need to specify aesthetic properties for a number
of components in the Objects listbox. We'll examine how to specify these properties for
each component one at a time in the next four subsections.

Aesthetic Properties That Apply to the Entire DataGrid

Any aesthetic properties that you want to be applied to the entire DataGrid should be
specified in the DataGrid object's aesthetic properties. One property that you typically
want to apply to the entire contents of the DataGrid is the font face. While you may want

certain parts of the DataGrid to have bold text or larger or smaller font sizes, it's often best to use a single font face for all of the DataGrid's text.

To set an aesthetic property for the entire DataGrid, simply click the DataGrid label from the Objects listbox in the Format screen. Then simply set the appropriate aesthetic property on the right. For our example simply select the font Verdana from the Font name drop-down list. If there are any other DataGrid-wide settings you'd like to set, specify them here.

Setting Aesthetic Properties for the Column Headers

To set aesthetic properties for the headers of all DataGrid columns, click the Header label in the Objects listbox and simply choose the various aesthetic property options to the right. For this exercise start by setting the Forecolor to white and the Back color to navy.

Note that the drop-down list provides you with only a small selection of color choices, not nearly as many color options as are present when setting the ForeColor and BackColor properties for other Web controls via the Properties pane. Also, as of the time of this writing, the buttons next to the drop-down lists, when clicked, do nothing. Keep in mind that the Web Matrix Project is still in progress and has a number of these little "surprises" here and there. (It's hard to complain, though, seeing as the Web Matrix Project's price is $0.00.)

If you cannot find the color you are looking for in the Forecolor or Back color drop-down lists, you can simply click in the drop-down list and type in a value in the hexadecimal format. (Hexadecimal format is given as #RRGGBB, where RR corresponds to the amount of red in the color, GG to the amount of green, and BB to the amount of blue.)

Next we want to set the font size to 16pt and make the header text bold and center-aligned. This can be accomplished with the following sequence of steps:

1. First select the Custom option from the Font size drop-down list. This will enable the textbox and drop-down list to the right of the Font size drop-down list.

2. In the textbox enter **16** and from the far right drop-down list, select pt.

3. To make the header text bold, simply check the Bold checkbox.

4. Finally, to have the header text centered, select Center from the Horizontal alignment drop-down list.

After specifying these settings, your screen should look similar to the screenshot in Figure 15.12.

FIGURE **15.12**

The Header aesthetic properties have been set.

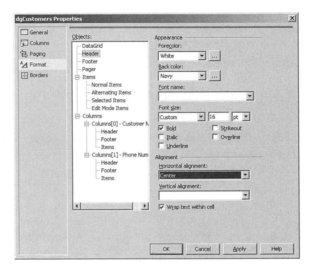

Specifying Aesthetic Properties for the Rows of the DataGrid

Our next step is to set the font size to 10pt for the rows of the DataGrid and to create rows of alternating background colors in the DataGrid. To accomplish this, we need to set aesthetic properties for the Items object.

As Figure 15.11 showed, the Items label in the Objects listbox can be expanded to show a number of items directly beneath it. If you haven't already, click the little plus sign next to the Items label to expand it. (Upon being clicked, the plus changes to a minus sign, as seen in the figure.)

Next click the Normal Items option from beneath the Items label. This will list the aesthetic properties for the rows of the DataGrid. Here we want to set the font size to 10pt. Similar to what we did with the Header aesthetic properties, set the font size to 10pt by selecting the Custom option from the Font size listbox, entering **10** into the textbox to the right of this listbox, and selecting pt from the far-right listbox.

In addition to the Normal Items option, there is also an Alternating Items option. The Alternating Items option specifies aesthetic properties for each alternating row. When displaying large amounts of data, it usually helps to give the rows alternating background colors. This helps the Web visitor discern one row from the next. All we need to do is specify different Back colors for the Normal Items and Alternating Items.

For this exercise let's have the Normal Items background be white. This is the default color, so you do not need to explicitly set the Normal Items Back color drop-down list to White, although you can, if you'd like. For every other item, let's make the background gray. Click the Alternating Items option from the Objects list and then select Gray from the Back color drop-down list.

Specifying Aesthetic Properties for the Columns of the DataGrid

If you have specified which columns should be present in the DataGrid, you can set column-specific aesthetic properties. Recall that to explicitly specify the DataGrid columns you have to add column types, such as Bound Columns, from the Columns screen in the Property Builder. We did this in the previous example, `ColumnsSpecified.aspx`, to display just two columns, one for the customer's name and one for the phone number. Recall that for this exercise we want to have the customer's phone number centered and displayed in an italicized font. Since these aesthetic properties apply to a specific column, we will need to set only this particular column's properties.

Expanding the Columns label from the Objects listbox shows a list of the columns that have been explicitly added to the DataGrid. Since the DataGrid for this example has two columns, there are two entries under the Columns label. Under each of these two column labels, there are additional labels—Header, Footer, and Items—which set the aesthetic properties for the specific column's header, footer, and rows. (Refer back to Figure 15.11 or Figure 15.12 to examine the full hierarchical structure of the Objects listbox.)

 If you didn't explicitly specify any columns for the DataGrid Web control, the Columns label in the Objects listbox will not be present.

Since we want to have the customer's phone number centered and displayed in italics, we need to set the aesthetic properties for the Phone Number column's Items. Click the Items label beneath the Columns[1] – Phone Number label. From here, check the Italics checkbox and select Center from the Horizontal align drop-down list.

The DataGrid after the Changes

Once you have set these properties, click the OK button. This will cause the Property Builder dialog box to close and the DataGrid in the designer to be updated to reflect the new aesthetic changes.

Figure 15.13 shows the designer after the DataGrid's aesthetic properties have been set. Note that the text is shown in a Verdana font, the column headers have a navy background and white foreground with a 16pt font size, the rows of the DataGrid are displayed in 10pt, and the phone numbers are centered and italicized.

FIGURE 15.13

The DataGrid's display in the designer reflects the specified aesthetic properties.

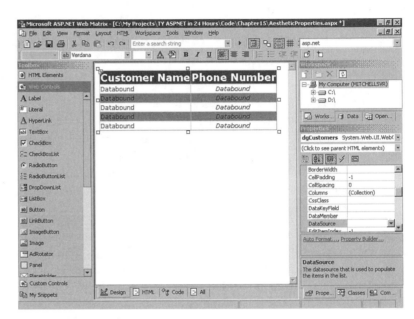

Take a moment to view the ASP.NET Web page through a browser, as well. The resulting Web page should look identical to the DataGrid shown in the designer in Figure 15.13, except that the text DataBound in each table cell will be replaced with the actual value from the appropriate DataSource field.

Learning More about the DataGrid

We've only begun to scratch the surface of the DataGrid in this hour. As we will see in future hours, the DataGrid provides an incredible feature set. In three upcoming hours, we'll look at a number of real-world examples that display data using the DataGrid. In Hour 18, "Allowing the User to Sort the Data in a DataGrid," for example, we will see how the DataGrid's data can be sorted by the Web visitor. In Hour 19, "Paging Through the DataGrid's Data," we will look at how to provide pagination for DataGrids that display a large amount of data. Finally, in Hour 20, "Editing the Data in a DataGrid," we will examine how to use the DataGrid to allow the user to edit existing database data.

Even after Hour 20 we will have covered only a portion of the DataGrid's immense set of features. The DataGrid is so feature rich that its features justify an entire book. If you want to learn all there is about using the DataGrid, pick up a copy of my book *ASP.NET Data Web Controls Kick Start*.

There are also a number of free online tutorials and articles that can help you move from DataGrid novice to DataGrid expert. One article series I suggest every ASP.NET developer read is *An Extensive Examination of the DataGrid Web Control*, available at `http://aspnet.4guysfromrolla.com/articles/040502-1.aspx`.

If you find yourself with questions about what the DataGrid can and cannot do or how to use the DataGrid to accomplish a particular feature, consider asking your questions at the DataGrid Forum: `http://asp.net/Forums/ShowForum.aspx?ForumID=24`.

Setting the Aesthetic Properties by Using the Auto Format Tool

With its numerous aesthetic properties, which can be applied at a number of components, the DataGrid allows for fine-grain control of its appearance. This control permits developers to craft intricate, visually pleasing DataGrids.

Of course, if you are as artistically challenged as me, you might find yourself having a hard time creating impressive looking DataGrids. (The DataGrid in Figure 15.13 is about as visually pleasing as I can make one.) Fortunately for those of us who aren't artistically inclined, the Web Matrix Project provides an Auto Format tool, which provides a list of eye-pleasing styles to choose from. Once a selection is made, the DataGrid's aesthetic properties are automatically set to correspond to the selected style.

Let's examine the Auto Format tool. Start by creating a new ASP.NET Web page named `AutoFormatTest.aspx`. Drag and drop a DataGrid Web control from the Toolbox onto the designer. Next click the DataGrid so its properties are displayed in the Properties pane. At the bottom of the Properties pane, you will find a hyperlink titled `Auto Format...`; clicking this link will display the Auto Format dialog box, which is shown in Figure 15.14.

FIGURE 15.14

The Auto Format dialog box is used to choose a visual style for the DataGrid.

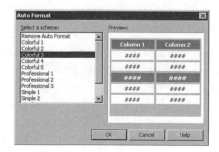

As Figure 15.14 shows, the Auto Format dialog box presents various styles that you can apply to the DataGrid. When you click a style, a preview of the style is shown in the Preview screen on the right side of the dialog box.

Once you choose a style, simply click the OK button. The Auto Format dialog box will close, and the DataGrid displayed in the designer will be updated with the new style settings. Behind the scenes the DataGrid's aesthetic properties are being set to match the style selected. Figure 15.15 shows a screenshot of the Web Matrix Project after style Colorful 3 has been selected.

FIGURE 15.15

The Colorful 3 style has been selected.

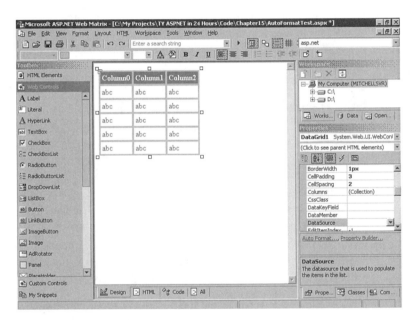

Summary

In this hour we examined the fundamentals of the DataGrid Web control. The DataGrid Web control was designed to display the results of a SQL SELECT query by using an HTML <table>, where each field in the SELECT query is represented as a column in the <table>, and each row in the query is represented as a row in the <table>.

In order to get a DataGrid to display a query's data, we need to bind the results of the query to a DataGrid. This can be accomplished, first, by using the SELECT Data Method Code Builder to create a function that returns a DataReader containing the results of the SELECT query, and then assigning this DataReader to the DataGrid's DataSource property. Next the DataGrid's DataBind() method is called. This process binds the data of a SELECT query to a DataGrid, and the code to do this should appear in the Page_Load event handler.

15

By default, the DataGrid creates a column for each field in its DataSource. We can, however, explicitly specify which columns should appear in the DataGrid and in what order. This is accomplished by adding Bound Columns to the DataGrid via the Columns screen in the Property Builder dialog box. When adding a Bound Column, we can indicate the DataSource field it should display by typing the DataSource field name into the Data Field textbox (refer back to Figure 15.8).

The DataGrid's appearance can be tweaked by means of the aesthetic properties, which can be applied either to the entire DataGrid or to certain components of the DataGrid. For example, aesthetic properties can be set specifically for the headers of every column or for just a particular column. And for us nonartistic individuals, the Web Matrix Project provides an Auto Format tool.

This hour is not the last we'll see of the DataGrid Web control. In the next hour we will examine a number of DataGrid examples. Additionally, Hours 18, 19, and 20 examine the DataGrid in further detail.

Q&A

Q In this chapter we saw how to bind a DataReader to a DataGrid. Other than the DataReader and DataSet, are there other types of objects that can be bound to a DataGrid?

A A number of other objects can be bound to a DataGrid. For example, there are a bevy of classes in the .NET Framework referred to as *collection classes*, which are used to store an arbitrary number of items. Instances of these classes can be bound to a DataGrid.

While there are other objects that can participate in data binding, DataSet and DataReaders are the most commonly used. This is because DataGrids are most often used to display database data, which is retrieved through DataReaders and DataSets.

Q What other DataGrid columns are there besides the Bound Column?

A One of the other column types, which we will explore in the next hour, is the HyperLink Column, which displays a hyperlink in each row of the column, where the hyperlink's text and URL can be bound to a DataSource column. Additionally, the DataGrid provides a Button Column, which adds a Button Web control to each row in the particular column. When the button in the Button Column is clicked, the Web form is submitted. The final DataGrid column type is the Template Column. When using a Template Column, you must specify the HTML and Web controls that appear within the column. Then this specified HTML markup and Web control syntax is repeated for each row.

Since the Bound Column is the most commonly used DataGrid column type, the majority of DataGrid examples will use Bound Columns. In the next hour we'll see HyperLink Columns, and in Hour 20, "Editing the Data in a DataGrid," we'll examine using the Edit, Update, Cancel Button Column, which is a special kind of Button Column. This book does not examine the Template Column.

Workshop

Quiz

1. Imagine that a DataReader was populated with the database results from the following SQL statement:

```
SELECT Name, Artist
FROM Albums
WHERE AlbumID > 7
```

Assume that this SQL query returned precisely nine records. If this DataReader were bound to a DataGrid, how many rows and columns would the DataGrid contain, assuming that the "Create columns automatically at run time" checkbox was left checked?

2. The DataGrid is rendered as what HTML element?

3. What does the term *data binding* mean?

4. Imagine that you had a DataSet with database content that you wanted to bind to a DataGrid. What source code would you need to add to the ASP.NET Web page to accomplish this?

5. Recall that with the Label Web control, the `BackColor` aesthetic property was one of those aesthetic properties that displayed only in uplevel browsers. Does the `BackColor` aesthetic property of the DataGrid share this same limitation, or will the DataGrid's `BackColor` property display for both uplevel and downlevel browsers?

6. Imagine that you have a DataReader that contains nine records, where each record has three columns: `Name`, `Artist`, and `DatePurchased`. If you wanted to display the name of the album and the date it was purchased in a DataGrid, how would you configure the DataGrid to display just these two values?

7. What will happen if you add a Bound Column to a DataGrid but forget to uncheck the "Create columns automatically at run time" checkbox?

Answers

1. There would be precisely two columns and nine rows, since the SQL query returns two columns (Name and Artist) and nine rows.

2. The DataGrid is rendered as an HTML <table>.

3. Data binding is the process of associating the data in a DataSet or DataReader to a Web control like the DataGrid.

4. Binding data to a DataGrid requires only two lines of code. First you must set the DataGrid's DataSource property to the DataSet or DataReader that you want to bind to the DataGrid. Next you need to call the DataGrid's DataBind() method. Assuming that we had a DataGrid whose ID property was dgAlbums, and a DataSet named recentAlbums, we could bind this DataSet to the DataGrid using the following two lines of code:

```
dgAlbums.DataSource = recentAlbums
dgAlbums.DataBind()
```

5. The BackColor property of the DataGrid will appear in both uplevel and downlevel browsers. This is because the DataGrid is rendered as an HTML <table>, which uses the bgcolor attribute to indicate its background color, and both uplevel and downlevel browsers support this <table> attribute.

6. First, you'd want to visit the DataGrid's Property Builder dialog box. From there you'd navigate to the Columns screen. Since you want to specify which columns should appear, you'd first need to uncheck the "Create columns automatically at run time" checkbox. Next you'd want to add two Bound Columns, setting the Data Field textbox of the first Bound Column to Name and the second to DatePurchased.

7. If the "Create columns automatically at run time" checkbox is left unchecked, the DataGrid will have a column for each of the fields in the DataSource. If you add a Bound Column, then the DataGrid will have all of the DataSource fields as well as the Bound Column you explicitly added.

Exercises

1. For this exercise please create an ASP.NET Web page that contains a DataGrid that displays the customers from the Customers table. The DataGrid should have precisely three columns. The first should show the customer's name, the second the zip code, and the third the customer I.D. Also, use the Auto Format tool to apply the Colorful 5 scheme to the DataGrid.

2. For this exercise create a DataGrid that displays all of the columns from the
   Customers database table. Format the DataGrid so that its contents are displayed in
   the font Tahoma with a white forecolor. The DataGrid rows should alternate
   between a black background and a gray background. Have the text in the column
   headers displayed in a bold font and a larger font size.

3. Recall that the SELECT Data Method Code Builder allows for parameterized WHERE
   clauses. For this exercise use the SELECT Data Method Code Builder to generate a
   function that returns the customers from the Customers table that have a
   CustomerID *greater than or equal to* a provided value. Also, take a few minutes to
   apply some aesthetic formatting to the DataGrid, either explicitly or through the
   Auto Format tool.

Hour 16

Examining Further DataGrid Examples

In the previous hour we took a first look at the DataGrid Web control, which is a Web control designed to display database data. In our initial examination of the DataGrid, we saw how to bind data to a DataGrid, how to specify what columns should appear in the DataGrid, and how to format the DataGrid either by setting its aesthetic properties or by using the Web Matrix Project's Auto Format tool.

During this hour we will continue our examination of the DataGrid Web control, delving into numerous examples that illustrate the utility of the DataGrid. This hour is designed to help you familiarize yourself with the DataGrid Web control. Because we will be using the DataGrid extensively throughout the remainder of this book, it is important that you feel comfortable working with the DataGrid. Oftentimes one of the best ways of familiarizing yourself with any given ASP.NET Web control is to simply work through a number of examples.

Specifically, in this hour we will look at DataGrid examples that do the following:

- Display information for a single customer
- Allow a user's input to determine the data to display in a DataGrid
- Explicitly specify the columns of a DataGrid
- Use data formatting to format the values in a particular column
- Demonstrate how to use the HyperLink Column

Using a DataGrid to Display Information about a Particular Customer

In the previous hour all of our DataGrid examples used a DataGrid to display information about *all* of the customers in the Customers database table. However, this would be impractical if the Customers table had thousands of records or more. More likely than not, the person visiting the Web page is only interested in viewing information about one particular customer. Rather than force the user to have to wade through all of the customers, it would be helpful to display just the customer information the user is interested in.

In order to accomplish this, we will use the DataGrid just like we did in the examples in the previous hour, "Displaying Data with the DataGrid Web Control." The difference arises in the function that the SELECT Data Method Code Builder creates. In the last hour's examples, we constructed queries without WHERE clauses, which causes all records in the table to be returned. We can limit the SELECT query to return only a particular customer by adding a WHERE clause whose condition checks for equality on the CustomerID column. For example, the following SQL SELECT statement would return customer information about Jisun Lee only:

```
SELECT *
FROM Customers
WHERE CustomerID = 1
```

The reason this SELECT statement returns information about only Jisun Lee is because Jisun Lee's CustomerID column equals 1, whereas every other customer's CustomerID is something other than 1.

Recall from our discussions about primary keys in Hour 14, "Understanding SQL, the Language of Databases," that the primary key column uniquely identifies each record in the table. Therefore, when using the WHERE condition,

```
WHERE CustomerID = someCustomerID
```

at most one row will be returned. (If there is no customer with the specified customer ID, then no row will be returned.)

In order to create an ASP.NET Web page that shows customer information for a particular customer, we must first create a new ASP.NET Web page. Do so and name the page `ShowSingleCustomer.aspx`.

For this page we are eventually going to be collecting user input; specifically, we'll be collecting the `CustomerID` of the customer whose customer information the user wants to view. As you know by now, to collect user input, we need to ensure that the Web controls responsible for user input collection appear within a Web form. Take a moment to have glyphs displayed so that you can be certain your Web controls are being placed within the Web form (go to the View menu and select Glyphs).

16

Once you have created the new ASP.NET Web page and turned on glyphs, add a DataGrid Web control to the Web page. This DataGrid does not have to be placed within the Web form (because it does not collect user input), although there's no reason why it shouldn't go there. Once the DataGrid has been added to the ASP.NET Web page, set its `ID` property to `dgCustomerInfo`.

Now that we have added the DataGrid, all that remains is retrieving the data from the database and binding the retrieved data to the DataGrid. In the next section we will examine how to retrieve the data from the database so that only the data for a particular customer is returned.

Building the Appropriate SELECT Query with the SELECT Data Method Code Builder

In Hour 14 we saw how to use the SELECT Data Method Code Builder to construct SQL queries that contain WHERE clauses. For this example we will want to build a SELECT query that has a WHERE clause on the `CustomerID` field.

To accomplish this, start by clicking the ASP.NET Web page's Code tab and then dragging and dropping the SELECT Data Method Code Builder from the Toolbox and onto the Code section. For the first screen you are asked to provide information on how to connect to the database. Use the same information you used when creating the `Customers` table. In the second screen you will be prompted to construct the query.

Start by selecting the * option from the Columns listbox. Next click the WHERE button and add a WHERE condition on the `CustomerID` column by using the = operator on the `filter@CustomerID`. When building this WHERE clause condition, your screen should look similar to Figure 16.1.

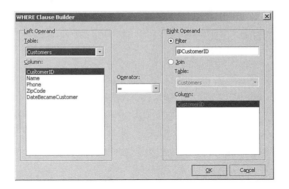

This is the only WHERE clause condition we need to add. Once the condition has been added, click the Next button to go to the Query Preview screen. Here you can test the query out (by clicking the Test Query button) and try inputting a value for the @CustomerID parameter. If you enter 1 as the @CustomerID parameter, you should be shown the customer information for Jisun Lee.

After previewing your query (which is optional), click Next to proceed to the final screen. At this final screen, name the function GetCustomerByCustomerID and opt to have a DataReader returned. Finally, click Finish, which will generate the suitable source code.

Binding the Data to the DataGrid

As we saw in the previous hour, the final step of having a DataGrid display database data is binding the data returned from the database to the DataGrid. This is accomplished by setting the DataGrid's DataSource property to the DataReader (or DataSet) that contains the database data and calling the DataGrid's DataBind() method. In the examples from the last hour, the code to perform this last step was placed in the Page_Load event handler, and looked like this:

```
Sub Page_Load(sender as Object, e as EventArgs)
    dgCustomers.DataSource = GetCustomer()
    dgCustomers.DataBind()
End Sub
```

However, the function we just created with the SELECT Data Method Code Builder is not named GetCustomers(). Rather, it is named GetCustomerByCustomerID(). Furthermore, if you examine the GetCustomerByCustomerID() source code, you'll note that this function takes a single input parameter, an Integer named customerID. This means that when calling this function, we need to pass in an Integer value. The function will then return the customer information for this particular customer.

For those not following along at a computer, the `GetCustomerByCustomerID()`
function looks like

```
Function GetCustomerByCustomerID(ByVal customerID As Integer) As
        System.Data.SqlClient.SqlDataReader
    ...
End Function
```

16

When setting our DataGrid's `DataSource` property, we need to use code like this:

```
dgCustomerInfo.DataSource = GetCustomerByCustomerID(1)
```

To demonstrate this, add the following code to the source code section of
`ShowSingleCustomer.aspx`:

```
Sub Page_Load(sender as Object, e as EventArgs)
    dgCustomerInfo.DataSource = GetCustomerByCustomerID(1)
    dgCustomerInfo.DataBind()
End Sub
```

After adding this code, save the ASP.NET Web page and view it through a browser. As
you can probably guess, the DataGrid will display the customer information for Jisun
Lee (because she is the customer whose `CustomerID` equals 1). Figure 16.2 shows a
screenshot of the `ShowSingleCustomer.aspx` ASP.NET Web page when viewed through
a Web browser.

FIGURE 16.2

*The DataGrid displays
information about just
one customer—
Jisun Lee.*

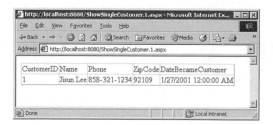

Allowing the User to Decide What Customer's Information to View

The current ASP.NET Web page is limited in its usefulness. Those users who want to
view customer information for Jisun Lee will find the page quite handy, but users who
want to view information about any other customer will find the page worthless. Ideally,
the users should be able to specify the `CustomerID` of the customer whose information
they are interested in viewing.

Extending `ShowSingleCustomer.aspx` to accommodate this extra functionality is not at all difficult. All that we need to do is add a TextBox Web control, which is where the user will enter the `CustomerID`, and a Button Web control.

Start by adding a TextBox Web control to the designer. Because we will be collecting user input via this TextBox, it is vital that the TextBox be placed within the Web form. Once the TextBox Web control has been added, set its `ID` property to `customerID` and its `Columns` property to 3. Also, you may want to type in some text to the left of the TextBox to indicate what the user is to enter into the TextBox. I chose the text label "CustomerID:".

Next add a Button Web control. As with the TextBox Web control, the Button must be placed within the Web form. Once the Button has been added, set its `Text` property to `View Customer` and its `ID` property to `btnView`. After adding these two Web controls, your screen should look similar to the screenshot in Figure 16.3.

FIGURE 16.3

TextBox and Button Web controls have been added to the ASP.NET Web page.

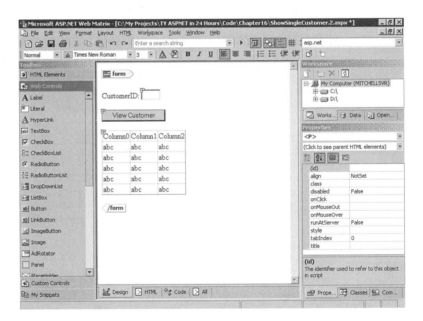

At this point the user visiting `ShowSingleCustomer.aspx` will see a textbox for entering a `CustomerID` and a button. When clicking the button, we want the customer corresponding to the entered `CustomerID` to appear in the DataGrid.

Because this action hinges on when the button is clicked, we can place the source code for displaying the customer information in the Button Web control's `Click` event handler. Recall that to add code to a Button Web control's `Click` event handler, simply double-click the Button in the designer. This action will take you to the Code tab and have your cursor inside the Button's `Click` event handler.

For the event handler we want to have the DataGrid display the appropriate customer's information. To do this, we need to set the DataGrid's DataSource property to the DataReader returned by GetCustomerByCustomerID() (passing in the CustomerID entered by the user) and then call the DataGrid's DataBind() method. The following code will accomplish this:

```
Sub btnView_Click(sender As Object, e As EventArgs)
    dgCustomerInfo.DataSource = GetCustomerByCustomerID(customerID.Text)
    dgCustomerInfo.DataBind()
End Sub
```

16

Note that the value passed into the GetCustomerByCustomerID() function is simply the CustomerID value entered by the user into the customerID TextBox Web control.

To complete the source code portion for this ASP.NET Web page, go ahead and remove the Page_Load event handler. The Page_Load event handler simply displays Jisun Lee's customer information via the dgCustomerInfo DataGrid whenever the page is visited. We don't want to do this, because we want to display the customer information based on the CustomerID provided by the user.

Once you have removed the Page_Load event handler, save the ASP.NET Web page and view it through a browser. You should see a textbox and a button. Enter a valid CustomerID into the textbox and click the button. The ASP.NET Web page will post back, and the customer information for the specific customer whose CustomerID you entered will be displayed. Figure 16.4 shows a screenshot of this ASP.NET Web page in action.

FIGURE 16.4

The information for a specified customer is displayed.

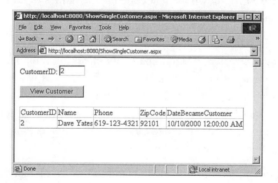

Improving the Example

If you play around with the ShowSingleCustomer.aspx ASP.NET Web page, you will likely find some areas for improvement. First, if the user enters a value for the CustomerID textbox in a nonnumeric format, such as a CustomerID value of "Scott," an "Input string not in correct format" error is displayed. This could be easily fixed by using a CompareValidator that ensures that the user's input is an integer data type and greater than 0.

Another shortcoming of the ASP.NET Web page is that if the user enters a `CustomerID` value that does not correspond to a customer in the `Customers` table, no message or indication is given that there is no customer matching the entered `CustomerID`. Rather, the DataGrid is simply not displayed, as Figure 16.5 shows.

FIGURE 16.5

The user has entered a `CustomerID` *value that doesn't correspond to an existing customer.*

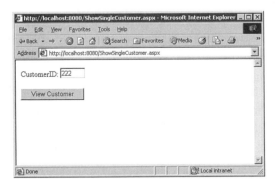

The reason the DataGrid isn't displayed is that the `GetCustomerByCustomerID()` function returns a DataReader with zero records. Therefore, no rows are created for the DataGrid, so the DataGrid isn't displayed.

You can work around this by allowing the user to view information only for a customer who already exists in the `Customers` table. One way to do this, which we'll examine during the next hour, "Working with Data-Bound DropDownList, RadioButton, and CheckBox Web Controls," is to use a drop-down list that contains the names of all of the customers. When the user selects one of the customers from the drop-down list, the customer's information is displayed via a DataGrid.

Another workaround involves programmatically checking how many rows the DataGrid contains. If it contains zero rows, then obviously no records were found for the particular `CustomerID`. In such a case, we can display a message like "No customers were found for the specified customer ID." If, however, the DataGrid contains a row, then we know that there was a customer with the specified `CustomerID`. This technique is discussed further in the "Q&A" section at the end of this hour.

An additional shortcoming of the current example lies in the fact that if you enter a customer ID into the textbox and hit the Enter key on your keyboard, the Web form submits, but the customer's information is *not* shown in the DataGrid. This is because the code that retrieves the information for the specified customer resides in the `btnView` Button Web control's `Click` event handler. This event handler fires only when the Web form is submitted by having the button clicked. In the "Q&A" section we'll discuss how to alter the ASP.NET Web page so that the customer's information is displayed if the button is clicked or if the user hits Enter after typing in a customer ID value into the textbox.

Finally, the ShowSingleCustomer.aspx ASP.NET Web page could certainly be prettied up; the DataGrid displaying the customer information is a bit bland. You are encouraged to use the Auto Format tool to provide a more visually appealing user experience.

Formatting the DataGrid's Data

In the previous example a selected customer's information is displayed. Looking back at Figure 16.4, you can see the customer's information displayed in the DataGrid. Notice that the DataGrid displays each field in the DataSource as a column in the DataGrid. This is because we have not specified which columns should appear in the DataGrid, so by default all of the DataSource's fields are added as columns. Additionally, note that the format of the DateBecameCustomer column displays both the date and time.

We can customize the output of the ShowSingleCustomer.aspx ASP.NET Web page by specifying which columns should appear in the DataGrid. When doing this, we can also specify a data-formatting style for each column. This means we can have the DataGrid's DateBecameCustomer column displayed as just a date, for example, instead of a date and time.

> You can't supply any sort of special data formatting to the contents of a string column. Data formatting is used for date/time and numeric values.

What is important to understand is that in order to specify that a particular column should have a specific data formatting, that column must be added by means of a Bound Column. In our quest to have the DateBecameCustomer column displayed as just a date, we need to have each column in the DataGrid specified, as opposed to just using the default DataGrid behavior that creates a column for each field in the DataSource.

Specifying the Columns to Appear in the DataGrid

Recall from the last hour that we can specify which columns should appear in a DataGrid through the Columns screen of the DataGrid's Property Builder. To display the DataGrid's Property Builder, click the DataGrid so that its properties are loaded in the Properties pane. At the bottom of the Properties pane, you'll find a hyperlink titled Property Builder..., which, when clicked, will display the Property Builder dialog box.

16

This example builds on the code from the `ShowSingleCustomer.aspx` example we examined earlier in this hour. Note, however, that we have a copy of the `ShowSingleCustomer.aspx` ASP.NET Web page named `FormatColumn.aspx` and are working from that.

The Property Builder has several screens—General, Columns, Paging, Format, and Borders—which are listed in the upper left-hand corner of the Property Builder dialog box. Click the Columns label to display the Columns screen. From here the first thing to do is uncheck the "Create columns automatically at run time" checkbox.

Next we need to add Bound Column columns for each column we want to appear in the DataGrid. Let's have our DataGrid display the customer's name, phone number, zip code, and the date he or she became a customer. This means that we will need to add four Bound Column columns. For each of these Bound Column columns, you will need to specify its Header text and Data Field. Recall that the specified Data Field refers to the name of the `DataSource` field whose value will be displayed in the column.

For the customer's name, use the Header text **Customer** and the Data Field **Name**. For the customer's phone number, use the Header text **Phone Number** and the Data Field **Phone.** For the customer's zip code, use the Header text **Zip Code** and the Data Field **ZipCode.** Finally, for the date the person became a customer, use the Header text **Date Became Customer** and the Data Field **DateBecameCustomer.** After having added these four Bound Columns, your screen should look similar to the screenshot in Figure 16.6.

FIGURE 16.6
Four Bound Columns have been added to the DataGrid.

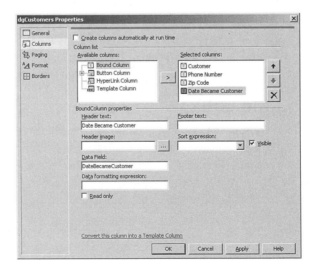

At this point click the Property Builder dialog box's OK button, which will return you to the designer. The DataGrid in the designer should have four columns with the appropriate text in the header of each column and the word "Databound" in the body of each cell. (Figure 16.7 shows a screenshot of the designer.)

FIGURE 16.7

The DataGrid has four databound columns.

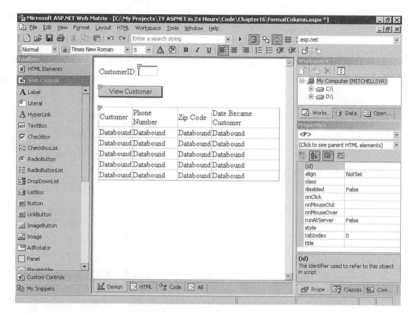

Now take a moment to test out the ASP.NET Web page through a browser. Note that when you enter a CustomerID, the customer's information is displayed with precisely four columns, as shown in Figure 16.8.

FIGURE 16.8

The ASP.NET Web page, when viewed through a browser.

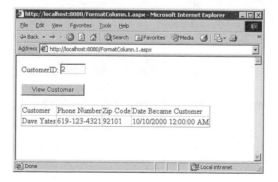

Specifying Data Formatting for a Bound Column

As Figure 16.8 shows, the Date Became Customer column still displays both the date and time the person became a customer. In order to format this value to show just the date, we need to specify the appropriate Bound Column's "Data formatting expression" option from the Columns screen in the Property Builder. To accomplish this, perform the following steps:

1. Reopen the Property Builder for the DataGrid and navigate to the Columns screen.

2. Next click the Date Became Customer Bound Column from the list of columns in the Selected columns listbox. (Refer back to Figure 16.6 to see what your screen should look like at this point.)

3. Beneath the Data Field textbox is a Data formatting expression textbox. Here we can specify how the data should be formatted. Enter the following value into the Data formatting expression textbox:

    {0:d}

4. Finally, click the OK button to close the Property Builder, save the ASP.NET Web page, and view it through a browser again.

This time, as Figure 16.9 shows, when you're viewing a customer's information, the Date Became Customer column shows only the date and not the time.

FIGURE 16.9

The date is shown, but not the time.

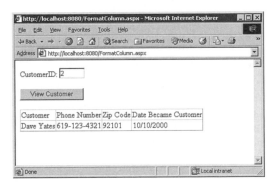

Understanding the Data Formatting Expression

You may be pleased to see that the Date Became Customer column shows just the date, but you are likely wondering how in the world the Data formatting expression {0:d} indicates that only the date should be shown.

First realize that when you are supplying a Data formatting expression, the format used is always as follows:

{0:*formatting rule*}

In the expression {0:d} only the d actually informs the DataGrid to display the DateBecameCustomer field by using just the date and not the time. The actual reason {0: and } are needed is beyond the scope of this book. Just understand that you must always include these characters when supplying a Data formatting expression.

> If you are interested in learning the details as to why {0: and } are needed, pick up a copy of *ASP.NET Data Web Controls* or read *An Extensive Examination of the DataGrid Web Control: Part 2,* available at http://aspnet.4guysfromrolla.com/articles/041702-1.aspx.

The next logical question is, Why does the character d cause the DateBecameCustomer field to be formatted using just the date and not the time? The .NET Framework contains a number of reserved formatting patterns for both numbers and dates. For dates the d specifies a short date pattern, which displays just the date and not the time.

The Date Formatting Patterns

Table 16.1 lists all of the reserved date formatting patterns and their respective outputs for the date August 27, 1989, and the time 3:32:00 p.m.. It is important to realize that the output of any particular date formatter is dependent upon the culture settings of the Web server. If the Web server is configured as English, U.S. culture, then the short date pattern emits

M/D/YYYY

where M is the month, D is the day, and YYYY is the year. If the setting is English, New Zealand, though, the short date pattern emits

D/M/YYYY

> For more information on the different outputs based on the Web server's culture settings, refer to http://msdn.microsoft.com/library/default.asp?url=/library/en-us/cpguide/html/cpcondatetimeformatstrings.asp.
>
> The output in Table 16.1 is for the English, U.S. culture, setting. Also, the output for Table 16.1 is for a Web server located -7 hours from Greenwich Mean Time.

TABLE 16.1   The Reserved Date Formatting Patterns

Format Pattern	Name	Example Output
d	Short date pattern	8/27/1989
D	Long date pattern	Sunday, August 27, 1989
t	Short time pattern	3:32 PM
T	Long time pattern	3:32:00 PM
f	Full date/time pattern (short time)	Sunday, August 27, 1989 3:32 PM
F	Full date/time pattern (long time)	Sunday, August 27, 1989 3:32:00 PM
g	General date/time pattern (short time)	8/27/1989 3:32 PM
G	General date/time pattern (long time)	8/27/1989 3:32:00 PM
M or m	Month day pattern	August 27
R or r	RFC 1123 pattern	Sun, 27 Aug 1989 8:32:00 GMT
s	Sortable date/time pattern	1989-08-27T15:32:00
u	Universal sortable date/time pattern	1989-08-27 15:32:00Z
U	Universal sortable date/time pattern (assumed date/time given in GMT)	Sunday, August 27, 1989 11:32:00 PM
Y or y	Year month pattern	August, 1989

Given the information presented in Table 16.1, you could easily change the data displayed in the Date Became Customer column. If you wanted this data displayed as just the month and the year, you could change the Data formatting expression value for the appropriate Bound Column from {0:d} to {0:y}.

There are a number of format patterns for numeric values, as well. We'll examine these format patterns in our next DataGrid example.

Using the HyperLink Column

Recall that to specify which columns should appear in the DataGrid, the Columns screen of the Property Builder dialog box is used. When adding a new column to the DataGrid, there are a number of types of columns that can be added. So far we have examined just one of these types, the Bound Column.

Another column type that can be added to a DataGrid is the HyperLink Column. As its name implies, the HyperLink Column displays a hyperlink in each row of the DataGrid. As we will see shortly, the URL and text of the hyperlink created by the HyperLink Column can be either a constant string value or a value from the DataGrid's DataSource.

Unfortunately, the Customers database table does not contain any columns that store URLs. In order to examine the HyperLink Column, then, we'll need to create a new database table, one that has a column that stores a URL.

Specifically, let's create a database table where we can store information about interesting books. This table's columns will store the various attributes of each book, such as the title, author, and price. Additionally, the table will have a URL column that will contain the URL to the book's page at the BarnesAndNoble.com Web site.

Creating and Populating the Books Database Table

Recall that in order to create a new database table via the Web Matrix Project, click the Data tab from the Workspaces pane. (If you haven't yet connected to a database, click the New Connection icon and connect to the database.) Next click the Tables label and then click the New Item icon. This will display the Create New Table dialog box. Name the new table **Books** and add the columns listed in Table 16.2.

TABLE 16.2 The Columns for the Books Table

Column Name	Data Type	Description
BookID	int (make it a primary key column as well, with an auto-increment)	A unique identifier for each row in the table
Title	varchar(50)	The title of the book
Author	varchar(50)	The book's author
Price	Money	The price of the book
URL	varchar(100)	A URL to view more information/ buy the book

Figure 16.10 shows a screenshot of the Edit Table Design dialog box after the five columns have been added.

16

FIGURE **16.10**

The structure of the
Books *database table.*

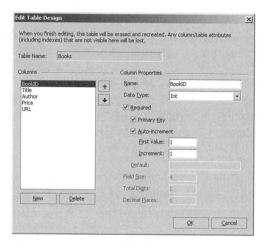

When creating table columns of type varchar, be sure to give a large
enough Field Size. The URL column has a Field Size of 100, meaning that the
URL column can store strings up to 100 characters. If you think you might
need more characters to store the URL, feel free to up the URL's Field Size to,
say, 150 or 200.

Once you have specified the table columns, click the OK button, which will save the table
and close the Create New Table dialog box. Doing so will add a Books label underneath
the Tables label in the Data tab. Double-click this label to edit contents of the Books table.

Feel free to enter whatever data you'd like into this table. For the example in this book,
we will be working from the data shown in Table 16.3.

TABLE 16.3 The Data Inserted into the Books Table

Title	Author	Price	URL
Designing Active Server Pages	Scott Mitchell	20.97	http://search.barnesandnoble.com/booksearch/ isbnInquiry.asp?isbn=0596000448
Professional ASP.NET 1.0	Alex Homer et al.	47.99	http://search.barnesandnoble.com/booksearch/ isbnInquiry.asp?isbn=1861007035
Atkins for Life	Robert Atkins	14.97	http://search.barnesandnoble.com/booksearch/ isbnInquiry.asp?isbn=0312315228
ASP.NET Data Web Controls	Scott Mitchell	31.99	http://search.barnesandnoble.com/booksearch/ isbnInquiry.asp?isbn=0672325012
Dorian	Will Self and Oscar Wilde	19.20	http://search.barnesandnoble.com/booksearch/ isbninquiry.asp?isbn=0802117295

When entering the price, enter just the dollars and cents, like 45.50, *without* using the dollar sign ($). For instance, when inserting the value for the Price column for the book *Atkins for Life*, use 14.97 instead of $14.97.

Also, note that if you enter a value that exceeds the column's Field Size, you will get an error message. If the title of the book is greater than 50 characters in length, you will not be able to add the long title to the database. (The lesson to learn here is to plan accordingly! If you are going to need to be able to store lengthy titles, then, when creating the database table, assign the Title column an appropriate Field Size.)

Using the HyperLink Column

Now that we have created the Books column, let's create a DataGrid that displays the Title, Author, Price, and URL fields of this table. To do so, we'll create a DataGrid that has three Bound Columns and one HyperLink Column.

First things first, though: Create a new ASP.NET Web page named HyperLinkColumn.aspx and drag and drop a DataGrid from the Toolbox and onto the designer. Next set this DataGrid's ID property to dgBooks.

Now, to add the needed columns, click the Property Builder... hyperlink in the DataGrid's Properties pane. Next navigate to the Columns screen. Here we want to start by adding three Bound Columns, one for the Title field, one for the Author field, and one for the Price field.

1. Before you add any Bound Columns, though, uncheck the "Create columns automatically at run time" checkbox.

2. Now add the first Bound Column, setting its Header text and Data Field textboxes to **Title.**

3. Add another Bound Column, this time setting its Header text and Data Field textboxes to **Author.**

4. Finally, add a third Bound Column and set its Header text and Data Field textboxes to **Price.**

After adding these three Bound Columns, your screen should look similar to Figure 16.11.

FIGURE **16.11**

*Three Bound Columns
have been added.*

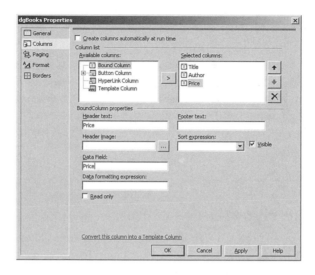

Now we need to add a HyperLink Column for the URL field. To accomplish this, click the
HyperLink Column type from the "Available columns" listbox; then click the > button,
which will add the HyperLink Column to the "Selected columns" listbox. Once the
HyperLink Column has been added, you will notice that a number of textboxes will
appear. Figure 16.12 shows a screenshot of the Property Builder after the HyperLink
Column has been added.

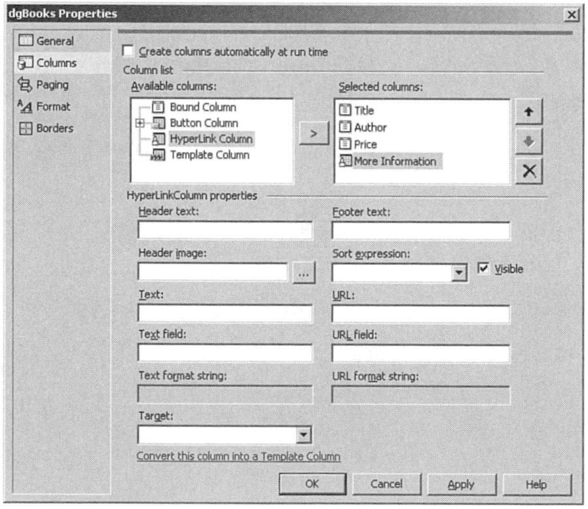

FIGURE **16.12**

*A HyperLink Column
has been added.*

Some of these textboxes, such as Header text, Header image, Footer text, and Sort expression, are identical to the ones for the Bound Column. However, there is no Data Field textbox for the HyperLink Column, and there are many new textboxes, such as URL field and Text format string.

The most important textboxes for the HyperLink column are Text, URL, Text field, and URL field. Understand that a hyperlink has two parts: a text part, which is displayed to the user, and a URL part, which indicates the Web location the user is whisked to when clicking the hyperlink.

The Text textbox specifies the hyperlink text to display for *every* row in the HyperLink Column. For this example, let's have every hyperlink's text be set to More Information. (Go ahead and enter the value **More Information** into the Text textbox at this time.) The URL textbox specifies the hyperlink URL to display for *every* row in the HyperLink Column. Rarely will you find yourself using this textbox, because you commonly will want every hyperlink in every row to direct the user to a unique URL when clicked.

The Text field and URL field textboxes allow for customizing the text and URL portions of the hyperlink on a row-by-row basis. Say you wanted the hyperlink's text to display the title of the book, as opposed to the static text More Information. Instead of setting the Text textbox to More Information, you'd set the Text field textbox to a value of **Title.** Then, because you want the URL portion of the generated hyperlink to send the user to the book's informational page on BarnesAndNoble.com, you set the URL field textbox to the value **URL.**

Notice that the value entered into the Text field or URL field textbox corresponds to a field name in the DataSource. It is this DataSource field that is displayed for the hyperlink's text or URL portions.

> You cannot set both the Text and Text field textboxes or both the URL and URL field textboxes. You must specify a value in either the Text *or* Text field textbox, just as you must specify a value in either the URL *or* URL field textbox.

Finally, add the value **More Information** into the Header text textbox. Once you have provided values for the Header text, Text, and URL field textboxes, your screen should look similar to the screenshot in Figure 16.13.

FIGURE 16.13

The HyperLink Column's properties have been set.

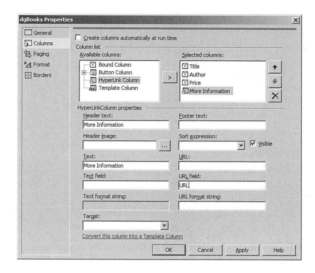

Retrieving the Records from the Books Table

The next step in creating our ASP.NET Web page is retrieving the database data that we want to be displayed by the DataGrid. Before we do, though, save the changes that you made in the Property Builder by clicking the Property Builder's OK button. This will return you to the designer. Note that after the addition of the four columns in the Property Builder, the DataGrid is now displayed as having four columns, with the last column displayed as a series of hyperlinks (see Figure 16.14).

FIGURE 16.14

The DataGrid has a HyperLink Column.

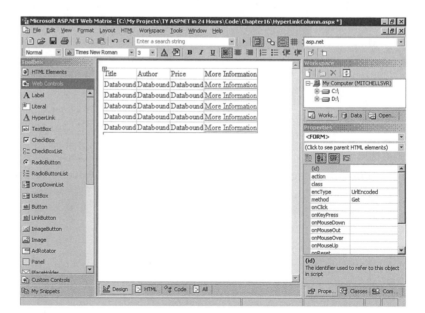

To add a function that returns the desired database data, use the SELECT Data Method Code Builder. From the Code Builder, build a query that selects all columns from the Books table. Name the resulting function **GetBooks** and have it return a DataReader.

Once this function has been generated, enter the following source code, which binds the DataReader returned by the GetBooks() function to the DataGrid whenever the page is visited:

```
Sub Page_Load(sender as Object, e as EventArgs)
  dgBooks.DataSource = GetBooks()
  dgBooks.DataBind()
End Sub
```

Viewing the ASP.NET Web Page through a Browser

Now let's test our ASP.NET Web page! Save the ASP.NET Web page and then view it through a Web browser. You should see the output shown in Figure 16.15. The output isn't particularly pleasing to the eye, but it demonstrates the use of the HyperLink Column. It may not be possible to determine from the screenshot, but each row's More Information hyperlink, when clicked, will whisk the user away to the proper page at BarnesAndNoble.com.

FIGURE 16.15

The four-column output as seen through a Web browser.

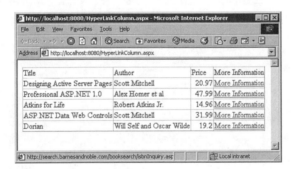

Formatting the Price Column

In Figure 16.15 you can see that the Price column of the DataGrid has undergone no formatting of any kind. The book *Dorian*, which costs $19.20, is displayed as "19.2" in the DataGrid. Ideally, this would be displayed as "$19.20," with the dollar sign and precisely two decimal places.

Earlier in this hour we examined how to use the Data formatting expression property of the Bound Column to format date/time values. Let's take a moment to examine how to use the property to format numeric values.

In order to specify a Bound Column's data-formatting expression, we must first open the Property Builder. To do so, return to the designer (if you're not already there), click the DataGrid, so as to load its properties in the Properties pane, and then click the `Property Builder...` hyperlink in the Properties pane. When the Property Builder dialog box loads, navigate to the Columns screen. Then, from the "Selected columns" listbox, choose the Price column.

To format a numeric value as a currency value, the formatting pattern c is used. Therefore, enter

`{0:c}`

into the "Data formatting expression" textbox. (Recall that the characters {0: and } must delimit the formatting pattern used.) Once you have specified this textbox setting, your screen should look like the screenshot in Figure 16.16.

FIGURE 16.16

The Price column's value is formatted as currency.

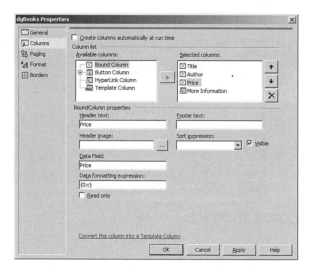

Click OK to close the Property Builder dialog box; then save the ASP.NET Web page and view it through a browser. As the screenshot in Figure 16.17 shows, the DataGrid's Price column displays its data in a currency format.

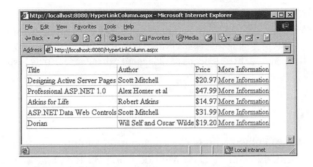

FIGURE 16.17
The Price column is formatted as currency.

The Numeric Formatting Patterns

In Table 16.1 we examined the reserved date formatting patterns. Table 16.4 lists the reserved numeric formatting patterns. The Example Output column in Table 16.4 is displaying the output for the number 65,537.257. The D format pattern and X format pattern work only with integers. For these two format pattern examples, the number 65,537 is used for the output.

For readers who have an interest in math, you might have noticed that both 65,537 and 257 are primes (note that the number chosen for the example output was 65,537.257). Furthermore, each of these numbers is one greater than a particular power of 2 (65,537 being $2^{16} + 1$, and 257 being $2^8 + 1$). Additionally, these two numbers are known as Fermat Primes, because they have the form $2^{2^n}+1$.

Note that the example output will differ on Web servers that have culture settings different from English, U.S.

TABLE 16.4 The Reserved Numeric Formatting Patterns

Format Pattern	Name	Example Output
C or c	Currency format	$65,537.26
D or d	Decimal format	*Works for integers only!* 65,537
E or e	Scientific (exponential) format	6.553726e+004
F or f	Fixed-point format	65537.26
G or g	General format	65537.257
N or n	Number format	65,537.26
P or p	Percent format	6,553,725.70%
X or x	Hexadecimal format	*Works with integers only!* 10001

For much more information on the reserved numeric formatting patterns, visit http://msdn.microsoft.com/library/default.asp?url=/library/en-us/cpguide/html/cpconstandardnumericformatstrings.asp.

Summary

In this hour we examined a number of DataGrid examples. Specifically, we saw how to use the DataGrid, the SELECT Data Method Code Builder, and a TextBox Web control to allow the user to view information about a particular customer in the Customers table. We looked at how to format the Date Became Customer column so that only the date, and not date *and* time, was shown. Finally, we created a Books database table and examined how to add a HyperLink column that would, when clicked, take the user to the book's informational page at BarnesAndNoble.com. We also saw how to format DataSource values as currencies.

The DataGrid is, in my opinion, the most useful and powerful ASP.NET Web control, so it is important that you feel comfortable using this control. This hour hopefully helped you accomplish that aim, although you are encouraged to play around with the DataGrid on your own, as well. In fact, if you're not yet comfortable with the DataGrid Web control, you may wish to become so before moving on to the next hour.

The next hour examines three other Web controls whose content can be bound to the results of a database query: the DropDownList, CheckBoxList, and RadioButtonList Web controls. Following that hour, we will turn our attention back exclusively to the DataGrid.

Q&A

Q **In the first example in this hour, we saw how to allow the user to specify a customer ID, which would cause the information for that particular customer to be displayed. However, if there were no customers with the supplied customer ID, then the DataGrid simply did not display. How can the Web page be enhanced so that if there are no matching customers, a helpful message like "There are no customers with the supplied Customer ID" is displayed instead of nothing?**

A In the ShowSingleCustomer.aspx example we examined in this hour, the user could enter a customer ID, and the customer with that particular customer ID would have his or her information displayed in a DataGrid. If, however, there were no customers whose customer ID matched the user-supplied customer ID, nothing appeared beneath the customer ID textbox, as shown back in Figure 16.5. That is, there was no helpful message explaining to the user that there were no customers with the specified customer ID.

The reason this happens is easy to understand. Assume that the user enters a customer ID of 222, and that there's no record in the Customers table with the value 222 in its CustomerID column. Therefore, when the GetCustomerByCustomerID() function executes, it will return an *empty DataReader*, which contains no records. When this empty DataReader is bound to the DataGrid, the DataGrid will not produce any rows, since the DataReader is empty and has no records. When the DataGrid's RenderControl() method (which produces the HTML markup for the DataGrid) is called, no HTML markup is returned, since the DataGrid has no rows. Therefore, there is nothing but a blank spot in the user's browser where the DataGrid would have been had a valid customer ID been entered.

What we'd like to have happen in the event that the DataGrid has no rows is that a message like "There are no customers with the supplied customer ID" is displayed. To determine whether the DataGrid has no rows, we can check the DataGrid's Items.Count property; if our DataGrid were named dgCustomerInfo, we could determine the number of rows in the DataGrid by using

```
dgCustomerInfo.Items.Count
```

After we've bound the DataReader to the DataGrid, we can check this property. If it's equal to 0, then there are no customers with the supplied customer ID. That is, using this property, we could rewrite the btnView Button Web control's Click event handler like so:

```
Sub btnView_Click(sender As Object, e As EventArgs)
    dgCustomerInfo.DataSource = GetCustomerByCustomerID(customerID.Text)
    dgCustomerInfo.DataBind()

    'Determine if a customer with the supplied customerID was found
    If dgCustomerInfo.Items.Count = 0 then
        'No customer found
    Else
        'A customer was found!
    End If
End Sub
```

To show a message when there is no customer found, we can add a Label Web control to the Web page. This Label Web control's Text property can then be set to the message you want displayed when no customer is found. Set the ID property to lblNoCustomer and set the Visible property to False. (The Visible property is a Boolean property of all Web controls. If Visible is True, the default, then the Web control is displayed in the Web page. If it's False, then the Web control is not rendered.)

Now, in the Button Web control's Click event, all we need to do is set the lblNoCustomer Label Web control's Visible property to True when dgCustomerInfo.Items.Count = 0, and to False otherwise. That is, the If statement in the event handler would look like this:

```
'Determine if a customer with the supplied customerID was found
If dgCustomerInfo.Items.Count = 0 then
    'No customer found
    LblNoCustomer.Visible = True
Else
    'A customer was found!
    LblNoCustomer.Visible = False'
End If
```

For practice applying this technique, be sure to work through Exercise 2.

Q As we saw in the first example, if the user enters a customer ID into the textbox and hits Enter, the Web form submits, but the data binding code in the Button Web control's event handler does not execute. Therefore, the appropriate customer information is not displayed. How can we fix this, so that hitting Enter when the Customer ID textbox has focus has the same effect as clicking the View Customer button?

A In order to have the DataGrid display the correct customer's information in the ShowSingleCustomer.aspx Web page, we simply needed to have the DataGrid's DataSource set to the DataReader returned by the GetCustomerByCustomerID() function and then call the DataGrid's DataBind() method. We placed this code in the btnView Button Web control's event handler. This code, then, executes whenever users click the View Customer button in their browsers.

However, users are also accustomed to submitting forms by hitting the Enter key when a textbox has focus. For example, if you visit ShowSingleCustomer.aspx through your browser, you may be tempted to simply click in the customer ID textbox, type in a customer ID, and hit Enter, expecting to then see the particular customer's information. Although hitting the Enter key when the textbox has focus does indeed submit the Web form, causing a postback, it does not cause the btnView Button's Click event to fire. Therefore, the Click event handler does not execute, and the DataGrid is not bound to the specified customer's information.

To overcome this limitation, all we need to do is have the same code in the btnView Button's Click event handler fire when the TextBox Web control's TextChanged event fires. To create an event handler for the TextBox Web control's TextChanged event, simply double-click the TextBox Web control in the designer. This will automatically take you to the Code tab, with your cursor in the TextChanged event. You can then copy and paste the code from the btnView Button Web control's Click event to the TextBox's TextChanged event. (A more modular approach would be to create a single subroutine and copy the code from the Click event handler there. Then both the Click and TextChanged event handlers could call this subroutine.)

Workshop

Quiz

1. What steps were taken to have the SELECT Data Method Code Builder create a function that returned the information for a customer specified by this user's CustomerID?

2. True or False: You can use the HyperLink Column to display either a hyperlink *or* a button.

3. True or False: When the DataGrid has its "Create columns automatically at run time" checkbox checked, you can format those columns of the DataGrid that are automatically generated.

4. If you wanted the value of a Bound Column formatted as a currency, what value would you enter into the Bound Column's Data formatting expression textbox?

5. In the HyperLinkColumn.aspx example, we saw how to have a HyperLink Column display a hyperlink for each row in the DataGrid. Specifically, in this example we had each hyperlink's text displayed as "More Information" and the URL portion as the value in the URL field of the DataSource. What changes would we need to make to have the value of the URL field displayed as *both* the text and URL portions of the generated hyperlink?

Answers

1. In the Build Query portion of the SELECT Data Method Code Builder, we added a WHERE clause by clicking the WHERE button. Specifically, we added a WHERE clause on the CustomerID column, using the = operator, and a filter, @CustomerID.

2. False. The HyperLink Column can display only hyperlinks.

3. False. Only Bound Columns can have their formatting specified.

4. {0:c}

5. We'd need to clear out the value of the HyperLink Column's Text textbox and enter the value URL into the HyperLink Column's Text field textbox.

Exercises

1. The first DataGrid example we examined in this hour allowed the user to enter a particular customer ID and then allowed display of the information from the customer with the entered customer ID. Create a similar ASP.NET Web page, but this time allow the user to enter a zip code as opposed to a customer ID. When entering a zip code and submitting the form, the user should be shown all of the customers that have the entered zip code.

2. Augment the ASP.NET Web page from Exercise 1 so that if there are no customers with the zip code entered by the user, the message "There are no customers with that zip code" is displayed. As discussed in the "Q&A" section, use the hidden Label Web control approach, displaying the Label only if there are no DataGrid rows after the `DataBind()` method.

HOUR **17**

Working with Data-Bound DropDownList, RadioButton, and CheckBox Web Controls

In the past two hours, you were introduced to a new ASP.NET Web control, the DataGrid, which is designed to display database data. By default the DataGrid essentially mirrors the structure of a database table in an HTML `<table>` tag, with an HTML `<table>` column for each field in the database table and an HTML `<table>` row for each record in the database table. Of course, the DataGrid allows for a large degree of customization, as we saw in the previous hour, "Further DataGrid Examples."

Recall that the first example we looked at in the previous hour involved allowing the user to enter the `CustomerID` in a TextBox Web control. Upon doing so and submitting the form, the ASP.NET Web page would be posted back, and the specific customer's information was shown in a DataGrid.

While this example illustrated a number of useful concepts, it had its shortcomings. For example, if the user entered an invalid CustomerID, no record would be shown. Also, a CompareValidator was needed to ensure that the user didn't enter a non-numeric input.

Part of the problem with this approach is that a TextBox Web control was used to specify the customer's CustomerID. Recall from our discussions in Hour 11, "Collecting Input by Using Drop-down Lists, Radio Buttons, and Checkboxes," that there are different classes of input and that certain Web controls are better suited for certain types of input than others. Typically, with input that is limited to a single choice from a list of legal choices, a drop-down list or series of radio buttons is a better choice than a textbox.

Fortunately, ASP.NET provides a means to bind database data to a drop-down list, a series of radio buttons, and a series of checkboxes. In this hour we will examine the three Web controls designed to provide this functionality.

Specifically, in this hour we will cover these tasks:

- Populating the list items in a DropDownList Web control with database data
- Examining the similarities between the DropDownList, RadioButtonList, and CheckBoxList Web controls
- Selecting a single customer from a list of customers by using a data-bound DropDownList
- Using the RadioButtonList Web control
- Working with the CheckBoxList Web control

Binding Database Data to a DropDownList Web Control

In Hour 11 we examined how to use the DropDownList Web control to display a drop-down list of options in a Web page. The drop-down list, as we discussed, is a means of collecting user input that is limited to one choice from a list of legal choices.

For example, an e-commerce site might use a drop-down list to prompt users for what type of shipping method they want their shipment sent by. Here the options might be U.S. Postal Service, 2-Day UPS, or Overnight FedEx. The drop-down list is a suitable means of collecting user input in this case because the user must choose precisely one shipping option from among the three options.

The options presented to the user in a DropDownList are referred to as *list items*. Each list item has two properties: Text and Value. The Text property specifies the text that is displayed to the user in the drop-down list; the Value is a hidden value that is associated with the list item. We'll see the utility of the Value property in an example shortly.

When working with the DropDownList in Hour 11, we specified the list items that were to appear in the resulting drop-down list. This was accomplished via the ListItem Collection Editor. For some applications, specifying the DropDownList Web control's list items is an acceptable option. If the drop-down list displays shipping options, and the shipping options never change, then specifying these list items is acceptable.

There are many situations, however, when the list items to be displayed in a DropDownList Web control are not known when the ASP.NET Web page is created, so they must instead be pulled from a database. For example, in the previous hour we examined a DataGrid example where the user could enter the CustomerID of the customer whose information he wished to view. The CustomerID was entered via a TextBox Web control.

This user interface is ideal only if the user knows the CustomerID for the customer whose information he is interested in. More often than not, the user will know the customer's name, not his or her CustomerID. For such a case, requiring the user to enter the CustomerID might be futile, because the user might know only the customer's name and have no idea what the CustomerID is.

A more ideal user interface would display all the customers on a drop-down list. The user could then select a customer from the list of customers, and then the customer's information would be displayed.

> The user interface from last hour's example, which had the user input the customer's CustomerID into a TextBox Web control, could be the ideal user interface in certain situations, such as a Web page used by staff who happen to know the CustomerID, and not the name, of the customer whose information they are interested in. It is important to realize that the ideal format for a user interface is heavily influenced by *who* is going to use the system, and *what* they want to accomplish.

Binding Database Data to the DropDownList Web Control

In order to have a DropDownList Web control's list items be populated from a database, we must bind database data to the DropDownList Web control. This process, fortunately, is exactly like binding data to the DataGrid Web control. To bind data to a DropDownList, the following steps must be taken:

1. Add a DropDownList Web control to the ASP.NET Web page.
2. Set the DropDownList's DataSource property to the DataSet or DataReader returned by a function that retrieves the appropriate database data.
3. Call the DropDownList's DataBind() method.

To demonstrate binding database data to a DropDownList, let's work through an example. Start by creating a new ASP.NET Web page named `DataDropDownList.aspx`.

Adding the DropDownList Web Control to the ASP.NET Web Page

Now that we have created an ASP.NET Web page, we are ready to add a DropDownList Web control. First, though, turn on glyphs. Next add a DropDownList Web control inside the Web form. Realize that this drop-down list will display the list of customer names. Set the drop-down list's `ID` property to `customers`.

In addition, be sure to set its `DataTextField` property to `Name` and its `DataValueField` property to `CustomerID`. The `DataTextField` and `DataValueField` properties must be set if you want to have the DropDownList populated by database data. Specifically, the `DataTextField` indicates the name of the `DataSource` field that is displayed as the `Text` property for each list item in the drop-down list; the `DataValueField` indicates the name of the `DataSource` field that is displayed as the `Value` property for each list item.

For example, assume that the DropDownList is bound to a DataReader that is composed of all of the columns and rows from the `Customers` database table. The drop-down list will have a list item added for each row in the `DataSource`. The text displayed in each of these list items will be the value of the `Name` field (the customer's name). The value of the list item, which is not displayed but can be programmatically accessed, is the customer's `CustomerID`.

If this doesn't quite make sense yet, don't worry; these concepts should become much clearer as we work through this example.

Creating the Function That Returns the Database Data and Binding Its Return Value to the DropDownList Web Control

Now that we have added the DropDownList and set its `ID`, `DataTextField`, and `DataValueField`, we need to set the DropDownList Web control's `DataSource` property to the DataSet or DataReader that contains the appropriate database data. As we've seen in the last few hours, we can use the Web Matrix Project's `SELECT` Data Method Code Builder to generate the needed source code.

Use the `SELECT` Data Method Code Builder to generate a function that returns all of the columns from the `Customers` table. Name this function `GetCustomers` and have it return a DataReader. As with the DataGrid example, we'll assign the DropDownList Web control's `DataSource` property in the `Page_Load` event handler. So, while still in the source code portion of the ASP.NET page, enter the following code:

```
Sub Page_Load(sender as Object, e as EventArgs)
    customers.DataSource = GetCustomers()
    customers.DataBind()
End Sub
```

Note that this accomplishes both steps 2 and 3—the DropDownList's `DataSource` property is first set, and then its `DataBind()` method is called.

At this point, let's test the ASP.NET Web page. Save the ASP.NET Web page and then view it through your browser of choice. The Web page, as Figure 17.1 shows, contains a drop-down list with a list item, the customer's name, for each of the customers in the `Customers` table.

FIGURE **17.1**

A drop-down list displays each customer from the Customers *table.*

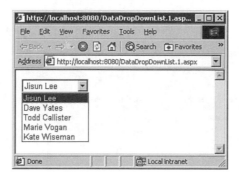

Displaying the List Item Selected

Currently, our ASP.NET Web page simply displays a drop-down list with the name of each of the customers from the `Customers` table. Because our end goal is to have the user select a customer and then view that customer's information, we need to have the Web form post back when the user selects a name from the drop-down list. One option is to add a Button Web control that users can click once they have selected the customers whose information they wish to view.

Another way is to set the DropDownList's `AutoPostBack` property to True. If set to True, the `AutoPostBack` property will cause the Web form to submit whenever a new list item is selected from the drop-down list. Oftentimes when the Web form is submitted, you will want to have certain source code executed. In our previous examples, where we used a Button Web control, we'd provide this source code in the Button's `Click` event handler. When using a DropDownList whose `AutoPostBack` property is set to True, we place our source code in the DropDownList Web control's `SelectedIndexChanged` event handler.

To create the `SelectedIndexChanged` event handler, simply double-click the DropDownList. This will take you to the Code tab and automatically place your cursor inside this event handler. For the time being, make sure the following code is in the source code portion of your ASP.NET Web page:

```
Sub customers_SelectedIndexChanged(sender As Object, e As EventArgs)
    Response.Write("<br>Text selected: " & customers.SelectedItem.Text)
    Response.Write("<br>Value selected: " & customers.SelectedItem.Value)
End Sub
```

This code will display the Text and Value properties from the selected list item in the cusomters DropDownList Web control. Note the syntax to access the selected item:

```
customers.SelectedItem
```

The Text and Value properties can then be referenced from the SelectedItem property, as shown in the SelectedIndexChanged event handler.

Take a moment to test the ASP.NET Web page. Upon loading the page in the browser, select an item from the drop-down list. What you will find is that no matter what customer you select, Jisun Lee will be the customer displayed in the drop-down list when the page is posted back, and the output will indicate that the Text and Value properties are Jisun Lee and 1 (see Figure 17.2).

FIGURE 17.2

Regardless of the customer chosen, Jisun Lee is displayed as the selected customer.

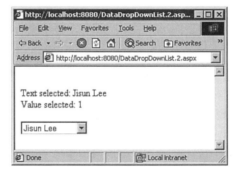

Why is this happening? Realize that whenever the user selects a drop-down list item, the ASP.NET Web page is posted back, and the ASP.NET Web page is reloaded with the submitted form values. What happens, though, when an ASP.NET Web page is loaded? The Page_Load event handler executes! Currently, the Page_Load event handler contains the following code:

```
Sub Page_Load(sender as Object, e as EventArgs)
    customers.DataSource = GetCustomers()
    customers.DataBind()
End Sub
```

This means that every time the ASP.NET Web page is loaded, even if it is due to a post-back from the Web form having been submitted, the customers DropDownList Web control is re-bound to the database data. This is why, regardless of the user's choice, he is continually shown Jisun Lee as his chosen customer.

Obviously, we want only the `customers` DropDownList to be bound to the database data when the page is not being posted back. Fortunately, we can accomplish this by changing the `Page_Load` event handler slightly, to

```
Sub Page_Load(sender as Object, e as EventArgs)
    If Not Page.IsPostBack then
      customers.DataSource = GetCustomers()
      customers.DataBind()
    End If
End Sub
```

The `Page.IsPostBack` returns a Boolean value—True if the page is being loaded due to a postback, and False otherwise. Therefore, the body of the `If` condition executes only if the page is *not* posted back. Hence, the `customers` DropDownList will be bound to the database data only if the page is not being loaded due to a postback.

With this small change, the ASP.NET Web page works as expected. As Figure 17.3 illustrates, once a customer is selected, the ASP.NET Web page is posted back, the customer who was selected is still displayed in the drop-down list, and the `Text` and `Value` properties are displayed on the Web page.

FIGURE 17.3

When a customer is selected, the ASP.NET Web page is posted back.

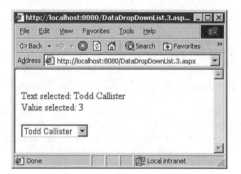

Adding a DataGrid to the ASP.NET Web Page

At this point we have added a DropDownList to the Web page whose list items are determined by the records returned via a `SELECT` query. We have also rigged up the DropDownList Web control so that whenever the user selects an item from the resulting drop-down list, the Web form is submitted.

What we want to do now is add to the Web page a DataGrid that displays the customer information for a single customer. The first step involved in this process is simply to add a DataGrid to the ASP.NET Web page, which you can do, as you know by now, by dragging and dropping the DataGrid Web control from the Toolbox and onto the designer. Once you have added the DataGrid, set its `ID` to `dgCustomer`.

Because this DataGrid will be used to display only one particular customer from the Customers table, we need to use the SELECT Data Method Code Builder to create a function that returns a single customer, based on the supplied CustomerID parameter.

This is precisely what we did in the first example from the last hour. Recall that to create such a function, we use the SELECT Data Method Code Builder. In the Query Builder a WHERE clause condition is added on the CustomerID column by using the = operator and @CustomerID for the filter value. Name this function GetCustomerByCustomerID and have it return a DataReader.

> For a more detailed explanation of creating the GetCustomerByCustomerID() function by using the SELECT Data Method Code Builder, refer back to the first example from Hour 16, "Examining Further DataGrid Examples."

Now that we have created the GetCustomerByCustomerID() function, we can bind it to the DataGrid by assigning the DataReader returned by this function to the DataGrid's DataSource property and then calling the DataGrid's DataBind() method. We want to perform this whenever the user selects a customer from the drop-down list. As we saw earlier, whenever a new customer is selected from the drop-down list, the ASP.NET Web page is posted back, and the DropDownList Web control's SelectedIndexChanged event handler executes. Therefore, we need to put the DataGrid's data-binding syntax in this event handler. Currently, this event handler has the following code:

```
Sub customers_SelectedIndexChanged(sender As Object, e As EventArgs)
    Response.Write("<br>Text selected: " & customers.SelectedItem.Text)
    Response.Write("<br>Value selected: " & customers.SelectedItem.Value)
End Sub
```

Replace this code with the following:

```
Sub customers_SelectedIndexChanged(sender As Object, e As EventArgs)
  dgCustomer.DataSource = GetCustomerByCustomerID(customers.SelectedItem.Value)
  dgCustomer.DataBind()
End Sub
```

This new code calls the GetCustomersByCustomerID() function passing in the Value property of the selected drop-down list item. The GetCustomersByCustomerID() function then gets the customer information for this particular customer and returns a DataReader containing this data. This DataReader is assigned to the DataGrid's DataSource property. Finally, the DataGrid's DataBind() method is called.

Figure 17.4 shows this ASP.NET Web page in action. Whenever the user selects a new option from the drop-down list, the ASP.NET Web page is posted back, and the selected customer's information is displayed.

FIGURE 17.4

The selected customer's information is shown in the DataGrid.

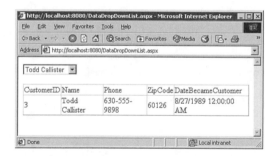

 As you can see in Figure 17.4, the DataGrid that contains the customer's information is quite an eyesore. Using the lessons you have learned over the past few hours, try improving the DataGrid's appearance.

Anytime the user selects a new customer from the drop-down list, the ASP.NET Web page will post back, and the selected customer's information will be displayed. But what happens when the page is first visited? Whose customer information is shown then?

To answer this question, we need to examine the `Page_Load` event handler, because this is the code that is executed whenever the page is loaded. Currently, the `Page_Load` event handler does not have any code to display customer information. This means that when the page is first visited, no customer information will be shown, even though the first customer is displayed (Jisun Lee). To see an example of this, examine Figure 17.5.

Figure 17.5 is a screenshot of the ASP.NET Web page when visited through a browser before a customer has been selected by the user. Note that the drop-down list shows the customer Jisun Lee but no customer information is displayed.

FIGURE 17.5

Jisun Lee's customer information is not displayed when the page is first visited.

To remedy this, we need to have the DataGrid set to display data when the page is first visited by a given user. To do this, we need to update our Page_Load event handler as follows:

```
Sub Page_Load(sender as Object, e as EventArgs)
    If Not Page.IsPostBack then
        customers.DataSource = GetCustomers()
        customers.DataBind()

        dgCustomer.DataSource =
                GetCustomerByCustomerID(customers.SelectedItem.Value)
        dgCustomer.DataBind()
    End If
End Sub
```

Here, after the customers DropDownList has been populated with the database data, the dgCustomer DataGrid's DataSource property is set to the DataReader returned by the GetCustomersByCustomerID() function. Note that the GetCustomersByCustomerID() function is passed to the Value property of the selected drop-down list option, which is customer Jisun Lee, the selected customer when the page is first visited.

With this small change to the Page_Load event handler, the user will see the customer information for Jisun Lee when first visiting the ASP.NET Web page, as Figure 17.6 illustrates.

FIGURE 17.6

Jisun Lee's customer information is displayed when the page is first visited.

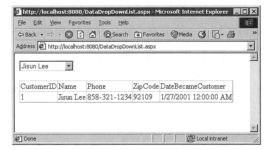

Using the RadioButtonList Web Control

In the previous section we saw how to bind database data to a DropDownList Web control. Along with being able to bind data to a DropDownList, database data can also be bound to a list of radio buttons and a list of checkboxes. In Hour 11 we examined the CheckBox and RadioButton Web controls, which could be used to create a single checkbox or radio button, respectively.

In Hour 11 we had to add a RadioButton Web control for each radio button we wanted to add to the page. While this approach works for situations where we know precisely the number of radio buttons we want on the page, it doesn't work when we need a variable number of radio buttons. For example, we could redo the example we examined in the previous section to allow the user to select from a series of radio buttons the customer whose information is wanted, as opposed to selecting the customer from a drop-down list.

We already saw that the each of the DropDownList's list items can be populated from a database. The same can be done with radio buttons by using a RadioButtonList Web control.

To examine how to use the RadioButtonList Web control, let's use radio buttons to display the list of books from the Books database. When selecting one of the radio buttons and clicking a Button Web control, the user is automatically whisked to the Web page specified by that particular book's URL table column value.

Recall that we created the Books table in the last example in Hour 16. The Books table contains columns such as Title, Author, Price, and URL.

17

Start by creating a new ASP.NET Web page named DataRadioButtonList.aspx. Because we are going to collect user input through this RadioButtonList, we need to ensure that it's placed within a Web form; therefore, turn on glyphs so that you can see where the Web form begins and ends. Next drag and drop a RadioButtonList from the Toolbox and onto the designer. Now you should see a single radio button with the text "Unbound" next to it (see Figure 17.7).

FIGURE 17.7
A RadioButtonList has been added to the designer.

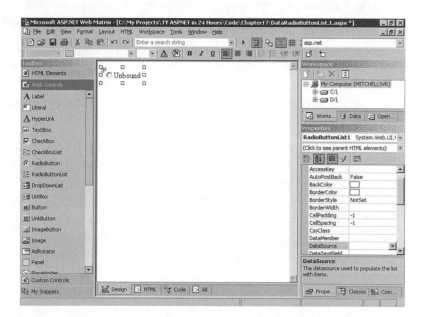

Once the RadioButtonList has been added to the ASP.NET Web page, set its `ID` property to `books`.

Binding Data to the RadioButtonList Web Control

As with the DropDownList in the earlier example in this hour, we now need to bind the appropriate database data to this RadioButtonList. Recall that each list item in a DropDownList had both a `Text` and `Value` property, which were specified by the DropDownList's `DataTextField` and `DataValueField` properties. To have each list item's `Text` property assigned to the value of the `DataSource`'s `Name` field, the DropDownList's `DataTextField` property was set to `Name`.

The RadioButtonList Web control works in a similar fashion. Each radio button produced by the RadioButtonList has a `Text` and a `Value` property; the RadioButtonList Web control has both `DataTextField` and `DataValueField` properties, which are semantically identical to the DropDownList Web control's `DataTextField` and `DataValueField` properties.

Therefore, to bind data to a RadioButtonList, the first step is to specify the `DataTextField` and `DataValueField` properties. For this exercise let's have the radio button for each book display the book's `Title` field and have the `Value` store the book's `URL` field. To indicate this, set the RadioButtonList's `DataTextField` property to `Title` and its `DataValueField` property to `URL`.

The next step in binding database data to the RadioButtonList is to create a function that returns the appropriate data (using the `SELECT` Data Method Code Builder) and then set the RadioButtonList's `DataSource` property to the return value of this function. Following that we need to make sure the RadioButtonList's `DataBind()` method is called.

Because we want to display a radio button for each book from the `Books` table, the data returned from the database should simply be all of the columns from the `Books` database table. To create a function that will return this data, use the `SELECT` Data Method Code Builder, specifying the query to return all columns of the `Books` table. Name the resulting function `GetBooks` and have it return a DataReader.

Once this function has been added to the source code portion of `DataRadioButtonList.aspx`, we need to assign this function's return value to the RadioButtonList's `DataSource` property. The code to perform this step needs to appear in the `Page_Load` event handler. Insert the following code into the source code of your ASP.NET Web page:

```
Sub Page_Load(sender as Object, e as EventArgs)
    If Not Page.IsPostBack then
        books.DataSource = GetBooks()
        books.DataBind()
    End If
End Sub
```

Note that in the Page_Load event handler, we set the books RadioButtonList's DataSource property and call its DataBind() method only if the page is not being visited via a postback. Recall that this is code we used in the drop-down list example earlier in this hour, and it is required if the ASP.NET Web page is to be posted back. Because we have not added a Button Web control to the DataRadioButtonList.aspx ASP.NET Web page yet (so far providing no means for a postback to occur), this If condition is superfluous. However, because we know that we *will* be adding a Button Web control, adding this code now will save us from having to add it later.

Once you have added this source code, save the ASP.NET Web page and view it through a browser. You should see five radio buttons, one for each record in the Books table, with the title of each book next to its radio button. Figure 17.8 contains a screenshot of the DataRadioButtonList.aspx ASP.NET Web page when viewed through a browser.

17

FIGURE 17.8

A radio button is displayed for each book.

Sending the User to the Selected Book's URL

The DataRadioButtonList.aspx ASP.NET Web page at this point simply displays the list of books in the Books table. What we want to be able to do, though, is allow the user to select a particular book and be whisked to its appropriate URL.

To accomplish this, we need to have the Web form submitted when the user selects a book. In the drop-down list example we saw earlier in this hour, this was accomplished by setting the DropDownList's AutoPostBack property to True and then placing the source code to execute when a new item was selected in the DropDownList's SelectedIndexChanged event handler. The RadioButtonList also has an AutoPostBack property; however, for this example, let's use a Button Web control, so to be whisked to the selected book's URL, the user will first have to choose the book from the list of books and then click the button to submit the Web form.

Add a Button Web control to the ASP.NET Web page by dragging and dropping the Web control from the Toolbox and onto the designer. Set the Button's ID property to btnSubmit and its Text property to Visit the Selected Book's URL. Once you have added this Button Web control, your screen should look similar to the screenshot in Figure 17.9.

FIGURE 17.9

*A Button Web control
has been added to the
ASP.NET Web page.*

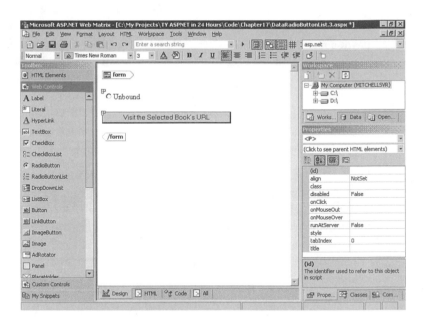

Now when the Button Web control is clicked, the ASP.NET Web page will post back, and the Button's `Click` event will fire. When the Web form is submitted, we want to write source code that sends the user to the selected book's URL. This source code, which we'll examine shortly, should be placed in the Button's `Click` event handler.

Recall that to add a `Click` event handler to a Button Web control, you simply double-click the Button Web control in the designer. Next add the following code to the source code portion of the ASP.NET Web page:

```
Sub btnSubmit_Click(sender As Object, e As EventArgs)
    Response.Redirect(books.SelectedItem.Value)
End Sub
```

The `Response.Redirect()` function accepts a single string parameter that must be a valid URL. The function then automatically sends the user to the specified URL parameter. Because we want to send the user to the selected book's associated URL, and because each radio button's `Value` property is the corresponding book's `URL` column value, the URL we want to direct the user to is simply `books.SelectedItem.Value`.

Next save the ASP.NET Web page and view it through a browser. Now when you select one of the radio buttons and click the Visit the Selected Book's URL button, you will be automatically redirected to the book's specified URL.

If the user does not select one of the radio buttons before clicking the Visit the Selected Book's URL button, an error will occur. In the Exercises section for this hour, we'll examine a couple of ways to ensure that the user is not presented with this error message.

Examining the CheckBoxList Web Control

While reading the "Using the RadioButtonList Web Control" section, you probably noticed the similarities between the RadioButtonList and the DropDownList Web controls. Each displayed a list of items specified by some `DataSource`. The DropDownList displayed each item as an option in a drop-down list; the RadioButtonList displayed its items as a series of radio buttons. The list items for both controls had two properties—`Text` and `Value`—and these values are bound to database data via the DropDownList and RadioButtonList's `DataTextField` and `DataValueField` properties.

Not surprisingly, the CheckBoxList Web control also shares many similarities with the DropDownList and RadioButtonList Web controls. The CheckBoxList, as its name implies, displays each item as a checkbox. Like the choices in the DropDownList and RadioButtonList, each checkbox in the CheckBoxList contains two properties—`Text` and `Value`—and these values are bound to database data via the CheckBoxList's `DataTextField` and `DataValueField` properties. Similarly, to bind database data to the CheckBoxList, the `DataSource` property needs to be assigned to a DataSet or DataReader containing the appropriate data, and then the `DataBind()` method needs to be called.

The major difference between the CheckBoxList Web control and the DropDownList and RadioButton Web controls is that with a drop-down list or a series of radio buttons, only *one* item from the list of data-bound items can be selected. With the CheckBoxList, however, the user can choose multiple items at one time.

Determining Which Checkboxes Have Been Checked in a CheckBoxList

In the DropDownList and RadioButtonList examples we examined earlier in this hour, the ASP.NET Web pages used the following source code to determine the item that was selected:

`WebControlID.SelectedItem`

While this code works well for the DropDownList and RadioButtonList, it is insufficient for the CheckBoxList, where the user may select multiple options. Rather, for the

CheckBoxList we must iterate through *all* of the available items to determine which ones (if any) have been checked by the user. To see how this is accomplished, let's work through an example of a CheckBoxList. Our example will use a checkbox list to display the list of books from the Books table, from which the user can choose which books sound interesting to him. Once the user makes selections and submits the Web form, the source code will simply display the titles of the books the user selected.

> Often checkbox lists are used in surveys or other information-collecting forms where the users are asked to choose which items from a list they are interested in learning more about. For example, when filling out a survey for Amazon.com, a checkbox list might display the various products Amazon.com is considering selling online. The survey might ask, "Which items from the list below would you consider purchasing from Amazon.com?" The user could then choose none, one, or many of the options.

To start the example, create a new ASP.NET Web page named `DataCheckBoxList.aspx`. Turn on glyphs and then drag and drop the CheckBoxList Web control from the Toolbox and onto the designer. You should see a single checkbox with the text "Unbound" next to it. Set the CheckBoxList's `ID` property to `books`.

Because we want to display the titles of the books in the Books table, set the `DataTextField` property of the CheckBoxList to `Title`. We could set the `DataValueField` property to some column name in the Books database table, but because our Web page is simply going to display the titles of the books, we don't need the `Value` property set for each of the checkbox items in the CheckBoxList.

The next step in having the CheckBoxList display the books from the Books table is to create a function that returns the appropriate data. As we have seen in previous examples, this can be accomplished by using the SELECT Data Method Code Builder to create a function that returns a DataReader that consists of all of the columns from the Books table. When creating this function, name it `GetBooks`.

> To save time, rather than using the SELECT Data Method Code Builder, you can simply cut and paste the `GetBooks()` function from the `DataRadioButtonList.aspx` example we examined earlier in this hour.

Once this function has been created, we need to assign its return value to the `books` CheckBoxList's `DataSource` property and then call the CheckBoxList's `DataBind()`

method. As with the DropDownList and RadioButtonList examples we've seen in this hour, this code should be placed in the Page_Load event handler and should be run only if the ASP.NET Web page has not been posted back. The Page_Load event handler code, which you should add to the DataCheckBoxList.aspx ASP.NET Web page's source code portion, is as follows:

```
Sub Page_Load(sender as Object, e as EventArgs)
  If Not Page.IsPostBack then
    books.DataSource = GetBooks()
    books.DataBind()
  End If
End Sub
```

Once this source code has been added, you can test your ASP.NET Web page. To do so, first save the ASP.NET Web page and then view it through your Web browser. You should see a list of checkboxes, one checkbox for each book in the Books database table. Figure 17.10 shows a screenshot of the DataCheckBoxList.aspx ASP.NET Web page when viewed through a browser.

FIGURE 17.10

The Web page displays a checkbox for each book.

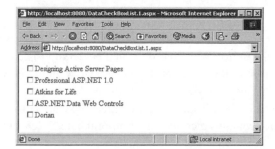

In order to take some action on the user's checkbox choices, we need to provide a means for submitting the Web form. To do this, we'll add a Button Web control and then provide a Click event handler for the button.

To accomplish this, start by navigating back to the Design tab and then add a Button Web control to the ASP.NET Web page by dragging and dropping it from the Toolbox and onto the designer. Set the Button Web control's ID property to btnSubmit and its Text property to Submit Book Choices. Realize that when this button is clicked, the ASP.NET Web page will be posted back and will display the titles chosen by the user.

Before we write the source code for the Click event handler, let's first add a Label Web control to the DataCheckBoxList.aspx Web page. This Label Web control will be used to display the output. Add a Label Web control, clear its Text property, and set its ID property to results. Once you have added the Button and Label Web controls, your screen should look similar to the screen in Figure 17.11.

17

FIGURE 17.11

*A Button Web control
and a Label Web
control have been
added.*

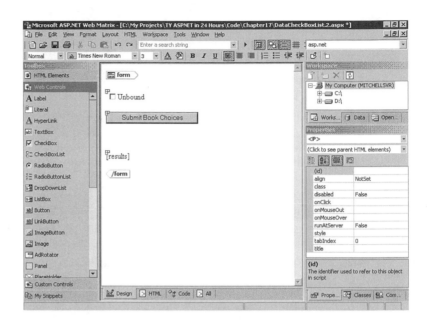

Before writing the source code for the Click event handler, we must create the Click
event handler for the Button Web control, which is accomplished by double-clicking the
button in the designer. In the Click event handler, we want to display the titles of the
books selected by the user. To determine which checkboxes have been selected, we need
to iterate through all of the CheckBoxList's items. The CheckBoxList contains a property
called Items, which contains a collection of all of the items (checkboxes) that constitute
the checkbox list.

To iterate through all of the items in the Items collection, we can use a For ... Next
loop with the following syntax:

```
Dim i as Integer
For i = 0 to CheckBoxListID.Items.Count - 1
  We can now access the ith item by using:
  CheckBoxListID.Items(i)
Next i
```

Recall that we discussed the For ... Next looping construct in Hour 6,
"Visual Basic .NET Control Structures."

There are two important things to note in this source code example. First, we can loop
through *all* of the items by looping from 0 to CheckBoxListID.Items.Count - 1. We
start at 0 because every collection in the .NET Framework is zero-based, meaning that its

first element is indexed as 0. *CheckBoxListID*.Items.Count returns the number of checkboxes in the checkbox list. Because we start counting at 0, we don't want to loop all the way up to Count, but rather Count - 1.

Second, inside the For ... Next loop, we can reference the current item by using

CheckBoxID.Items(i)

We can reference the item's Text and Value properties with the following code:

CheckBoxID.Items(i).Text
CheckBoxID.Items(i).Value

The item also has a property called Selected, which is a Boolean value and indicates whether it was selected by the user. In the case of a CheckBoxList, the Selected property is true for a particular checkbox if it has been checked. The Selected property can be accessed with the following code:

CheckBoxID.Items(i).Selected

Therefore, in order for our Click event handler to display the titles of the selected books, we simply need to iterate through the Items collection and, for each selected item, display the title of the book. (Recall that the Text property of the checkbox is precisely the title of the book.)

Insert the code from Listing 17.1 into the source code portion of the ASP.NET Web page. (Make sure that you have double-clicked the Button Web control in order to create the Click event handler.)

LISTING 17.1 The Titles of the Selected Books Are Displayed

```
 1: Sub btnSubmit_Click(sender As Object, e As EventArgs)
 2:     results.Text = "You selected the following books:<p>"
 3:
 4:     Dim i as Integer
 5:     For i = 0 to books.Items.Count - 1
 6:         If books.Items(i).Selected then
 7:             results.Text &= "<li>" & books.Items(i).Text & "<br>"
 8:         End If
 9:     Next i
10: End Sub
```

Listing 17.1 displays the titles of the selected books in the results Label Web control. On line 2 the Label Web control's Text property is set to the text You selected the following books:<p>. Following that, in lines 5–9, a For ... Next loop iterates through the books CheckBoxList's Items collection. In each iteration of the loop, the current item's Selected property is checked. If it is True, then the results Label Web control's Text property has the title of the book appended to it, along with some HTML markup for formatting.

17

Figure 17.12 shows a screenshot of the `DataCheckBoxList.aspx` Web page when viewed through a browser after the user has selected some checkboxes and clicked the Submit Book Choices button.

FIGURE **17.12**

The user has submitted multiple choices from the checkbox list offered.

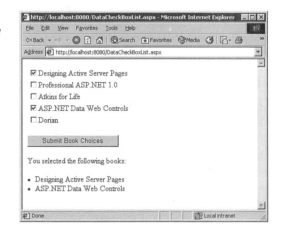

Summary

In this hour we examined three input Web controls whose contents are determined by database data. These three controls—the DropDownList, RadioButtonList, and CheckBoxList—share much in common. They all display a series of items, each of which has the properties `Text` and `Value`. The three Web controls each has a `DataTextField` property that specifies the `DataSource` field, whose value is assigned to each item's `Text` property, and a `DataValueField`, which specifies the field whose value is assigned to each item's `Value` property. Finally, all three controls have a `DataSource` property, which specifies the data to be bound to the control, and a `DataBind()` method, which actually performs the work of binding the data to the Web control.

The first control we examined was the DropDownList Web control. The DropDownList displays each of its items as an option in a drop-down list. In this hour we used the data-bound DropDownList to enhance an example from Hour 16. Specifically, we saw how we could display a list of customers from the `Customers` table by using a DropDownList Web control. Then, whenever the user selected a customer from the drop-down list, the customer's information would be displayed in a DataGrid.

Next we turned our attention to the RadioButtonList Web control, which displays each item as a radio button. We saw an example of using the RadioButtonList to list the titles of the books in the `Books` database. The user could select a particular book and then, at the click of a button, be automatically redirected to the selected book's URL.

The DropDownList and RadioButtonList Web controls both allow for only one item from a list of items to be selected. The CheckBoxList, on the other hand, displays a checkbox for every item and allows the user to select any number of them simultaneously. In order to determine which checkboxes were selected, the CheckBoxList's Items collection must be enumerated through. To determine what items have been selected, we can check the Selected property, which returns True if the item is selected and False otherwise.

We now turn our attention back to the DataGrid Web control. Over the next three hours, we will examine three of the DataGrid's most useful features: its ability to allow the user to sort, page through, and edit the DataGrid's data. The next hour examines sorting the DataGrid's data.

Q&A

17

Q In the examples using the DropDownList, I noticed that we have to set the DataTextField and DataValueField properties of the DropDownList to the names of fields in the DataSource. What happens if we forget to set these properties?

A In the "Binding Database Data to a DropDownList Web Control" section of this hour, we used a DropDownList to list the various customers from the Customers table. In this particular example, we set the DropDownList's DataTextField to Name and its DataValueField to CustomerID. This had the effect of having one list item in the DropDownList for each customer in the Customers table. The text of each list item was the value of the Name column in the Customers table, and the value associated with each list item was the value of the CustomerID column.

If you forget to set these properties through the Properties pane, the DropDownList will still display. However, the text and value for each of its list items will be System.Data.Common.DbDataRecord if the DropDownList is bound to a DataReader, or System.Data.DataRowView if the DropDownList is bound to a DataSet. The reason for this is that if you do not specify either the DataTextField or DataValueField properties, the DropDownList simply emits the name of the object it is iterating over in its DataBind() method for the text and value properties of the list item.

If you do not fully understand why the particular messages are emitted, don't worry. What's important to take away from this discussion is that if you are using a data-bound DropDownList and, in testing the ASP.NET Web page, see the DropDownList containing either System.Data.Common.DbDataRecord or System.Data.DataRowView as the text for each list item, it likely means that you simply forgot to specify the DataTextField and DataValueField properties.

Q **In the RadioButtonList example we examined in this hour, when the user first visits the page with the list of radio buttons, no radio button is selected. This means that the user can submit the Web form without having selected a radio button option. Is there some way to automatically have one of the radio buttons selected when the user first visits the page?**

A There is an easy way to have the first in a list of radio buttons selected. Immediately after the RadioButtonList Web control's `DataBind()` method has been called, simply add the following line of code:

```
RadioButtonListID.Items(0).Selected = True
```

The `Items` property of the RadioButtonList Web control returns the list items that make up the RadioButtonList. Therefore, we can access the first such radio button in the list of radio buttons by using the code `Items(0)`. Once we have a reference to the first radio button, we can set its `Selected` property to True. This code has the effect of having the first radio button in the list of radio buttons already selected when the user first visits the Web page.

For practice at implementing this technique, see Exercise 1.

Workshop

Quiz

1. In this hour we saw how to use the DropDownList Web control to display a drop-down list populated with items from a database. We first saw this Web control, though, in Hour 11, where we discussed manually adding a number of list items to the DropDownList Web control. Contrast the steps required for displaying a hard-coded, static set of list items versus those for displaying a set of items from a database.

2. The steps for binding database data to DropDownList, RadioButtonList, or CheckBoxList Web controls are the same. List these steps.

3. Which of the three Web controls that we examined in this hour would you use to create an ASP.NET Web page that allowed the user to select an arbitrary number of customers from the `Customers` table?

4. What happens if the DataReader or DataSet you bind to a DropDownList, RadioButtonList, or CheckBoxList is an empty DataReader or empty DataSet? (Recall that an empty DataReader or empty DataSet is a DataReader or DataSet that has no records.)

5. True or False: The code to determine which radio button was selected in a RadioButtonList Web control is the same code that is used to determine which checkboxes were checked in a CheckBoxList.

Answers

1. Recall that when adding list items to a DropDownList manually, we clicked the ellipsis next to the `Items` property in the Properties pane. This displayed the ListItem Collection Editor dialog box, with which we could add new list items. For each added list item, we could choose whether or not it should be the selected one and what its `Text` and `Value` properties should be.

   To bind database results to a DropDownList Web control, we needed to programmatically assign the DataReader or DataSet containing the database items to the DropDownList's `DataSource` property and then call the DropDownList's `DataBind()` method. In addition to this, we needed to specify the `DataTextField` and `DataValueField` properties. These properties indicate which `DataSource` field should be used for each list item's `Text` and `Value` properties.

2. To bind database data to a DropDownList, RadioButtonList, or CheckBoxList Web control, first set the Web control's `DataTextField` and `DataValueField` properties to the proper fields in the `DataSource`. Next assign the DataReader or DataSet to the Web control's `DataSource` property. Finally, call the Web control's `DataBind()` method.

3. You would want to use the CheckBoxList Web control, since only it allows for multiple items to be selected.

4. For the RadioButtonList and CheckBoxList, no radio buttons or checkboxes are displayed. For the DropDownList Web control, an empty drop-down list is displayed.

5. False. With a RadioButtonList, since only one item can be selected, we can use the `SelectedItem` property. With a CheckBoxList, which can have multiple items selected, we must iterate through the `Items` property to determine which checkboxes have been checked.

Exercises

1. In the "Q&A" section in this hour, we saw how to enhance the RadioButtonList so that the first in a list of radio buttons would be already selected when the user first visited the page. Please update the `DataRadioButtonList.aspx` example we examined in the "Using the RadioButtonList Web Control" to include this functionality.

2. In the "Binding Database Data to a DropDownList Web Control" section, we examined how to display the list of customers in a DropDownList Web control. The information of a particular selected customer would be displayed in a DataGrid. Create a new ASP.NET Web page that provides this functionality, but instead of listing the customers in a DropDownList Web control, list the customers by using a RadioButtonList Web control. Furthermore, use the technique practiced in Exercise 1 so that the first radio button in the list is selected when the page is first visited.

17

(Hint: Don't forget—you will need to set the RadioButtonList's `AutoPostBack` property to True and create an event handler for the RadioButtonList's `SelectedIndexChanged` event. This event handler can be created by simply double-clicking the RadioButtonList in the designer.)

3. For this Exercise create an ASP.NET Web page that allows the user to choose one or more of the customers from the `Customers` table. (Hint: Use a CheckBoxList Web control.) After choosing an arbitrary number of customers, the user should be able to click a button to display the phone numbers for all of the selected customers. Figure 17.13 shows a screenshot of the ASP.NET Web page that you are to create.

FIGURE 17.13

The phone numbers of the selected customers are displayed.

PART IV

Advanced Data Display with the DataGrid

Hour

HOUR 18

Allowing the User to Sort the Data in a DataGrid

In Hours 15, "Displaying Data with the DataGrid Web Control," and 16, "Examining Further DataGrid Examples," we took an introductory look at the DataGrid Web control. We saw how to bind the database to the DataGrid, how to format the DataGrid, specifying Bound Column and HyperLink Column, and many other techniques. Of equal importance, in these two hours (as well as in the previous hour, "Working with Data-Bound DropDownList, RadioButton, and CheckBox Web Controls") we saw how to use the SELECT Data Method Code Builder to create functions that return the proper database data in the form of a DataReader.

This hour, as well as the next two hours, examines some of the more advanced features of the DataGrid Web control. In this hour we'll see how to allow the user to sort the DataGrid's data; in the next hour, "Paging Through the DataGrid's Data," we'll look at how to allow the user to page through data; and in Hour 20, "Editing the Data in a DataGrid," we'll see how to provide functionality so that the user can edit the data displayed in the DataGrid.

In order to understand the concepts that will be presented in this hour and the next two, it is important that you are comfortable using the DataGrid and creating data-accessing functions with the SELECT Data Method Code Builder. If you still need more experience with the DataGrid and SELECT Data Method Code Builder, consider rereading the previous hours or trying out some examples with the DataGrid and Code Builder on your own.

In this hour we will cover the following topics:

- A high-level overview of how sorting works in the DataGrid Web control
- Specifying which columns in the DataGrid are sortable
- Sorting the results of an SQL SELECT query
- Tweaking the function produced by the SELECT Data Method Code Builder to provide dynamic sorting
- Configuring the DataGrid to allow for sorting
- An example of a DataGrid with sorting capabilities

Making a High-Level Overview of DataGrid Sorting

As we have seen in the DataGrid examples throughout the last few hours, the DataGrid displays data from a database table in a two-dimensional grid format, using an HTML <table> tag. The purpose of a DataGrid is to display data, ideally in a form that is easy for the user to utilize. But what makes data easily utilizable by the user? It depends largely on what information the user wants to extract from the data.

For example, imagine that you want to find the least expensive book on home improvements available on Amazon.com. Going to Amazon.com, you could run a search on "home improvements," which may return hundreds of books. Finding the least expensive of these hundreds of books would be quite a chore unless Amazon.com provided some way to sort the results by price. Of course, another user may want to buy the most recently published book on home improvements. To satisfy this user's needs, Amazon.com would want to allow users to search sort results by the books' publication dates.

As this example illustrates, by providing the ability for the user to to sort data, the data becomes that much more useable. The DataGrid Web control includes properties, methods, and events to assist with sorting of the DataGrid's data. Before we delve into the technical details of sorting data in the DataGrid, let's discuss the sorting process in high-level terms first.

Sorting the DataGrid—From the User's Perspective

Before we can examine what we, the developers, need to do to provide DataGrid sorting, we need to examine sorting from the user's perspective. We should ask ourselves how the user can tell whether a DataGrid is sortable and what actions the user must take to sort the DataGrid by a particular column.

When a DataGrid is configured to allow sorting, every sortable column of the DataGrid has its header displayed as a hyperlink. When this header is clicked for a particular DataGrid column, the data in the DataGrid is sorted by this column. Figure 18.1 shows a screenshot of a sortable DataGrid. Note that the two sortable columns' headers are displayed as hyperlinks. When one of these hyperlinks is clicked, the DataGrid's data will be sorted by that column.

FIGURE 18.1

Each sortable column's header is a hyperlink.

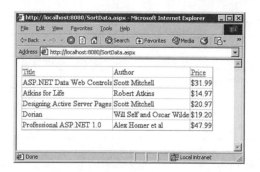

18

When you create a sortable DataGrid whose columns are implicitly created, all columns will be sortable. This means that each column will display its header as a hyperlink. If you explicitly specify the DataGrid columns through the Property Builder dialog box's Columns screen, you can specify whether a particular column should be sortable or not. If a column is *not* sortable, the header will be displayed as normal text and not as a hyperlink.

DataGrid Sorting—From the Developer's Perspective

To make a DataGrid sortable, we, the developers, have to perform a number of tasks that may be quite involved. Before we enumerate these tasks, though, let's first discuss what happens behind the scenes when a user opts to sort the DataGrid data by a particular column.

Recall that by clicking a column's hyperlink header, the user can select which column the data should be sorted by. This hyperlink causes the Web form to submit, posting back the ASP.NET Web page. This postback causes the DataGrid's SortCommand event to fire. Because we want to re-sort the data in the DataGrid whenever this event fires, we will need to provide an event handler for this event. The event handler will requery the database, obtaining the database data sorted by the column the user clicked, and then bind this sorted data to the DataGrid. Figure 18.2 is a graphical representation of the sequence of steps that occurs whenever a user opts to sort the DataGrid by a particular column.

FIGURE **18.2**

A graphical representation of DataGrid sorting from the developer's perspective.

Step 1: The DataGrid's `DataSource` property is set, and the `DataBind()` method is called. The user is shown the data in an HTML table, with the column headers displayed as hyperlinks.

Name	Age	Gender
Scott	24	M
Jisun	23	F
Chris	21	M

Step 2: The user clicks one of the column header hyperlinks, which causes the ASP. NET Web page to be posted back.

For example, if the Name column hyperlink is clicked…

Click

Name	Age	Gender
Scott	24	M
Jisun	23	F
Chris	21	M

Step 3: …the DataGrid's SortCommand event fires, which causes the associated event handler to execute. This event handler rebinds the database data to the DataGrid, but this time sorts the data based on the column whose hyperlink header was clicked. This sorted DataGrid is then displayed to the user.

Name	Age	Gender
Chris	21	M
Jisun	23	F
Scott	24	M

The important concept to grasp is that whenever the user chooses to view the DataGrid sorted in a different order, the ASP.NET Web page is posted back, a database query must be issued that obtains the data in the properly sorted order, and the results of this SELECT query must be bound to the DataGrid.

Recall that the results of an SQL SELECT query can be ordered by a particular table field by using the ORDER BY clause. Refer back to Hour 14, "Understanding SQL, the Language of Databases," for more information on ORDER BY.

In order to create a sortable DataGrid, we'll need to perform the following steps:

1. Add a DataGrid Web control to the ASP.NET Web page.
2. Specify, via the Property Builder, that the DataGrid should allow sorting.
3. If the DataGrid's columns are to be explicitly added, every column that is sortable must have its field name entered into the "Sort expression" textbox in the Columns screen of the Property Builder.
4. Use the SELECT Data Method Code Builder to create a function that returns the DataGrid data.
5. Edit this function so that it accepts a string input parameter specifying the column name to sort by.
6. Alter the function's body so that the SQL SELECT query used is sorted by the passed-in column name.
7. Bind the data to the DataGrid in the Page_Load event handler, performing this binding only when the page is not being loaded on a postback.
8. Provide an event handler for the DataGrid's SortCommand event. This event handler needs to rebind the DataGrid according to the column the DataGrid is to be sorted by.

The brief descriptions for some of the steps may sound a bit confusing at this point. Don't worry; we'll thoroughly examine each one of these steps. We will spend the remainder of this hour examining how to perform these eight tasks. Steps 1 through 3 are discussed in the next section, "Specifying That a DataGrid Is to Be Sortable." The section "Obtaining the Database Data in Properly Sorted Order" discusses steps 4–6. Finally, steps 7 and 8 are covered in the section "Sorting the Data when a Sortable Column's Header Hyperlink Is Clicked."

Specifying That a DataGrid Is to Be Sortable

As we have seen in our previous DataGrid examples, a DataGrid, by default, is not considered sortable. To make a DataGrid sortable, we must check the "Allow sorting" checkbox in the DataGrid's Property Builder. Furthermore, if we are explicitly specifying which columns should appear in the DataGrid, it is vital that we specify which of these columns is sortable.

To examine the steps needed to make a DataGrid sortable, create a new ASP.NET Web page named SortData.aspx. Drag and drop a DataGrid Web control from the Toolbox and onto the designer. (You may want to turn glyphs on, as sortable DataGrids must be placed within the page's Web form.) Set the DataGrid's ID property to **dgBooks**.

18

This DataGrid will be used to display the books from the Books table. Once the DataGrid has been added, we can specify that it should be sortable by visiting the DataGrid's Property Builder and checking the "Allow sorting" checkbox. This checkbox can be found in the General screen of the Property Builder, which is the screen shown when first launching the Property Builder dialog box. The checkbox is at the bottom of the General screen, just below the Behavior label. Figure 18.3 shows a screenshot of the Property Builder dialog box after the "Allow sorting" checkbox has been checked.

FIGURE 18.3

The "Allow sorting" checkbox has been checked.

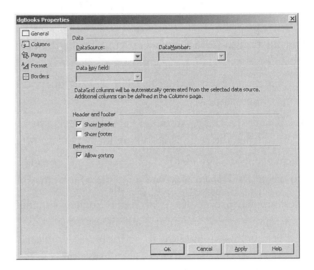

If you do not want to specify the columns that should be displayed in the DataGrid, this is all you need to make the DataGrid sortable. If, however, you plan to specify explicitly the DataGrid columns, then, when adding each column, you will need to specify whether or not the column is sortable.

Let's examine how to accomplish this. For this exercise let's have the DataGrid use three Bound Columns: one to display the Title field, one to display the Author field, and the last to display the Price field. To add these Bound Columns to the DataGrid, navigate to the Columns screen of the Property Builder. Uncheck the "Create columns automatically at run time" checkbox and then add three Bound Columns.

For the first Bound Column, set the Header text and Data Field textboxes to **Title**. For the second Bound Column, set the Header text and Data Field textboxes to **Author**. Finally, for the last Bound Column, set the Header text and Data Field textboxes to **Price** and the Data formatting expression textbox to **{0:c}**, which, as we saw in Hour 16, will format the values in this column as currency.

The "Sort expression" textbox for the BoundColumn indicates whether the column is sortable. To make a Bound Column sortable, simply enter the field name into the "Sort expression" textbox. If you do not want a Bound Column to be sortable, don't enter anything into the "Sort expression" textbox. For this exercise let's make the Title and Price columns sortable. Therefore, for the Title Bound Column enter the value **Title** into the "Sort expression" textbox, and for the Price Bound Column enter the value **Price**. Because we do not want the Author Bound Column to be sortable, leave the "Sort expression" textbox blank.

Figure 18.4 shows a screenshot of the Columns screen of the Property Builder after the aforementioned settings have been made. It shows the values for the Title Bound Column. Note that the Sort expression contains the value Title.

FIGURE 18.4

The Title column of the DataGrid is now sortable.

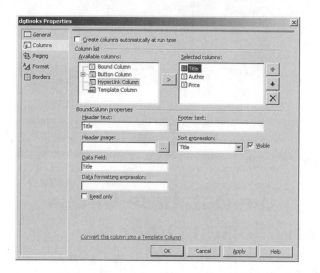

18

Once the three Bound Columns have been added and their properties set, click the Property Builder's OK button to return to the designer. Upon returning to the designer, you should notice that the appearance of the DataGrid has changed. As Figure 18.5 shows, the DataGrid now has three columns (because we explicitly specified that the DataGrid have three Bound Columns), and the sortable columns' headers are displayed as hyperlinks.

FIGURE **18.5**

The DataGrid's appearance in the designer has been updated.

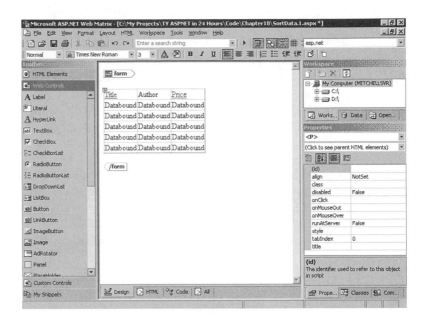

With these steps we have indicated that the DataGrid is sortable and that the Title and Price columns are sortable. We have not yet, however, performed the needed steps to have the DataGrid's data sorted when a user clicks one of the column header hyperlinks.

Obtaining the Database Data in Properly Sorted Order

Whenever a user clicks the hyperlink header of a sortable DataGrid column, the ASP.NET Web page is posted back, and the DataGrid's SortCommand event is fired. In the DataGrid's SortCommand event handler, we must provide code that queries the database, returning the results sorted by the database table field that corresponds to the clicked DataGrid column. To accomplish this, we will need first to create a data access function via the SELECT Data Method Code Builder, and then tweak the resulting source code.

Start by clicking the Code tab and creating a function that returns all of the records from the Books table via a DataReader. Recall that this can be easily accomplished by using the SELECT Data Method Code Builder, specifying that all rows should be returned for the Books table. Make sure that you name the resulting function **GetBooks** and that you have it return a DataReader. Listing 18.1 shows the source code for the GetBooks() function that was created by the SELECT Data Method Code Builder.

LISTING 18.1   The `GetBooks()` Function Returns All of the Records
from the `Books` Table

```
 1: Function GetBooks() As System.Data.SqlClient.SqlDataReader
 2:     Dim connectionString As String = "server='localhost'; user id='sa';
                password='xxxx'; Database='ASPExamples'"
 3:     Dim sqlConnection As System.Data.SqlClient.SqlConnection = New
                System.Data.SqlClient.SqlConnection(connectionString)
 4:
 5:     Dim queryString As String = "SELECT [Books].* FROM [Books]"
 6:     Dim sqlCommand As System.Data.SqlClient.SqlCommand = New
                System.Data.SqlClient.SqlCommand(queryString, sqlConnection)
 7:
 8:     sqlConnection.Open
 9:     Dim dataReader As System.Data.SqlClient.SqlDataReader =
                sqlCommand.ExecuteReader(System.Data.CommandBehavior.CloseConnection)
10:
11:     Return dataReader
12: End Function
```

While the `GetBooks()` function does a great job at returning all of the records from the
`Books` table, it does not permit any way to specify how the results should be sorted.
Because we need to be able to specify by which table column the results should be
sorted, we need to alter the `GetBooks()` function so that it can be passed a string parameter
that specifies the name of the column to sort by.

To make this change, specify that the `GetBooks()` function can accept a single parameter.
That is, edit line 1 so that it becomes

```
Function GetBooks(sortBy as String) As System.Data.SqlClient.SqlDataReader
```

Here we have added an input parameter named `sortBy` of type `String`. While the
`GetBooks()` function now accepts a parameter by which the results are to be sorted, we
have yet to add the code needed to indicate that the results should indeed be sorted. To
do this, we need to alter the query on line 5 to contain an `ORDER BY` clause.

Recall from Hour 14 that the `ORDER BY` clause of an `SQL` `SELECT` statement appears at the
end of the `SELECT` statement and has the following syntax, where our *"ColumnName"*
replacement will specify the name of the column the results should be sorted by:

```
ORDER BY ColumnName
```

Because the input parameter `sortBy` specifies the name of the column by which the
results should be sorted, we only need to change line 5 slightly. Edit line 5 so that it contains
the following source code:

```
Dim queryString As String = "SELECT [Books].* FROM [Books] ORDER BY " & sortBy
```

18

As you can see, we have simply added an ORDER BY clause at the end of the query and then appended the value of the sortBy parameter.

To see how the code works, consider what happens when the GetBooks() function is called with the following code:

```
GetBooks("Title")
```

Here the value of the input parameter sortBy is Title. Therefore, the SELECT query issued to the database is

```
SELECT [Books].*
FROM [Books]
ORDER BY Title
```

Alternatively, if the GetBooks() function is called using

```
GetBooks("Price")
```

then the value of the input parameter sortBy is Price, and the SELECT query issued to the database is

```
SELECT [Books].*
FROM [Books]
ORDER BY Price
```

By changing two lines of code in the GetBooks() function, we have converted the GetBooks() function from one that blindly returns the records from the Books table to one that returns the records from the Books table sorted by the user's specified column. As we will see in the next section, this function will be called whenever the user opts to sort the DataGrid results by a particular column.

Sorting the Data when a Sortable Column's Header Hyperlink Is Clicked

At this point we have specified that the DataGrid should be sortable by checking the "Allow sorting" checkbox in the General screen of the DataGrid's Property Builder. This setting has the effect of displaying the sortable columns' headers as hyperlinks. We have also added the GetBooks() function to the ASP.NET Web page via the SELECT Data Method Code Builder and modified the function to accept a single input parameter that determines by which table column the results of the SQL query are sorted.

With these pieces in place, all that we have left to do is create an event handler for the DataGrid's SortCommand event and have the source code for this event handler retrieve the database data in the properly sorted order. Realize that the DataGrid's SortCommand event is fired whenever the user clicks one of the sortable column headers. More specifically, when one of these column headers is clicked, the ASP.NET Web page is posted back, and the ASP.NET Web page can tell that the reason the postback occurred was because a sortable column header was clicked.

Adding an Event Handler

In previous hours we have created a number of event handlers. For example, we've seen that to create a Click event handler for the Button Web control, all we have to do is double-click the button in the designer. Similarly, double-clicking the DropDownList Web control in the designer will create the SelectedItemChanged event handler.

Realize that whenever you create an event handler in this manner, two things happen. First, the Web Matrix Project creates the suitable event handler subroutine in the ASP.NET Web page's source code section. For example, for the Button Web control's Click event, the event handler created is

```
Sub ButtonID_Click(sender as Object, e as EventArgs)

End Sub
```

It is inside this subroutine that you add the source code to execute when the Button's Click event fires. Second, the Web Matrix Project indicates in the Web control's declaration that when a particular event fires, a particular event handler should be executed.

For example, when creating an event handler for the Button Web control by double-clicking the button in the designer, the Web Matrix Project adds the following to the Button Web control declaration:

```
OnClick="ButtonID_Click"
```

> More generally, when specifying the event handler for any event for any Web control, the syntax is
> ```
> OnEventName="EventHandlerName"
> ```

If the Button Web control's declaration prior to adding the event handler were, say,

```
<asp:Button id="btnSubmit" runat="server" Text="Click Me"></asp:Button>
```

after creating the event handler for the Click event, the Button's declaration would be changed to

```
<asp:Button id="btnSubmit" runat="server" Text="Click Me"
      OnClick="btnSubmit_Click"></asp:Button>
```

18

All of this is done automatically for you by the Web Matrix Project when you add an event handler to a Web control by double-clicking it in the designer. Unfortunately, each Web control can have only one event handler that is automatically wired up to it when double-clicking. If you want to add an event other than the one assigned to be added when the Web control is double-clicked, you must perform the two steps just described by hand.

We have delved into this explanation because, as you might have already guessed, when you double-click the DataGrid Web control, an event handler for the `SelectedIndexChanged` event is added. So, to add an event handler for the `SortCommand` event, we'll have to edit the DataGrid declaration and add the needed subroutine by hand.

Adding the Subroutine in the Source Code Portion

Let's first add the subroutine for the `SortCommand` event handler in the source code portion. Start by clicking the Code tab so that you can edit the ASP.NET Web page's source code. Then add the following:

```
Sub SortDataGrid(sender as Object, e as DataGridSortCommandEventArgs)

End Sub
```

> I have chosen to name this event handler `SortDataGrid` (the name of the subroutine). You can, however, choose any name you want for the subroutine. For example, this event handler could have been named `dgBooks_Sort`, which would have meant that the subroutine would have been defined as
>
> ```
> Sub dgBooks_Sort(sender as Object, e as DataGridSortCommandEventArgs)
> End Sub
> ```

For now we won't write any source code for this event handler. However, we'll come back to this subroutine later in this hour and add the source code needed to implement paging.

If you have a sharp eye, you might have noticed that the event handlers we have examined before have had the form

```
Sub EventHandlerName(sender as Object, e as EventArgs)

End Sub
```

The `SortCommand` event handler is slightly different, however. The `SortCommand` event handler's second input parameter is of type `DataGridSortCommandEventArgs` instead of `EventArgs`. While most event handlers expect a second parameter of type `EventArgs`, there are a handful of events that require alternate types for their second parameters. The reason for this is beyond the scope of this book. What is important to realize, though, is that there can be a difference, and the difference is on an event-by-event basis.

Wiring Up the `SortCommand` Event to the `SortDataGrid` Event Handler

The next step is to specify that when the DataGrid's `SortCommand` event fires, the `SortDataGrid` event handler should execute. This is accomplished by adding the following code to the DataGrid's declaration:

```
OnSortCommand="SortDataGrid"
```

This can be accomplished most easily by going to the designer, right-clicking the DataGrid, and selecting the Edit Tag option (see Figure 18.6).

FIGURE 18.6

Right-click the DataGrid and choose the Edit Tag option.

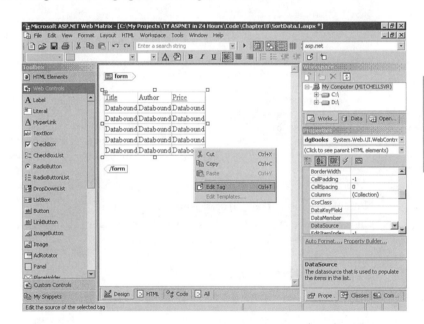

Selecting the Edit Tag option will display the Quick Tag Edit dialog box, as shown in Figure 18.7.

FIGURE 18.7
The DataGrid's declaration is displayed.

Here we need to wire up the DataGrid's SortCommand event to the SortDataGrid event handler. To do this, move the cursor immediately after the `<asp:DataGrid` and type

```
OnSortCommand="SortDataGrid"
```

Once you have done this, the DataGrid tag should look similar to this:

```
<asp:DataGrid OnSortCommand="SortDataGrid" id="dgBooks" runat="server"
        AllowSorting="True" AutoGenerateColumns="False">
  <Columns>
    <asp:BoundColumn DataField="Title" SortExpression="Title"
        HeaderText="Title"></asp:BoundColumn>
    <asp:BoundColumn DataField="Author" HeaderText="Author"></asp:BoundColumn>
    <asp:BoundColumn DataField="Price" SortExpression="Price"
        HeaderText="Price" DataFormatString="{0:c}"></asp:BoundColumn>
  </Columns>
</asp:DataGrid>
```

Note the addition of `OnSortCommand="SortDataGrid"` from the screenshot in Figure 18.7. Once you have entered `OnSortCommand="SortDataGrid"` to the DataGrid tag, click the OK button, which will return you to the designer.

Writing the Source Code for the `SortDataGrid` Event Handler

Now that we have added the SortDataGrid subroutine and wired up the DataGrid's SortCommand event to the SortDataGrid event handler, all that remains is to write the source code for the SortDataGrid event handler. In order to comprehend the code that needs to be written, it is vital that we understand when this event handler executes and what tasks need to be accomplished.

Recall that when the user clicks a sortable column's header hyperlink, the ASP.NET Web page is posted back, and the DataGrid's SortCommand event handler fires. This causes the SortDataGrid event handler to execute. What this event handler must do is retrieve the data to be displayed in the correctly sorted order and then bind this data to the DataGrid.

In order to get the data in the properly sorted format, we need to know which column of the DataGrid the user wants to sort the results by. Fortunately, this is quite simple to determine. Earlier we saw that the definition of the SortDataGrid event handler is given as

```
Sub SortDataGrid(sender as Object, e as DataGridSortCommandEventArgs)

End Sub
```

The second input parameter, e, has a string property called SortExpression, which returns the Sort expression property for the clicked column. Recall from earlier in this hour, that when we explicitly added the three Bound Columns to the DataGrid, we also entered in the name of the column into the "Sort expression" textbox. The value returned by the e.SortExpression property is the value entered into this textbox. The value we entered into the "Sort expression" textbox was precisely the name of the field that was being displayed in the Bound Column.

Due to this fact, we can get the database data in the properly sorted format simply by making a call to the GetBooks() function that is passing in the value of the e.SortExpression property. Just use the following code:

```
GetBooks(e.SortExpression)
```

To see how and why this works, consider the DataGrid's Title column, which displays the title of each book. This Bound Column's "Sort expression" textbox value is Title. Therefore, when the user clicks the hyperlink for this sortable column, the value of e.SortExpression in the SortDataGrid event handler is Title, meaning the function call

```
GetBooks(e.SortExpression)
```

is synonymous to

```
GetBooks("Title")
```

Both of these return the rows from the Books table ordered alphabetically by the books' titles.

> If you do not explicitly specify which columns should appear in the DataGrid, the e.SortExpression property returns the DataSource field name that is bound to the DataGrid column.

18

Now, to bind the sorted data to the DataGrid, all we have to do is set the DataGrid's `DataSource` property to the DataReader returned by the `GetBooks()` function and then call the DataGrid's `DataBind()` method.

The complete code for the `SortDataGrid` event handler is quite brief:

```
Sub SortDataGrid(sender as Object, e as DataGridSortCommandEventArgs)
  dgBooks.DataSource = GetBooks(e.SortExpression)
  dgBooks.DataBind()
End Sub
```

All that we need to add now is the code for the `Page_Load` event handler, which binds the database results to the DataGrid only when the page is not being posted back. Here is this code:

```
Sub Page_Load(sender as Object, e as EventArgs)
  If Not Page.IsPostBack then
    dgBooks.DataSource = GetBooks("Title")
    dgBooks.DataBind()
  End If
End Sub
```

Realize that we want to bind the data to the DataGrid only when the page is not being posted back, because each time the user clicks one of the sortable columns' header hyperlinks, the ASP.NET Web page is posted back. Also note that when calling the `GetBooks()` function, we have to pass in the name of the table column by which the results should be sorted. For example, the code presented uses

```
GetBooks("Title")
```

This will have the DataGrid sorted by the Title column when first visited. If you want to change this to some other `Books` column name, feel free.

Testing the ASP.NET Web Page

At this point we have added a DataGrid to the ASP.NET Web page and specified that it be sortable. We have added a function to return the contents of the `Books` database table in a specified sorted order, and we have created an event handler for the DataGrid's `SortCommand` event. Whew! Accomplishing all of these tasks took quite a bit of time and explanation, but our hard work has paid off—we now have a sortable DataGrid!

Save the ASP.NET Web page and view it through a browser. When you first load the page, the data will be sorted by the Title column (assuming you did not change the `Page_Load` event handler). Figure 18.8 shows a screenshot of the ASP.NET Web page when first loaded in a Web browser.

FIGURE **18.8**
The books are sorted
alphabetically
by their titles.

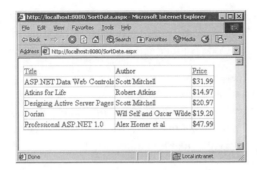

Now, if you click the hyperlink in the Price column header, the contents will be sorted by their prices (in ascending order). Figure 18.9 shows a screenshot of the ASP.NET Web page after the Price column header hyperlink has been clicked.

FIGURE **18.9**
The books are now
sorted by price.

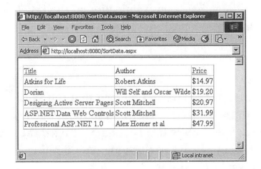

18

The default sortable DataGrid can sort the columns in only one direction. A discussion on how to enhance the DataGrid to allow bidirectional column sorting is beyond the scope of this book, but, if you are interested, you can find a thorough discussion on the topic in *ASP.NET Data Web Controls*.

Summary

In this hour we examined how to create a sortable DataGrid. The sortable DataGrid allows the user to sort the data in the DataGrid according to a particular column by clicking the column's hyperlink header.

In order to make a sortable DataGrid, we, the developers, must undertake a number of steps. The first step is simply to add the DataGrid to the ASP.NET Web page. Next we have to specify that the DataGrid should be sortable by checking the "Allow sorting" checkbox in the DataGrid's Property Builder.

Next we need to create a function that takes an input parameter that specifies by which column the database data should be sorted. To assist in creating this function, we can use the SELECT Data Method Code Builder and then modify the source code generated by the Code Builder.

Finally, we need to create an event handler for the DataGrid's SortCommand event. To accomplish this, we must not only provide an appropriate subroutine in the ASP.NET Web page's source code portion but must also wire up the SortCommand event to the created event handler. This is accomplished by adding the following code to the DataGrid's declaration:

```
OnSortCommand="EventHandlerName"
```

The simplest way to edit the DataGrid's declaration is to right-click the DataGrid in the designer and choose the Edit Tag option.

In the next hour we will continue our examination of the DataGrid's more advanced features, turning our attention to paginating data.

Q&A

Q **In the SortData.aspx Web page, I noticed that the Page_Load event handler binds the data to the DataGrid only on the first page load (when Page.IsPostBack is False). Is this necessary? I tried the example without the If condition, thereby always performing data binding in the Page_Load event handler, and it worked just fine.**

A As we've discussed before, whenever a user visits an ASP.NET Web page, be it for the first time or via a postback, the Page_Load event handler is executed. In fact, this event handler is executed before any of the Web control event handlers is executed.

If we alter the Page_Load event handler from the SortData.aspx Web page so it does not contain an If clause, checking if the Page.IsPostBack property is False, then we'd have:

```
Sub Page_Load(sender as Object, e as EventArgs)
  dgBooks.DataSource = GetBooks("Title")
  dgBooks.DataBind()
End Sub
```

This means that with *every* visit to the ASP.NET Web page, the DataGrid will be bound to the list of books sorted by the Title. So what happens when a user visits the SortData.aspx Web page and sorts the data by, say, the Price? Well, upon the user's first visit, the Page_Load event handler executes, and the DataGrid displays the data sorted alphabetically by the Title column. When the user clicks the header hyperlink in the Price column, the ASP.NET Web page is posted back. The Page_Load event executes again, and the DataGrid is bound to the list of books ordered by the Title column.

However, after the Page_Load event handler has executed, the DataGrid's SortCommand event handler executes. This event handler sorts the database data by the Price column (because this was the hyperlink header clicked by the user) and then binds the results to the DataGrid. Following this, the DataGrid is rendered into an HTML <table>, with its data sorted by the Price column. This is then what the user sees in his browser.

Since the DataGrid's SortCommand event handler executes after the Page_Load event handler, the DataGrid sorting example will work whether or not the If condition is in the Page_Load event handler. However, realize that by omitting the If condition, *two* database queries are executed on every page visit, whereas only one is needed. That is, every time the user opts to have the DataGrid data sorted by a particular column, the ASP.NET Web page is first getting the data sorted by the Title, which is wasteful if the user is asking to have the data sorted by the Price. Therefore, you are strongly encouraged to leave the If statement in the Page_Load event handler, even though the ASP.NET Web page will work fine without it.

18

Workshop

Quiz

1. True or False: You must check the "Allow sorting" checkbox in the General screen of the Property Builder dialog box in order to provide DataGrid sorting.

2. How can you specify that a particular Bound Column not be sortable?

3. When creating a sortable DataGrid, we need to make a few small changes to the function generated by the SELECT Data Method Code Builder. What specific changes need to be made?

4. Explain how the designers of the Web Matrix Project might be able to modify the SELECT Data Method Code Builder to remove the need to alter the generated function when wanting to provide DataGrid sorting support.

5. What DataGrid event fires when the user clicks one of the sortable columns' header hyperlink?

6. True or False: DataGrid sorting works only on uplevel browsers.

Answers

1. True.

2. To make a particular Bound Column unsortable, simply do not enter a value into the Bound Column's "Sort expression" textbox.

3. The function created by the SELECT Data Method Code Builder needs to be altered to accept a String input parameter, which specifies which column to sort the results on. Additionally, the SQL SELECT query must be modified so that it contains an ORDER BY clause based on the input parameter value.

4. If the SELECT Data Method Code Builder had some way to add an ORDER BY clause based on a passed-in column name, then we would not need to make changes to the resulting function.

5. The SortCommand event fires.

6. False. DataGrid sorting works on all browsers.

Exercises

1. Create an ASP.NET Web page that lists the customers from the Customers database table in a sortable DataGrid. The DataGrid should display three columns, one for the customers' IDs, one for the customers' names, and one for the customers' phone numbers. The user should be able to sort the DataGrid either by customer ID in ascending order or by name in alphabetical order. Also, to improve the appearance of the DataGrid, apply the Simple 3 style from the Auto Format dialog box.

2. Imagine that you wanted to create an ASP.NET Web page that contained a DataGrid listing each customer's customer ID, name, and phone number. Furthermore, you want to allow the user to sort the data by any of the three columns. However, rather than using the built-in DataGrid sorting via the column header hyperlinks, you decide to have a DropDownList Web control that lists the three columns in the DataGrid. The user can then select one of the column names, and the DataGrid will automatically be sorted according to the user's choice.

   For this exercise please create such an ASP.NET Web page. To accomplish this, you will first need to add a DropDownList Web control and add three list items via the ListItem Collection Editor. (Refer back to Hour 11, "Collecting Input by Using Drop-down Lists, Radio Buttons, and Checkboxes," for more information on adding static list items to the DropDownList Web control.)

   Once the drop-down list has been added and its items specified, be sure to set the AutoPostBack property to True, so that the page will be posted back whenever the user makes a new selection. Also, you will need to create an event handler for the drop-down list's SelectedIndexChanged event. (To accomplish this, simply double-click the drop-down list in the designer.) In this event handler you will need to make the code similar to the code that you had previously put in the DataGrid's SortCommand event handler.

Realize that for this exercise, you do not need to check the DataGrid's "Allow sorting" checkbox, and you do not need to specify values for the various Bound Columns' "Sort expression" textboxes.

18

HOUR 19

Paging Through the DataGrid's Data

In the DataGrid examples we have worked on thus far, the DataGrid has been used to show only a handful of records. The Books and Customers tables each contains a measly five records. More often, though, database tables contain tens, hundreds, thousands, hundreds of thousands, or millions of rows. For example, a Customers table at a phone company like Southwestern Bell would have millions of entries.

In the examples, we have used the DataGrid to show *all* of the records of these database tables at once. With just five table records, it's no big deal, but imagine displaying ten thousand items in a DataGrid on a single Web page! The more data shown to a user, the harder it is for the user to digest that data, so displaying one million records in one ASP.NET Web page would essentially make the data unreadable.

The solution is to display the data in digestable portions through a technique called *paging*. Rather than displaying one million records at once, it would be ideal to display just 10 records at a time. The user could then step through one page at a time.

Virtually all Web sites that contain large amounts of data use paging. For example, when searching for "Microsoft" at the search engine Google, roughly 37,700,000 results are found, but thankfully, Google shows only 10 of these more than 37 million results at a time. Similarly, if you search for "ASP.NET" at Amazon.com, more than 155 books are found, but only 10 matches are shown at a time.

In this hour we will examine how to implement paging with the DataGrid Web control. As you will see, adding paging support to the DataGrid is simpler than adding sorting support. Here we will cover the following topics:

- How to configure a DataGrid to support paging
- How the user pages through the data in a DataGrid
- Why a pageable DataGrid's `DataSource` must be a DataSet and not a DataReader
- How a user steps through the pages of data
- What pieces of information the DataGrid needs to know in order to provide pagination of its data
- Creating an event handler for the DataGrid's `PageIndexChanged` event
- Creating and testing a pageable DataGrid

A High-Level Overview of DataGrid Paging

In all of the previous DataGrid examples, the DataGrid creates an HTML `<table>` based on the data in its `DataSource`. The resulting HTML `<table>` contains a table row for each record in the `DataSource`. This approach guarantees displaying all of the `DataSource`'s data in the DataGrid Web control.

With `DataSources` that contain large amounts of data, however, we don't necessarily want to display all of the `DataSource` at once. Rather, to make the data easier for the user to read and understand, we'd like to display only a portion of the data at a time. In addition, the user should be provided with some means for navigating to the data that is not currently being displayed.

These goals are accomplished by paging. When the DataGrid Web control is configured to page its data, only a subset of the data in the `DataSource` is displayed. Additionally, the DataGrid displays either one of two navigation modes: a Next, Previous buttons mode or a Page numbers mode. In the Next, Previous buttons mode, the user is presented with two hyperlinks. One, when clicked, displays the previous page of data, and the other displays the next page of data. With the Page numbers mode, the user is given a list of page numbers, each being a hyperlink. The user can then click a hyperlink to be taken to the corresponding page of data. Figures 19.1 and 19.2 illustrate these two paging modes; note the differences in the paging hyperlinks at the bottom of the DataGrid.

The screenshots in Figures 19.1 and 19.2 show paging through the Customers table, which has only five records. The paging has been configured to display two records per page. Hence, there are three pages, with the first page displaying the first two customers (Jisun Lee and Dave Yates), page two displaying the second two customers (Todd Callister and Marie Vogan), and the last page displaying the last customer (Kate Wiseman).

FIGURE **19.1**

The Next, Previous buttons mode.

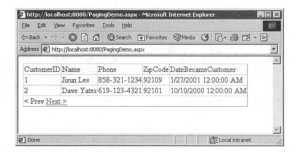

FIGURE **19.2**

The Page numbers mode.

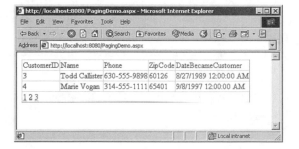

19

Examining the Steps to Implement Paging

As we saw in the previous hour, "Allowing the User to Sort the Data in a DataGrid," adding sorting support to the DataGrid Web control involved a number of steps, such as specifying that the DataGrid should support sorting through the Property Builder, creating a function to retrieve the database results in a specified sorted order, and creating an event handler for the DataGrid's SortCommand event.

Adding paging support to a DataGrid can also be broken down into a series of steps. The first is specifying that the DataGrid is to page data. This specification is made by checking a checkbox in the DataGrid's Property Builder, just as was done with enabling sorting support. In addition to indicating that the DataGrid should support paging, you can also specify a number of other criteria, such as how many rows to show per page, what paging mode to use, where the paging navigational hyperlinks should be displayed in the

DataGrid, and other information. We will examine these settings in detail in the "Configuring the DataGrid to Support Paging" section.

The next step involves creating a function to retrieve the database data that the DataGrid is to page through. We have performed this step a number of times before using the SELECT Data Method Code Builder. The same approach can be taken here; the only difference is that it is vital that the function created returns a DataSet instead of a DataReader. We'll discuss why this is the case, and cover more details on this matter, in the "Getting the Data to Page Through" section.

> Recall that when providing sorting support, you needed to edit the resulting function so it could accept as an input parameter the name of the table column to sort by. For paging we don't need to edit the function generated by the SELECT Data Method Code Builder at all.

The final step involves creating an event handler for the DataGrid's PageIndexChanged event. The PageIndexChanged event fires whenever the ASP.NET Web page has been posted back due to the user's clicking one of the navigational hyperlinks. The event handler must determine which page the user wants to view and then rebind the data to the DataGrid. We'll examine the code needed for this event handler in the "Displaying a Different Page Of Data" section.

As you can see, the steps required to implement paging support are similar to the steps for implementing sorting.

Configuring the DataGrid to Support Paging

In order to provide paging support in a DataGrid, the DataGrid must be configured to support paging. This is accomplished through the setting of a few properties via the DataGrid's Property Builder. Let's create a new ASP.NET Web page to demonstrate how to provide paging support for a DataGrid. Name this new ASP.NET Web page **PagingDemo.aspx** and drag a DataGrid Web control from the Toolbox and onto the designer. This DataGrid will eventually allow the user to page through the records in the Customers table.

> When the user clicks the navigational hyperlinks to view a different page of data, the ASP.NET Web page is posted back. For this reason the DataGrid must be placed within a Web form. You are encouraged to turn on glyphs to ensure that the DataGrid you add to the designer is indeed within the Web form.

Once you have added the DataGrid to the designer, set its ID property to **dgCustomers**. Next view the DataGrid's Property Builder by clicking the Property Builder . . . hyperlink in the Properties pane. From the Property Builder, visit the Paging screen by clicking the Paging label in the upper left corner. Figure 19.3 shows a screenshot of the Paging screen in the Property Builder.

FIGURE 19.3

The Property Builder Paging screen.

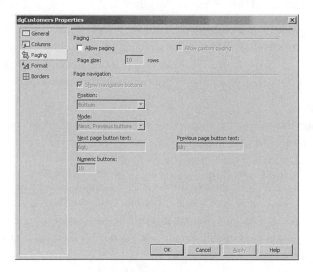

To specify that the DataGrid should provide sorting capabilities, simply check the "Allow paging" checkbox. Once you do, the disabled checkboxes, textboxes, and drop-down lists shown in Figure 19.3 become enabled, as can be seen in Figure 19.4.

19

FIGURE 19.4

The Paging screen after the "Allow paging" checkbox has been checked.

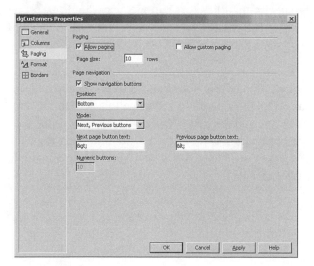

The first textbox to examine is the "Page size" textbox, which has a default value of 10. This corresponds to the number of records that are shown per page. Because we are going to be implementing paging through the Customers table's data, and because the Customers table has only five records, we need to set the "Page size" textbox to a value less than 5. If we left the value at 10, then all five customers would be displayed in the first page of data. Set the "Page size" textbox to **2**.

The "Show navigation buttons" checkbox determines whether the navigational hyperlinks are displayed or not. By default, this checkbox is checked. If you uncheck it, the navigational hyperlinks will not be displayed, and the user will not be able to move from one page to another. For this reason, keep this checkbox checked.

The Position drop-down list determines where the navigational hyperlinks are displayed in the DataGrid. The default value is Bottom, although you can choose to have these hyperlinks displayed at the top or at the top and bottom.

Recall that the navigational hyperlinks for a pageable DataGrid can be displayed in one of two modes: in Next, Previous buttons mode or Page numbers mode. The default mode is the Next, Previous buttons mode. The navigational mode is specified via the Mode drop-down list. For this exercise leave the Mode drop-down list as Next, Previous buttons.

If the Next, Previous buttons mode is being used, the "Next page button text" and "Previous page button text" textbox values determine what text is displayed for the Next and Previous buttons, respectively. The default value is > for the Next button and < for the Previous button. Although > and < may look cryptic, they simply specify that the Next button's text should be > and the Previous button's text should be <. The reason > and < are used instead of > and < is because > and < are reserved characters in HTML syntax, since they represent the end and start of a tag.

If you want the Next and Previous buttons to display something different, you can provide your own values here. Let's change this so that the text Next > is displayed for the Next button and the text < Prev is displayed for the previous button. Simply set the "Next page button text" textbox's value to **Next >** and the "Previous page button text" textbox's value to **< Prev**. Your screen should now look like the screenshot in Figure 19.5.

FIGURE 19.5

The Paging screen after the various properties have been set.

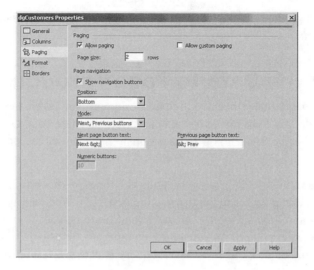

FIGURE 19.5

The Paging screen after the various properties have been set.

Click the OK button to close the Property Builder. Upon returning to the designer, the DataGrid's appearance will be updated, showing only two rows (since we set the page size to 2) and containing < Prev and Next > navigational hyperlinks at the bottom of the DataGrid (see Figure 19.6).

FIGURE 19.6

The DataGrid in the designer has two rows and navigational hyperlinks.

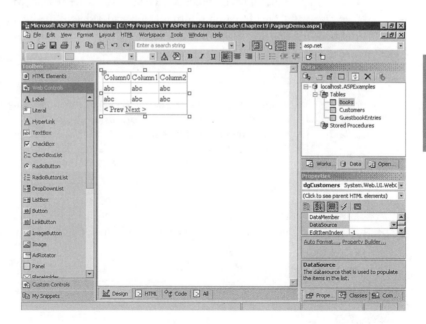

19

At this point the DataGrid is configured to support paging. What remains to be done is grabbing the data from the database and then binding the data to the DataGrid as the user pages through the data. We'll examine how to retrieve the particular database data in the next section.

Getting the Data to Page Through

After the DataGrid has been configured to support paging, we need to create a means for the DataGrid to be bound to the appropriate database data. Over the past several hours, we have examined how to accomplish this using the SELECT Data Method Code Builder.

We can use this technique for generating the function that returns the needed data. Start by clicking the Code tab to view the ASP.NET Web page's source code portion. Next drag and drop the SELECT Data Method Code Builder from the Toolbox and onto the source code portion. As you've done numerous times before, connect to the ASPExamples database and construct a query that returns all of the columns from the Customers table.

When you reach the final step of the SELECT Data Method Code Builder, where you are asked to provide a name for the function and specify whether the function should return a DataSet or a DataReader, name the function **GetCustomers** and have it return a DataSet. In past examples in which we've used the SELECT Data Method Code Builder, we've always had the function return a DataReader due to the increased performance benefits of the DataReader. However, for the data to be paged, it is vital that the data be returned in the form of a DataSet.

> If you forget to have the GetCustomers() function return a DataSet, you will later get an error reading, "*AllowCustomPaging must be true and VirtualItemCount must be set for a DataGrid with ID dgCustomers when AllowPaging is set to true and the selected datasource does not implement Icollection*" when you test the ASP.NET Web page.

Figure 19.7 shows a screenshot of the last stage of the SELECT Data Method Code Builder; note that the GetCustomers function is specified to return a DataSet.

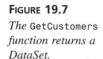

Figure 19.7

The GetCustomers
function returns a
DataSet.

Why a DataSet Must Be Used for Paging

In Hour 14, "Understanding SQL, the Language of Databases," we examined the differences between the DataSet and DataReader. Recall that the DataReader is more efficient than the DataSet because it only allows for its data to be accessed from the first record to the last, one record at a time. Additionally, there is no DataReader property that indicates how many records are contained in the DataReader. The DataSet, on the other hand, allows the records to be accessed in random order and contains a property that indicates how many records are present.

For paging, the DataGrid displays only a subset of its DataSource's data. The subset displayed depends on what page of data is being viewed and the number of records to display per page. In order to display just a subset of the records and to determine how many total pages of data exist, the DataGrid needs to be able to access a particular subset of the data and to be able to determine how many total records exist in the DataSource. These tasks can be accomplished only if the DataGrid's DataSource is a DataSet. For this reason, for paging to work, you must have the function that is generated by the SELECT Data Method Code Builder return a DataSet and not a DataReader.

Now that the GetCustomers() function has been added, we're ready to move on to the final steps required for implementing a pageable DataGrid: providing the needed source code to allow for the DataGrid to display the proper page of data.

Displaying a Different Page of Data

At this point we have configured the DataGrid to support paging, and have created a function that retrieves the data to be paged through, returning it as a DataSet. All that remains to be done is to specify what page of data should be displayed in the DataGrid.

Earlier we discussed that with paging enabled, the DataGrid displays only a subset of the data in the DataSource, but we didn't delve into the details of how this is accomplished. In addition to knowing what subset of records to display from the DataSource, the DataGrid must also be able to determine how many total pages of data there are in order to render the navigational controls. (For example, if the DataGrid is using the Next, Previous buttons navigation mode and the user is viewing the last page of data, then the DataGrid will display the Next button as text instead of as a hyperlink.)

To know what data from the DataSource to display, and to be able to render the paging navigational controls correctly, the DataGrid must know three things:

- How many records to show per page
- What page of data is to be displayed
- How many total records exist in the DataSource

We specified how many records to show per page when configuring the DataGrid for paging support by providing a value for the "Page size" textbox in the Paging screen of the Property Builder. The total number of records in the DataSource can be determined automatically by the DataGrid due to the fact that the DataSource is a DataSet. Recall that the number of records in a DataSet can be easily determined.

The page of data to be displayed depends on the user's interaction with the DataGrid. Initially, the first page of data is to be shown. If the user clicks the Next navigational button, then the second page of data should be displayed. Following this, if the user clicks the Previous navigational button, the first page should be shown again.

The DataGrid provides a CurrentPageIndex property that indicates which page of data the DataGrid will display. It is our job to set this property correctly and then bind the database data to the DataGrid. With the CurrentPageIndex property set, the DataGrid will know how to display the correct records from the DataSource and will be able to render the navigational controls correctly.

Creating an Event Handler for the PageIndexChanged Event

The CurrentPageIndex property is an Integer property that is zero based. That is, to display the first page of data, CurrentPageIndex should be set to 0, to display the second page of data, `CurrentPageIndex` should be set to 1, and so on. The value of the `CurrentPageIndex` is 0 by default, meaning that we do not need to set the `CurrentPageIndex` property when first binding the data to the DataGrid, since we want the first page of data shown by default.

However, when the user clicks one of the nagivational hyperlinks, we need to update the `CurrentPageIndex` property and rebind the database data to the DataGrid. Whenever the user clicks one of the navigational hyperlinks, the ASP.NET Web page is posted back, and the DataGrid's `PageIndexChanged` event fires. In order to provide paging support, we'll need to create an event handler for this event that contains source code that sets the DataGrid's `CurrentPageIndex` property accordingly and then rebinds the database data to the DataGrid.

Recall from our discussions from the previous hour that in order to create an event handler for one of the DataGrid's events, we need to add the appropriate source code in the ASP.NET Web page's source code portion and then wire the event to the created event handler. An event is wired to an event handler by adding the following to the DataGrid's declaration:

On*EventName*="*EventHandlerName*"

The event handler for the DataGrid's `PageIndexChanged` event must have the following definition:

```
Sub EventHandlerName(sender As Object, e As DataGridPageChangedEventArgs)

End Sub
```

The second input parameter to the event handler is of type `DataGridPageChangedEventArgs`, which has the property `NewPageIndex`. This property indicates the page of data the user has requested to view. Therefore, in this event handler we'll simply set the DataGrid's `CurentPageIndex` property to the value of the `NewPageIndex` property and then rebind the data to the DataGrid.

Click the Code tab of your ASP.NET Web page and enter the following source code:

```
Sub dgCustomers_Page(sender As Object, e As DataGridPageChangedEventArgs)
  ' Assign the CurrentPageIndex property to the new page index value
  dgCustomers.CurrentPageIndex = e.NewPageIndex

  ' Rebind the data to the DataGrid
  dgCustomers.DataSource = GetCustomers()
  dgCustomers.DataBind()
End Sub
```

Adding the source code for the `dgCustomers_Page` event handler is only the first step. In order to have this event handler execute when the DataGrid's `PageIndexChanged` event fires,

19

we need to wire the event to the event handler. To do this, click the Design tab to return to the designer and then right-click the DataGrid. Choose the Edit Tag option, which will display the Quick Tag Edit dialog box. Add the text **OnPageIndexChanged="dgCustomers_Page"** to the DataGrid's declaration so your screen looks like the screenshot in Figure 19.8.

FIGURE 19.8

The DataGrid declaration after the PageIndexChanged *event has been wired to the* dgCustomers_Page *event handler.*

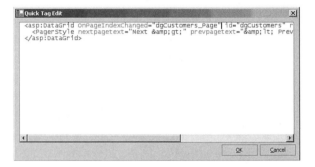

After you have made this change, click the OK button, which will close the Quick Tag Edit dialog box and return you to the designer. We have now created an event handler for the PageIndexChanged event that will display the correct page of data, based on whatever steps the user decides to take through the various pages of data.

Binding the Data to the DataGrid in the Page_Load Event Handler

The DataGrid has been configured to support paging, a GetCustomers() function exists that returns the records from the Customers table, and the DataGrid's CurrentPageIndex is updated whenever the user requests seeing an alternate page. But we are still missing one very important piece of the puzzle: We need to bind the database data to the DataGrid when the user first visits the page (before any postbacks).

To do this, we need to provide a Page_Load event handler that binds the data to the DataGrid only if the page is not being posted back. The code for this, as you learned in the previous two hours, looks like this:

```
Sub Page_Load(sender as Object, e as EventArgs)
   If Not Page.IsPostBack then
      dgCustomers.DataSource = GetCustomers()
      dgCustomers.DataBind()
   End If
End Sub
```

Add this code to the ASP.NET Web page's source code portion, and the steps needed to implement paging have now been completed.

To review: We started by configuring the DataGrid for paging by visiting the Paging screen in the DataGrid's Property Builder and checking the "Allow paging" checkbox. Next we used the SELECT Data Method Code Builder to create a function that retrieved the database data that we wanted the DataGrid to page through. Remember that it is vital that this function return a DataSet and not a DataReader. Finally, we wired up the DataGrid's PageIndexChanged event to an event handler. The source code for the event handler simply assigned the DataGrid's CurrentPageIndex to the page the user requested to view and then re-bound the data to the DataGrid.

Testing the ASP.NET Web Page

Now that we have created an ASP.NET Web page that includes a pageable DataGrid, let's test the page and examine the paging capabilities. Save the ASP.NET Web page and then view it through a browser. When you first visit the page, you should see a DataGrid that displays two customers, as shown in Figure 19.9. (Recall that we set the "Page size" textbox in the Paging screen to a value of 2.)

FIGURE 19.9

The first two customers are displayed.

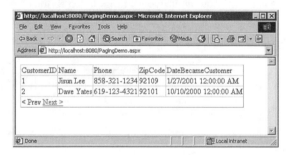

19

If, in testing the ASP.NET Web page, you do not see Figure 19.9 but instead see an error message reading, "*AllowCustomPaging must be true and VirtualItemCount must be set for a DataGrid with ID dgCustomers when AllowPaging is set to true and the selected datasource does not implement Icollection*," then the GetCustomers() function is returning a DataReader rather than a DataSet. To remedy this problem, delete the source code for the GetCustomers() function and then recreate the function by using the SELECT Data Method Code Builder, ensuring that the function returns a DataSet and not a DataReader.

At the bottom of the DataGrid, the Next > and < Prev links are displayed. Note that the < Prev text is *not* a hyperlink. This is because we are viewing the first page, so there's no way we could view a previous page of data. To view the second page of data, click the Next > hyperlink, which will take you to the second page of data (see Figure 19.10). Since we are viewing the second of three total pages, both the < Prev and the Next > hyperlinks are enabled.

FIGURE 19.10
The second page of data is shown.

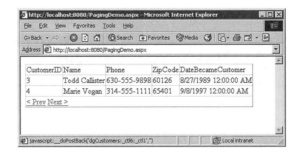

If you click the Next > button again, you will be taken to the third and final page. Since there are five customers, the last page of data, as Figure 19.11 shows, has only one row. Also, since it is the last page of data, the Next > hyperlink is disabled.

FIGURE 19.11
The third and final page of data is displayed.

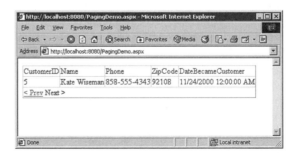

Summary

In this hour we saw how to add paging capabilities to a DataGrid Web control. As with creating a sortable DataGrid, creating a pageable DataGrid can be broken down into a number of steps. The first step involves configuring the DataGrid to support paging, which is done by checking the "Allow paging" checkbox in the Paging screen of the Property Builder. From the Paging screen, we can also specify the exact number of records to show per page, what paging mode should be used (Next, Previous buttons or Page numbers), and other optional information.

Once the DataGrid has been configured to support paging, we need to create a function that returns the data that is to be paged through by the DataGrid. We can use the SELECT Data Method Code Builder to generate this function, but we must keep in mind that this function must return a DataSet and not a DataReader.

Finally, we need to create an event handler for the DataGrid's PageIndexChanged event. The PageIndexChanged event fires whenever the user clicks one of the navigational hyperlinks to view a different page of data. In the event handler, we need to assign the DataGrid's CurrentPageIndex property to the value of NewPageIndex, which is the index of the page the user wants to view. Then we need to rebind the database data to the DataGrid.

In the next hour we will examine yet another powerful feature of the DataGrid—the ability to edit the DataGrid's contents.

Q&A

Q In the previous hour we saw how to sort the DataGrid. In this hour we examined how to page through the DataGrid's data. Is there a way to build a DataGrid that's *both* sortable and pageable?

A It is quite possible to build a DataGrid whose data can be both sorted and paged through, but it is not as easy or straightforward as you might initially think. Due to its difficulty, this book does not include a discussion on building a sortable, pageable DataGrid. Once you have had ample experience with the DataGrid, though, you can learn how to build a sortable, pageable DataGrid by picking up a copy of *ASP.NET Data Web Controls Kick Start*, where the matter is discussed in detail.

Q When using a pageable DataGrid, is it possible to display information like which page of data the user is currently viewing or how many total records there are?

A Yes, it's quite possible. In fact, upcoming Exercise 3 asks you to create an ASP.NET Web page that contains a pageable DataGrid and a display mentioning what page of data is being viewed and how many total pages of data there are.

The secret to accomplishing this is simply to add a Label Web control to the ASP.NET Web page. The Text property of this Label Web control needs to be updated whenever its underlying information might change. For example, if we are using a Label Web control to display which page of data is currently being displayed, then whenever the user pages to the next page of data, we need to update the Label Web control's Text property so that the message displayed to the user is updated, as well.

19

To determine the total number of pages in a DataGrid, use the DataGrid's `PageCount` property. (This property is discussed briefly in Question 3 in the upcoming quiz.) To determine how many records are in a DataSet, you can use the following code:

```
DataSetID.Tables(0).Rows.Count
```

Workshop

Quiz

1. True or False: When paging through a DataGrid's data, you can bind either a DataSet or a DataReader to the DataGrid.

2. What are the difference between the Next, Previous buttons and the Page numbers navigational modes?

3. The DataGrid contains an integer property called `PageCount`, which returns the total number of pages of data that the DataGrid contains. Give an equation expressing the value of this property. (*Hint:* it involves the number of total items in the DataGrid's `DataSource` as well as the number of items to be shown per page.)

4. What are the steps required to create the `PageIndexChanged` event handler?

5. Describe what the DataGrid's `CurrentPageIndex` property indicates.

6. Why does the `Page_Load` event handler bind the data to the DataGrid only when the `Page.IsPostBack` property is False?

7. True or False: DataGrid paging is supported only by uplevel browsers.

Answers

1. False. In order to provide DataGrid paging, you must use a DataSet, and *not* a DataReader.

2. The Next, Previous buttons navigation mode displays only two navigational hyperlinks: one that sends the user to the previous page of data, and one that sends the user to the next page of data. The Page numbers navigation mode, on the other hand, displays a series of hyperlinks, allowing the user to jump directly to a particular page of data.

3. The number of pages is simply the number of items to be paged through divided by the size per page, rounded up. For example, if we binded a DataSet with 13 records to a DataGrid configured to display 5 records per page, the total number of pages in the DataGrid would be 13 divided by 5, which is 2.6, rounded up, which is 3.

4. To create a `PageIndexChanged` event handler, we must perform two steps. First the actual event handler needs to be created. This event handler must accept two input parameters, the first of type `Object` and the second of type `DataGridPageChangedEventArgs`. For example, the following code creates a suitable event handler named `HandlePaging`:

```
Sub HandlePaging(sender as Object, e as DataGridPageChangedEventArgs)
  '... Write event handler code here ...
End Sub
```

Once the event handler has been created, the DataGrid's `PageIndexChanged` event must be wired up to this event handler. This is accomplished by adding the following to the DataGrid's declaration:

```
OnPageIndexChanged="EventHandlerName"
```

Recall that to edit the declaration of a Web control easily, right-click the Web control in the designer and choose the Edit Tag option.

5. The `CurrentPageIndex` property indicates which page of data is currently being displayed in the DataGrid. This property is zero based, meaning that when the first page of data is being viewed, `CurrentPageIndex` equals 0.

6. When the page is first visited, the `Page.IsPostBack` property is True. In this case we want to bind the data to the DataGrid. However, subsequent postbacks occur whenever the user clicks one of the navigational hyperlinks. This causes the `PageIndexChanged` event handler to fire. In the `PageIndexChanged` event handler, the `CurrentPageIndex` property is updated, and the data is rebound to the DataGrid. Since the data is rebound to the DataGrid in the `PageIndexChanged` event handler, there is no need to bind it also in the `Page_Load` event handler.

7. False. DataGrid paging support does not involve any features or functionality that is browser-specific. Therefore, DataGrid paging can be experienced in all browsers.

Exercises

1. Create an ASP.NET Web page that displays the customers from the `Customers` table, three customers to a page. The DataGrid should display all of the columns from the `Customers` table. Use the Page number navigation mode, and use the Auto Format tool to apply the Colorful 4 formatting.

2. For this Exercise display the customers in a pageable DataGrid showing two customers per page. The DataGrid should use the Next, Previous buttons navigation mode. Furthermore, the DataGrid should use two Bound Columns to display only the customer's name and zip code. Also, be sure to apply some of the DataGrid's aesthetic properties to make the appearance of the DataGrid more eye-pleasing.

19

3. To determine the total number of pages in a DataGrid, we can use the DataGrid's
PageCount property. Armed with this knowledge, create an ASP.NET Web page
that, in addition to a pageable DataGrid, contains a Label Web control that displays
which page of data is being displayed and how many total pages of data there are.
That is, when first visiting the pageable DataGrid, if there are a total of 5 pages of
data, the Label Web control would read, "You are viewing page 1 of 5."

(Hint: The Label Web control's Text property will need to be set whenever the
DataSet is bound to the DataGrid. This occurs in two places: in the Page_Load
event handler and in the PageIndexChanged event handler.)

Hour 20

Editing the Data in a DataGrid

In the previous two hours, we saw how to enhance the DataGrid to allow for sorting and pagination. The DataGrid also can be configured to support inline editing of its data on a row-by-row basis. That is, a DataGrid can be configured so that each row of data contains an Edit button. When this Edit button is clicked, the row displays its data in textboxes, and the user can alter the values.

In this hour we will examine how to provide editing capabilities for a DataGrid. To implement the DataGrid's editing features, we will need to perform a series of steps, just as we needed to perform a series of steps to provide sorting and paging support.

In the first section, "Examining the Steps Required for Providing Editing Support," we'll look at an overview of the steps required for providing editing capabilities. Then we'll delve into the details of each step. By the end of this hour, we'll have created an ASP.NET Web page that displays the records from the Customers table and allows them to be edited. This hour will cover the following topics:

- The DataGrid's editing interface and editing a row in the DataGrid
- Using the Edit, Update, Cancel Button Column
- How to display a DataGrid row as editable
- Creating a function to update a database table by using the UPDATE Data Method Code Builder
- Updating the database table with the edited values the user supplies
- Testing the editable DataGrid

Examining the Steps Required for Providing Editing Support

Before we look at the required steps, let's take a moment to examine the editable DataGrid's user interface. As you know, a DataGrid displays data in a two-dimensional grid, with each record of the database query represented as a row in the DataGrid and each field in the database query represented as a DataGrid column.

Like a noneditable DataGrid, the editable DataGrid contains columns for each database query field; however, it also contains an additional column. This additional column displays an Edit button for each row, as shown in Figure 20.1.

FIGURE 20.1

Each row of the DataGrid has an Edit button.

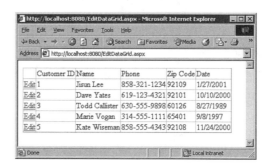

When a given row's Edit button is clicked, that particular DataGrid row becomes editable. The editable DataGrid row's Edit button changes from a single Edit button to two buttons: an Update button and a Cancel button. Additionally, each column in the DataGrid that displays database data will change from displaying text to displaying a textbox with the column's value as the text inside the textbox. Figure 20.2 shows a screenshot of an editable DataGrid after the user has clicked the Edit button for a particular row.

FIGURE 20.2

The row whose Edit button was clicked is now editable.

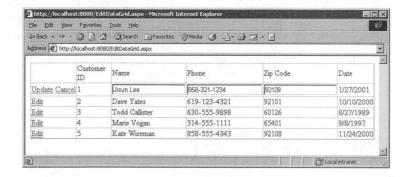

> As Figure 20.2 shows, not all columns in the DataGrid row being edited need be displayed as textboxes. Certain DataGrid columns can be marked as read-only, meaning that when the user opts to edit a DataGrid row, those read-only columns are not displayed as textboxes. We'll see how to mark DataGrid columns as read-only later in this hour in the "Specifying Which DataGrid Columns Are Editable" section.

From this editing interface, the user can make changes to the various columns by entering new values into the textboxes. Having made the desired changes, the user can click the Update button to save the changes or Cancel to disregard the changes. If either the Update or Cancel button is clicked, the DataGrid returns to its preediting mode, where each row has just an Edit button (as in Figure 20.1).

Now that we have seen an example of the DataGrid editing interface, we're ready to examine the steps required to provide the editing capabilities.

1. Add a DataGrid to the ASP.NET Web page and explicitly specify which columns should be displayed. When adding the various columns, add an Edit, Update, Cancel Button Column to the DataGrid along with the various added Bound Columns. This Edit, Update, Cancel Button Column displays the Edit, Update, and Cancel buttons for each row in the DataGrid.

2. Use the SELECT Data Method Code Builder to generate a function to obtain the data to display in the DataGrid. The function should return a DataReader.

20

3. Create three event handlers and wire them up to the DataGrid's `EditCommand`, `UpdateCommand`, and `CancelCommand` events. These three events are fired when the Edit, Update, and Cancel buttons are clicked, respectively.

4. Write the complete code for the `EditCommand` and `CancelCommand` event handlers, and the preliminary code for the `UpdateCommand` event handler.

5. Use the `UPDATE` Data Method Code Builder to generate a function that updates a particular record in the database table.

6. Complete the code for the `UpdateCommand` event handler by writing code to read in the values the user entered into the textboxes, and calling the function created in step 5 to update the database.

Over the remainder of this hour, we will examine how to implement these six steps.

Adding the Edit, Update, Cancel Button Column to the DataGrid

The first step in creating an editable DataGrid is to add the Edit, Update, Cancel Button Column, as follows:

1. We first need to add a DataGrid to our ASP.NET Web page. To follow along, start by creating a new ASP.NET Web page named **EditDataGrid.aspx** and turn glyphs on.

2. Then drag and drop a DataGrid from the Toolbox and onto the designer, within the Web form.

3. Set this DataGrid's `ID` property to **dgCustomers**.

4. Next open the DataGrid's Property Builder dialog box and navigate to the Columns screen.

5. Since we will be specifying which columns should appear in the DataGrid, be sure to uncheck the "Create columns automatically at run time" checkbox.

6. Under the "Available columns" listbox, there is a Button Column label that has a plus sign next to it. Clicking this plus reveals three Button Columns: Select; Edit, Update, Cancel; and Delete (see Figure 20.3). Add the Edit, Update, Cancel Button Column to your DataGrid.

FIGURE 20.3

One of the "Available column" types is the Edit, Update, Cancel Button Column.

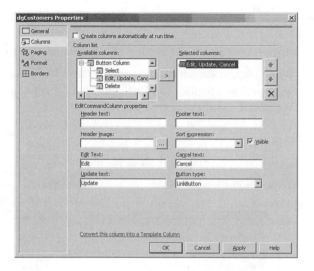

7. Once you add the Edit, Update, Cancel Button Column, the column's properties are displayed in textboxes (as seen in Figure 20.3). The "Header text" textbox value indicates the value that is displayed in the column's header. The "Edit Text," "Update text," and "Cancel text" textboxes—which have default values of Edit, Update, and Cancel, respectively—indicate the text displayed in the Edit, Update, and Cancel buttons. Finally, the "Button type" drop-down list can be used to specify whether the Edit, Update, and Cancel buttons should be displayed as LinkButtons, meaning that they are displayed as hyperlinks, or as PushButtons, meaning that they are displayed as traditional buttons, such as the buttons displayed using a Button Web control.

Feel free to change the default values for the "Header text," "Edit Text," "Update text," or "Cancel text" textboxes. The examples in this hour will be working with the default options.

Adding the Bound Columns

Once we have added the Edit, Update, Cancel Button Column, we can proceed with adding a Bound Column for each column we want to appear in the DataGrid, as follows:

1. For this example let's have DataGrid columns for each field of the Customers table. That is, we'll have columns for the CustomerID, Name, Phone, ZipCode, and

DateBecameCustomer fields. Add five Bound Columns. For the first Bound Column, display the CustomerID; for the second, the Name; and so on, displaying the DateBecameCustomer field as the fifth and final Bound Column.

2. For formatting purposes, set the DateBecameCustomer Bound Column's Data formatting expression textbox to **{0:d}**, which will display just the date and not the time of the DateBecameCustomer field.

3. Once you have added the Bound Columns, click the OK button on the Property Dialog box to return to the designer. Figure 20.4 contains a screenshot of the designer after the Edit, Update, Cancel Button Column and five Bound Columns have been added to the DataGrid.

FIGURE 20.4

The DataGrid is composed of an Edit, Update, Cancel Button Column and five Bound Columns.

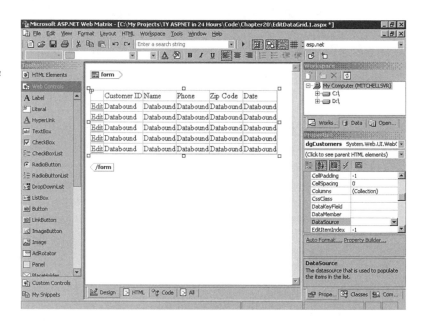

 If you see more than six columns on your screen, it may be because you forgot to uncheck the "Create columns automatically at run time" checkbox in the Columns screen of the Property Builder dialog box.

Using the SELECT Data Method Code Builder to Generate the GetCustomers() Function

The next step is to generate the function that will return the database data with which to populate the DataGrid. As we've seen in a number of previous hours, this can be easily accomplished using the SELECT Data Method Code Builder, here as follows:

1. Click the Code tab of the EditDataGrid.aspx Web page and drag and drop the SELECT Data Method Code Builder from the Toolbox and onto the source code portion of the ASP.NET Web page.

2. Construct the SELECT query such that it returns all columns from the Customers table. Figure 20.5 shows a screenshot of the query constructed by the SELECT Data Method Code Builder.

FIGURE 20.5

The SELECT query returns all rows from the Customers database.

3. On the last page of the SELECT Data Method Code Builder, have the function return a DataReader and specify the name of the function as **GetCustomers()**.

20

Understanding the `EditCommand`, `UpdateCommand`, and `CancelCommand` Event Handlers

The DataGrid's editing interface contains three buttons, the Edit, Update, and Cancel buttons. Whenever one of these buttons is clicked, the ASP.NET Web page is posted back, and the appropriate DataGrid event is fired. If the Edit button is clicked, the DataGrid's `EditCommand` event fires; if the Update button is clicked, the DataGrid's `UpdateCommand` fires; and if the Cancel button is clicked, the DataGrid's `CancelCommand` is fired.

Recall that the Edit button is displayed for each row and that when it is clicked, the row becomes editable. This editable row then has the Update and Cancel buttons displayed. Then, if the Update button is clicked, the database needs to be updated with the values entered into the editable row's textboxes. Regardless of whether the Update or Cancel button is clicked, the row that was editable must be turned back into a normal row, displaying its columns as text and not as textboxes.

In order to accomplish all these tasks, we'll first need to create event handlers for the Edit, Update, and Cancel buttons and wire them up to the associated DataGrid events. Following this, we must add the source code for each of these event handlers so the appropriate action transpires when the button is clicked.

Adding the Event Handlers and Wiring Them Up to the Appropriate Events

As we saw in Hours 18 and 19, "Allowing the User to Sort the Data in a DataGrid" and "Paging Through the DataGrid's Data," respectively, to add an event handler to the DataGrid, we must first create the event handler in the ASP.NET Web page's source code portion and then wire up the event handler to an event via the DataGrid's declaration. We will need to create an event handler for the `EditCommand`, `UpdateCommand`, and `CancelCommand` events, and each event handler must have the following definition:

```
Sub EventHandlerName(sender as Object, e as DataGridCommandEventArgs)
    ' Event handler source code goes here...
End Sub
```

Let's name our three event handlers **dgCustomers_Edit**, **dgCustomers_Update**, and **dgCustomers_Cancel**. Click the Code tab of the `EditDataGrid.aspx` Web page and add the following source code:

```
Sub dgCustomers_Edit(sender as Object, e as DataGridCommandEventArgs)

End Sub


Sub dgCustomers_Update(sender as Object, e as DataGridCommandEventArgs)

End Sub


Sub dgCustomers_Cancel(sender as Object, e as DataGridCommandEventArgs)

End Sub
```

Now that we have added the event handlers in the source code portion, we need to wire up the DataGrid's EditCommand, UpdateCommand, and CancelCommand events to the appropriate event handlers. This is accomplished by adding the following content to the DataGrid's declaration:

```
OnEditCommand="dgCustomers_Edit"
OnUpdateCommand="dgCustomers_Update"
OnCancelCommand="dgCustomers_Cancel"
```

Recall that the DataGrid declaration can be edited by right-clicking the DataGrid in the designer and selecting the Edit Tag option. Figure 20.6 shows a screenshot of the Quick Tag Edit dialog box after the three events have been wired up to the three event handlers.

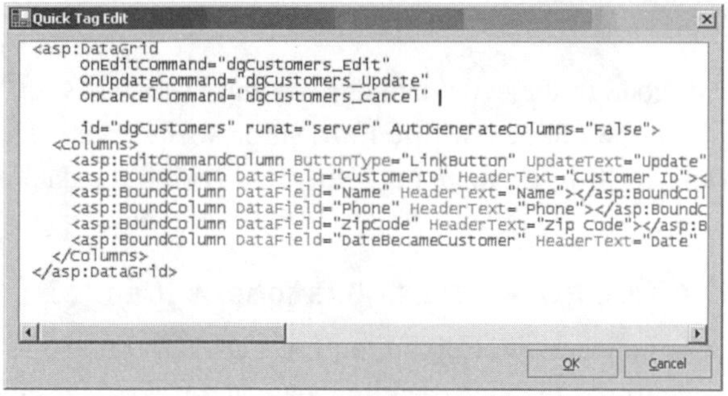

FIGURE 20.6

The events are now wired up to the event handlers.

20

Writing the Source Code for the Event Handlers

Now that we have created the event handlers, we can write the source code for them. At this point we can write the complete code for the dgCustomers_Edit and dgCustomers_Cancel event handlers and the preliminary code for the dgCustomers_Update event handlers. Let's start with the dgCustomers_Edit event handler.

Writing the Code for the dgCustomers_Edit Event Handler

The dgCustomers_Edit event handler is executed in response to a DataGrid row's Edit button's being clicked. The dgCustomers_Edit event handler then needs to make that row editable, but how is this accomplished? First understand that each row in a DataGrid has a zero-based index. That is, the first row of the DataGrid has the index value 0, the second row has the index value 1, and so on.

Furthermore, the DataGrid has an integer property called EditItemIndex. When the DataGrid is being rendered, it determines whether the row it is adding has an index value equal to the EditItemIndex property. If it does, then that particular row is displayed as editable.

Therefore, to make a row editable, all we need to do is set the DataGrid's EditItemIndex property to the index of the row whose Edit button was clicked. Then we need to rebind the data to the DataGrid and call the DataGrid's DataBind() method so the DataGrid is rerendered.

All of this can be accomplished in three lines of code. Edit the source code portion of your ASP.NET Web page so the dgCustomers_Edit event handler has the following content:

```
Sub dgCustomers_Edit(sender as Object, e as DataGridCommandEventArgs)
    dgCustomers.EditItemIndex = e.Item.ItemIndex

    dgCustomers.DataSource = GetCustomers()
    dgCustomers.DataBind()
End Sub
```

The first line of code in the event handler sets the DataGrid's EditItemIndex property to the index of the DataGrid row whose Edit button was clicked. The last two lines simply specify the DataGrid's DataSource property and rebind the data through the DataBind() method.

Writing the Code for the dgCustomers_Cancel Event Handler

After the user has clicked the Edit button for a DataGrid row, the row becomes editable, meaning that the row is displayed with Update and Cancel buttons and that the columns of the row are displayed as textboxes rather than as text. If the user then clicks the Cancel button, we simply want to return the DataGrid to its preediting state. This can be accomplished by setting the DataGrid's EditItemIndex property to −1.

As with the dgCustomers_Edit event handler, our dgCustomers_Cancel event handler is a scant three lines of code. Go ahead and ensure that your dgCustomers_Cancel event handler looks as follows:

```
Sub dgCustomers_Cancel(sender as Object, e as DataGridCommandEventArgs)
    dgCustomers.EditItemIndex = -1

    dgCustomers.DataSource = GetCustomers()
    dgCustomers.DataBind()
End Sub
```

Writing the Preliminary Source Code for the dgCustomers_Update Event Handler

The dgCustomers_Update event handler is a bit more complicated than the dgCustomers_Edit and dgCustomers_Cancel event handlers. This is because the dgCustomers_Update event handler must do more than simply toggle the DataGrid's editing interface; the dgCustomers_Update event handler must determine the values the user entered into the textboxes and then update the database.

Realize that after the user clicks the Update button, we do not want only to update the database with the user's entered values but also to return the DataGrid to its preedit state. Therefore, the dgCustomers_Update event handler must contain source code quite similar to the dgCustomers_Cancel event handler.

For now let's just write the source code for the dgCustomers_Update event handler identical to the dgCustomers_Cancel event handler. Later in this hour we'll return to the dgCustomers_Update event handler and add the code needed to update the database with the user's entered values. Go ahead and alter the dgCustomers_Update event handler so it looks like the following:

```
Sub dgCustomers_Update(sender as Object, e as DataGridCommandEventArgs)
    ' We will later add the code to update the database here

    dgCustomers.EditItemIndex = -1

    dgCustomers.DataSource = GetCustomers()
    dgCustomers.DataBind()
End Sub
```

20

Using the UPDATE Data Method Code Builder

In order to update the Customers database table with the values entered by the user, we need to use the UPDATE Data Method Code Builder to generate a function that will perform the database update. The function that will be generated by the UPDATE Data Method Code Builder will accept an input parameter for each column that is editable as well as an input parameter that uniquely identifies which record in the database table to update.

Here's the procedure:

1. To use the UPDATE Data Method Code Builder, click the Code tab and then drag and drop the UPDATE Data Method Code Builder from the Toolbox and onto the source code portion, just as we have done for the SELECT Data Method Code Builder numerous times before.

2. The UPDATE Data Method Code Builder begins with a Connect to Database dialog box. As with the SELECT Data Method Code Builder, connect to the database that contains the Customers table. The next screen in the UPDATE Data Method Code Builder (see Figure 20.7) looks just like the query construction screen in the SELECT Data Method Code Builder.

FIGURE 20.7

The second screen of the UPDATE *Data Method Code Builder.*

3. Now, for each DataGrid column that is editable, we need to check the corresponding field checkbox. For example, if we plan on letting the user edit the customer's name, we need to check the Name field checkbox.

4. Upon checking the checkbox, a Set Value dialog box will appear in which you can provide the value that will appear in the SQL UPDATE query (see Figure 20.8). The default value in the Set Value checkbox will be

   @FieldName

   Leave this as the default for all checked checkboxes.

FIGURE 20.8

The Set Value dialog box.

5. For this example we will allow the user to edit the Name, Phone, and Zip Code DataGrid columns. Therefore, we need to check the checkboxes for the Name, Phone, and ZipCode fields.

6. For each checked field, the Set Value dialog box will appear—just use the default *@FieldName* value.

> At this point our DataGrid is configured such that *all* DataGrid columns are editable. However, in the "Specifying Which DataGrid Columns Are Editable" section, we will change this so only the Name, Phone, and Zip Code columns are editable and the Customer ID and Date columns are read-only.

7. After we have checked the Name, Phone, and ZipCode fields in the UPDATE Data Method Code Builder, we still need to add a WHERE clause. This WHERE clause indicates which record from the Customers database table we want to update. To add a WHERE clause, click the WHERE button; this will display the WHERE Clause Builder dialog box (see Figure 20.9).

FIGURE 20.9

The WHERE Clause Builder dialog box.

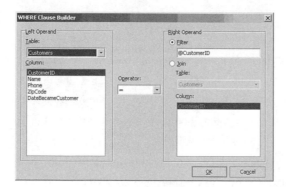

20

8. Because we want to add a WHERE clause that ensures that the CustomerID equals a passed-in value, we want to select the CustomerID column from the Column list-box, the = operator from the Operator dropdown list, and the Filter value @CustomerID. (Note that these are the default values in the WHERE Clause Builder.) To add the WHERE clause, click the OK button. Figure 20.10 shows a screenshot of the UPDATE Data Method Code Builder after the WHERE clause has been added. Note that the SQL query in the preview window reads:

```
UPDATE [Customers] SET [Name]=@Name, [Phone]=@Phone, [ZipCode]=@ZipCode
        WHERE ([Customers].[CustomerID] = @CustomerID)
```

FIGURE 20.10

The needed properties have been set.

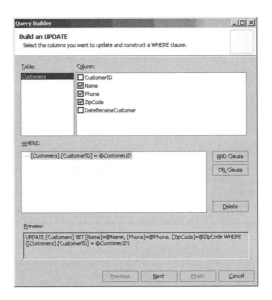

9. After verifying that your screen looks like Figure 20.10, click the Next button.

10. This will take you to the Query Preview screen. Click the Next button again to proceed to the final screen of the UPDATE Data Method Code Builder.

11. On the final screen you will be prompted to enter the name for the generated function. Enter a value of **UpdateCustomer**.

Now the UPDATE Data Method Code Builder dialog box will close, returning you to the source code portion of the EditDataGrid.aspx ASP.NET Web page. A function named UpdateCustomer() has been added. This function takes four input parameters: The first parameter specifies the `CustomerID` of the customer whose information is to be updated; the second through fourth parameters specify the new values for the `Name`, `Phone`, and `ZipCode` fields.

For example, if we wanted to update customer Jisun Lee's zip code to 92109 and phone number to 858-555-7372, we could call the `UpdateCustomer()` function like so:

```
UpdateCustomer(1, "Jisun Lee", "858-555-7273", "92109")
```

Here we pass in the value **1** as the first parameter since customer Jisun Lee's `CustomerID` is 1.

Specifying Which DataGrid Columns Are Editable

At this point all of the columns in the DataGrid are marked as editable. This means that when the user opts to edit a DataGrid row, all of the DataGrid columns will be displayed as textboxes, meaning that the user can change the value of any of these columns.

However, we don't necessarily want to allow the user to edit *all* of the columns. For example, the `CustomerID` field is a primary key column, meaning that each customer's Customer ID must be unique. If we allowed the user to alter a customer's Customer ID, the user could try to give two customers the same Customer ID. (In actuality, the database would not allow this to happen. If a user attempted to do this, the database would raise an error, which would be displayed on the ASP.NET Web page.)

There may be other DataGrid columns that should not be editable, too. In our customer's example, perhaps it is important that a customer's `DateBecameCustomer` field never be edited.

In any event, it is quite easy to make a DataGrid column noneditable. Such noneditable columns are referred to as *read-only*. To mark a column as read-only, open the DataGrid's Property Builder dialog box and navigate to the Columns screen. Select the Bound column you want to make read-only from the "Selected columns" listbox. This will display the Bound Column's properties, including a checkbox titled "Read only." Simply check this box to indicate that the Bound column is read-only.

Go ahead and make both the DataGrid's Customer ID and Date columns read-only. Figure 20.11 shows a screenshot of the Property Builder after the Customer ID Bound Column has been marked read-only.

20

FIGURE 20.11

The Customer ID Bound Column has been marked as read-only.

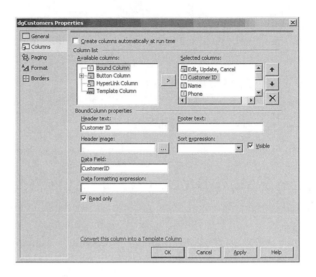

When a Bound Column is marked as read-only, its content is always displayed as text, even when a DataGrid row becomes editable. To see an example of this, refer back to Figure 20.2, which shows the DataGrid in edit mode with the Customer ID and Date columns as read-only.

Completing the Source Code for the `dgCustomers_Update` Event Handler

Now that we have created the function to update the `Customers` database table for a particular customer, we are ready to complete the source code portion for the `dgCustomers_Update` event handler. Before we can update the database table, we must first retrieve the values entered into the textboxes by the user. Furthermore, we must determine the value of the Customer ID column for the edited row.

In previous examples we've been able to reference the value of a TextBox Web control by simply doing

```
TextBoxID.Text
```

However, for the editable row we don't know the ID of the various TextBoxes. All we have to work with is a reference to the row being edited. Fortunately, this row has a `Cells` collection property. This property can be accessed like so:

```
e.Item.Cells(i)
```

This would access the *i*th column in the edited row. If the column is read-only, then it contains only text and not a TextBox Web control. In this case the text can be retrieved using the following syntax:

```
e.Item.Cells(i).Text
```

If, however, the column is editable, then a TextBox Web control resides in the column and can be accessed like so:

```
e.Item.Cells(i).Controls(0)
```

Listing 20.1 contains the complete source code for the dgCustomers_Update event handler. Take a moment to update the dgCustomers_Update event handler so it contains this code. Note that earlier in this hour we already entered lines 12 through 15.

LISTING 20.1 The dgCustomers_Update Event Handler

```
 1: Sub dgCustomers_Update(sender as Object, e as DataGridCommandEventArgs)
 2:     'Determine the value of the Customer ID Column
 3:     Dim customerID as Integer = e.Item.Cells(1).Text
 4:
 5:     'Reference each TextBox
 6:     Dim nameTextBox as TextBox = e.Item.Cells(2).Controls(0)
 7:     Dim phoneTextBox as TextBox = e.Item.Cells(3).Controls(0)
 8:     Dim zipTextBox as TextBox = e.Item.Cells(4).Controls(0)
 9:
10:     UpdateCustomer(customerID, nameTextBox.Text, phoneTextBox.Text,
                zipTextBox.Text)
11:
12:     dgCustomers.EditItemIndex = -1
13:
14:     dgCustomers.DataSource = GetCustomers()
15:     dgCustomers.DataBind()
16: End Sub
```

On line 3 the value in the Customer ID column is retrieved by using the e.Items.Cells(1).Text syntax. We use this syntax because the Customer ID column is read-only, meaning that there is text in the column as opposed to a textbox. Also, the Cells(1) is used because the Customer ID column is the *second* DataGrid column (the first is the Edit, Update, Cancel Button Column). Cells(1) retrieves the second column because the Cells collection is zero-based, meaning that the first column is referenced via Cells(0).

The reason we need to retrieve the Customer ID column value is that when we call the UpdateCustomer() function (line 10), we must know which customer to update. Recall that the value of the Customer ID column is the value of the customer's CustomerID field, which uniquely identifies the customer.

20

Next, on lines 6 through 8, the three TextBox Web controls are referenced. Here we use the syntax `e.Item.Cells(i).Controls(0)`, because these DataGrid columns contain TextBox Web controls.

On line 10 a call to the `UpdateCustomer()` function is made. The first parameter passed in is the `customerID` variable. The next three parameters are the values the user entered in the Name, Phone, and Zip Code textboxes. These values are obtained as stored in the `Text` property of the TextBox Web control. That is, to retrieve the value the user entered into the Name column textbox, we use `nameTextBox.Text`.

After calling the `UpdateCustomer()` function, the database has been updated with the new values. All that remains is to revert the DataGrid to its preediting state. This is accomplished, as we saw earlier in this hour, by setting the DataGrid's `EditItemIndex` property to –1 (line 12) and rebinding the DataGrid (lines 14 and 15).

Note that the DataGrid in the `EditDataGrid.aspx` ASP.NET Web page displays as one of its columns the customer's `CustomerID`. In the `dgCustomers_Update` event handler, we determined the `CustomerID` of the customer whose information was being edited by retrieving the value of the Customer ID column.

Because the `CustomerID` field uniquely identifies each customer, and because we need to be able to specify which customer's information needs to be updated in the `UpdateCustomer()` function call, it is vital that the DataGrid include a column for the `CustomerID` so we can determine the edited customer's `CustomerID`. More generally, when using an editable DataGrid, it is essential that the database data's primary key column be included in the list of DataGrid columns.

There are a couple techniques that can be employed that manage to associate the primary key value for each DataGrid row without explicitly including a DataGrid column for the primary key. However, they are beyond the scope of this book. For more information on these topics, be sure to read *ASP.NET Data Web Controls Kick Start*.

Completing and Testing the EditDataGrid.aspx ASP.NET Web Page

At this point we have nearly completed the `EditDataGrid.aspx` Web page. All that remains is to add the `Page_Load` event handler. The `Page_Load` event handler needs to bind the data from the GetCustomers() function to the DataGrid only when there is not a postback. Therefore, just as in Hours 18 and 19, our Page_Load event handler must look like this:

```
Sub Page_Load(sender as Object, e as EventArgs)
    If Not Page.IsPostBack then
        dgCustomers.DataSource = GetCustomers()
        dgCustomers.DataBind()
    End If
End Sub
```

Take a moment to add this code to the EditDataGrid.aspx Web page's source code portion.

Once the Page_Load has been added, we're ready to test the editable DataGrid. Start by viewing EditDataGrid.aspx through the browser of your choice. Figure 20.12 shows a screenshot of the Web page when first visited.

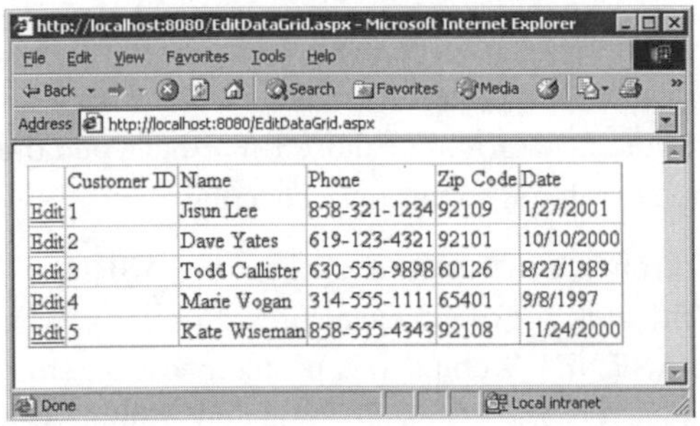

FIGURE 20.12

The DataGrid displays an Edit button for each row.

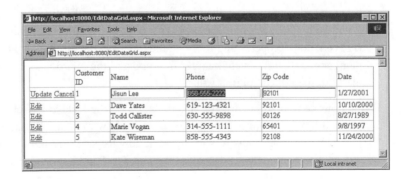

Figure 20.13 shows a screenshot of the Web page after the Edit button has been clicked for a particular row. Note that each of the editable row's columns is displayed as a textbox except for those columns marked read-only (the Customer ID and Date columns).

FIGURE 20.13

The edited row displays Update and Cancel buttons and textboxes for each editable column.

20

Finally, Figure 20.14 shows a screenshot of the Web page after some of the editable row's values have been edited and the Update button has been clicked.

FIGURE 20.14

The edited column's altered values have been saved to the database.

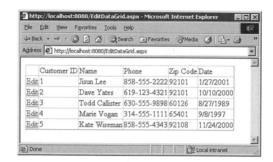

Summary

In this hour we examined how to create an editable DataGrid. The first step is to add an Edit, Update, Cancel Button Column to the DataGrid and then a Bound Column for each row to be displayed in the DataGrid. For those rows that you do not want to be editable, simply check the Bound Column's read-only checkbox.

Whenever a DataGrid row's Edit button is clicked, the ASP.NET Web page is posted back, and the DataGrid's `EditCommand` event fires. Similarly, when the Update or Cancel button is clicked, the ASP.NET Web page is posted back, and the DataGrid's `UpdateCommand` or `CancelCommand` fires. To create an editable DataGrid, we need to be able to have certain code execute when these events fire. To accomplish this, we created three event handlers: `dgCustomers_Edit`, `dgCustomers_Update`, and `dgCustomers_Cancel`. These three event handlers were then wired up to the DataGrid's `EditCommand`, `UpdateCommand`, and `CancelCommand` events.

All three of these event handlers altered the DataGrid's `EditItemIndex` property. The `EditItemIndex` property indicates which row is to be displayed in edit mode. Whereas the `dgCustomers_Edit` and `dgCustomers_Cancel` event handlers simply set the `EditItemIndex` property and rebound the database data to the DataGrid, the `dgCustomers_Update` event handler first updated the appropriate record in the `Customers` table with the edited column values.

This hour concludes our focused examination on the DataGrid Web control. We have now seen how to display data in the DataGrid, how to create Bound Columns and HyperLink Columns, how to sort the data, how to page through the data, and how to edit the data. For a more in-depth look at the DataGrid and its many facets, check out my article series *An Extensive Examination of the DataGrid Web Control*, available online at `http://aspnet.4guysfromrolla.com/articles/040502-1.aspx`.

For the remainder of this book, we'll be applying the knowledge we've amassed over the past 20 hours to creating an online guestbook application. In Hour 21, "Devising a Plan for the Guestbook Application," we'll start by examining the feature requirements, user interface, and needed database tables.

Q&A

Q **The editable DataGrid features are great for editing one row at a time, but what I'd like to be able to do is have *all* the rows in the DataGrid editable. That is, I would like to have each editable column in each row of the DataGrid displayed as a textbox. The user could then update whichever columns in whatever rows he wanted. Once these updates had occurred, the user could simply click an Update All button, and all of the changes would be saved to the database. Is such a scenario possible?**

A Creating such a DataGrid is quite possible, but this is far beyond the scope of this book. As we have seen in this hour, the DataGrid contains a number of built-in editing capabilities, but these capabilities are designed to support an editing interface that allows for only one row to be edited at a time.

In order to create a DataGrid that allows all of its content to be edited at once, you have to use a bit more tricky Web control syntax and much more complex source code. For more information on this technique, be sure to read *ASP.NET Data Web Controls Kick Start*, where such an editable DataGrid is discussed.

Workshop

Quiz

1. What type of DataGrid column needs to be added to a DataGrid in order to make the DataGrid editable?

2. If a DataGrid has six rows and the DataGrid's `EditItemIndex` property equals 3, what row will be in edit mode?

3. If a DataGrid has six rows and the DataGrid's `EditItemIndex` property equals 6, what row will be in edit mode?

4. In creating a DataGrid event handler, we must create three event handlers for three of the DataGrid's events. Please list what these three events are and when each of them fires.

20

5. Why do the `UpdateCommand` and `CancelCommand` event handlers contain this line of code:

```
DataGridID.EditItemIndex = -1
```

6. True or False: Editable DataGrids are a feature of DataGrids that work only with uplevel browsers.

Answers

1. An Edit, Update, Cancel Button Column.

2. The fourth row. (Remember that the `EditItemIndex` is zero based.)

3. No row will be in edit mode.

4. The DataGrid events that we need to create event handlers for are the `EditCommand` event, the `UpdateCommand` event, and the `CancelCommand` event. The `EditCommand` event fires when the user clicks the Edit button. The `UpdateCommand` event fires when the user clicks the Update button. Finally, the `CancelCommand` event fires when the user clicks the `Cancel` button.

5. By setting the `EditItemIndex` property to –1 and then rebinding the DataGrid, none of the DataGrid's rows will be editable. This is performed in the `UpdateCommand` and `CancelCommand` event handlers because when these events fire, the user has just completed editing the row and is ready to return to the preediting DataGrid state.

6. False.

Exercises

1. In the `EditDataGrid.aspx` example we worked through in this hour, the editable DataGrid's appearance was quite unattractive. Update the DataGrid so that it is more eye-pleasing. You may either use the Auto Format tool or set various aesthetic properties through the DataGrid's Property Builder dialog box.

2. For this exercise create an ASP.NET Web page that displays the contents of the `Books` database table in an editable DataGrid. The DataGrid should have a column each for the book's ID, title, author, price, and URL, as well as an Edit, Update, Cancel Button Column. The Book ID and Title column should be read-only.

Once you have created the editable DataGrid and have it working, take a moment to enhance its appearance either by using the Auto Format tool or by specifying various aesthetic properties manually through the DataGrid's Property Builder.

PART V

Building a Guestbook Web Application with ASP.NET

Hour

HOUR **21**

Devising a Plan for the Guestbook Application

Over the past 20 hours, you have learned a number of topics, including ASP.NET basics, Visual Basic .NET, SQL syntax, and working with the various ASP.NET Web controls. In the remainder of this book, we'll take the knowledge you've amassed and use it to build a real-world Web application— an online guestbook.

This hour focuses on planning for the guestbook application and creating the needed database tables. As we discussed back in Hour 3, "Creating Our First ASP.NET Web Page," when creating an ASP.NET Web application, it is important to spend adequate time planning the application before you jump straight into creating the individual ASP.NET Web pages. The planning phase involves a number of preparatory steps, such as deciding precisely what features the Web application will provide and outlining the application's user interface. In addition to deciding on the feature set and user interface, in the planning phase it is also important to determine what database tables are needed and how many separate ASP.NET Web pages the Web application will comprise.

In the first section, "Specifying the Guestbook's Features and Functionality," we will focus on just the features that will be provided for the guestbook. In the next section, "Deciding on the User Interface," we'll devise a suitable user interface and see that we'll need precisely two ASP.NET Web pages for this Web application. Finally, in the section "Storing the Guestbook Entries," we'll discuss what information we'll need to store for each guestbook entry and create an appropriate database table.

In the next hour, we'll look at creating an ASP.NET Web page that allows users to create new guestbook entries. In Hour 23, "Displaying the Guestbook's Contents," we'll see how to display the contents in an ASP.NET Web page by using a DataGrid Web control with pagination. Finally, in Hour 24, "Sending E-Mail when a New Guestbook Entry Is Added," we'll see how to enhance our application so that you can receive an e-mail whenever a visitor adds a new guestbook entry on your Web site.

Again, in this hour we will cover the following topics:

- What features we will be adding to the guestbook
- Specifying the user interface
- What information the user will need to provide when adding a new guestbook entry
- Creating the database table where the guestbook entries will be stored

Specifying the Guestbook's Features and Functionality

If you've visited many personal home pages, you've likely encountered online guestbooks, which can be "signed" by Web visitors. In signing an online guestbook, a user is asked, at minimum, to leave a name and a brief message. Some guestbooks allow users to provide other information as well, such as an e-mail address, a home page URL, and geographic information. In addition to being able to leave an entry in the guestbook, Web visitors can view guestbook entries from other users.

In determining what features and functionality a Web application should include, it often helps to list the things we'd like users to be able to accomplish with our Web application. Take a moment to think of such a list of things for the guestbook application that we'll be creating, and then compare it to mine:

- The user should be able to add a guestbook entry.
- The user should be able to provide name, e-mail address, and message when adding a guestbook entry.

- The user should not be required to provide an e-mail address but should be required to leave at least a name and a message.

- The user should be able to view the entries of the guestbook.

- Submitted guestbook entries should be presented to the user in an easy-to-read, tabular format.

- In the event of a large number of guestbook entries, the user should be able to page through them, as opposed to having to view all of them on one page.

- For user viewing, the submitted guestbook entries should be listed in order from the most recently added entry to the oldest entry.

Notice that some of the functionality items listed are very generic, such as the items "The user should be able to add a guestbook entry" and "The user should be able to view the entries of the guestbook." At first glance these items might seem obvious and superfluous. You may wonder why we even need to mention that a guestbook should allow the user to make a guestbook entry.

The reason for listing these obvious cases is twofold. First, it helps us define what exactly the application will do, even if it is obvious; and second, it provides a springboard for future ideas. Once we list, "A user can leave a guestbook entry," we can then ask ourselves what is involved in leaving a guestbook entry. This would take us to reasoning that a user should be able to enter name, e-mail address, and message—items we would want to add to our list. In noting these items, we may further decide that the e-mail address should be optional but the name and message required.

Building up a functionality list is an iterative process. First start out with the obvious functionality. Once you have written it down, you can ask yourself more specific questions pertaining to the generic functionality. This will lead to more functionalities, which you should include in your list. This process can be iteratively repeated until you arrive at a comprehensive list.

Looking back at our list, we can easily see what features the guestbook application needs to provide. First comes the ability for a user to leave a guestbook entry, including name, an optional e-mail address, and a brief message. The guestbook must provide a means for the user to view a list of the existing guestbook entries, ordering the results from the most recent entry to the least recent entry. Finally, for a large guestbook, the user should be able to page through the various entries.

Now that we have a good idea as to the functionality of the guestbook application, we can move on to designing the user interface.

21

Deciding on the User Interface

With the guestbook features mapped out, let's discuss the guestbook user interface, or UI. Because the user needs to be able to perform two general tasks—adding a guestbook entry and viewing existing guestbook entries—the guestbook application will consist of two ASP.NET Web pages. One ASP.NET Web page will allow the user to enter a new guestbook entry, while the other will allow the user to view existing ASP.NET Web pages.

For entering a guestbook entry, the user will be presented with three textboxes and a button. One textbox will prompt the user for his or her name, another for an e-mail address, and the third for a guestbook message. Upon entering this information, the user will click the button to add the entry to the guestbook.

> Recall that one of the functionalities we discussed for our guestbook application was to allow for displaying the existing guestbooks from the most recent to the oldest. In order to do this, we need to record the date and time each guestbook entry is made. However, notice that our user interface does not include a textbox for entering the date and time the guestbook entry was made. This is because we can have the Web server's current date and time automatically recorded when the user submits the guestbook entry information.

When you are thinking about user interfaces, it often helps to sketch out on paper what you envision the user interface will look like (see Figure 21.1).

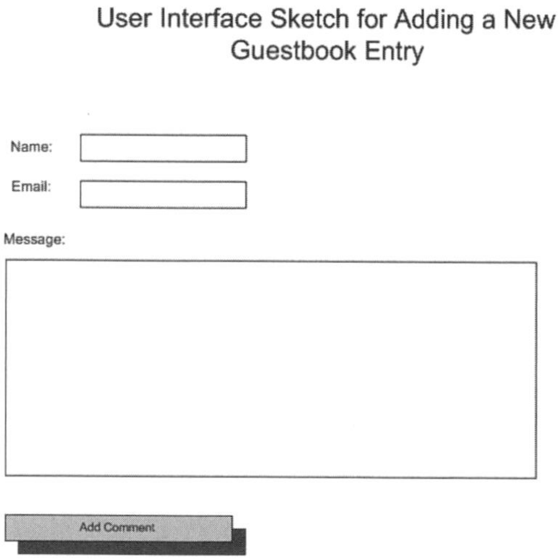

FIGURE 21.1

A sketch of the user interface for entering a guestbook entry.

User Interface Sketch for Adding a New
Guestbook Entry

Name:

Email:

Message:

Add Comment

The benefit of sketching user interface ideas on paper is that it allows you to grasp visually what various user interface ideas, when implemented, will look like. Once you have settled on a user interface drawing, you can use the Web Matrix Project to implement the UI quickly.

We also need to conceptualize a user interface for the ASP.NET Web page that will display the existing guestbook entries. As decided in the "Specifying the Guestbook's Features and Functionality" section, the existing guestbook entries should be displayed in a DataGrid that employs paging. Furthermore, the guestbook entries should be sorted chronologically, with the most recent entry shown first.

Figure 21.2 shows a sketch of the user interface for displaying existing guestbook entries. Note that a DataGrid is used, which shows the person who made the guestbook entry in the first column, the person's e-mail address (if provided) in the second column, the message in the third column, and the date and time the message was added in the fourth and final column.

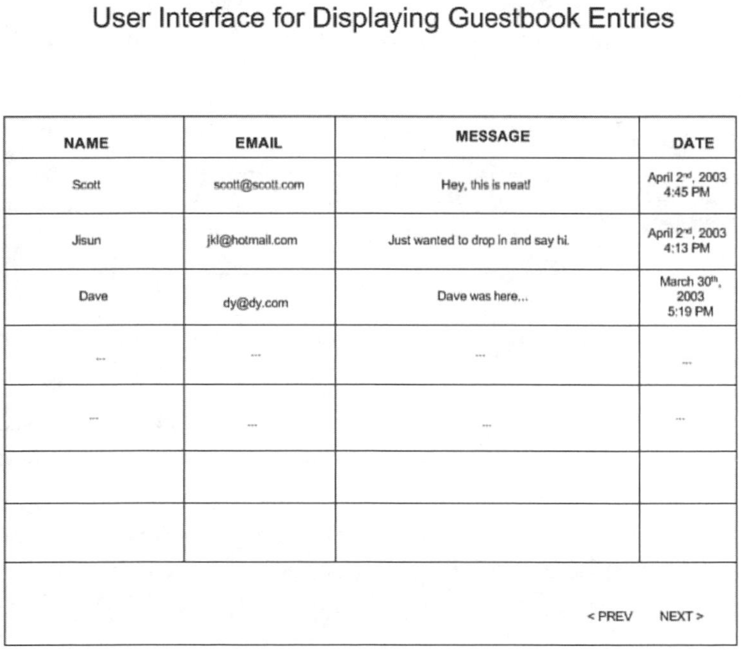

FIGURE 21.2

A sketch of the user interface for viewing existing guestbook entries.

User Interface for Displaying Guestbook Entries

NAME	EMAIL	MESSAGE	DATE
Scott	scott@scott.com	Hey, this is neat!	April 2nd, 2003 4:45 PM
Jisun	jkl@hotmail.com	Just wanted to drop in and say hi.	April 2nd, 2003 4:13 PM
Dave	dy@dy.com	Dave was here...	March 30th, 2003 5:19 PM
...	...	...	...
...	...	...	...
			< PREV NEXT >

21

Now that we have a general idea of the user interface and the application's functional requirements, we can better determine what information we'll need to store for each guestbook entry. Armed with this information, we can design the database table needed to store the guestbook entries, which we'll do in the next section.

Storing the Guestbook Entries

Because we want to store the various guestbook entries made by visitors to our Web site, we'll need to store each user's guestbook entry in a database table. Each separate piece of information we need to store concerning a guestbook entry should become a column in the database table, with an appropriate column type. Let's take a moment to review what needs to be stored with each guestbook entry:

- The user's name
- The user's e-mail address
- The user's message
- The date and time the guestbook entry was made

The user's name, e-mail address, and message will be strings, so we'll want to use appropriate-length varchar column types. A DateTime column type will suffice for the date and time the guestbook entry was made.

 We need a table column to store the date and time a guestbook entry was made because we want to be able to display guestbook entries in descending chronological order.

Let's go ahead and create a database table named GuestbookEntries that contains the needed columns with the appropriate column types, following these steps:

1. Start by clicking the Data tab in the Web Matrix Project. Recall from our discussions in Hour 13, "An Introduction to Databases," that the Data tab is in the upper right corner.

2. Once you have clicked the Data tab, you will need to create a connection to the database where you plan on creating the GuestbookEntries table. Click the New Connection icon, which is shown in Figure 21.3.

FIGURE 21.3

Click the New Connection icon to connect to a database.

If you have not shut down the Web Matrix Project since you last created a connection via the Data tab, there will already be an existing connection in the Data tab. If this is the database where you want to create the GuestbookEntries table, there's no need to establish a new connection.

3. Once you click the New Connection icon, a Connect to Database dialog box will appear, as shown in Figure 21.4. Specify the Server where the database resides and enter the correct User name and Password. If you installed MSDE locally, recall that you should set the server to **localhost**, the User name to **sa**, and the password to the password you chose when installing MSDE.

4. Next select from the Database drop-down list which database to connect to. For this application simply use the ASPExamples database we created in Hour 13 (see Figure 21.4) and click OK.

FIGURE 21.4

Specify the database to connect to in the Connect to Database dialog box.

Connect to Database	✕
Connect to SQL or MSDE Database Enter the connection information and select a database.	

Server: `localhost`

○ Windows authentication
● SQL Server authentication

User name: `sa`

Password: `******`

Database: `ASPExamples` ▼

Create a new database   [OK]   [Cancel]

21

5. The Connect to Database dialog box has now closed, and the Data tab will contain the Tables and Stored Procedures for the database. To create a new table, click the Tables label in the Data tab, and then click the New Item icon.

6. In the Create New Table dialog box now displayed, specify the Table Name as **GuestbookEntries**.

7. Recall that when creating a new table through the Web Matrix Project, you must create a primary key column. As we discussed in Hour 13, a primary key column guarantees that the value in the column is unique for every row in the table. To create this primary key column, click the New button underneath the Columns listbox. In the Column Properties, enter the Name as **GuestbookEntriesID** and its Data Type as int. Also, be sure to check the Required, Primary Key, and Auto-increment checkboxes. Figure 21.5 shows a screenshot of the Create New Table dialog box after adding the GuestbookEntriesID column.

FIGURE 21.5

The primary key column GuestbookEntriesID *has been added.*

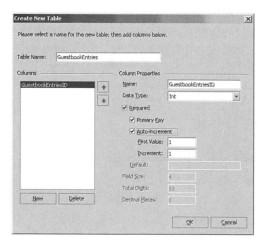

8. Now we're ready to add the remaining table columns. Let's first add the column for the user's name, which we'll call Name. Click the New button underneath the Columns listbox to create the new column. Then, for its properties, choose **Name** as its Name, and varchar as its Data Type. Feel free to leave its Field Size at 50.

9. Next add a column for the user's e-mail address. Repeat the steps used for adding the Name column, but this time give the column the name **Email** (note no hyphen) and make its Data Type a varchar with a Field Size of **100**.

10. Now add the column for the user's message. Let's call this column **Message** and make it a varchar with Field Length **5000**.

11. Finally, add a column for the date and time the guestbook entry was made. This column should be called **DateSigned** and have a `DateTime` Data Type. Figure 21.6 shows a screenshot of the Create New Table dialog box after all of the table columns have been specified.

FIGURE 21.6

The `GuestbookEntries` *table's five columns have been added.*

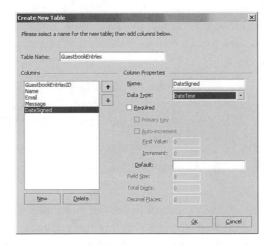

12. Once you have created these five columns, click the OK button. This will create the new database table, adding a new label underneath the Tables label in the Data tab.

At this point we have created a database table to hold guestbook entries submitted by the visitors to our Web site. In the next hour we'll see how to create an ASP.NET Web page to allow users to insert data into this table through the user interface outlined in Figure 21.1.

Summary

This hour was spent planning an online guestbook application. We started by enumerating the functionality the application should support. These base features include allowing a user to add a guestbook entry and providing a means for viewing previous guestbook entries. From these base features, we arrived at other features, such as the submitted guestbook entries being shown in descending chronological order in a paginated DataGrid and the user's being able to supply his or her e-mail address.

Once the feature requirements were laid out, we moved on to creating a user interface. When thinking about what the user interfaces should look like, it often helps to sketch out some ideas on paper, as we did in Figures 21.1 and 21.2. Once these user interfaces are down on paper, we can see, roughly, what the corresponding Web page will look like

21

and make any changes necessary. In addition, thinking about the application's user interface often helps us determine how many separate ASP.NET Web pages will be needed for the Web application.

This hour concluded with creating the database table needed to store each guestbook entry. As discussed, we need to create a database table column for each bit of information we want to have stored in a guestbook entry. This means we needed a column for the user's name, e-mail address, and message, along with a column to indicate when the guestbook entry was made.

In the next hour, "Allowing Users to Add Guestbook Entries," we'll examine how to create the ASP.NET Web page to enter a new guestbook entry. In Hour 23, "Displaying the Guestbook's Contents," we'll turn our attention to creating the ASP.NET Web page for displaying the existing guestbook entries.

Q&A

Q **In this hour we outlined the features of the guestbook application. But what are we to do if, half way through creating the application, we realize there are features that we forgot to plan for when preparing the application's design?**

A This is a common occurrence when designing software applications. To combat this, software is usually designed in an iterative process. That is, an initial feature requirements document is drafted, along with a proposed data model and associated user interface. Following this, actual coding for the application begins. During this time it is quite common for the developers to discover that there are other pressing features that need to be added.

After adding the first set of features, the process begins again. As before, a feature requirements document is created, which contains, in addition to the original features, the newly discovered ones. The user interface diagrams are updated, and the data model augmented. Coding then continues on the project, adding the necessary features.

This process can continue indefinitely, but it usually terminates due to time constraints.

Workshop

Quiz

1. What are the two most basic features of the guestbook application?

2. How many columns are there in the GuestbookEntries table? Briefly describe the purpose of each column.

3. Imagine that we wanted to allow the guestbook user to optionally enter a home page URL. What changes would need to be made to the user interface and GuestbookEntries table in order to accommodate this additional feature?

Answers

1. To be able to enter a guestbook entry and to be able to view the existing guestbook entries.

2. There are five columns in the GuestbookEntries table. The first column, GuestbookEntriesID, is an auto-incrementing primary key column that uniquely identifies each guestbook entry. The Name column specifies the name of the person who has made the guestbook entry. The Email column specifies the person's e-mail address. The Message column contains the actual guestbook entry message. Finally, the DateSigned column contains the date and time the guestbook entry was made.

3. To allow the user to optionally provide a home page URL, you would need to update the user interface to include a textbox for the user's home page URL. When displaying the guestbook entries, you would need to add a column to the DataGrid to show the value of the user's home page URL. Finally, the GuestbookEntries database table would need to be updated to include a column to store the URL. This column might be named home pageURL and could be of type varchar(100).

Exercise

Spend some time writing down additional features you think would improve the usability of the guestbook application. Once you have a list of such features, sketch out how the user interface would need to change, if at all, to accommodate said features. Furthermore, if the additional features would require altering the GuestbookEntries table, such as adding columns, note what changes you would need to make.

21

HOUR **22**

Allowing Users to Add Guestbook Entries

The previous hour was spent planning for the online guestbook application. In this hour we'll start developing the first of the two ASP.NET Web pages needed, the ASP.NET Web page for creating a new guestbook entry.

The first thing we'll need to do to create this ASP.NET Web page is implement the user interface sketched in Figure 21.1. This involves adding the needed Web controls to the Web page and setting their properties accordingly. We'll discuss these aspects in the first section, "Implementing the User Interface."

Once the Web controls have been added, the ASP.NET Web page's HTML portion will have been completed, leaving only the source code portion to implement. The source code portion will do the work of collecting the user's input and inserting a new record into the GuestbookEntries database table. Fortunately, inserting data into a database table is quite a quick and simple process with the aid of the Web Matrix Project's INSERT Data Method Code Builder. We'll examine the ASP.NET Web page's source code portion in the other major section, "Examining the Source Code."

At the conclusion of this hour, we will have created a fully functional ASP.NET Web page for entering new guestbook entries, and we will have covered the following topics:

- Implementing the user interface for adding a new guestbook entry
- Adding RequiredFieldValidator validation controls to ensure that the user provides a name and a message
- Adding a RegularExpressionValidator validation control to ensure that the user's e-mail address, if provided, is in a legal format
- Using the `INSERT` Data Method Code Builder to insert a new record into the `GuestbookEntries` database table
- How to call the function created by the `INSERT` Data Method Code Builder

Implementing the User Interface

In the last hour, "Devising a Plan for the Guestbook Application," we spent some time discussing the functional requirements for the guestbook Web application as well as sketching out a user interface (UI). Armed with the user interface drawing we examined in Figure 21.1, we are ready to create an ASP.NET Web page that implements this UI by adding the necessary Web controls to the page and setting their properties.

Start by creating a new ASP.NET Web page named `AddEntry.aspx`. Also, be sure to turn on glyphs, as we will need to make sure that the various TextBox Web controls and the Button Web control that we'll be adding to this page are placed within the Web form.

Take a minute to refer back to Figure 21.1 to get a solid understanding of the user interface we're trying to implement. Once you have a good idea of this UI design, start creating it via the Web Matrix Project's WYSIWYG designer. Start by typing in the text **Name:** (note colon). Add a TextBox Web control, setting its `ID` property to **name** (no colon here). Recall that the Name column in the `GuestbookEntries` database table was defined as a `varchar` with field size 50. Therefore, we do not want the user to enter a value longer than 50 characters. To help protect against this, set the TextBox Web control's `MaxLength` to **50**.

Next add the text **Email:**. After this text add another TextBox Web control, this time setting the TextBox Web control's `ID` to **email** and its `MaxLength` property to **100**.

Now we need a multiline textbox for the user's guestbook message. Start by adding the text **Message:** and hitting the Enter key. Below this text add a TextBox Web control. For this textbox set the `ID` to **message** and its `TextMode` to **MultiLine**. You can tweak the `Columns` and `Rows` properties to get a multiline TextBox Web control that is big enough.

(The TextBox Web control shown in Figure 22.1 has its Columns and Rows properties set to 45 and 8, respectively.) Because the Message table column is a varchar of field size 5000, set the Message textbox's MaxLength property to **5000**.

Finally, add a Button Web control, setting its ID to **btnSubmit** and its Text property to **Add Comment**. Once you have added these Web controls, your screen should look similar to the screenshot in Figure 22.1.

FIGURE 22.1
Three TextBox Web controls and a Button Web control have been added.

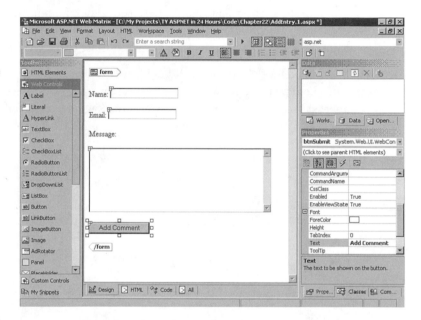

Adding Validation Web Controls

When creating a guestbook entry, the user is required to provide a name and a message. An e-mail address, however, is optional. As we saw in Hour 12, "Validating User Input with Validation Controls," ASP.NET provides a number of helpful validation Web controls that can help ensure that the user's supplied data is considered valid.

Before you can decide which validation Web controls are needed on the ASP.NET Web page, you must first define clearly what user input is considered invalid. If not providing a or a message, a user's input is invalid. Furthermore, we want to make sure that the e-mail address entered by the user is in a valid format, in the form

sometext@sometext.sometext

Therefore, if the user enters foobar as an e-mail address, the input should be considered invalid.

Ensuring that the User Enters a Name and a Message

Recall that to ensure that the user provides a value for a textbox, the RequiredFieldValidator can be used. Therefore, we will need to add two RequiredFieldValidators to the AddEntry.aspx Web page: one for the Name textbox and one for the Message textbox.

To add a RequiredFieldValidator, simply drag and drop the RequiredFieldValidator Web control from the Toolbox and onto the designer, adding it immediately after the Name TextBox Web control. For this RequiredFieldValidator, set the ControlToValidate property to **name** and the ErrorMessage property to **You must enter your name.**

Next add an additional RequiredFieldValidator after the "Message:" text. For this RequiredFieldValidator, set the ControlToValidate property to **message** and the ErrorMessage property to **You must enter a message.** Upon adding these two RequiredFieldValidators, your screen should look similar to the screenshot in Figure 22.2.

FIGURE 22.2

Two RequiredFieldValidators have been added.

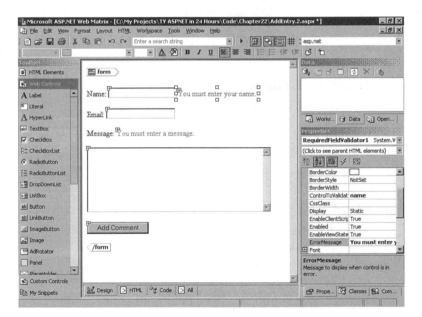

Ensuring That the E-Mail Is in a Proper Format

Note that we did not add a RequiredFieldValidator to the e-mail TextBox Web control, because users are not required to enter their e-mail addresses. However, if users do provide their e-mail addresses, it would be nice to ensure that they're in a legal format. As we saw in Hour 12, the RegularExpressionValidator is useful for ensuring that a user's input is in the proper format, such as making sure the user's e-mail address is in a legal e-mail address format.

22

To add the RegularExpressionValidator, drag and drop the RegularExpression Validator Web control from the Toolbox onto the designer. Set its `ControlToValidate` property to **email** and its `ErrorMessage` property to **Your email address is not in a valid format.** Next, in the Properties pane, click the RegularExpressionValidator's `ValidationExpression` property. Once you do this, you will see a button labeled "..." (an ellipsis)—click this button to display the Regular Expression Editor dialog box (see Figure 22.3). From the Regular Expression Editor dialog box, choose the Internet E-mail Address option and click the OK button, which will close the dialog box and set the `ValidationExpression` property to the Internet E-Mail Address regular expression pattern.

FIGURE 22.3

Select the Internet E-mail Address regular expression pattern.

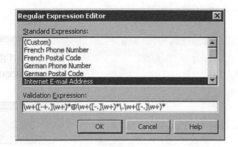

The Internet E-mail Address regular expression pattern is given by

`\w+([-+.]\w+)*@\w+([-.]\w+)*\.\w+([-.]\w+)*`

If you are not familiar with regular expressions, the syntax may look like complete nonsense, and understandably so! Don't worry, though—the preceding regular expression pattern is one of the many expressions already provided by the Web Matrix Project's regular expression library.

In case you're wondering what this regular expression pattern means in English terms, it can be translated as follows: "The pattern must begin with one or more alphanumeric characters; followed by zero or more alphanumeric characters or minus signs or plus signs or periods; followed by an "at" sign (@); followed by one or more alphanumeric characters; followed by zero or more alphanumeric characters, minus signs, or periods; followed by a period; followed by one or more alphanumeric characters; followed by zero or more alphanumeric characters, minus signs, or periods." (Try saying that fast three times!)

Therefore, input such as `mitchell@4guysfromrolla.com` would match the pattern, while input like `fred` would not. While this may sound great, realize that a number of *illegal* e-mail addresses would also match the input. For example, `8@8.8` would match the pattern. The regular expression pattern that can accurately differentiate between all legal and illegal e-mail address formats is quite lengthy and hard to read and understand. For our purposes, we'll settle for this simpler regular expression pattern.

> To see more advanced e-mail format regular expression patterns, visit
> http://www.regexlib.com, where there are literally hundreds of regular
> expression patterns for a wide variety of common formats.

Figure 22.4 shows a screenshot of the designer once the RegularExpressionValidator has been added and all of its properties have been set.

FIGURE 22.4

A RegularExpression Validator has been added to the ASP.NET Web page.

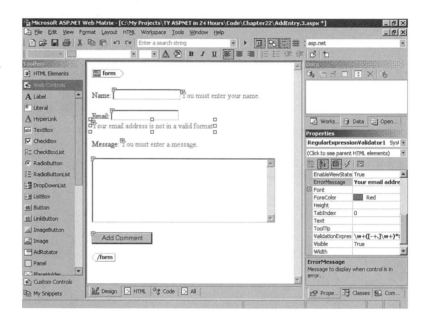

Testing the User Interface

Before we move on to the next section, where we'll be creating the source code portion for the AddEntry.aspx ASP.NET Web page, let's take a moment to test the user interface by visiting the ASP.NET Web page through a browser. Figure 22.5 shows the Web page when first visited through a browser.

FIGURE 22.5

AddEntry.aspx *when visited through a browser.*

Figure 22.6 shows the Web page if the user submits the page without providing any input. Finally, Figure 22.7 shows the AddEntry.aspx Web page when the user provides an invalid e-mail address format.

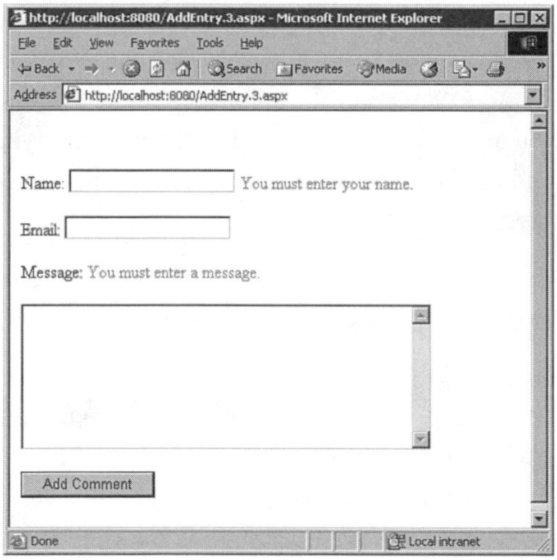

FIGURE 22.6

An error message is displayed if the user fails to enter a name or a message.

FIGURE 22.7

An error message is displayed if the e-mail address is in an invalid format.

This concludes implementing the user interface for a Web page. Notice how quickly the UI can be designed with such WYSIWYG tools as the Web Matrix Project designer. Of course, as Figure 22.1 shows, this particular user interface won't win any awards for its visual appeal. However, with a bit of time and artistic skill, you can touch up the user interface through the designer in a number of ways. Some of these include displaying the "Name:," "Email:," and "Message:" text in an eye-pleasing font, setting the visual properties of the TextBox and Button Web controls, and using HTML tables for alignment and background colors. You are encouraged to spend some time prettying up the user interface. (An exercise at the end of this hour gives you practice using HTML tables to enhance the appearance of a Web page.)

Examining the Source Code

When visiting the AddEntry.aspx Web page, the user will enter name, message, and perhaps e-mail address. Upon entering this information, the user will click the Add Comment button, which will submit the Web form, causing the ASP.NET Web page to be posted back. When this postback occurs, we want to make sure that the validation Web controls report valid data (that is, that Page.IsValid is True) and then add a new record to the database table GuestbookEntries.

Throughout the past eight hours, we have seen numerous examples of how to retrieve information from a database by using the SELECT Data Method Code Builder. With this helpful tool, we are able to visually construct an appropriate SQL query, which then automatically generates the needed source code for accessing this data from the database.

Fortunately, the Web Matrix Project includes an INSERT Data Method Code Builder. This Code Builder, as its name implies, is useful for creating the source code needed for inserting data into the database. In this section we'll be examining the INSERT Data Method Code Builder and how to use it to generate the source code needed to insert user input into the GuestbookEntries table.

Using the INSERT Data Method Code Builder

Recall that the SELECT Data Method Code Builder automatically creates a function that runs a SQL SELECT statement and returns the results as either a DataSet or a DataReader. The INSERT Data Method Code Builder is similar in the fact that it too automatically creates a function. The function created by the INSERT Data Method Code Builder, however, inserts data into a specified database table.

The function created by the INSERT Data Method Code Builder has a number of input parameters, one for each of the table's columns that you wish to specify a value for. For example, the GuestbookEntries table has five columns: GuestbookEntriesID, Name, Email, Message, and DateSigned. The created function can have, at most, four input parameters, one each for the Name, Email, Message, and DateSigned columns. The function might look like this:

```
Function InsertGuestbookEntry(name as String, email as String, message as
        String, dateSigned as DateTime)
 ... Insert passed in data into a new record in the GuestbookEntries table...
End Function
```

To add a new record to the GuestbookEntries table from a visitor named Sam with e-mail address sam@hotmail.com and the message "Hello!" the function could be called like this:

```
InsertGuestbookEntry("Sam", "sam@hotmail.com", "Hello!", DateTime.Now)
```

Note that DateTime.Now returns the current date and time.

Realize that there is no way to create a function from the INSERT Data Method Code Builder that allows the primary key column to be automatically specified. In the InsertGuestbookEntry() function we just looked at, the GuestbookEntriesID column is not specified via an input parameter. This is because the database system itself must determine the value for a table's auto-incrementing primary key column to ensure that the value inserted into the column is unique across all of the rows of the table.

Using the INSERT Data Method Code Builder to Create the Function

To create the function to insert a new record into the GuestbookEntries table, start by clicking the ASP.NET Web page's Code tab. Next drag and drop the INSERT Data Method Code Builder onto the source code portion, just as we've done numerous times before with the SELECT Data Method Code Builder.

The Connect to Database dialog box will now appear (see Figure 22.8). This is the same Connect to Database dialog box that we are first shown when using the SELECT Data Method Code Builder. Use the Connect to Database dialog box to specify the database where the table exists that you want to insert a new record into.

FIGURE 22.8

Specify the database where the table to insert into exists.

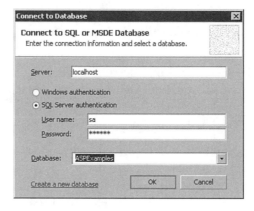

Once you select a database, you will be taken to a dialog box, where you are prompted to select the table that you want to insert data into. As Figure 22.9 shows, a list of the selected table's columns is shown, each with a checkbox next to it. Initially, all table columns except the primary key column are unchecked.

FIGURE 22.9

The primary key column checkbox cannot be unchecked.

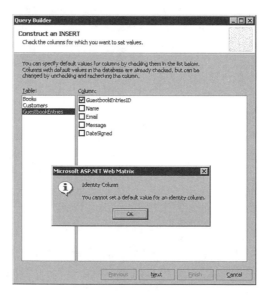

Recall that the INSERT Data Method Code Builder creates a function that inserts a record into the specified table, based on the parameters passed into the function. If a column is unchecked, the generated function will contain a parameter that then expects a value to be passed in and specifies the value of that column for the newly added record.

Because the database system is responsible for assigning the value to the primary key column, the primary key column's checkbox is checked. In fact, the Web Matrix Project won't let us uncheck the primary key column. Attempting to uncheck the primary key column will result in the dialog box shown in Figure 22.9.

You can check (and then uncheck) any of the other columns. If you check a column, the Set Value dialog box appears, which prompts you for the value that should be inserted into this column whenever a new record is added (see Figure 22.10).

FIGURE 22.10
The Set Value dialog box.

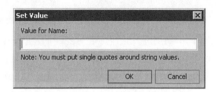

Realize that by checking a column, you are essentially saying to the INSERT Data Method Code Builder, "I do not want to provide a value for this particular column when inserting a new record. Therefore, whenever a new record is created, always set the column to the following value." That "following value" is the value that you enter into the Set Value dialog box.

For example, if for some reason we wanted everyone's e-mail address to be entered as billg@Microsoft.com, we could check the Email table column and enter the value

`'billg@Microsoft.com'`

into the Set Value dialog box.

Notice that when entering a string value into the Set Value dialog box, you must surround the string value with single quote marks.

Rarely will we find ourselves needing to set some column value to a hard-coded string value. The `DateSigned` column shows the much more common application of having a default value entered into a particular column when a new record is inserted. When a new record is inserted into the `GuestbookEntries` table, the value of the `DateSigned` column should be equal to the current date and time. We can ensure that this occurs by checking the `DateSigned` column and entering the value **getdate()** into the Set Value dialog box (as can be seen in Figure 22.11).

FIGURE 22.11

The `DateSigned`
column's default value
is set to `getdate()`.

`getdate()` is a built-in function in MSDE and SQL Server that returns the database server's current date and time. By checking the `DateSigned` column's checkbox, the resulting function created will not expect a parameter for the `DateSigned` value. Rather, when a new record is creating, the value of the `DateSigned` column will always show the result of the `getdate()` function.

We could optionally leave the `DateSigned` column unchecked. This, however, would require us to pass in a value for the `DateSigned` column when inserting a new record. The value we would pass in is `DateTime.Now`, which in VB.NET returns the current date and time.

Once you have specified that the value of the `DateSigned` column should be `getdate()`, click the Next button to advance to the final screen of the `INSERT` Data Method Code Builder. The last screen, shown in Figure 22.12, allows you to specify the name of the created function. Choose the name **InsertGuestbookEntry**.

After specifying the name of the function, click the Finish button. This will close the `INSERT` Data Method and add the `InsertGuestbookEntry()` function to your ASP.NET Web page's source code.

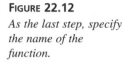

FIGURE 22.12

As the last step, specify the name of the function.

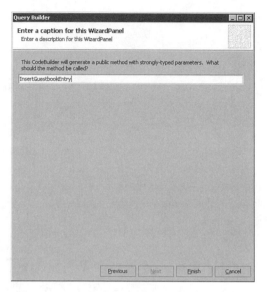

Calling the `InsertGuestbookEntry()` Function from the Button's `Click` Event Handler

At this point we have created the `InsertGuestbookEntry()` function with the help of the `INSERT` Data Method Code Builder. This function expects three string input parameters, which specify the values that should be inserted into the Name, Email, and Message columns, respectively.

Once a user submits the Web form with valid data, we want to call the `InsertGuestbookEntry()` function, passing in the values specified by the user. To accomplish this, we'll need to provide an event handler for the Button Web control's `Click` event. Return to the designer by clicking the Design tab, and then double-click the Button Web control. This will take you back to the Code tab, where a suitable event handler will be in place.

Recall from Hour 12 that if all of the validation controls report that the data they are checking is indeed valid, the `Page.IsValid` property will be True; otherwise, it will be False. Therefore, before calling the `InsertGuestbookEntry()` function, we first want to ensure that `Page.IsValid` is True. After this we can call the `InsertGuestbookEntry()` function, passing in the values specified by the user.

The code to accomplish all of this is only a few lines long. Add the following code to your source code portion.

```
Sub btnSubmit_Click(sender As Object, e As EventArgs)
    If Page.IsValid then
        InsertGuestbookEntry(name.Text, email.Text, message.Text)
        Response.Redirect("ViewGuestbook.aspx")
    End If
End Sub
```

Notice that after the `InsertGuestbookEntry()` function is called, the `Response.Redirect()` method is called. `Response.Redirect()` automatically directs the user's browser to a specified URL. Therefore, after adding a guestbook entry, the user will be automatically forwarded to the Web page `ViewGuestbook.aspx`, which will display the existing guestbook entries.

Testing the `AddEntry.aspx` ASP.NET Web Page

Before moving on to the next hour, "Displaying the Guestbook's Contents," where we'll create the `ViewGuestbook.aspx` ASP.NET Web page, let's take a moment to test the `AddEntry.aspx` Web page. View the `AddEntry.aspx` Web page through a browser. Enter your name, e-mail address, and a short message and click the Add Comment button.

The ASP.NET Web page will be posted back, and the Button's `Click` event handler will execute. Assuming the input is valid, the `InsertGuestbookEntry()` function will be called, which will add a new record to the `GuestbookEntries` table. Finally, you will be automatically redirected to the `ViewGuestbook.aspx` Web page. Of course, this Web page doesn't exist yet, so you should see some sort of error in your Web browser indicating that it can't find the requested URL (such as the one shown in Figure 22.13).

FIGURE 22.13

A 404 error is displayed because the `ViewGuestbook.aspx` *Web page has yet to be created.*

22

Although you can't view the guestbook entries via an ASP.NET Web page yet, you can examine the contents of the GuestbookEntries table by going to the Web Matrix Project's Data tab and double-clicking the GuestbookEntries label. This will display the Edit Table dialog box, which lists the records of the table.

 If you add a guestbook entry without specifying an e-mail address, the new record's Email column will be a blank string.

Summary

In this hour we created the first of the two ASP.NET Web pages that comprise the online guestbook application. The AddEntry.aspx Web page contains three TextBox Web controls, for the user's name, e-mail address, and message, as well as a Button Web control. RequiredFieldValidator Web controls were added for the Name and Message TextBox Web controls to ensure that the user supplies a name and a message, while a RegularExpressionValidator was added to the Email textbox to ensure that the provided e-mail is in a legal e-mail address format.

Next we used the INSERT Data Method Code Builder to add a function (InsertGuestbookEntries()) that performed the actual work of inserting a new record into the GuestbookEntries database table. This created function was configured to accept three inputs, one each for the Name, Email, and Message columns. The DateSigned column was configured to receive the current date and time via the built-in SQL function getdate().

After creating the InsertGuestbookEntries() function, we added an event handler for the Button Web control's Click event. This event handler's code starts by checking to see whether Page.IsValid is True. If it is, the event handler calls the InsertGuestbookEntries() function, inserting a new row into the GuestbookEntries table. After that the user is automatically redirected to the ASP.NET Web page ViewGuestbook.aspx, which displays the existing guestbook entries via a pageable DataGrid.

Now that we have created the AddEntry.aspx Web page, users can add guestbook entries. All that remains is create the ViewGuestbook.aspx Web page, which we'll do in the next hour.

Q&A

Q In the `AddEntry.aspx` Web page, the textboxes use the `MaxLength` property to limit the number of characters to the respective database table's column's size. (For instance, the Name textbox's `MaxLength` property is set to 50 because the Name column is a `varchar(50)`.) Since the `MaxLength` property is browser dependent, certain browsers may not support the property. Is there any way to use a validation Web control to ensure that the user's input is within a certain number of characters?

A The RegularExpressionValidator can ensure that a user's input into a textbox falls within a certain range of characters. For example, in a user account–creation Web page, you might want the user to choose a password that you can ensure is from 6 to 15 characters. This check can be performed using a RegularExpressionValidator. Specifically, here is the `ValidationExpression` to limit a textbox to contain from m to n characters:

`^(.|\n){m,n}$`

A thorough discussion as to what this regular expression pattern does is beyond the scope of this book, but let's take a cursory look at the pattern. The period (`.`) is a special character in regular expressions that matches any character other than the new line character, which is denoted as `\n`. The `|` is a special character in regular expressions meaning *or*. For example, a|b means match a *or* b. Therefore, `.|\n` matches *any* character, since `.` matches any character but the new line character, and `\n` is the new line character.

The `{m,n}` indicates matches whatever expression is to its immediate left m to n times. That means `(.|\n){m, n}` matches a sequence of m to n characters. Finally, the `^` and `$` indicate that the string being searched must start and end with the pattern.

An example of this technique in application would be to limit the number of characters in the Name textbox to no more than 50 characters. To accomplish this, you would simply add a RegularExpressionValidator, assign its `ControlToValidate` property to the Name TextBox Web control, and then set its `ValidationExpression` to

`^(.|\n){0,50}$`

If the user enters more than 50 characters, the RegularExpressionValidator will display its `ErrorMessage`, and the `Page.IsValid` property will be False.

22

Workshop

Quiz

1. In the `btnSubmit_Click` event handler, the `Page.IsValid` property is checked and the user's guestbook entry added to the database only if this property is True. Why is this check made? Is it necessary?

2. What validation Web controls were added to the ASP.NET Web page, and what sort of data validity do they provide?

3. In the `INSERT` Data Method Code Builder, each database column other than the auto-increment primary key column could be checked. What effect does checking a column have?

4. Regarding question 3, why did we check the `DateSigned` column, and what was the value entered into the Set Value dialog box?

5. True or False: The `Response.Redirect()` method automatically redirects the user's Web browser to a specified URL.

Answers

1. Whenever validation Web controls are being used, it is vital that the `Page.IsValid` property be True before using the user input that is being validated by the validation controls. This is because users visiting the Web page with downlevel browsers, or with uplevel browsers with client-side JavaScript disabled, will not have their input checked on the client side. This means that the Web form can be submitted with invalid data.

2. Three validation Web controls were added to the `AddEntry.aspx` Web page. A RequiredFieldValidator was added for both the Name and Message textboxes, and a RegularExpressionValidator was added to the Email textbox to ensure that the user's supplied e-mail was in a valid format.

3. Checking a database table column in the `INSERT` Data Method Code Builder displays the Set Value dialog box. This dialog box allows you to specify the value that should always be inserted into this particular column whenever a new row is added via the generated function.

4. Since we wanted to have the current date and time automatically inserted into the DateSigned column, the `DateSigned`'s checkbox was checked in the `INSERT` Data Method Code Builder, and the value `getdate()` was entered.

5. True.

Exercises

1. In the "Q&A" section, we discussed how to use a RegularExpressionValidator to ensure that the number of characters entered into a TextBox Web control was within certain bounds. Use this technique to augment the AddEntry.aspx Web page to guarantee that the user enters at most 50 characters for the name, 100 characters for the e-mail, and 5,000 characters for the message. (Note that to test to ensure that your RegularExpressionValidator is working properly, you will need to up the MaxLength property on the TextBox Web controls.)

2. For this exercise let's improve the aesthetics of the AddEntry.aspx Web page. A simple way to improve the appearance of any form is to use an HTML table with two columns. The user input elements, such as textboxes, radio buttons, checkboxes, and so on, appear in the right column, while the title for each input element appears in the left column.

   Figure 22.14 shows a screenshot of the AddEntry.aspx Web page after an HTML table has been used to improve the aesthetics. For this exercise add an HTML table to the AddEntry.aspx Web page and move the TextBox Web controls and text elements into the table so that it appears like Figure 22.14. Recall that to add an HTML table through the Web Matrix Project designer, go to the HTML menu and select the Insert Table... option.

   (Hint: All of the properties that you need to set in order to have your AddEntry.aspx Web page look like the one in Figure 22.14 can be set through the Properties pane in the designer. For example, to right-align the titles for each textbox in the HTML table's left column, you can click inside the appropriate table cell and set the align property to Right.)

FIGURE 22.14

An HTML table has been used to align the display of the textboxes and their titles.

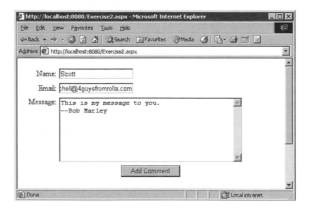

HOUR 23

Displaying the Guestbook's Contents

In Hour 21, "Devising a Plan for the Guestbook Application," we determined that for our online guestbook application, we needed to create two ASP.NET Web pages. The first one, AddEntry.aspx, which was created in the previous hour, allows a user to add a new entry to the guestbook. The second one, ViewGuestbook.aspx, displays the existing guestbook entries to the user through a pageable DataGrid. This hour focuses on creating this second ASP.NET Web page.

Like the last hour, "Allowing Users to Add Guestbook Entries," this hour is divided into three main sections. In the first section, "Implementing the User Interface," we'll examine turning the user interface ideas discussed in Hour 21 into an actual ASP.NET Web page. We'll discuss what columns the DataGrid will need to contain, along with formatting issues and configuring the DataGrid to support paging.

Once the user interface portion of the ASP.NET Web page has been created, we'll turn our attention to the code in the "Examining the Source Code Portion" section. Here we will use the SELECT Data Method Code Builder to create a function that retrieves the guestbook entries from the GuestbookEntries database table. Additionally, we will add the event handlers necessary to implement DataGrid paging.

In the final section, "Testing the ViewGuestbook.aspx ASP.NET Web Page," we'll view the completed ASP.NET Web page through a browser to test the functionality of the ViewGuestbook.aspx Web page.

So, in this hour we will be covering the following topics:

- Implementing the user interface for viewing the existing guestbook entries
- Adding a DataGrid and configuring it to support paging
- Providing formatting information for the DataGrid's navigational paging controls
- Creating a function that retrieves the existing guestbook entries in the properly sorted order
- Creating the DataGrid's PageIndexChanged event handler
- Testing the guestbook application

Implementing the User Interface

Back in Hour 21 we sketched out a user interface design for the Web page that would display the existing guestbook entries. This sketch, which you can find in Figure 21.2, displayed the guestbook entries in a grid with a row for each guestbook entry and a column for the name, e-mail address, message, and date signed. As you know by now, the DataGrid Web control will serve as an ideal Web control for this user interface because it displays database data in a grid format.

It's now time to create an ASP.NET Web page that implements this interface. Start by creating a new ASP.NET Web page named ViewGuestbook.aspx. Next turn on glyphs; because we will be using a pageable DataGrid to display the guestbook entries, it is vital that the DataGrid be placed within the Web form. Now add a DataGrid Web control to the designer, making sure that it is placed within the Web form, and set its ID property to entries.

From the user interface we sketched out in Figure 21.2, we need the DataGrid to have four columns. We'll represent each of these columns as a Bound Column. Click the Property Builder... hyperlink in the DataGrid's Properties pane and then select the Columns screen from the Property Builder.

Recall that we can explicitly indicate what columns should appear in a DataGrid through the Columns screen of the Property Builder. For more information on this process, refer back to Hour 15, "Displaying Data with the DataGrid Web Control."

To create the four Bound Columns, complete the following steps:

1. First uncheck the "Create columns automatically at run time" checkbox.

2. Next add a Bound Column and enter the value **Name** into both its Header text and its Data Field textboxes.

3. Then add another Bound Column, this time setting its Header text and Data Field textboxes to **Email**.

4. Next add the third Bound Column, setting its Header text and Data Field textboxes to the value **Message**.

5. Finally, add the fourth Bound Column, setting its Header text textbox to **Date** and its Data Field textbox to **DateSigned**. Also take a moment to set the Data formatting expression textbox to **{0:g}**, which will format the DateSigned field as a general date format. (Recall from Hour 16, "Examining Further DataGrid Examples," that the general date format displays the date August 27, 2003, and time 4:23:03 p.m. as "8/27/2003 4:23 PM.")

Figure 23.1 shows a screenshot of the Property Builder dialog box after the four Bound Columns have been added.

FIGURE 23.1
Four Bound Columns have been added to the DataGrid.

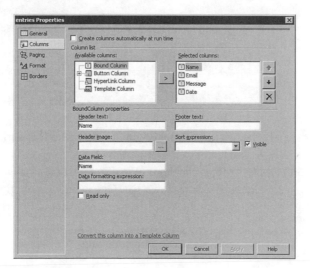

Formatting the Four Bound Columns

Now that we have added the needed Bound Columns to the DataGrid, let's take a moment to specify their formatting. We can specify formatting settings for the header of each column, such as making the header column text a larger, bold font. Furthermore, we can increase the aesthetic properties of the DataGrid by using a more attractive font than the default system font. To specify formatting options, follow these steps:

1. Click the Format label in the upper left corner of the Property Builder dialog box.

2. Doing so will take you to the Format screen. Let's indicate that the DataGrid's contents should be displayed using the Arial font. To accomplish this, click the DataGrid label in the Objects listbox and choose the Arial font from the "Font name" drop-down list.

3. Also specify that the font should be size 10pt. To do this, choose the Custom option from the "Font size" drop-down list and enter **10** into the textbox to the drop-down list's right (see Figure 23.2).

FIGURE 23.2

The DataGrid's contents will be rendered using the Arial font in 10pt size.

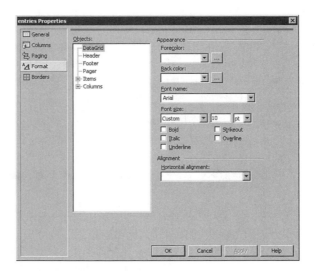

4. Next specify the header's formatting by clicking the Header label from the Objects listbox. Set the Forecolor to White and the Back color to Navy. Set the font size to **15**pt and check the Bold checkbox. Finally, select the Center option from the "Horizontal alignment" drop-down list. Once you have configured these formatting settings, your screen should look like the screenshot in Figure 23.3.

FIGURE 23.3

Each column's header will be displayed in a larger, centered, bold font.

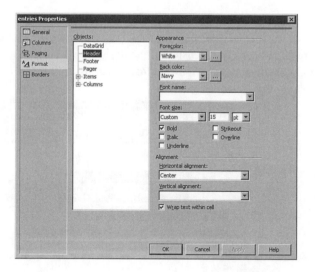

23

5. To enhance the readability of the DataGrid, let's give alternating items in the DataGrid different background colors. For this, expand the Items label in the Object listbox. This will display a number of labels underneath the Items label, such as Normal Items, Alternating Items, and so on. Click the Alternating Items label and set the Back color to Gray (see Figure 23.4).

FIGURE 23.4

Every other guestbook entry will have a gray background.

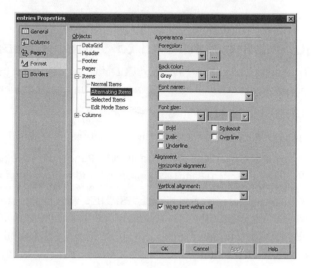

Once you have specified all of these formatting settings, click the OK button of the Property Builder.

6. Upon returning to the designer, you will notice that the DataGrid's appearance has changed to reflect the changes we made to the number of columns and the formatting. Figure 23.5 shows a screenshot of the designer after specifying the DataGrid's four Bound Columns and configuring the formatting properties.

FIGURE 23.5

The DataGrid's appearance has changed to reflect the specified formatting.

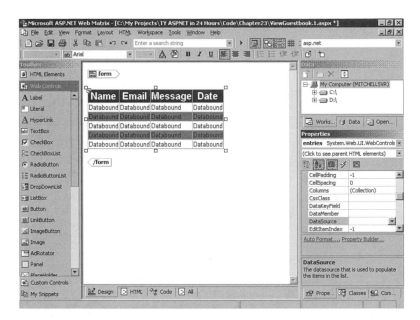

Configuring the DataGrid to Support Paging

In Hour 19, "Paging Through the DataGrid's Data," we discussed the steps required for creating a pageable DataGrid. These steps, briefly summarized, include

1. Configuring the DataGrid to support paging

2. Creating a function that retrieves the DataSet that contains the data to page through

3. Writing an event handler for the DataGrid's PageIndexChanged event that updates the DataGrid's CurrentPageIndex property and rebinds the DataGrid

Steps 2 and 3 involve creating code in the ASP.NET Web page's source code portion. Step 1, however, is accomplished by setting properties in the DataGrid's Property Builder. Therefore, before moving on to the next section, "Examining the Source Code Portion," let's take a moment to configure the DataGrid to support paging.

Start by opening the DataGrid's Property Builder dialog box and navigate to the Paging screen. To enable paging, simply check the "Allow paging" checkbox. For this application set the "Page size" textbox to **5**. Also, change the "Next page button text" textbox value from > to **Next >** and the "Previous page button text" from < to **< Prev** (see Figure 23.6).

23

FIGURE 23.6

The DataGrid's paging properties have been set.

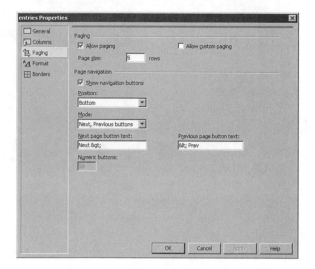

Once you have made these changes, click the Property Builder's OK button, which will return you to the designer. The DataGrid's appearance should have been updated to include a <Prev and Next> set of hyperlinks.

Formatting the Paging Navigational Controls

As Figure 23.6 shows, the paging navigational controls are composed of a < Prev and Next > pair of hyperlinks. These are displayed at the bottom of the DataGrid and are left-aligned. But what if we want to set these hyperlinks right-aligned or displayed in a font different from the rest of the DataGrid?

To specify formatting properties for the paging navigational controls, start by opening the DataGrid's Property Builder dialog box and selecting the Format screen. Next click the Pager label in the Objects listbox. From here you can specify the same formatting options as can be specified for the DataGrid's Header, Footer, or Items.

For this application let's give the paging navigational controls a White foreground color and Navy background color (just like the Header). Set these by choosing White from the Forecolor drop-down list and Navy from the "Back color" drop-down list. Next, set the font size to **11**pt and check the Bold checkbox. Finally, choose the Right option from the "Horizontal alignment" drop-down list. Upon specifying these settings, your screen should look similar to Figure 23.7.

FIGURE 23.7

FIGURE 23.7

Specifying formatting for the paging navigational controls.

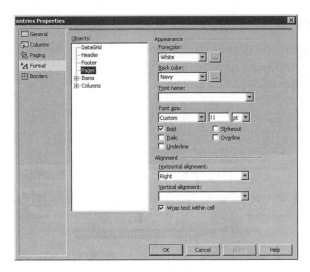

Once you have set the formatting properties accordingly, click the OK button. Upon returning to the designer, you will see that the < Prev and Next > hyperlinks are right-aligned on a navy background with a white, bold, 11pt foreground. Figure 23.8 shows a screenshot of the designer after the paging formatting changes have been specified.

FIGURE 23.8

The DataGrid has been updated to reflect the new paging navigational control formatting.

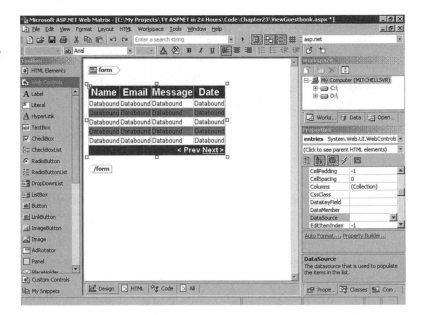

Examining the Source Code Portion

Since we have added the DataGrid to the Web page, specified what columns it contains, set a number of formatting properties, and configured it for paging, we are ready to tackle the source code portion of the ASP.NET Web page.

First we will need to use the SELECT Data Method Code Builder to create a function that returns the guestbook entries via a DataSet. Start by clicking the Code tab of the ASP.NET Web page. Next drag and drop the SELECT Data Method Code Builder from the Toolbox and onto the source code portion, just as we have done numerous times before. When constructing the SELECT query, have all Columns returned from the GuestbookEntries table (see Figure 23.9). Name the function **GetGuestbookEntries** and be sure that it returns a DataSet.

FIGURE 23.9

Build a query to return all columns from the GuestbookEntries *table.*

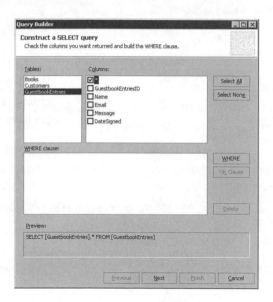

It is vital that you have the created function return a DataSet as opposed to a DataReader. As we discussed in Hour 19, the DataGrid must be bound to a DataSet in order to utilize the DataGrid's paging features.

Returning the GuestbookEntries Records in Sorted Order

Once we have completed all of the steps of the SELECT Data Method Code Builder, the source code presented in Listing 23.1 will be automatically added to our ASP.NET Web page. This function, GetGuestbookEntries(), returns all of the records from the GuestbookEntries table in a DataSet object.

LISTING 23.1   The Source Code Created by the SELECT Data Method Code Builder

```
 1: Function GetGuestbookEntries() As System.Data.DataSet
 2:     Dim connectionString As String = "server='localhost'; user id='sa';
               password='password'; Database='ASPExamples'"
 3:     Dim sqlConnection As System.Data.SqlClient.SqlConnection = New
               System.Data.SqlClient.SqlConnection(connectionString)
 4:
 5:     Dim queryString As String = "SELECT [GuestbookEntries].* FROM
               [GuestbookEntries]"
 6:     Dim sqlCommand As System.Data.SqlClient.SqlCommand = New
               System.Data.SqlClient.SqlCommand(queryString, sqlConnection)
 7:
 8:     Dim dataAdapter As System.Data.SqlClient.SqlDataAdapter = New
               System.Data.SqlClient.SqlDataAdapter(sqlCommand)
 9:     Dim dataSet As System.Data.DataSet = New System.Data.DataSet
10:     dataAdapter.Fill(dataSet)
11:
12:     Return dataSet
13: End Function
```

The actual SQL SELECT statement that is used to query the database can be seen in line 5 of Listing 23.1. Note that this SQL query does not contain an ORDER BY clause, which means the results will be sorted by the primary key column, GuestbookEntryID, in ascending order.

Since we want the results sorted by the DateSigned column, we'll need to edit the SQL SELECT query. Specifically, change line 5 from

```
Dim queryString As String = "SELECT [GuestbookEntries].* FROM
[GuestbookEntries]"
```

to

```
Dim queryString As String = "SELECT [GuestbookEntries].* FROM [GuestbookEntries]
      ORDER BY DateSigned DESC"
```

Note that the change adds ORDER BY DateSigned DESC to the SELECT statement. This added ORDER BY clause will sort the results chronologically from the most recent guestbook entry to the oldest.

Adding the PageIndexChanged Event Handler

At this point we have created the GetGuestbookEntries() function and altered the function's SQL query to retrieve the guestbook entries in the properly sorted order. To provide paging support, we still need to create an event handler for the DataGrid's PageIndexChanged event.

Recall from Hour 19 that whenever the user clicks one of the navigational control hyperlinks, the ASP.NET Web page is posted back, and the DataGrid's `PageIndexChanged` event fires. When this event fires, we need to update the DataGrid's `CurrentPageIndex` property so that it equals the page of data the user wants to view. Following this, we need to rebind the DataGrid to the database data.

Adding an event handler for the `PageIndexChanged` event is a two-step process. First we must create an event handler in the source code portion of the ASP.NET Web page. Second, we need to wire up the DataGrid's `PageIndexChanged` event to the event handler created in the first step.

To create the event handler, simply add the following code to the source code portion of the `ViewGuestbook.aspx` ASP.NET Web page:

```
Sub entries_Page(sender As Object, e As DataGridPageChangedEventArgs)
    ' Assign the CurrentPageIndex property to the new page index value
    entries.CurrentPageIndex = e.NewPageIndex

    ' Rebind the data to the DataGrid
    entries.DataSource = GetGuestbookEntries()
    entries.DataBind()
End Sub
```

This event handler, `entries_Page`, updates the `entries` DataGrid's `CurrentPageIndex` property, assigning it to `e.NewPageIndex`. Following this, the `entries` DataGrid is rebound to the data. This last step is accomplished by assigning the DataGrid's `DataSource` property to the DataSet returned by the `GetGuestbookEntries()` function and then calling the `DataBind()` method.

The next step is to wire the DataGrid's `PageIndexChanged` event to the `entries_Page` event handler. As discussed in Hour 19, this is accomplished by adding the following syntax to the DataGrid's declaration:

```
OnPageIndexChanged="entries_Page"
```

To edit the DataGrid's declaration, go to the designer, right-click the DataGrid Web control, and select the Edit Tag option from the menu. This will display the Quick Tag Edit dialog box, which will contain the DataGrid's declaration (see Figure 23.10).

23

FIGURE 23.10
The Quick Tag Edit dialog box is displayed.

The DataGrid's declaration should contain the following markup:

```
<asp:DataGrid id="entries" runat="server" AllowPaging="True" PageSize="5"
        Font-Names="Arial" Font-Size="10pt" AutoGenerateColumns="False">
  <HeaderStyle font-size="15pt" font-bold="True" horizontalalign="Center"
        forecolor="White" backcolor="Navy"></HeaderStyle>
  <PagerStyle nextpagetext="Next &amp;gt;" font-size="11pt" font-bold="True"
        prevpagetext="&amp;lt; Prev" horizontalalign="Right" forecolor="White"
        backcolor="Navy"></PagerStyle>
  <AlternatingItemStyle backcolor="Gray"></AlternatingItemStyle>
  <Columns>
    <asp:BoundColumn DataField="Name" HeaderText="Name"></asp:BoundColumn>
    <asp:BoundColumn DataField="Email" HeaderText="Email"></asp:BoundColumn>
    <asp:BoundColumn DataField="Message" HeaderText="Message">
        </asp:BoundColumn>
    <asp:BoundColumn DataField="DateSigned" HeaderText="Date"
        DataFormatString="{0:g}"></asp:BoundColumn>
  </Columns>
</asp:DataGrid>
```

The `OnPageIndexChanged="entries_Page"` syntax should be placed after the
`<asp:DataGrid` and before the `id="entries"`. That is, in the first line of the Quick Tag
Edit dialog box, enter `OnPageIndexChanged="entries_Page"` so that it looks like this:

```
<asp:DataGrid OnPageIndexChanged="entries_Page" id="entries" runat="server"
        AllowPaging="True" PageSize="5" Font-Names="Arial" Font-Size="10pt"
        AutoGenerateColumns="False">
```

This addition wires the DataGrid's `OnPageIndexChanged` event to the `entries_Page`
event handler.

Creating the `Page_Load` Event Handler

The only part of the source code that has yet to be coded is the `Page_Load` event handler.
When the page is visited for the first time—that is, when the page is not loaded because
of a postback—we need to bind the DataSet returned by the `GetGuestbookEntries()`
function to the `entries` DataGrid.

This, as we have seen in previous hours, can be easily accomplished via an `If` statement to check whether `Page.IsPostBack` is False. If this is the case, then the DataGrid's `DataSource` is set and its `DataBind()` method is called.

To complete the source code for `ViewGuestbook.aspx`, add the following to the source code portion:

```
Sub Page_Load(sender as Object, e as EventArgs)
    If Not Page.IsPostBack then
        entries.DataSource = GetGuestbookEntries()
        entries.DataBind()
    End If
End Sub
```

23

Testing the `ViewGuestbook.aspx` ASP.NET Web Page

With the finishing touches on the `ViewGuestbook.aspx` Web page we added in the last section, we have completed the online guestbook application. Let's take a moment to test the `ViewGuestbook.aspx` Web page.

Figure 23.11 shows a screenshot of `ViewGuestbook.aspx` when viewed through a browser. Note that because there are only two guestbook entries, the DataGrid does not exhibit its paging capabilities. (Recall that we set the Page size to 5, which means the DataGrid will display 5 guestbook entries per page.)

FIGURE 23.11

Two guestbook entries are displayed.

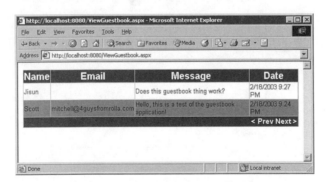

Let's go ahead and add some additional guestbook entries so that we can see the paging features in effect. To enter new guestbook entries, simply visit the `AddEntry.aspx` ASP.NET Web page we created in Hour 22. Take a few minutes to add at least another five guestbook entries. Once you do so, you will have enough guestbook entries to illustrate the `ViewGuestbook.aspx` DataGrid's paging capabilities.

Figure 23.12 shows a screenshot of `ViewGuestbook.aspx` after a number of other guestbook entries have been added. Note that only the first page of guestbook entries is shown, with the `Next >` hyperlink enabled.

FIGURE 23.12
The first page of guestbook entries is displayed.

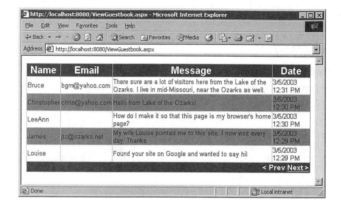

After the `Next >` hyperlink is clicked, the user will be taken to the second page of guestbook entries, which is shown in Figure 23.13.

FIGURE 23.13
The second page of guestbook entries is displayed.

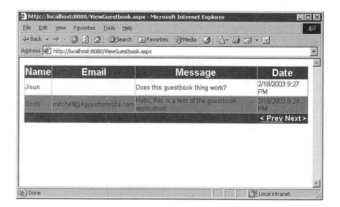

Notice that the guestbook entries shown in Figures 23.11, 23.12, and 23.13 are all sorted by date and time, starting with the most recent guestbook entry to the oldest.

Summary

In this hour we created the final ASP.NET Web page for the online guestbook application `ViewGuestbook.aspx`. This Web page displays the existing guestbook entries, sorted in chronological order from the most recent to the oldest entries, through a pageable DataGrid.

To create the source code portion of this Web page, we used the SELECT Data Method Code Builder to generate the `GetGuestbookEntries()` function, which returns all of the records from the `GuestbookEntries` tables in the properly sorted order. Because the results are displayed in a pageable DataGrid, this function returns the data in a DataSet as opposed to a DataReader.

Along with the `GetGuestbookEntries()`, we created an event handler for the DataGrid's `PageIndexChanged` event. This event handler, `entries_Page`, simply updates the DataGrid's `CurrentPageIndex` property. In addition, we needed to wire up the DataGrid's `PageIndexChanged` event to the event handler, which was accomplished by adding

```
OnPageIndexChanged="entries_Page"
```

to the DataGrid's declaration.

With the `ViewGuestbook.aspx` and `AddEntry.aspx` Web pages, we have the two pages needed for our guestbook application. To add a new guestbook entry, a user can simply visit `AddEntry.aspx`. Once having added an entry, the user will be automatically forwarded to the `ViewGuestbook.aspx` Web page, where can be sees his or her guestbook entry as well as all of the other entries.

In the next hour we will examine how to enhance this application by having the `AddEntry.aspx` Web page automatically send an e-mail to us (or whomever we like) whenever a new guestbook entry is added. We'll also examine some subtle problems the current guestbook application has and some fixes for these issues.

Q&A

Q Rather than show *all* of the past guestbook entries, I want `ViewGuestbook.aspx` to only show the 10 most recent guestbook entries. How can I accomplish this?

A Databases like Microsoft SQL Server 2000 and MSDE support a SQL command called TOP that returns only a specified number of records from the database. If you wanted to return only the 10 most recent guestbook entries, you would need to modify the SQL SELECT statement in the GetGuestBookEntries() function from

```
SELECT [GuestbookEntries].* FROM [GuestbookEntries] ORDER BY DateSigned
DESC
```

to

```
SELECT TOP 10 [GuestbookEntries].* FROM [GuestbookEntries]
        ORDER BY DateSigned DESC
```

Notice that the TOP 10 comes *before* the list of columns in the SELECT statement.

Workshop

Quiz

1. The GetGuestBookEntries() function, which we created using the SELECT Data Method Code Builder, returns a DataSet instead of a DataReader. Why did we do this?

2. What did we have to do to have the guestbook entries ordered from the most recent to the least recent?

3. Imagine that we wanted to change the paging navigational interface to use page numbers instead of the next and previous hyperlinks. What would we have to do to make this change?

4. True or False: It would be difficult to alter the ViewGuestbook.aspx Web page to have the guestbook entries ordered alphabetically by the name of the person who made the guestbook entry.

5. Quiz question 3 in Hour 21 asked what changes would need to be made to the user interface and data model if we wanted to allow the user to record a home page URL when making a guestbook entry. Assume that to make these changes, a new column called HomePageURL was created in the GuestbookEntries table. How would you use a HyperLink Column in the ViewGuestbook.aspx Web page to show the user's home page URL as a hyperlink?

Answers

1. To provide paging support, the DataGrid's DataSource must be a DataSet and *not* a DataReader. Therefore, we had the GetGuestBookEntries() function return a DataSet.

2. After creating the GetGuestBookEntries() function with the SELECT Data Method Code Builder, we needed to alter the SQL SELECT query by hand, adding an ORDER BY clause.

3. To change the navigation mode from the Next, Previous buttons to the Page number mode, all that we'd have to do is open the DataGrid's Property Builder... dialog box, navigate to the Paging screen, and change the value in the Mode drop-down list from Next, Previous buttons to Page numbers. That's it!

4. False. To have the existing guestbook entries listed alphabetically by the `Name` field, we'd simply need to make one tiny change to the `GetGuestBookExtries()` function. Where we previously had

   `ORDER BY DateSigned DESC`

   we'd change this to

   `ORDER BY Name`

5. First you'd need to add a HyperLink Column through the Columns screen of the DataGrid's Property Builder. Imagine that we wanted to have the URL of the created hyperlink point to the value in the `HomepageURL` field of the `DataSource`, and we wanted the text of the hyperlink to read, "Visit my Home Page!" To accomplish this, we could enter into the HyperLink Column's Text textbox the value **Visit My Home Page!** In the HyperLink Column's URL Field textbox, we'd want to enter the value **HomePageURL**. This would have the effect of creating a DataGrid column where each row had a hyperlink whose text read, "Visit My Home Page!" and that, when clicked, would send the user to the appropriate URL.

Exercise

For this exercise update the `ViewGuestbook.aspx` Web page so that the DataGrid displays the Email column as a HyperLink Column. That is, change the Email column from a Bound Column to a HyperLink Column. Have it so that the column displays the e-mail address as the text of the column. The hyperlink URL should be

`mailto:emailAddress`

23

HOUR 24

Sending E-Mail when a New Guestbook Entry Is Added

Over the past three hours, we planned for, designed, and tested an online guestbook application. The application was designed using the specifications outlined in Hour 21, "Devising a Plan for the Guestbook Application," and consisted of two ASP.NET Web pages, AddEntry.aspx and ViewGuestbook.aspx.

Because the guestbook was designed and created according to the plan outlined in Hour 21, you might think that our job is done. In the real world, this is hardly ever the case. Once an application has been created and deployed, users invariably start itching for new features.

In this hour we'll examine adding two features to the guestbook application. The first involves having the e-mail address displayed in the guestbook displayed as a mailto hyperlink. As we'll see in the "Displaying the E-Mail

Address as a Mailto Hyperlink" section, this feature can be added quickly with minimal changes to the ViewGuestbook.aspx Web page.

In the "Sending E-Mail upon a New Guestbook Entry" section, we'll update the AddEntry.aspx Web page so we receive an e-mail whenever a guestbook entry is added. Without this feature, if we were interested in the popularity of the guestbook on our Web page, we'd need to visit the guestbook periodically to see what, if any, entries had been added.

In this hour we will cover the following topics:

- Using a HyperLink Column to display the e-mail address by using a mailto hyperlink
- Using the URL format string property of the HyperLink Column
- Sending an e-mail from an ASP.NET Web page
- Sending HTML-formatted e-mails
- Using the Send Email Code Builder

Displaying the E-Mail Address as a Mailto Hyperlink

Recall from Hour 22, "Allowing Users to Add Guestbook Entries," that when entering a guestbook entry, a user can optionally provide an e-mail address. In Hour 23, "Displaying the Guestbook's Contents," we displayed this e-mail address, if provided, in the guestbook entry listing (see Figure 24.1).

FIGURE 24.1

The user's e-mail address, if provided, is displayed.

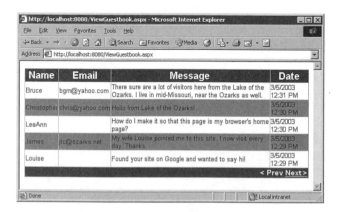

Rather than just displaying the user's e-mail address as text, it would be nice to display the e-mail address as a *mailto hyperlink,* which is a hyperlink that has the form

```
<a href="mailto:emailAddress">emailAddress</a>
```

It is called a mailto hyperlink because the href attribute of the a tag starts with mailto:, as opposed to http://. When this hyperlink is clicked, the user's default mail program will be launched with a new message to be sent to the specified e-mail address.

To accomplish this, we need to alter the DataGrid so a HyperLink Column for the Email column is used instead of a Bound Column.

> Recall that we first discussed using the HyperLink Column in Hour 16, "Examining Further DataGrid Examples."

Changing the Email Bound Column to a HyperLink Column

24

When creating the DataGrid to display the existing guestbook entries in the previous hour, we explicitly specified the DataGrid's four columns. The four Bound Columns displayed the Name, Email, Message, and DateSigned fields from the DataSource. Each of these columns displays its associated DataSource field as plain text. In order to have the DataGrid's Email column display the Email field as a mailto hyperlink, we must use a HyperLink Column instead of a Bound Column.

To change the Bound Column to a HyperLink Column, start by opening the ViewGuestbook.aspx ASP.NET Web page in the Web Matrix Project. Next open the DataGrid's Property Builder dialog box and navigate to the Columns screen. Figure 24.2 contains a screenshot of what your screen should look like. Note that there are four Bound Columns listed in the "Selected columns" listbox: Name, Email, Message, and Date.

FIGURE 24.2

The Columns screen shows four Bound Columns.

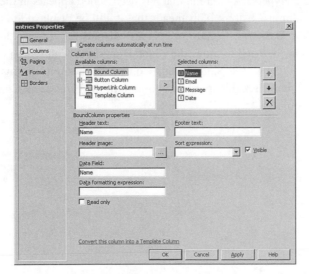

To change the Email Bound Column to a HyperLink Bound Column, you must first remove the Email Bound Column from the "Selected columns" listbox. Click the Email Bound Column and then click the button with the black X label on it, which is positioned at the bottom right of the "Selected columns" listbox.

Once you have removed the Email Bound Column, add a new HyperLink Column by using the HyperLink Column option from the "Available columns" listbox and then clicking the > button. This will add a new HyperLink Column at the bottom of the "Selected columns" listbox, as shown in Figure 24.3.

FIGURE 24.3

A HyperLink Column has been added.

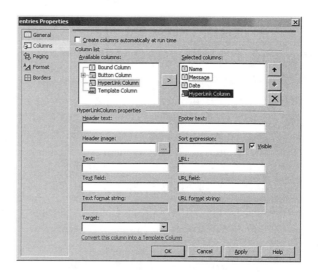

Note that the HyperLink Column that has been added appears at the bottom of the "Selected columns" listbox. This means that it will be displayed to the right of the Date column in the DataGrid. Because we want to display the Email column to the right of the Name column, we need to move the added HyperLink Column up the list of Selected columns so it follows the Name Bound Column. To accomplish this, click the HyperLink Column and then click the up arrow button until the HyperLink Column is in place, as shown in Figure 24.4.

FIGURE 24.4

The HyperLink Column has been moved to appear after the Name Bound Column.

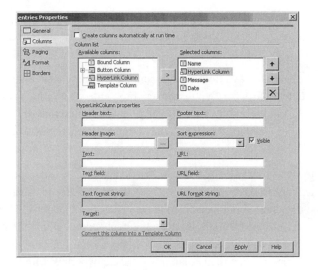

Setting the HyperLink Column Properties

Now all that remains is setting the HyperLink Column's various properties. Start by setting the "Header text" textbox to the value **Email**. This, as we've discussed in previous hours, will display the text "Email" in the header of the DataGrid's Email column.

Recall that hyperlinks have two properties: the actual URL that the user is directed to when the hyperlink is clicked and the clickable text that is displayed in the user's browser. These hyperlink properties can be set for the HyperLink Column via the "Text," "Text field," "URL," and "URL field" textboxes. In some cases we want the text of the generated hyperlink to be the same value for each row of the DataGrid. If so, we can specify this static text value in the Text textbox. Similarly, if we want each hyperlink in the HyperLink Column to have the same URL, we can specify a static URL in the URL textbox.

However, if we want the value of the generated hyperlink's text attribute to differ for each DataGrid row as based on a `DataSource` field, we need to specify the name of the field in the "Text field" textbox. Similarly, if we want the URL specified based on a `DataSource` field, we can specify the field name in the "URL field" textbox.

Because we want to have the e-mail address displayed as the text of the generated hyperlink, enter the value **Email** into the "Text field" textbox. For the URL part of the hyperlink, we want to have **mailto:***emailAddress*, where *"emailAddress"* is replaced by the value of the `Email` `DataSource` field.

At this point you may be wondering how we can specify that we want the URL `mailto:`*emailAddress* to appear. Obviously, if we just wanted the static text `mailto:` for the URL, we could specify that as the value for the URL textbox. Similarly, if we wanted just the value of the `Email DataSource` field as the URL, we could enter **Email** into the URL field textbox.

However, we want to have both a static and a dynamic URL value. To accomplish this, we need to enter values for two textboxes. First enter the value **Email** into the "URL field" textbox. Once you enter a value here, you'll notice that the "URL format string" textbox becomes enabled. Into the "URL format string" textbox, enter the value **mailto:{0}**.

The URL format string value specifies the static text that should appear in the URL portion of the generated hyperlink. Any instances of {0} in the URL format string are replaced by the value of the `DataSource` field specified in the "URL field" textbox. Therefore, if there are two guestbook entries—one by John Smith with e-mail address john@johnsmith.com, and one by Scott Mitchell with e-mail address mitchell@4guysfromrolla.com—the DataGrid will contain two rows. The first row's e-mail column will have a hyperlink with the URL `mailto:john@johnsmith.com` and the text `john@johnsmith.com`, while the second row's e-mail column will have a hyperlink with the URL `mailto:mitchell@4guysfromrolla.com` and the text `mitchell@4guysfromrolla.com`.

Figure 24.5 shows a screenshot of the Property Builder dialog box after the various properties for the Email HyperLink Column have been set.

FIGURE 24.5

The various HyperLink Column properties have been set.

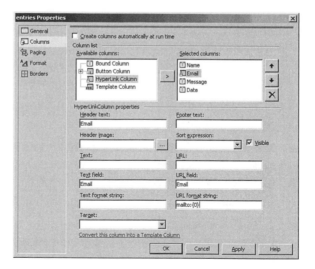

> As Figure 24.5 shows, the HyperLink Column also contains a Text format string, which has the same semantics as the "URL format string" textbox. For example, if you wanted the Email HyperLink Column to have each hyperlink's text property read `Send an Email to emailAddress`, you could set the Text format string to
>
> `Send an Email to {0}`

Testing the New Changes to the DataGrid

Once you have set the HyperLink Column settings as shown in Figure 24.5, click the Property Builder dialog box's OK button. This will close the Property Builder, returning you to the designer. Notice that the DataGrid in the designer has been updated to illustrate that the Email column is a HyperLink Column (see Figure 24.6).

FIGURE 24.6
The designer shows that the DataGrid's second column is a HyperLink Column.

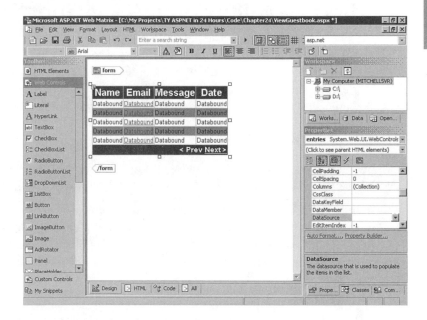

Finally, take a moment to view the updated ASP.NET Web page through a Web browser. Note that when visiting the page, every guestbook entry for which an e-mail address was provided displays the e-mail as a mailto hyperlink. A guestbook entry that does not include an e-mail address shows nothing (see Figure 24.7).

FIGURE 24.7

The e-mail addresses are displayed as mailto hyperlinks.

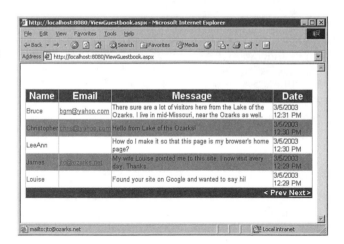

Sending E-Mail upon a New Guestbook Entry

One cool feature that is worth adding to our guestbook application is to have the application automatically send an e-mail to us whenever a user leaves a guestbook entry. Without an e-mail notification, in order to see if the guestbook has had any new entries, we'd have to visit the ViewGuestbook.aspx Web page. While this takes only a few moments, it can be a disheartening process if we continually check this page yet find no new guestbook entries.

Therefore, let's extend the AddEntry.aspx Web page so that whenever a user leaves a guestbook entry, we are sent a short e-mail detailing who left the message, the e-mail address (if supplied), the message, and the time the guestbook entry was made.

In order to send an e-mail through an ASP.NET Web page, we need to add a number of lines of source code. As we'll see shortly, creating this source code is a breeze with the Send Email Code Builder. But before we use the Send Email Code Builder, let's take a moment to think about where this code should be added.

Recall from Hour 22 that the AddEntry.aspx Web page's source code section contains an InsertGuestbookEntry() function and an event handler named btnSubmit_Click, which is executed whenever the "Add Comment" button is clicked. The InsertGuestbookEntry() function, created using the INSERT Data Method Code Builder, simply inserts a new row into the GuestbookEntries database table. The btnSubmit_Click event handler contains the following code:

```
Sub btnSubmit_Click(sender As Object, e As EventArgs)
    If Page.IsValid then
        InsertGuestbookEntry(name.Text, email.Text, message.Text)
        Response.Redirect("ViewGuestbook.aspx")
    End If
End Sub
```

This code first checks to ensure that the data entered by the user is valid. If the data is indeed valid, then the InsertGuestbookEntry() function is called, and then the user is automatically redirected to the ViewGuestbook.aspx Web page.

So where in this mess of code do we want to add the code for sending an e-mail? Because we don't want to send the notification e-mail until after the user has successfully submitted a guestbook entry, we'll add the needed code inside the If statement in the btnSubmit_Click event handler.

Using the Send Email Code Builder

To add the source code needed for sending an e-mail message, click the Code tab of AddEntry.aspx. This will display the Code Builders in the Toolbox. Click the Send Email Code Builder and, holding down the mouse button, drag the cursor so it is in the If statement of the btnSubmit_Click event handler, and then release the mouse button. This will display the Send Email Message Code Builder dialog box, as shown in Figure 24.8.

24

FIGURE 24.8

The Send Email Message Code Builder dialog box.

In the Send Email Message Code Builder dialog box, you are prompted to enter an address to send the e-mail to, the e-mail address from where the e-mail was sent, the e-mail's subject line, whether the e-mail should be sent in plain text or HTML format, and what SMTP server to use to send the e-mail.

For this example, because you want the e-mail sent to yourself, simply enter your e-mail address into the To textbox. Similarly, because we do not know whom the e-mail is from (remember, the user making the guestbook entry might not leave an e-mail address), enter your e-mail address in the From textbox, as well. In the Email Subject textbox, enter the value A New Guestbook Entry. Leave the Mail Format set to Plain Text.

The final Send Email Code Builder setting is the SMTP server setting. An *SMTP server* is a program that sends e-mails on the Internet. SMTP stands for Simple Mail Transfer Protocol, which defines the way e-mail is transferred across the Internet.

If your computer is running Windows 2000, Windows XP Professional, or Windows Server 2003, you likely already have an SMTP server running on your machine. In this case leave the SMTP server setting as `localhost`. (The `localhost` setting simply indicates that the SMTP server is on the same computer on which the Web server is located.)

Windows XP Home, on the other hand, does not have SMTP server capabilities. If you are using Windows XP Home, you will need to enter a known SMTP server address into the SMTP server setting. For example, you might be able to use your Internet Service Provider's SMTP server (the same one you have specified in your e-mail client). That is, if in your e-mail client you use the SMTP server `smtp.myisp.com`, you can enter this value in the SMTP server textbox in the Send Email Code Builder.

If you are using Windows XP Home and your Internet Service Provider requires that you provide a username and password to use the SMTP server, or it simply does not provide an SMTP server, you will not be able to send an e-mail from an ASP.NET Web page hosted on your computer.

If you are hosting your ASP.NET Web pages through a Web hosting company, you may need to contact the Web hosting company to determine what SMTP server to use to send an e-mail from an ASP.NET Web page.

Figure 24.9 shows the Send Email Message Code Builder dialog box after the values have been entered into the various textboxes. Of course, when following along on your computer, please use your own e-mail address and not mine!

FIGURE 24.9

The properties for the Send Email Code Builder have been set.

Once you have set these values, click the OK button. This will close the Send Email Message Code Builder dialog box, returning you to the source code portion of the `AddEntry.aspx` Web page. Note that the following source code has been automatically added by the Code Builder:

```
' Build a MailMessage
Dim mailMessage As System.Web.Mail.MailMessage = New System.Web.Mail.MailMessage
mailMessage.From = "mitchell@4guysfromrolla.com"
mailMessage.To = "mitchell@4guysfromrolla.com"
```

```
mailMessage.Subject = "A New Guestbook Entry"
mailMessage.BodyFormat = System.Web.Mail.MailFormat.Text

' TODO: Set the mailMessage.Body property

System.Web.Mail.SmtpMail.SmtpServer = "localhost"
System.Web.Mail.SmtpMail.Send(mailMessage)
```

As you can see by the TODO comment, we still have to provide the text for the body of
the e-mail message.

Specifying the E-Mail Message's Body Text

Because the intent of the notification e-mail is to alert us that a new guestbook entry has
been added, it would be wise to have the e-mail not only include this notification but also
include the name, e-mail address (if provided), the message, and the date and time of the
guestbook entry.

To specify the body of the e-mail message, we need to set the Body property of the
mailMessage object through the following syntax:

```
mailMessage.Body = "text to appear in the body of the email message"
```

This line of code needs to appear before the last two lines of code added by the Code
Builder. That is, this code should appear where the

```
' TODO: Set the mailMessage.Body property
```

comment appears.

The following source code will set the Body property so the e-mail message contains the
guestbook entry's information.

```
mailMessage.Body = "A new guestbook entry has been added!" & vbCrLf & vbCrLf
mailMessage.Body &= "From: " & name.Text & vbCrLf
mailMessage.Body &= "Email: " & email.Text & vbCrLf
mailMessage.Body &= "Message: " & message.Text & vbCrLf
mailMessage.Body &= "Date: " & DateTime.Now
```

The vbCrLf that you see at the end of each line of code is a special symbol that inserts a
carriage return in the e-mail body. If you did not include these vbCrLfs, the contents of
the e-mail would contain no line breaks, making it quite difficult to read. Notice that we
are displaying the name, e-mail address, and message added to the guestbook by simply
referencing the Text properties of the name, e-mail, and message TextBox Web controls.

Testing the E-Mail–Sending Capabilities

Once you have added the source code that specifies the Body property, save the ASP.NET
Web page and then view it through a Web browser. The AddEntry.aspx Web page

24

prompts the visitor to enter a new guestbook entry. Take a moment to add a new guest-book entry. Upon doing so, you will be whisked to the `ViewGuestbook.aspx` Web page.

Now fire up your e-mail client. In a few minutes you should find that you have a new e-mail message with the subject "A New Guestbook Entry." The body of the e-mail message should show the name, e-mail address, and message you entered when creating the new guestbook entry. Figure 24.10 shows a screenshot of a sample e-mail sent by the `AddEntry.aspx` Web page.

FIGURE 24.10

The e-mail notifies us that a new guestbook entry has been made.

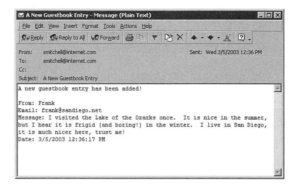

Sending HTML-Formatted E-Mail

As Figure 24.10 shows, the e-mail sent by the ASP.NET Web page was sent as plain text, which is not as aesthetically pleasing as HTML-formatted e-mail. Fortunately, the Send Email Code Builder allows for HTML-formatted e-mails. When filling out the various properties in the Send Email Message Code Builder dialog box, one option is the Mail Format, which can be set to either Plain Text or HTML (refer back to Figure 24.9). If you set this option to HTML, the e-mail message will be HTML formatted.

With an HTML-formatted e-mail, you can use HTML markup in the body of the e-mail message. For example, we could have the e-mail message displayed in a particular font, with various portions displayed in bold.

To try out sending an HTML-formatted e-mail message, simply delete the code the Send Email Code Builder generated and then launch the Send Email Code Builder again. This time, however, instead of specifying Plain Text format, set the Mail Format to HTML. After finishing the Send Email Message Code Builder dialog box settings, add the fol-lowing code immediately after the `TODO` comment:

```
mailMessage.Body = "<font face=Arial size=3>"
mailMessage.Body &= "<b>A new guestbook entry has been added!</b><p>"
mailMessage.Body &= "<b>From:</b> " & name.Text & "<br>"
mailMessage.Body &= "<b>Email:</b> " & email.Text & "<br>"
mailMessage.Body &= "<b>Message:</b> " & message.Text & "<br>"
```

```
mailMessage.Body &= "<b>Date:</b> " & DateTime.Now
mailMessage.Body &= "</font>"
```

Here you can see that the Body property contains HTML markup. For example, the <font> tag is used so that the body of the e-mail is displayed in Arial font. Also, certain parts of the e-mail message are displayed in bold. Figure 24.11 shows a screenshot of the HTML-formatted e-mail as viewed through an e-mail client.

FIGURE 24.11

The notification e-mail is HTML formatted.

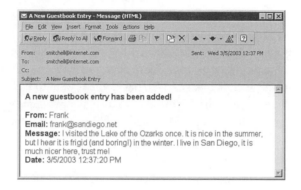

24

Notice that with the HTML-formatted e-mail, we did not need to include the vbCrLf symbol to insert line breaks. Rather, we used the HTML tags associated with inserting line breaks, such as <p> and <br>.

Summary

In this hour we looked at two ways to enhance the online guestbook application. The first added feature was in the ViewGuestbook.aspx Web page. In the display of the existing guestbook entries, we changed the DataGrid's Email column from a Bound Column to a HyperLink Column. The HyperLink Column displayed the e-mail address associated with each guestbook entry as mailto hyperlinks.

The second enhancement was added to the AddEntry.aspx Web page. Here we had an e-mail automatically sent to us whenever a new guestbook entry was added. As we saw in the "Using the Send Email Code Builder" section, the source code needed to send an e-mail from an ASP.NET Web page can be easily added by using the Send Email Code Builder.

With the Send Email Code Builder, we simply indicate the e-mail address to send the e-mail to, the address the e-mail is from, the e-mail's subject line, the e-mail format, and the SMTP server to use in sending the e-mail message. With these settings in place, the Send Email Code Builder automatically generates the needed source code. All that we have left to do is specify the body of the e-mail via the Body property.

Q&A

Q **Since guests to the Web site might make obscene comments in their guestbook entries, I'd like to be able to not have a guestbook entry displayed on the Web page until I approve it. How could I go about adding this functionality?**

A To add this functionality, you would need to update the data model, adding a Show column to the GuestbookEntries table. This column could be of type bit, which essentially is a Boolean since it allows for only two values, 0 and 1.

The idea here is that a guestbook entry with a 0 value in its Show column has yet to be approved, while one with a 1 has been approved. Since you do not want a guest-book entry to display until it has been approved, when inserting a new guestbook entry from the AddEntry.aspx Web page, you'd want to have a value of 0 inserted into the Show column. Since you want to display only approved guestbook entries, in the ViewGuestbook.aspx Web page, you'd want to use the WHERE clause builder in the SELECT Data Method Code Builder to only return rows whose Show column equaled 1.

The final piece of the puzzle would be creating a new ASP.NET Web page that listed the unapproved guestbook entries and allowed you to approve them. This could be done using an editable DataGrid that displays all records from the GuestbookEntries table where Show equals 0. To approve a guestbook entry, you could simply edit the row, changing the value of the Show column from a 0 to a 1. This editable DataGrid approach would also give you the opportunity to edit the Message column, if needed, before approving. For example, if a person used a profane word in the guestbook entry message, you might want to edit the Message column, removing the obscene word, and then approve the entry.

Workshop

Quiz

1. True or False: Using the Send Email Code Builder, you can send HTML-formatted e-mails.

2. True or False: You can use the Send Email Code Builder to send an e-mail from a computer using the Windows XP Home operating system.

3. Imagine that we wanted to have an e-mail sent to ourselves *whenever* someone viewed the guestbooks. (That is, whenever someone visited ViewGuestbook.aspx, we wanted to be sent an e-mail.) How would we accomplish this? Where would we place the code to send the e-mail message?

4. To display an e-mail address as a mailto link, what type of DataGrid column did we need to use?

Answers

1. True.

2. False. The ASP.NET e-mail component can work only on Windows 2000, Windows XP Professional, or Windows 2003 Server.

3. To have an e-mail sent whenever the `ViewGuestbook.aspx` Web page was visited, we'd want to place the code to send an e-mail message in the page's `Page_Load` event handler. Since we'd likely want to get e-mails only when persons first visit the Web page, and not one each time that they page through the DataGrid of existing guestbook entries, we'd want to make sure to place this code inside the `If Not Page.IsPostBack` block.

4. A HyperLink Column.

Exercise

In Hour 16 we saw how to use a TextBox Web control and a `WHERE` clause in the `SELECT` Data Method Code Builder to create an ASP.NET Web page that allows the user to enter a customer's ID, and that particular customer is displayed in the DataGrid.

For this exercise repeat this process, but instead of having a TextBox Web control that prompts the user for a customer ID, have the TextBox prompt the user for the name of the person whose guestbook entries the user wants to view. Once the name of a person has been entered and the Web form submitted, the guestbook entries by that person should be shown in a pageable DataGrid. Figure 24.12 shows a screenshot of such an ASP.NET Web page in action.

FIGURE 24.12

Guestbook entries by Scott are displayed.

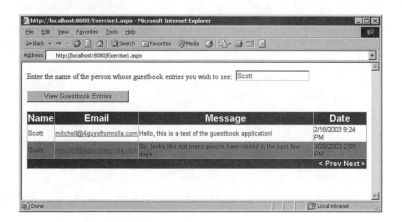

Conclusion

Congratulations on the great progress you've made over the past 24 hours! At the beginning of this book, you likely had never created an ASP.NET Web page before, but now you can quickly create data-driven ASP.NET Web pages by using the Web Matrix Project. Your accomplishment is no small feat—in my teaching experience I've found ASP.NET to be one of the most difficult computer technologies to teach to beginners, due to its breadth.

Hopefully, this book has you excited about ASP.NET and ready to move on to more challenging projects. You may be wondering what book to read next to continue your education. I'd adamantly recommend that you pick up a copy of Stephen Walther's *ASP.NET Unleashed* (Sams Publishing). This book is nearly 1,500 pages in length but covers all facets of ASP.NET in an easy-to-follow manner. If you are looking for books that provide ASP.NET examples using the Web Matrix Project, consider picking up the *Web Matrix Developer's Guide* (APress) or *Microsoft ASP.NET Web Matrix Starter Kit* (Microsoft Press).

In addition to learning via books, I would encourage you to consider using the multitude of online resources at your disposal. The online ASP.NET community is extremely helpful, and there exists a plethora of articles, tutorials, message boards, and listservs scattered across the Internet that cater specifically to ASP.NET. Some of my personal-favorite Web sites for ASP.NET resources include

- http://www.4GuysFromRolla.com
- http://www.asp101.com
- http://www.asp.net
- http://www.aspalliance.com

In addition to Web sites, there are a number of listservs and message boards where you can ask your ASP.NET questions and get helpful answers, usually within minutes. Some of the more popular online message boards and listservs include

- http://www.aspmessageboard.com
- http://www.asp.net/forums
- http://www.aspadvice.com
- http://www.aspfriends.com

I hope you have enjoyed learning about ASP.NET as much as I enjoyed writing this book. If you have any questions, comments, feedback, or suggestions, I invite you to get in touch with me—I can be reached at mitchell@4guysfromrolla.com.

Happy Programming!

Scott Mitchell
mitchell@4guysfromrolla.com

INDEX

C